This book is an account, based on previously unused material, of the events that marked the troubled relationship between Louis XV, the clergy of France, and the *Parlement* of Paris in the mid-eighteenth century.

The author shows how religious disputes drove a wedge between the King and the leading magistrates of his kingdom, leading to the exile of the *Parlement* in 1753-4. He describes the way in which legal and procedural conflicts gave rise to a debate about the nature of the Monarchy itself, the exercise of royal authority, and the rights of the subject under the protection of law. Rejecting the notion that the activities of the *Parlement* can be defined simply as 'political' or 'judicial', the book challenges traditional views about the nature of absolutism and also demonstrates that it is possible to write a history of the constitutional debates without reference to social conflict. Attention is given to the rôle of factions and intrigues at court and elsewhere, and debates inside the *Parlement* are analysed for the first time, using the newly discovered reports of highly placed government spies and agents. New light is shed on the part played by Louis XV himself in exacerbating the disputes or in resolving the crisis by means of the 'Law of Silence' of 1754.

LOUIS XV AND THE *PARLEMENT* OF PARIS, 1737–1755

Plate 1 Louis XV in 1748, pastel by M.Q. Delatour (Louvre, Paris)

LOUIS XV
AND THE
PARLEMENT
OF PARIS,
1737–1755

JOHN ROGISTER

CAMBRIDGE
UNIVERSITY PRESS

Published by the Press Syndicate of the University of Cambridge
The Pitt Building, Trumpington Street, Cambridge CB2 1RP
40 West 20th Street, New York, NY 10011-4211, USA
10 Stamford Road, Oakleigh, Melbourne 3166, Australia

First published 1995

Printed in Great Britain at the University Press, Cambridge

A catalogue record for this book is available from the British Library

Library of Congress cataloguing in publication data
Rogister, John.
Louis XV and the *Parlement* of Paris, 1737–1755/John Rogister.
p.   cm.
Includes bibliographical references and index.
ISBN 0 521 40395 2
1. Louis XV, King of France, 1710–1774.
2. France. *Parlement* (Paris) – History – 18th century.
3. France – Politics and government – 1715–1774 – Religious aspects.
4. Despotism – France – History – 18th century.
I. Title.
DC133.4.R64 1995
944'.034 – dc 20   94–10668 CIP

ISBN 0 521 40395 2 hardback

CE

*Studies presented to the International Commission for the
History of Representative and Parliamentary Institutions*
LXXIV
*Etudes présentées à la Commission internationale pour
l'histoire des Assemblées d'états*

TO THE MEMORY OF MY PARENTS

L'ordre a esté institué de Dieu, pour estre le père de la paix, union & concorde; comme le désordre est l'autheur de la désunion, & discorde ... Et certainement l'ordre fait des choses estranges, & pleines d'admiration. Il n'y a rien en l'univers, rien en tout le monde, où cet ordre ne soit observé. Le monde sans cet ordre, seroit un désordre. Au ciel l'ordre y est establi, si que les basses sphères ont leur mouvement de ce premier mobile. La mer se meust soubs le mouvement de la Lune; la terre se laisse conduire au mouvement du soleil. L'ordre des saisons y est establi. L'Esté suit le Printemps, l'Automne suit l'Esté, & l'Hyver l'Automne. Après le iour arrive la nuict, après le serein vient la pluye, & la pluye après le beau temps. Que si cet ordre se trouve sans variation en la nature, à plus forte raison le doibt-il estre en la Iustice, qui est la mère tutrice & conservatrice de l'ordre ...

La Roche Flavin, *Treize livres des Parlemens de France* (1617)

CONTENTS

PLATES

FIGURES

TABLES

xv

ABBREVIATIONS

AAE	Archives du Ministère des Affaires Etrangères, Paris
ADD	Archives départementales de la Drôme, Valence
ADG	Archives départementales de la Gironde, Bordeaux
AN	Archives nationales, Paris
AS	Archivio di Stato (Florence and Turin)
BL	British Library, London
BMReims	Bibliothèque municipale, Reims
BN	Bibliothèque nationale, Paris
BPR	Bibliothèque de la Société de Port-Royal, Paris
BS	Bibliothèque du Sénat, Paris
BUP	Bibliothèque universitaire, Poitiers
BVC	Bibliothèque Victor Cousin, Sorbonne, Paris
CA	Archives du Comte d'Argenson (BUP)
FL	Fonds Lamoignon (Rosanbo and Tocqueville MSS)
JF	Collection Joly de Fleury (BN)
LP	Collection Le Paige (BPR)
n.a.fr.	Nouvelles acquisitions françaises (BN)
RP	Richelieu Papers (BVC)

PREFACE

ON 6 OCTOBER 1789 Louis XVI and the royal family were brought back to Paris by the mob after the invasion of the Palace of Versailles the previous night. Protocol required that whenever the King came to stay in Paris for any length of time, the magistrates who made up his *Parlement* should present their respects to him. The King had arrived safely at the Tuileries, but it could hardly be said that he had come of his own free will. A further complication was that the King had come unexpectedly in the middle of the vacation, and there were therefore few *parlementaires* left in the capital. Nevertheless, the first president, Bochart de Saron, hastily assembled those of his colleagues who still happened to be in town to decide what they should do. They resolved that tradition should be observed, and so the *gens du roi* were sent on their customary mission to ask the 'seigneur Roi' when it would please him to receive the homage of the first court of the realm. Louis XVI had more pressing concerns on his mind, and it took him a while to fix a date for the deputation. When the King finally saw the *parlementaires* the first president delivered a speech that was a somewhat terse statement of the profound attachment to the sovereign. Louis XVI's reply was equally perfunctory: 'Je recevrai toujours avec satisfaction les témoignages de fidélité de mon Parlement de Paris.' Shortly afterwards, the National Assembly put the *Parlement* into abeyance. As for Louis XVI, he was now on the slippery slope that was to lead to the abolition of the Monarchy and to his own execution.

That final confrontation between Louis XVI and his leading magistrates was the last of a long series of *dialogues des sourds* that had marked the relationship between the Crown and the *Parlement* of Paris over the previous sixty years. In a broad sense this book represents an attempt to explain the failure of that dialogue during the first part of the personal rule of the King's grandfather, Louis XV, between 1737 and 1754. A subsequent work will take up the story during the period of the Seven Years'

War and broaden it out to include the rôle of the provincial *parlements*. A final volume will conclude with the events of the Maupeou *coup* of 1770–1 directed against the *parlements*.

The history of the relations between Louis XV and the *Parlement* of Paris in the mid-eighteenth century has long suffered from being studied from stale sources, such as the journals of undeniably observant contemporaries like the lawyer Barbier, the Marquis d'Argenson, and the Duc de Luynes, and not from official records or from the private papers of those who played a part in the decisions that were made. Jules Flammermont's edition of *Les Remontrances du Parlement de Paris au xviiiᵉ siècle* (Paris, 1888–98) with its linking commentary was often the only primary source used. Many historians still tend to assume that the story of the events of the 1750s has been told many times, particularly where it concerns denials of the sacrament and confession certificates, and some dismiss it in a few sentences. With earlier works, like those of E. Régnault on Christophe de Beaumont (1882) and M. Marion on Machault d'Arnouville (1891), there was a clericalist or 'royalist' bias, which was subsequently taken up by Pierre Gaxotte in his celebrated and influential study of Louis XV (1933).[1] Recently, thanks to the work of English and American scholars – James D. Hardy (1967), J. H. Shennan (1968), Dale Van Kley (1975 and 1984), and B. Robert Kreiser (1978) – this area is being explored anew and fresh manuscript sources used.[2] However, there remains a bias, albeit an unconscious one, towards presenting the subject matter as a prelude to the Revolution, or as an aspect of the so-called Enlightenment, or else as a sign of a new burgeoning 'political culture'. The story itself, moreover, remains untold.

This book is therefore also an attempt at writing narrative history with a strong element of analysis. I make no apologies for writing 'histoire événementielle': how events happen often provides the key to why they happened. My first aim has thus been to present an extended account of the tripartite conflict between the King, the clergy of France, and the *Parlement* of Paris based on official sources and on the private papers of the chief participants. My second aim has been to draw attention to the importance of procedural questions and legal niceties on which much of the action turned. Thirdly, I have tried to bring into focus the personalities and

---

[1] Père E. Régnault, *Christophe de Beaumont* (Paris, 1882), 2 vols.; M. Marion, *Machault d'Arnouville: étude sur l'histoire du contrôle général des finances de 1749 à 1754* (Paris, 1891); Pierre Gaxotte, *Louis XV* (Paris, 1933, re-edition with illustrations, 1979).

[2] James D. Hardy, *Judicial politics in the Old Régime: the Parlement of Paris during the Regency* (Baton Rouge, La., 1967); J.H. Shennan, *The Parlement of Paris* (London, 1968); Dale Van Kley, *The Jansenists and the expulsion of the Jesuits from France, 1757–1765* (New Haven, Conn., 1975); *ibid.*, *The Damiens affair and the unraveling of the Ancien Régime 1750–1770* (Princeton, N.J., 1984), reviewed by J.M.J. Rogister in *British Journal for Eighteenth-century Studies*, ix (1986), pp. 239–42; B. Robert Kreiser, *Miracles, convulsions, and ecclesiastical politics in early eighteenth-century Paris* (Princeton, N.J., 1978).

factions that contributed more to the political uncertainty than has previously been recognised. The system produced stresses and tensions
amongst its practitioners. My efforts have gone into looking at the problems faced by members of the Government, *parlementaires*, and leading
clerics in a way that might have been familiar to them, and in trying to
discern what Sainte-Beuve, in a celebrated passage in his *Port-Royal*, aptly
described as 'les variétés de l'espèce, les diverses formes de l'organisation
humaine, étrangement modifiée au moral dans la société et dans le dédale
artificiel des doctrines'. I cannot hope to have succeeded more than
partially in any of these aims. There are still many events that have not
been elucidated; there are many points of procedure, 'subtilités d'avocats'
as Chancellor de Lamoignon called them, and, above all, many subter-
ranean intrigues, that have eluded me. I shall not feel that my efforts have
been wasted, however, if I have been able to show that the internal
political history of France under Louis XV is an interesting subject, worthy
of being studied in the light of new evidence.

In passing I may also have confirmed the wisdom of those historians
who, like Roger Mettam in his *Power and faction in Louis XIV's France* (1988),
have usefully cast doubt on the traditional view of 'Absolutism'. As the
Papal diplomatic observer Raimondo Cecchetti (of Oderzo) commented in
1754: 'one is forced to conclude that a foreigner who comes to France full of
ideas about the certain despotism of the King over his subjects is con-
strained to relinquish no small part of that opinion upon seeing from such
examples with what caution, with what dissimulation, and with what
moderate use of power His Majesty deals with the bodies of the State'.

Private papers are the most important source for the political history of
Louis XV's reign. I was fortunate in being able to gain access to the
extensive D'Argenson and Lamoignon archives which contain a wealth of
information, especially when used in conjunction with other important
collections that have never been systematically exploited, like the Durey de
Meinières papers in the Library of the Senate and in the Bibliothèque
Nationale or the Le Paige manuscripts at the Bibliothèque de la Société de
Port-Royal. The Maurepas papers, now dispersed on both sides of the
Atlantic, have also been an invaluable source for my work. I have not
translated my quotations into English because I felt that, as so many of
them came from documents that were not readily available or even inven-
toried, it was best to leave them in the original to avoid any subsequent
confusion. That confusion can easily arise when so many letters are unsigned and undated. I also accept full responsibility for dating them, wherever
possible, and identifying their writers and recipients. I have also tended to
keep the legal terminology in French; that terminology is complicated
enough without my adding a further layer of complexity. I have taken care,

however, to outline the meaning of legal and procedural terms when I use them.

Much of my primary material is in private hands, and this book could not have been produced without the willingness of those who opened their archives to me or who introduced me to those of others. The Duc and the Duchesse de Praslin have a particular claim on my gratitude for all the help and kindness which they have given me over the last thirty years. The Marquis d'Argenson enabled me to continue working on his family papers after his father's death, when they were placed on deposit at the Bibliothèque universitaire at Poitiers. I am grateful to him and to his brothers, the Abbé Pierre-Armand d'Argenson and Monsieur Jean-Denis d'Argenson, for their help with this archive over the years. At the Bibliothèque universitaire, my thanks are due to the successive librarians, Mademoiselle S. Guyotat, Madame M. S. Regnier, and Monsieur A. Dubreucq. My gratitude goes also to my colleagues of the *Société pour le rayonnement des Archives d'Argenson*, and especially to Monsieur Bernard Delhaume, who gave me his transcription of an important document.,

The Marquis de Rosanbo allowed me to use the papers of Chancellor de Lamoignon and of the Le Peletier family in his possession. The Marquise de Chabrillan gave me free access to the papers of Maurepas inherited by his nephew, the Duc d'Aiguillon. Monsieur Michel Vinot Préfontaine showed particular kindness in lending me a transcript of the memoirs of his ancestor, Robert de Saint-Vincent, while at the same time directing my attention to several other sources which I wish I had had time to explore. The Marquis de Beaucourt and Professor Eric de Dampierre kindly lent me valuable material that will help towards the second volume of this work. To the Princesse de Robech, the Duc de Noailles, the Duc de La Rochefoucauld, and Comte Jean d'Ormesson (of the Académie française), I am also indebted for assistance in one way or another.

To fellow scholars I owe a great debt. In this country my thanks are due first to Dr John Roberts of Merton College, Oxford, who supervised the D.Phil. thesis which, in time, gave rise to this book. When needed, his advice was unerring and promptly delivered. Professor Douglas Johnson has remained a source of encouragement to his former student. With Dr Rohan Butler, unrivalled expert on Choiseul, I have enjoyed an enriching dialogue on eighteenth-century French history (and much else besides) over many years. I remember that during my year in France on a state studentship in 1965–6 I was greatly stimulated by my conversations with William Doyle, then working on the *Parlement* of Bordeaux. My thanks are especially due to Dr Robert Oresko, who amongst other kindly gestures, introduced me to a publisher, and to Mr William Davies at the Cambridge University Press, who was that publisher, and whose patience and forbearance with me are truly meritorious. I am particularly grateful to the Rev Professor John McManners, who read the typescript and made most helpful comments upon it drawn from his deep knowledge of the *ancien régime*. In Durham my colleagues Dr David Sweet and Dr David Barry kindly undertook to do my teaching during periods of sabbatical leave.

Some of the intellectual stimulus has come through my experiences in France and Italy. Professor Michel Antoine was very helpful in my early days when he was working at the Archives nationales; his knowledge of the primary material is unrivalled. When I was at the University of Paris X-Nanterre, I had some lively exchanges with Professor François Bluche, historian of the social and economic background of the *parlementaires*. In 1987 Professor Emmanuel Le Roy Ladurie arranged for me to give a series of lectures at the Collège de France. Since then, he has taken an interest in my work and more recently, as *Administrateur général* of the Bibliothèque nationale, he has facilitated my research there. I have constantly benefited from my conversations with my colleague and friend at the Ecole pratique des Hautes études (IVe section), Monsieur Bruno Neveu, who has made an impressive contribution to our knowledge of the religious background to *Unigenitus*. Madame Nadine Marchal has helped me enormously, not only by drawing one of the plans but also over the topography of the *Parlement*, an activity which involves an absorbing quest for documents, some of which still elude us. Père Paul Duclos SJ, archivist at the Centre culturel Les Fontaines at Chantilly, was of assistance in tracking down inmates of the Collège Louis-le-Grand after the librarian at its successor, the Lycée Louis-le-Grand, had proved obstructive. I should like to record my thanks to those hospitable friends and scholars: Professor and Madame René Pillorget and Professors André and Philippe Cocatre-Zilgien.

In Italy I have been fortunate in knowing the two leading scholars in my field. Professor Paolo Alatri shared with me the breadth of vision that went into his *Parlamento e lotta politica nella Francia del '700* (1977). Professor Furio Diaz, author of *Filosofia e politica nel settecento francese* (1962) and more recently of an impressive *Dal movimento dei lumi al movimento dei popoli* (1986), invited me to give some lectures on the *Parlement* at the Scuola Normale Superiore in Pisa in 1988. With both these scholars I learned much about the pervasive influence of ideas in the eighteenth century. In return, they may possibly gain a little from the British obsession with day-to-day politics which my work perhaps exemplifies. My debt to scholars in Italy would not be complete if I did not mention Professor Marta Pieroni Francini, Professor Alberto Postigliola, and Doctor Mireille Gille-Pirchio.

I have also greatly benefited from regular contact with my friends of the International Commission for the History of Representative and Parliamentary Institutions, and here I should single out Professor Michel Péronnet.

My debt to archivists and librarians in several countries is great. In France, at the Archives nationales, I should like to thank Madame d'Huart and Monsieur Jean-Pierre Brunterc'h; at the Bibliothèque nationale, Mademoiselle Kleindienst; at the Bibliothèque du Sénat, Monsieur Jean Bécarud; and the curators and librarians at the Quai d'Orsay, at the Bibliothèque Victor Cousin, at the Bibliothèque de la Sorbonne, at the bibliothèque Sainte-Geneviève, at the Mazarine, at the Institut, at the Archives de l'Académie française, at the Bibliothèque historique de la ville de Paris, at the Bibliothèque de l'Ordre des Avocats (where I have not forgotten the kindness of Monsieur Albert Tropénat, then its chief librarian). In the provinces, the archivists at the Archives départementales de la Côte d'Or(Dijon), de la Drôme (Valence), de la Gironde (Bordeaux), du Rhône (Lyon), and the librarians of the municipal libraries of Avignon, Beauvais, Besançon, Bourges, Dijon, Grenoble, Lyon, Mantes, Nantes, Reims, and Rouen, either gave assistance to me on the spot or patiently answered my inquiries and at times supplied photocopies of documents. I should like to thank the staff of the Archivi di Stato in Florence and Turin (especially here, Dr Marco Carassi). At Cornell University I should like to thank Mr George H. Healey of the Department of Rare Books, and at the Pierpont Morgan Library, Mr H. Cahoon. In this country my thanks are due to the librarians of the British Library and the Bodleian Library. In Durham, my gratitude is owed to Dr Ian Doyle, to Mr Brian Cheesman (former deputy librarian), Miss Beth Rainey, and Mrs Hilda Guy.

Much of the excitement in the research has come through the chance discovery of documents that come up periodically on the autograph market. Here the kindness of two persons who have a desire to help scholars is greatly appreciated: Monsieur Michel Castaing has always been willing to show me what goes through the Maison Charavay; in England, thanks to Dr A. R. A. Hobson, formerly of Sotheby's, I was able to see parts of the Phillipps Collection before they went under the hammer in 1976.

I owe a great debt to those who converted a complicated manuscript into a typescript: Mrs Mary Holcroft-Veitch, Mrs Joan Pearce, and especially Miss Wendy Duery, whose skill, reliability, and patience far exceeded my own. I am also very grateful to Mrs V. Catmur, a painstaking and meticulous copyeditor. For any mistakes that remain, as well as for the views expressed, I accept full responsibility.

Research abroad is an increasingly expensive activity. I should like to put on record my thanks to the Research Fund Committee of the University of Durham for several grants received over the years, to the Twenty-

Seven Foundation for a grant, and to the French Ministry of Education which pays a research allowance to visiting professors.

My wife's comments on the manuscript invariably helped me to improve it.

One cannot undertake a task that takes twenty years to complete without having a feeling of sadness at the loss of those who are no longer there to be thanked. My lengthy conversations with my friends John Bromley, Robert Shackleton, Hugh Murray Baillie, and Roland Mousnier deeply enriched my knowledge of the *ancien régime*. André Gazier welcomed me to the austere riches of the Bibliothèque de la Société de Port-Royal, thus continuing a family tradition. Jean Marchand and Roger Gourmelon provided helpful introductions. Maurice Piquard granted me permission to consult the Richelieu papers, and Suzanne Solente helped me with her knowledge of the Joly de Fleury Collection, of which she was the cataloguer.

In France I also owe a great debt of gratitude to the late Marquis d'Argenson. Until his death in 1975 he regularly had me to stay at Les Ormes, near Châtellerault. There it was that I discovered and worked on the letters of *Avocat général* Jean-Omer Joly de Fleury to the Comte d'Argenson; by a curious irony Marc was descended from both of them, albeit through a regicide. As I worked on the papers at Les Ormes or sat in front of the crackling fire in the superb library, my thoughts often turned to that winter of 1757 when the Comte d'Argenson returned there, sent into exile after fourteen years in high office. What must have been his morose meditations as he gazed into that same fireplace, alone, save for the presence of his evil genius, Madame d'Estrades?

The Comte de Tocqueville, *inspecteur des finances*, allowed me to consult the Lamoignon and Malesherbes papers in his possession, and his permission reached me for greater speed by that vanished means of postal communication, the *pneumatique*. Comte Pierre de Leusse, *ambassadeur de France*, gave me details of the Lamoignon papers in his possession. The Marquis de Beaucourt searched in vain at Coulans for the papers which his son later unearthed for me.

The Duchesse Edmée de La Rochefoucauld took a permanent interest in my work and effected many useful introductions. She invited me to stay at Montmirail on several occasions and gave me unrestricted access to the magnificent library that had once belonged to the Duc de Liancourt. Here too, as at Les Ormes, the spirit of old France worked its evocative charm. It is sad that this wonderful friend did not see the work in print. During a couple of summers, the writing of the early chapters took place in a different environment: overlooking the tranquil Chiemsee in Bavaria, thanks to the kindness of Dr Ing. Wolfgang Herbold. Finally, the dedication of the book expresses my deepest debt of all: to my parents, whose encouragement never wavered and whose support made possible so much that would otherwise have been impossible. Sadly, they, too, did not see the finished product.

The living and the dead are thus remembered, and in selecting the opening epigraph for the book, I have chosen a passage from the first historian of the French *parlements* that usefully reminds one of a different concept of the passage of time and of the seasons.

A NOTE ON NAMES

As a general rule surnames have been reproduced here as their bearers signed them. However, it has proved impossible to find signatures for all those mentioned in the book. Some further, imperfect, guidelines have therefore been observed. On the whole, the surname was used by the heads of families, with eldest sons or younger brothers adding to it the name of one or other of the different *seigneuries* held by the family. Thus, one has Monsieur Clément, Monsieur Clément de Feillet, or Monsieur Clément de Blavette. Unfortunately, this rule has many exceptions: Gilbert de Voisins, a former *avocat général*, was always referred to with the name of his *seigneurie* once he became a member of the Royal Council, whereas his son was plain President Gilbert. Le Fèvre d'Ormesson, *doyen* of the Royal Council, was usually referred to as Monsieur d'Ormesson, his eldest son (also in the Royal Council) confusingly as Monsieur d'Ormesson and his second son, the *avocat général*, also as Monsieur (and later as President) d'Ormesson, with only the latter's son adding a name as Monsieur d'Ormesson de Noyseau. There was confusion between Chancellor Daguesseau and his eldest son, Monsieur Daguesseau, whose younger brothers helpfully used the names Daguesseau de Fresnes and Daguesseau de Plainmont. President Potier de Novion was usually referred to as President de Novion. Although he signed official acts and letters as M. P. de Voyer d'Argenson, the minister of war was always referred to as the Comte d'Argenson; it was his son who was known as the Marquis de Voyer. The guidelines observed here have been to follow the current practice of the time with all its inconsistencies.

I

THE BACKGROUND: THE
PARLEMENT AND THE KING

Autrefois notre seule liberté, notre seul moyen de résist-
ance à l'oppression était ce refus de concourir activement
à l'exécution d'une opération qu'on désaprouvait [*sic*].

Condorcet to Loménie de Brienne, 23 January 1791

MANY VISITORS to the heart of Paris will see the Ile-de-la-Cité; there, even
if they only go round the Conciergerie with its tragic memories of Marie-
Antoinette, they become aware of the imposing buildings which surround
them. Perhaps the sight of a sealed police van sweeping briskly into the
main courtyard and disgorging handcuffed prisoners may suggest to them
that the place is in use as a court of criminal justice. Few, however, will
realise that it has been in constant use as such for over six hundred years
and that over two hundred years ago it was the seat of France's most venerable court, the *Parlement* of Paris. Between 1715 and 1771 the *Parlement* was
made up of 250 men from 592 noble or recently ennobled families who had
bought their offices and with it the right to dispense the King's justice over
an area that covered about a third of France.[1]

The kings of France had always regarded the dispensation of justice as
the most exalted of their kingly duties after their Christian obligations, and
the splendid ceremonies of the *sacre* at Reims, where they received the
sceptre known as the 'Hand of Justice', solemnly reminded them and their

---

[1] For these and other details concerning the social composition of the *Parlement* in the
eighteenth century, see François Bluche, 'Le Rôle des offices dans la mobilité sociale des
familles du Parlement de Paris', in *Amterkäuflichkeit: Aspekte sozialer Mobilität im Europäischen
Vergleich (17. und 18. Jahrhundert)*, ed. Klaus Malettke (Berlin, 1980), pp. 69–76 which
completes and corrects the same author's *thèse complémentaire, L'Origine des magistrats du
Parlement de Paris au xviii*ᵉ *siècle (1715–1771): Dictionnaire généalogique* in *Paris et Ile-de-France:
Mémoires publiés par la Fédération des sociétés historiques et archéologiques de Paris et de l'Ile-de-
France*, vvi (Paris, 1953–4 [1956]), referred to hereafter as Bluche, *L'Origine des magistrats*;
and his *thèse principale, Les Magistrats du Parlement de Paris au xviii*ᵉ *siècle, 1715–1771* (Paris,
1960), *passim*; see also David D. Bien, 'Aristocratie et anoblissement au xviii*ᵉ *siècle', *Annales,
économies, sociétés, civilisations*, xxix (1974), pp. 23–48, 505–34, especially pp. 510–12.

Table 1. *Calendar of sessions of the* Parlement

Sessions of the Parlement
St Martin's Day (11 November) to the eve of the Nativity of the BVM (7 September).

Holidays and Feast Days
Christmas (25–28 December)
Three Meat Days and Ash Wednesday
Holy Tuesday (*mardi-saint de Pâques*) to the Monday after Quasimodo (13 days)
Eve of Whit Sunday to Trinity Monday (9 days)
Ascension Day
Corpus Christi (*fête-Dieu*)
Foire St Denis (9 October)
St Nicholas (6 December)
New Year's Day
Ste Geneviève (3 January)
St Hilaire (13 January)
St Charlemagne (28 January)
'Reduction of Paris' (22 March)
Translation of St Gatien (2 May)
Foire St Denis (June)
Assumption of the BVM and 'Vœu de Louis XIII' (14–16 August)
If a feast occurred on a Sunday, it was celebrated also the next day.

Vacations
7 September to 11 November, though a vacation chamber sat from 9 September until
27 October, the eve of the feast of Sts Simon and Jude.

This table has been established with the information supplied in Bluche, *Les Magistrats du Parlement de Paris*, pp. 53–54, and the *Handbook of dates for students of English history*, ed. C. R. Cheney (London, 1955), pp. 40–65.

---

subjects of this duty. They had created the *Parlement*, and in 1301 Philip the Fair had made it a sedentary court in Paris, where it occupied a royal palace.[2] Reminding the eighteenth-century *parlementaires* of the origin of their institution was the *Palais* itself, the adjoining Sainte-Chapelle with its relic of Our Lord's crown of thorns brought back and venerated by St Louis, their founder. However, the character of the place is still that stamped upon it by the passage of the *parlementaires*. Despite the destruction of its bustling complex of mediaeval streets and houses in the first half of the nineteenth century and their replacement by some grim instances of Third Republic state architecture, the *Palais* remains their building, and its main façade on the street after one has crossed the pont de la Cité is the one which they left to posterity: it was built after the fire of 1776 and is in the neo-classical style

---

[2] On the history of the *Parlement* throughout the ages, see particularly E. Glasson, *Le Parlement de Paris, son rôle politique depuis le règne de Charles VII jusqu'à la Révolution* (Paris, 1901), 2 vols.; J. H. Shennan, *The Parlement of Paris* (London, 1968); Françoise Autrand, *Naissance d'un grand corps de l'Etat, les gens du Parlement de Paris* (Paris, 1981); on its history during the eighteenth century, see James D. Hardy, *Judicial politics in the Old Régime: the Parlement of Paris during the Regency* (Baton Rouge, La., 1967); Jean Egret, *Louis XV et l'opposition parlementaire 1715–1774* (Paris, 1970), a work which has the undeserved reputation of being 'revisionist' in its approach (cf. this author's review of it in *French Studies*, xxvi (1972), p. 201); and Bailey Stone, *The Parlement of Paris, 1774–1789* (Chapel Hill, N.C., 1981), which is also based on the late Jean Egret's research.

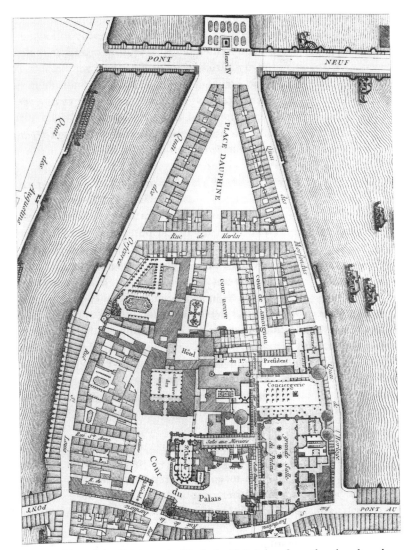

Figure 1 Plan of the *Palais* on the Ile-de-la-Cité, taken from the plan done by the Abbé Delagrive and known as the Bernage Plan (1754). The *salle Saint-Louis* was the room marked *Tournelle*.

of the period. As *parlementaires* were classicists by training and inclination and tended to compare themselves to the Roman senate, their new façade was a fitting entrance to what they regarded as the temple of Themis.[3]

The courtyard was the *cour de may*, where on 1 May each year the first

[3] A plan of the *Palais* appears at Figure 1; for this and other details, see Pierre d'Espezel, *Le Palais de Justice de Paris: château royal* (Paris, 1938), *passim*, and especially pp. 163 and 195; and also Bluche, *Les Magistrats du Parlement de Paris*, pp. 392–3 (on the *buvettes*).

president of the *Parlement* planted a may tree to symbolise the renewal of justice. The judicial year began on 12 November, the day following St Martin's day, and ended on 6 September; a Vacation chamber then sat between 9 September and 27 October to deal with urgent cases. The judicial year was further interrupted by holidays and feast days (see Table 1). Some of these were also days for ceremonial. The *messe rouge* at the start of the judicial year was when the *parlementaires* led by the first president and the nine *présidents à mortier* wearing the short toga (*épitoge*) trimmed with ermine over their red robes and the high, round cap (or *mortier*) on their heads led their colleagues on foot to mass in the *grande salle* of the *Palais*. On 22 March, this time 'en robes rouges et chaperons fourrés', *messieurs* went in state to the *Grands Augustins*, their ushers 'frappant de leurs baguettes', for the anniversary mass commemorating Henry IV's 'Reduction' of Paris.[4] Avoiding the dilapidated and perilous *escalier du may*, the procession wound its way down a tricky flight of steps leading into the north side of the courtyard, went through the porte de la Colindre, into the rue de la Barillerie, across the pont Saint-Michel and along the quai des Augustins by the river to the church (which was demolished in 1794). Occasionally there were special ceremonies, for the birth or death of a member of the royal family, perhaps a *Te Deum* for some military victory: on 27 November 1766, for instance, at the requiem mass for the dowager queen of Spain at Notre-Dame, the Duc de Luynes, governor of Paris, went to fetch *messieurs* and led them down the steps into the courtyard flanked by the first president and President d'Ormesson, the ushers again striking their rods, and, preceded by 'des gardes dudit gouverneur de paris et cottoyés des archers de la ville', they walked to the cathedral.[5]

In the society of the *ancien régime* public ceremonies had an ancillary purpose: that of enhancing their participants in the eyes of the populace. Hence, no hitch was allowed to go unnoticed. In November 1746 at a requiem service for the Dauphine, again at Notre-Dame, the *parlementaires* were refused admission through the main doors by the guards on duty; they had to gain entry by the side doors. The first president, according to one account, 'se plaignit hautement et dit que le roy en seroit informé'. The King was duly informed and he assured the first president that he had given orders that such an incident should not be repeated.[6] The *Parlement*

---

[4] Bibliothèque du Sénat (hereafter BS), MS 805: 'Journal de Mr Flandre de Brunville', f. 305, entry for 7 Apr. 1769.

[5] *Ibid.*, MS 802, f. 39.

[6] Archives nationales, Paris (hereafter AN), 342 AP 2 (Joly de Fleury Papers): 'Mémoires commencés au mois de Juin 1746 de tout ce qui m'a paru Intéressant' (hereafter 'Mémoires' (1746–50) of J. O. Joly de Fleury), pp. 15–16; these are the autograph memoirs of Jean-Omer Joly de Fleury (1715–1810), *avocat général* (1746) and later *président à mortier* (1768) of the *Parlement*; see also Archives de Paris, 4 AZ 410: Maupeou to [Maurepas], 24 Nov. 1746.

LE ROY LOUIS XV· Tenant son lit de Justice pour la premiere fois en son Parlement A Paris le 12ᵐ Septᵉ 1715·

Plate 2 View of the *grand'chambre* of the *Parlement* during the *Lit de justice* of 12 September 1715, engraving by De Poilly after a drawing by F. Delamonce

was the most powerful lay institution in the capital: within France it was the most senior of the thirteen *parlements* of the kingdom.

Within the *Palais* itself, the *Parlement* dispensed justice through a *grand'-chambre*, five chambers of *enquêtes* and two of *requêtes*. The *grand'chambre* was the most important of these. It was made up of the first president, who was appointed by the King, the nine *présidents à mortier*, and thirty-three *conseillers* (twenty-one lay and twelve clerks). In addition there were honorary members: retired presidents who had received their *lettres d'hono-raires* from the King, two ecclesiastical *conseillers d'honneur nés* (the arch-bishop of Paris and the abbot of Cluny), six lay *conseillers d'honneur*, eight honorary presidents from the *enquêtes* and *requêtes*, and forty-four other honorary *conseillers*. And finally, the princes of the blood (as peers by birth), the dukes and peers and the six ecclesiastical peers could sit in the *grand'-chambre*. Although they and the honorary members had a vote, they could not take part in the preparation of judicial proceedings: only the *présidents à mortier* and the thirty-three *conseillers* could do this.[7]

The *grand'chambre* dealt with the important cases and was the court of appeal from the lesser tribunals within the jurisdiction of the *Parlement*. It

[7] Bluche, *Les Magistrats du Parlement de Paris*, p. 49.

was the only chamber of the *Parlement* before which the advocates pleaded. The *enquêtes* were concerned chiefly with the appeals from minor civil and criminal cases. The *requêtes* gave judgements in cases involving all privileged persons, namely those who enjoyed the privilege of *committimus*. It was in the chambers of *enquêtes* and *requêtes* that the young and sometimes boisterous *parlementaires* began their careers: as they gained seniority, so they moved up to the *grand'chambre*. Despite its division into chambers, the *Parlement* existed as a corporate body, and seniority within it – except for the *présidents à mortier* – was determined by the date of the magistrate's reception into the court, irrespective of the chamber to which he belonged (hence, the older ones tended to be concentrated in the *grand'chambre*).

The *gens du roi*, or the *parquet* (from the spot in the chamber where they took up their position), consisted of the *procureur général*, three *avocats généraux*, and the twelve *substituts* of the *procureur général*. The *procureur général* was at their head and his duties included the maintenance of discipline within the *Parlement*. He also acted as prosecutor for the Crown in criminal cases. Laws, whether edicts or declarations, for registration at the *Parlement* (and other orders from the King) were sent directly to him, and it was his duty to present the laws to the *Parlement* with his written opinion (or *conclusions*) as to the course of action which the *parlementaires* should adopt. The *procureur général* rarely spoke before the *Parlement*: that task fell to the *avocats généraux* (in order of seniority of appointment) who would use the resources of their rhetorical eloquence to support the course adovcated by the *procureur général*. The *gens du roi* could not attend the debates of the *Parlement*; they withdrew from the chamber once the *conclusions* had been presented or the *avocat général* had made his *réquisitoire*.[8]

Historians are familiar with the office-holding system of the *ancien régime*. In addition to the magistrates and the *gens du roi*, the *Parlement* included a plethora of minor officials from clerks to *buvetiers*, surgeons and apothecaries. The most highly prized offices were the nine *présidences à mortier*. On the whole, however, they had become the preserve of a few famous dynasties whose names were linked to the history of the *Parlement*: Lamoignon, Talon, Molé, Le Peletier, Potier de Novion, Le Fèvre d'Ormesson. This did not prevent them from being sold from time to time when families ran into difficulties or were unable to provide an incumbent for the office. The average price of a *présidence à mortier* was 750,000 *livres* in the eighteenth century. The lesser offices of *conseillers* (worth about 40,000 *livres* in the 1750s) remained the basic channel of entry to the *Parlement* for well over a hundred families in the course of Louis XV's reign.[9]

---

[8] On the *gens du roi*, see *ibid.* and Paul Bisson de Barthélemy, *Les Joly de Fleury, procureurs généraux au Parlement de Paris au xviiiᵉ siècle* (Paris, 1964), *passim*. The *avocat général* was expected to learn his *réquisitoire* by heart: see AN, 342 AP 2: 'Mémoires' of J. O. Joly de Fleury, p. 38.

[9] Bluche, *Les Magistrats du Parlement de Paris*, pp. 160–74, especially pp. 167–8.

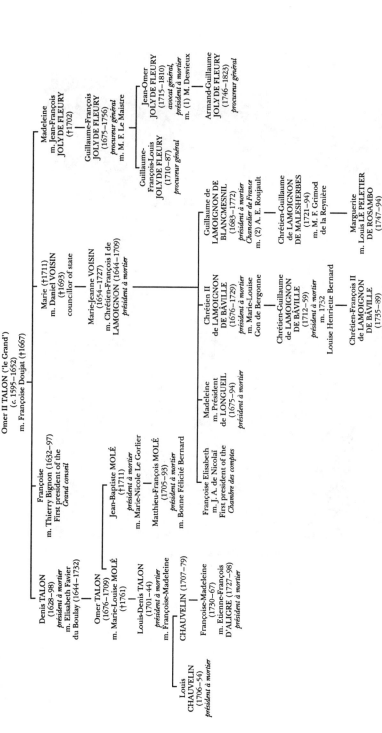

Figure 2 Table of some *parlementaire* dynasties and their alliances (by the author)

Plate 3 The wife of a *parlementaire*: the *Présidente* Bernard de Rieux, pastel by M.Q. Delatour (Musée Cognacq Jay, Paris)

Why did families divert a substantial amount of their wealth into purchasing judicial offices? After all, the offices carried with them some onerous duties. The financial returns were not great: a few leading *parlementaires* were given royal pensions (but they were rich men anyway). Those who actively involved themselves in their judicial duties received the *épices*, a sum which they were awarded by the first president at the expense of the litigants in civil cases.[10] Although this system was decried at the time and

[10] On the system of the *épices*, see *ibid.*, p. 171 and Stone, *The Parlement of Paris*, pp. 18, 45–52, 58, 67 and 74. In his account Stone has overlooked an interesting memoir of 1783 on the *épices* by First President d'Aligre in the Archives de l'Assistance Publique, Paris, Fonds

was open to abuse, it was not the prospect of the *épices* that chiefly drew men of noble families to enter the *Parlement*. There were many absentee magistrates who did not receive the *épices*, and indeed the burden of judicial work was unevenly divided as a result. It was more likely to be the social and professional status – the *état* – that membership of this august body conferred upon them. A senior magistrate in the government, Gilbert de Voisins, a former *parlementaire* himself, observed:

> il n'est permis à personne d'ignorer que la noblesse est une qualité qui suit le sang, et que la robe est une profession de choix dont la noblesse est susceptible comme de celles de l'église et des armes. Les familles les plus distinguées ont fourni, et souvent dans le mesme temps, des prélats à l'église, et au Roi des magistrats, aussi bien que des officiers militaires...[11]

Moreover, because the distinction between government service and the administration of justice was blurred under the *ancien régime*, the robe tended to supply the Crown with many of its administrators. Hence, it could be a matter of temperament or of family decision whether a young man remained a judge or steered his career towards the Royal Council. A stage, however brief, as a young judge in the *Parlement* was essential to a majority of those intending to enter the royal administration.[12]

Members of the *Parlement* were also drawn to it by its *esprit de corps*. Courtiers and writers tended to scoff at the robe, and 'the president' or 'the magistrate' was indeed a stock literary type: severe in manner, austere in his obligatory black clothes, pompous, haughty – *la morgue de la robe* – generally humourless; his wife remained a prude and *une bourgeoise*, even if seduced by these very courtiers and writers. Naturally, these types were a caricature of the reality. In his memoirs Cardinal de Bernis paid tribute to the magistracy by describing it as 'la partie de la nation qui a encore conservé le plus de mœurs et d'intégrité'.[13] In his journal, the Marquis d'Argenson wrote that Keeper of the Seals Chauvelin 'a pris les manières et l'attitude d'un bon et ancien magistrat de race, grave et mesuré, ne soupant point et n'ayant point de maîtresse'.[14] For many, membership of the robe amounted to a sacred calling. A new entrant was expected to live up to the

---

Montyon, *carton* 15; D'Aligre states therein that complaints that first presidents did not always apportion the *épices* fairly (citing the case of First President Le Peletier in 1742) led him to decide that he would henceforth apportion them in consultation with the *bureau* of the whole *Parlement*.

[11] AN, U 870 (Gilbert de Voisins Papers): unnumbered and undated notes in the hand of P. Gilbert de Voisins (1684–1769) on a memorandum by Daguesseau de Fresnes on the garb to be worn by councillors of state.

[12] Michel Antoine, *Le Conseil du Roi sous le règne de Louis XV* (Geneva and Paris, 1970), pp. 247–64. See also Vivien R. Gruder, *The royal provincial intendants: a governing elite in eighteenth-century France* (Ithaca, N.Y., 1968), *passim*.

[13] *Mémoires et lettres de François-Joachim de Pierre Cardinal de Bernis, 1715–1758*, ed. F. Masson (Paris, 1903), 2 vols., i, p. 324.

[14] *Mémoires du Marquis d'Argenson*, ed. René d'Argenson (Paris, 1825), p. 318. The celebrated Marquise de Monconseil had been Chauvelin's mistress at one time.

reputation of his father or of some other worthy relative; in 1748 the young Robert de Saint-Vincent was received by Chancellor Daguesseau upon entering the *Parlement* and he recalled later: 'Je me souviens très bien qu'il insista tout particulièrement sur l'éloge de M. Robert et qu'il m'exhorta à soutenir la réputation d'un nom qui méritoit d'être soutenu avec honneur.'[15] When a *parlementaire* died, it might be said of him, as First President Molé said of Revol, a president of the *requêtes*: 'C'est une perte réel [*sic*] pour le service du Roy, et pour le parlement; beaucoup d'esprit, des connaissances étendues, et un parfaittement honette [*sic*] homme.'[16] These were the qualities required, and that was the language of the robe.

Its permanent corporate existence had enabled the *Parlement* to preserve a strong *esprit de corps*.[17] However, the *parlementaires* themselves should not be regarded as a social caste despite their tendency to inter-marry. Certainly, they were all noble and they or their families had chosen to enter the *Parlement* because of the social status which it conferred; but in the majority of cases their nobility was very recent and the antecedents of some families still marked out certain social differences. Out of 592 families that were in the *Parlement* during Louis XV's reign, 260 owed their ennoblement to the simple expedient of purchasing an office of *secrétaire du roi* which conferred nobility at the first generation.[18] This was a consequence of the rapid social mobility that characterised the second half of the seventeenth century.[19]

In his memoirs *Avocat général* Joly de Fleury concluded his unflattering portrait of President Durey de Meinières with the tart comment that he saw in him 'tout l'orgueil de la platte finance dont il tirait son origin'.[20] The Joly de Fleurys owed their ennoblement in 1629 to the exercise of magisterial office over a few generations, while the Dureys were financiers who

[15] Collection Michel Vinot Préfontaine, Paris: 'Mémoires de P. A. Robert de Saint-Vincent' (typescript copy of these memoirs which are still in the possession of his descendants), p. 114. Unfortunately, names and dates are not always accurately transcribed in the typescript copy, and the date of P. A. Robert de Saint-Vincent's admission to the *Parlement* is wrongly given as 1743 instead of 1748. The author also confused the sequence of certain events when writing his memoirs late in life during the Emigration.

[16] Fonds Lamoignon (hereafter FL), Chartrier du château de Tocqueville (catalogued by the Archives nationales in their private archives series under the reference 154 AP II and available for consultation on microfilm with the owner's permission at the AN: 177 Mi 70–152 (hereafter Tocqueville MSS)), Mi 73, *dossier* 6, *pièce* 119: Molé to Chancellor de Lamoignon, 15 June 1760.

[17] J. H. Shennan, 'The political role of the *Parlement* of Paris under Cardinal de Fleury', *English Historical Review*, lxxxi (1966), p. 521.

[18] Bluche, 'Le Rôle des offices', pp. 70 and 72: 'La charge vénale et anoblissante de secrétaire du Roi domine donc et marque toute la société parlementaire.' See also, in the same collection, *Amterkäuflichkeit*, ed. K. Malettke, Bluche's other article, 'Von Monsieur Jourdain zu Monsieur Necker. Ein Porträt des "secrétaire du roi" (1672–1789)', pp. 77–86, and also his 'Les Magistrats des cours parisiennes au xviiie siècle: hiérarchie et situation sociale', *Revue historique de droit français et étranger* (1974), p. 95.

[19] Bluche, 'Le Rôle des offices', p. 76.

[20] AN, 342 AP 2 ('Mémoires' of J. O. Joly de Fleury), p. 52.

briskly ennobled themselves in 1685 through the purchase of a *charge* of *secrétaire du roi*.[21] It is typical of the double standards of the age, however, that, for all his sarcasm at Durey's expense, the *avocat général* was himself married to the daughter of a financier whose father had been ennobled in 1672 in the same way as the Dureys.[22] There are some indications of the contrast in style and manners among these *parlementaires* from different backgrounds: Durey de Meinières again, whom Diderot once observed with his round wig and displaying a natural dignity in an encounter with a churlish lawyer, or else insinuating himself into the family secrets of others, if Joly de Fleury is to be believed; and the urbane patrician, President de Lamoignon, whom Jean-Jacques Rousseau dined with in the 1740s at the house of Madame de Bezenval and who had 'ce petit jargon de Paris, tout en petits mots, tout en petites allusions fines'.[23]

The *Parlement* was not simply a judicial court: it had what would nowadays be described as political attributions as well. All edicts and declarations had to be 'registered', or transcribed in its records; the *Parlement* was then able to publicise and enforce the new laws throughout its jurisdiction. Registration was no mere formality. In the entry under 'Enregistrement' in the *Encyclopédie* of Diderot and D'Alembert, Boucher d'Argis concluded his exhaustive account with a neat summary of its full implications:

> Les enregistrements des nouvelles ordonnances n'est pas comme on voit un simple cérémonial et en insérant la loi dans les registres, l'objet n'est pas seulement d'en donner connoissance aux magistrats et aux peuples, mais de lui donner le caractère de loi, qu'elle n'aurait point sans la vérification et enregistrement, lesquels se font en vertu de l'autorité que le roi lui-même a confié à son Parlement.[24]

For this reason, edicts and declarations were placed before the *Parlement* by the *procureur général*, usually at an assembly of all the chambers. The *Parlement* had the right of making 'remonstrances' to the King before registering any law. In 1673 Louis XIV had curtailed this right by insisting that registration should always precede any remonstrances the *Parlement* might wish to make; the reluctant registration of this measure was accompanied by a protest which Daguesseau later described as 'le dernier

---

21 Bluche, *L'Origine des magistrats*, entries under Durey de Meinières (p. 167) and Joly de Fleury (p. 220).

22 *Ibid.*, entries under Jean-Omer Joly de Fleury (p. 221) and under Desvieux (p. 149).

23 D. Diderot, *Correspondance*, ed. Georges Roth (Paris, 1959), v, p. 55, letter of 21 July 1765 to Sophie Volland; Jean-Jacques Rousseau, *Les Confessions*, ed. A. Van Bever (Paris, 1926), ii, pp. 89–90: the editor (p. 360, n. 44) identifies the president as the future Chancellor de Lamoignon, but this attribution is probably inaccurate: he was more likely the latter's nephew, Lamoignon de Basville (1712–59), who became a *président à mortier* in 1730.

24 *Encyclopédie, ou Dictionnaire raisonné* (Paris, 1752), v, p. 702.

cri de la liberté mourante'.[25] The argument that the *parlementaires* had little cause for apprehension at the King's suppression of their right of presenting remonstrances to him before they registered new laws because that stipulation applied only to letters patent is a flawed one. Letters patent necessarily accompanied edicts and *déclarations*, and the 1673 stipulation was therefore a means of facilitating the passage of these more significant pieces of legislation through the *Parlement*. The declaration of 1673 was rescinded by the Regent Philip of Orleans in September 1715, when he needed the support of the *Parlement* to quash Louis XIV's will.[26] Thereafter, the *Parlement* took advantage of its right to examine laws carefully and, if need arose, to make remonstrances before it gave them formal recognition by the essential act of registration.

It was the first president's task to draft the remonstrances on these and on other occasions, and in a memoir of 1747 for his guidance, his secretary, Boizot, dealt neatly with the question of their scope:

les Remontrances roulent ordinairement

1°   sur les entreprises de la Cour de Rome et des gens d'église, sur l'autorité et les droits du souverain et de la couronne
2°   sur l'enregistrement ordonné par le Roy d'édits et de déclarations qui sont préjudiciables, ou à ses intérêts, ou à ceux de ses peuples
3°   sur les entreprises contre les privilèges de la compagnie.

Finalement le Parlement ayant été étably pour conserver les droits de la Couronne et rendre la justice au nom du Roy, à tous ses sujets, dans tous les cas où les intérêts de S.M. et ceux de ses peuples peuvent être attaqués, il est obligé d'user de remontrances, pour se mettre à l'abry des reproches qu'on pourroit lui faire, ce droit de remontrances est même dans son institution.[27]

No extract better summarises the exact rôle which remonstrances played in the life of the *Parlement* under Louis XV or conveys the untranslatable flavour of *parlementaire* language than this. The *Parlement* did not and could not see itself as existing in opposition to the King: it was an emanation of his authority, a reflection of his sovereignty: its purpose was to enlighten him, to warn him, to remind him and, if need be, to endeavour to correct him by respectful means. For this reason remonstrances were replete with expres-

[25] Daguesseau, *Œuvres complètes*, ed. André (Paris, 1769-89), xiii, p. 545, quoted in F. Monnier, *Le Chancelier Daguesseau ... son influence sur le mouvement des esprits 1700-1750* (Paris, 1860), p. 256.
[26] On the events of September 1715, see Hardy, *Judicial politics*, pp. 3-50; and J. H. Shennan, 'The political role of the *Parlement* of Paris, 1715-23', *The Historical Journal*, viii, 2 (1965), pp. 179-200, especially pp. 185-6.
[27] BS, MS 435: 'Le Premier Président du Parlement de Paris dans l'exercice de ses fonctions', by C. L. Boizot, pp. 438-9.

sions of respect, loyalty and obedience where the Monarch was concerned.[28]

When *parlementaires* assembled to discuss the sort of issues which Boizot described, they did so in the *grand'chambre* with its fine Gothic ceiling and on the far wall, above the bench reserved for the presidents, there was a Flemish altar piece (now in the Louvre) depicting Calvary and the figures of St Louis, their founder, St Denis and Charlemagne in the foreground (see Plate 2).[29] It was here that the councillors of the *grand'chambre* normally held their meetings. At one corner of the room was a raised dais. In a moving speech to his assembled colleagues on 9 March 1767, Monsieur Drouyn de Vandeuil described it:

> Dans l'angle des deux bancs d'en haut est un siège en forme de cube, symbole de stabilité, sur lequel on place le Dais, les coussins et le Tapis où le Roi s'assied quand il vient au Parlement tenir son Lit de Justice. Cette place est toujours censée remplie par le Roi, et personne ne l'occupe en son absence.[30]

Before their eyes, *parlementaires* had a permanent reminder of the origin of their power, and even if their eyes strayed they would light only upon the royal fleur-de-lis on the surrounding tapestries.

These fundamental beliefs concerning the nature of sovereignty and the origins of their authority were to retain a lasting hold over the minds of *parlementaires*, though their interpretation and application were to create tensions and dilemmas for them. Boizot described some of these when listing the qualities required of a first president, who was

> partagé continuellement entre la cour et sa compagnie dont les intérêts sont presque toujours opposés. Le P.P. est pour ainsi dire celui qui tient l'équilibre et un médiateur qui travaille sans cesse à les réunir; dans une position si délicate, quelle supériorité de génie et de talents ne faut-il pas pour parvenir à

[28] Daguesseau, *Œuvres complètes*, xiii, pp. 554–6: 'Fragment sur l'origine et l'usage des Remontrances'; Monnier, *Le Chancelier Daguesseau*, pp. 208–9, 256–7, 260–3. For the text of the remonstrances, see *Les Remontrances du Parlement de Paris au xviii* siècle, ed. Jules Flammermont (Paris, 1888–98), 3 vols. (hereafter referred to as Flammermont, *Rems.*).

[29] Jean Guiffrey, 'Le Retable du Parlement de Paris au Musée du Louvre', *Les Arts* (1904), pp. 9–12 (with illustrations, especially that on p. 11). Attributed at one time erroneously to Van der Weyden, the reredos was given as 'Ecole de Paris, vers 1475' by Guiffrey but is now once again attributed to the Flemish school, if not to Van der Weyden. The reredos was damaged in the fire at the *Palais de Justice* during the Paris Commune of 1871 and was restored in 1891 when it was also transferred to the Louvre. It appears in several paintings and prints representing the *grand'chambre* in the eighteenth century; see, for instance, Sarah Hanley, *The 'Lit de Justice' of the Kings of France: constitutional ideology in legend, ritual and discourse* (Princeton, N.J., 1983), pp. 285, 308–9; and Plate 5. The recent interpretation of the reredos given by Christian de Mérindol in 'Le Retable du Parlement de Paris: nouvelles lectures', *Histoire de la Justice*, v (1992), pp. 19–34 is highly questionable.

[30] BS, MS 802: 'Journal de Mr Flandre de Brunville', f. 182: speech given on 9 March 1767. Drouyn de Vandeuil's interpretation of the symbolism of the cube has not been considered by Sarah Hanley; see her *The 'Lit de Justice'*, passim.

ramener tant d'esprits d'un côté à la douceur et à la clémence, de l'autre à la soumission en éteignant le feu de la Discorde toujours prêt à s'allumer.[31]

Few first presidents possessed all the necessary qualities, but most of them did their best to maintain the harmony that was supposed to exist between the King and his leading magistrates. Why at times did they fail? Did events show that the task was beyond them? Was the system itself to blame?

The system itself and the complicated procedures governing the conduct of public affairs at the *Parlement* need to be described in some detail.[32] When edicts and declarations were presented for registration (or when remonstrances were discussed), it was the normal practice for all the chambers to assemble in the *grand'chambre*. The *procureur général* was then summoned and after producing the sealed originals of the proposed laws, he would leave his own *conclusions* in writing. After he had withdrawn, a member of the *grand'chambre* known as the *rapporteur* read out the text of the laws and the *conclusions* of the *gens du roi*; he then recommended a particular course of action usually elaborating the arguments contained in the *conclusions* in an introductory speech to the assembly. His purpose was usually to make the new laws as palatable as possible to his colleagues in order to facilitate their registration.[33] The *rapporteur* had to possess the confidence of the Government and of the first president. Until 1757 the duties of *rapporteur* were performed by the Abbé de Salabéry, whose status was enhanced when Madame Le Normand d'Etioles became the King's favourite in 1745: Salabéry was an old friend of hers and had rendered services to her family.[34]

The next stage was usually for the assembly to decide that the measures would be examined in detail by *commissaires*. It was the first president's right to appoint the *commissaires*, though in practice he limited his choice to

[31] BS, MS 435, pp. 174–5 (Boizot).

[32] These procedures have not received the attention they deserve from historians: they can be studied only by inference from different souces: in particular, see the account given by Durey de Meinières of the events of November–December 1751 reproduced in Flammermont, *Rems.*, i, pp. 651–713, and also two articles: Madeleine Dillay, 'Les "Registres secrets" des chambres des enquêtes et des requêtes au Parlement de Paris', in *Bibliothèque de l'Ecole des Chartes*, cviii (1949–50), pp. 75–93; and John Rogister, 'Le Gouvernement, le Parlement de Paris et l'attaque contre *De l'esprit* et *l'Encyclopédie* en 1759', *Dix-huitième siècle*, xi (1979), pp. 321–54, especially pp. 340–1.

[33] Flammermont, *Rems.*, i, pp. 680–1 (Durey de Meinières); and Madeleine Dillay, 'Conclusions du procureur général au Parlement de Paris, relatives à la vérification et à l'enregistrement des lettres patentes', *Revue historique de droit français et étranger*, 4th series (1955), pp. 255–66.

[34] FL, Archives du château de Rosanbo (catalogued by the Archives nationales in their private archives series under the reference 263 AP and available for consultation on microfilm with the owner's permission at the AN: 162 Mi 1–2, 8–11 (hereafter Rosanbo MSS)), *carton* 2, *dossier* 2, *pièce* 2: Madame de Pompadour to Chancellor de Lamoignon, 19 Sept. 1757. Through her influence Salabéry obtained one of the few posts of councillor of state reserved for clerks (1758).

the fourteen most senior members present from the *grand'chambre* (i.e. just under half of its total membership) to represent that chamber; as for the seven other chambers, he simply chose the two most senior members present from each (either a president and a *conseiller* or two *conseillers*). The *présidents à mortier* were *ex officio commissaires*, and the total number of *commissaires* was therefore thirty-seven.[35] Seniority in the *Parlement* was determined by date of entry into it in whatever capacity. There was an old dispute about whether *commissaires* from the *enquêtes* and *requêtes* ought not to be chosen by those chambers themselves rather than by the first president. The dispute was revived on 13 December 1743 and again on 23 April 1751. On the first occasion the proponents got nowhere, but on the second they had more success and, on 24 April, they nominated their own *commissaires*. However, in nominating two of their members who had not been present at the previous debate, the 2nd chamber of *enquêtes* irritated the other chambers. It is instructive to investigate this incident more closely. According to the other chambers, the 2nd chamber of *enquêtes* should have nominated Clément and Lambert who had been present at the debate. Had they done so, they would have been represented by a pair of young, active *zélés*. Instead, they chose President Bernard de Boulainvilliers, who promptly went off to England, and the aged Mayneaud, who showed no interest in the issue under discussion.[36] Thus, in one instance at least, the assumption by the chambers of the right to appoint their own *commissaires* had produced a pair of senior and uninterested representatives. Besides, whichever way the *commissaires* of the *enquêtes* and *requêtes* were selected, it is clear that they were always outnumbered by the solid phalanx of the *présidents à mortier* and the *commissaires* from the *grand'chambre*. They could face a difficult task in convincing this conservative majority, and some indication of the problems faced by the *zélés* is provided in a description of the *commissaires* of the *grand'chambre* left by President Durey de Meinières:

> A l'égard de Mrs. de grand chambre, le personnage qu'ils jouent dans ces sortes d'assemblées de commissaires, c'est de marquer l'ennuy le plus profond et l'indifférence la plus parfaitte. Ou ils ne disent mot, ou ils disent des riens qui n'en valent pas la peine. Ils sont toujours portés à laisser le premier président s'en tirer comme il voudra, disposés à l'approuver et à l'admirer en tout.
> Les enquestes au contraire font tout et discutent les questions avec âme et

[35] Flammermont, *Rems.*, i. pp. 664 (for the various chambers the first president selected the *doyen* or the member 'qui se trouvait ce jour-là le doyen'), 671–3.

[36] BS, MS 800: 'Journal du Président de Meinières', 7 Jan. 1749 to 27 May 1751, f. 70: account of the debate on 23 April 1751. BS, MSS 800–1 (Durey de Meinières Papers) comprise the journals of parliamentary debates kept by Durey de Meinières, Rolland d'Erceville, Lambert, Moreau, Potier de Novion, and others.

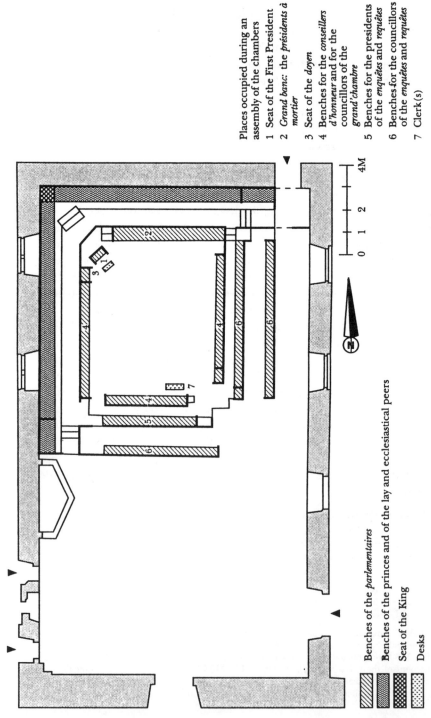

Places occupied during an assembly of the chambers

1 Seat of the First President

2 *Grand banc*: the *présidents à mortier*

3 Seat of the *doyen*

4 Benches for the *conseillers d'honneur* and for the councillors of the *grand'chambre*

5 Benches for the presidents of the *enquêtes* and *requêtes*

6 Benches for the councillors of the *enquêtes* and *requêtes*

7 Clerk(s)

▨ Benches of the *parlementaires*

▨ Benches of the princes and of the lay and ecclesiastical peers

▨ Seat of the King

▨ Desks

0 1 2 4M

Figure 3 Reconstruction of the seating arrangements in the *grand'chambre* for an assembly of the chambers (by Nadine Marchal and the author)

vivacité comme s'il s'agissoit de leur intérest personnel. Alors quelques uns de Mrs. de la grand chambre se réveillent, se détachent de leurs confrères, la vérité et l'honneur prennent le dessus et l'on voit Mrs. de la grand chambre revenir du blanc au noir, les uns par conviction, les autres pour abréger des séances qui les excèdent et qui occuppent [*sic*] un temps qu'ils emploieraient d'une manière plus lucrative. Il faut cependant retrancher de ce tableau un Pajot de Malzac, un abbé de Vougny, et un abbé d'Héricourt.[37]

After the *commissaires* had met a few times at the first president's lodgings in the precinct of the *Parlement*, the Hôtel du Bailliage, they were in a position to report back to the assembly of the chambers. Again the *rapporteur* spoke first, endeavouring to sum up the views of the *commissaires*. Then, the first president asked the *commissaires* present to give their views: in order of seniority if they belonged to the *grand'chambre* and in turn by chambers for the others. When they had given their opinion, the first president asked for the views of the remainder of the assembly starting with the *grand'chambre* (including the *conseillers d'honneur*) and continuing with the *conseillers* from the other chambers, though there is some uncertainty as to the order in which the members of the *enquêtes* and *requêtes* gave their opinions: whether by chamber, by order of seniority in the *Parlement*, or simply in the order in which they chose to sit on the benches that were reserved for them (see Figure 3). The *présidents à mortier* gave their views last of all, in order of seniority on the *grand banc*; in other circumstances, when there was no *rapporteur*, they were the first to speak.[38] At an assembly of the chambers it may have been easier to get the ordinary members of the *enquêtes* and *requêtes* to speak in the order in which they had chosen to sit on the benches in the *grand'chambre*. One should not assume that the rigidity of the seating arrangement by chambers necessarily prevented physical contact between senior members of the *Parlement* and the *enquêtes*; on 18 April 1752 Robert de Saint-Vincent (5th *enquêtes*) found himself sitting at the end of the first *banc* of the *enquêtes* on the small seat (see Figure 3) that the clerk had the right to occupy during sessions ('à côté et plus bas que ne sont assis les conseillers de grand'chambre, qui sont sur le premier banc de la grand-

---

[37] BS, MS 800, f. 87: account of a meeting of *commissaires* on 17 May 1751; see Durey de Meinières's description of another such meeting in Flammermont, *Rems.*, i, p. 672, wherein it may be inferred that the first president would ask the *commissaires* to give their opinion in order of seniority unless the chambers had mandated them by means of a *vœu*; in that case, he was expected to ask the *commissaires* from each chamber in turn to speak.

[38] Flammermont, *Rems.*, i. pp. 680–1 (*rapporteurs* and *commissaires*), 684 (*grand'chambre*), 684–5 (*enquêtes* and *requêtes*); a comparison with Bluche, *L'Origine des magistrats*, would suggest that the order of speakers given by Durey de Meinières does not agree with the date of their reception into the *Parlement*: e.g. Bélanger d'Essenlis (2nd *enquêtes*, 12 May 1741) precedes Murard (4th *enquêtes*, 5 Dec. 1738). In BS, MS 800, f. 96, Durey de Meinières also implies that the *enquêtes* and *requêtes* did not always speak in strict order of seniority. See also Flammermont, *Rems.*, i, p. 679 and BS, MS 800, f. 92 (*présidents à mortier*) and Rogister, 'Le Gouvernement, le Parlement de Paris', pp. 336–7, 353–4.

'chambre'); this arrangement meant that he was sitting next to Thomé, a leading figure of the *grand'chambre*.[39] In the same way on one occasion, Anjorrant (a councillor of the *grand'chambre*) sat 'sur le premier banc des princes à droite de M. le Premier Président'.[40]

It is necessary to turn next to the voting procedures in the *Parlement*. Each *parlementaire* expressed his opinion, or *avis*, once only in the course of a debate (this rule was broken on two known occasions, by President Durey de Meinières in November 1751 and by President de Maupeou in a crucial debate in February 1753), and his *avis* might end with a proposed text for an *arrêt* or *arrêté*; alternatively, he might wish simply to endorse an *avis* that had been expressed earlier in the debate or to propose a different *arrêt*, or to make an amendment to one which had been proposed. In this way, after the first president had asked each *parlementaire* for his opinion, any number of different *avis* could have been expressed, at times up to sixty, some enjoying greater support than others. But on a typical occasion in an important debate, like that of 3 December 1751 on the *Hôpital général* affair for instance, there were seventeen different *avis* expressed.[41] The next step was to break down these *avis* so that only two remained. This was done by asking those whose *avis* had received little or no support to opt for one of the others. Eventually it was possible to reduce the number of *avis* to three by the same process. The *parlementaires* whose *avis* enjoyed the least support of the three then had to choose between the two others, and of the two remainig *avis*, the one which thereby obtained the support of the majority was carried (see Table 2).[42]

Any discussion of voting and other procedures in the *Parlement* raises the question whether these could be manipulated in the interests of any group. To a great extent, the answer to that question helps to dispel the prevailing notion that the *Parlement* was increasingly dominated, even led, in the 1750s by those who are described as the *zélés*: young, active and usually Jansenist members of the *enquêtes* and *requêtes*. It is certainly evident that, in an assembly attended by about 136 *parlementaires*, a handful of *zélés* were usually eager to activate the *Parlement* on questions relating to the Bull *Unigenitus* and its effects. But the twin assumptions that these five or six *zélés* were Jansenists and that they led the *Parlement* need to be questioned. One of the *zélés*, Rolland d'Erceville, questioned the first of these assumptions in his account of the origins of the *Grandes Remontrances* of 1753.[43] He would not be

[39] Collection Michel Vinot Préfontaine (Paris), 'Mémoires de P. A. Robert de Saint-Vincent' (typescript copy), p. 134.

[40] *Ibid.*, p. 166.   [41] Flammermont, *Rems.*, i, p. 701 (Durey de Meinières's account).

[42] *Ibid.*; see also Rogister, 'Le Gouvernement, le Parlement de Paris', p. 341; Flammermont, *Rems.*, i, pp. 684 and 691.

[43] Bibliothèque nationale, Paris (hereafter BN), Cabinet des MSS, MSS Fonds français 8496 (Collection Lamoignon), ff. 124–5. On President Rolland's memoirs see also Chapter 6, note 29.

Table 2. *Opinions expressed at an assembly of the chambers with their reduction to form an arrêt* (1 July 1752)

No.	*Avis*	No. of votes	*Arrêt*
	Conclusions des gens du roi: à décréter Daguet d'ajournement personnel et Belleguelle d'assigné pour être ouï; informations continuées		
1	à l'avis des conclusions	65	68*
2	à l'avis de décréter Daguet de prise de corps; rien contre Belleguelle	4	
3	à l'avis de décréter Daguet de prise de corps, Belleguelle d'ajournement personnel	38	65
4	à l'avis de décréter Daguet d'assigné pour être ouï	22	
5	à l'avis de décréter Daguet de prise de corps, Belleguelle d'ajournement personnel, et Lecler [a third chaplain implicated in the affair] d'assigné pour être ouï	4	
6	à l'avis de décréter Daguet et Belleguelle de prise de corps	2	
	Number of votes expressed	135	133

Note: An asterisk indicates the opinion that prevailed and formed the *arrêt*.
The matter under discussion related to a refusal of the sacrament to Barbe Dufossé by two chaplains at Abbeville.
Source: Bibliothèque universitaire de Poitiers, Archives d'Argenson, CA 59, nos. 1 and 6: secret reports from the Councillor Titon to the Comte d'Argenson.

drawn on a quibble about what constituted a Jansenist, but he allowed the term to be applied freely to opponents of *Unigenitus*, not because they upheld the errors contained in the propositions attributed to Jansenius, but because, thanks to the efforts of those whom he equally freely described as 'the Jesuits', 'cette qualification est devenue inhérente avec l'opposition à la constitution Unigenitus et qu'il faut se conformer à la façon de parler réelle dans le monde'.[44] According to this definition, some *zélés* like Clément, Lambert and Robert de Saint-Vincent were Jansenists, but others were not: President Gilbert (a *président à mortier*), Presidents Durey de Meinières, Gaultier de Besigny and Frémont du Mazy, together with the Abbé Chauvelin, Chavanon, Davy de La Fautrière, and Béze de la Belouse, all from the *enquêtes* and *requêtes*. Although those whom Rolland d'Erceville did describe as Jansenists were, in his words, 'la cheville ouvrière de tout ce qui se passe', it was his opinion that they led the *Parlement* not because they were Jansenists but because they were more active and learned in legal and historical precedents than the majority of their colleagues. He made the further point that the real extremists in the *Parlement* were few in number, never carried the day, and were not Jansenists.[45]

   Rolland d'Erceville's analysis concerning the *zélés* can be corroborated in part from other sources and helps to dispel the notion that they were all Jansenists, even in his loose definition. But his view that they led the *Parlement* was advanced almost exclusively on the basis of his close knowledge of the events leading up to the *Grandes Remontrances* of 1753; as will be seen later, he was dealing there with a special case. Perhaps it was also believed in some court and governmental circles that the *zélés* led the *Parlement*; Madame de Pompadour complained to President Durey de Meinières in 1757 of the 'contrainte et tyrannie' which they wielded over the rest of *Parlement*.[46] However, neither court nor government was noted for a perceptive analysis of the different groups within the *Parlement*. Certainly, the *zélés* could usually ensure that a few, if not all, of their number were made *commissaires* for their respective chambers (in place of elderly, absent colleagues) to discuss matters that were of great concern to them. They could also manipulate their colleagues in those chambers to secure a request, or *vœu*, from the *enquêtes* and *requêtes* for the first president to call an assembly of the chambers.[47] Finally, they could draft *avis* and texts of *arrêts* and *arrêtés*

---

[44] BN, MS franç. 8496 (Collection Lamoignon), f. 124.   [45] *Ibid.*, f. 125.

[46] B[aron] J[érôme] P[ichon] (ed.), 'Conversation de la Marquise de Pompadour et du Président de Meinières', *Mélanges de littérature et d'histoire recueillis et publiés par la Société des bibliophiles françois, 1ère partie* (1856), pp. 133–62, 158. The conversation took place in Madame de Pompadour's apartment at Versailles on 26 January 1757.

[47] Flammermont, *Rems.*, i, p. 678 (Durey de Meinières), and BS, MS 732: 'Registre de la deuxième chambre des enquêtes', f. 101 (deliberation of 7 Feb. 1759 in that chamber leading to the formulation of a *vœu*).

which they proposed or could induce others further down the line of *opinants* to propose when giving their *avis*; literally back-bench intrigue.[48] But an examination of voting and other procedures clearly shows that it was practically impossible for any single group of junior *parlementaires* to dominate the assembly on a permanent or systematic basis. That possibility was reserved for the real leaders of the *Parlement*: the first president, the *présidents à mortier* and their generally loyal gerontocracy of the *grand'chambre*. The use of *rapporteurs* and *commissaires* also gave added weight to the men who really mattered. The voting procedures gave disproportionate influence to the *grand'chambre* in assemblies both of *commissaires* and of all the chambers, where their fourteen *commissaires* spoke immediately after the *rapporteur*. By speaking last on these occasions, the *présidents à mortier* could propose such *avis* as might be necessary to repair the damage done by those who had already spoken. By speaking first when there was no *rapporteur*, the *présidents à mortier* gave the line to the *grand'chambre*, and they had even more agents and opportunities than the *zélés* when it came to getting others to propose *avis* or possible *arrêtés* at the subsequent stages in a debate. These men of influence were usually reluctant to take anything but the mildest course of action: *supplications* to the King were preferable to making representations to him, representations were preferable to remonstrances, and remonstrances were preferable to any more serious proceeding.

Nevertheless, the best-laid schemes may go awry. As the political crisis of the 1750s demonstrated, the system could break down. Division could appear among the ranks of the *présidents à mortier* and of the stalwarts of the *grand'chambre*, and the *zélés* had a chance to take the initiative. Could the explanation for breakdowns of this nature lie in the disruptive effects of the religious and financial issues of the day? Certainly, the political crises of those years cannot be understood properly without reference to the conflict over *Unigenitus* and the cumulative effect of the Crown's financial demands. Yet there were other developments that also help to explain the crises. These lesser-known developments were concerned with the *Parlement* itself. There, the conflict over *Unigenitus* and issues of finance simply added fuel to the latent struggle of personalities and factions. A striking example was the fall of Keeper of the Seals Chauvelin in 1737. Chauvelin was dismissed in part because his adherents in the *Parlement* were trying to create trouble there and to overthrow First President Le Peletier: an issue concerning the validity of papal bulls in France had provided them with the opportunity

---

[48] Flammermont, *Rems.*, i, p. 700 (Durey de Meinières's account of the debate on 3 Dec. 1751); on this occasion the Abbé Chauvelin (3rd *enquêtes*) seated himself at one point behind Presidents Chauvelin and Gilbert of the *grand'chambre* and drafted an *arrêté* which was then passed down the line to Titon, Pasquier, and Davy de La Fautrière for their comments. Once the draft had been amended, it was sent down to Goguet (5th *enquêtes*) who proposed it as part of his own *avis* when his turn came to speak in the debate.

they needed.[49] It was not uncommon for ministers like Chauvelin, and later Machault and D'Argenson, to have factions in the *Parlement* as well as at court. Chauvelin's fall was also significant in that it did not destroy his faction either at court or in the *Parlement*, as events as late as 1753–4 were to demonstrate. Moreover, his fall had significant repercussions on the handling of religious and financial questions at the *Parlement*.

It was not only faction that influenced *parlementaires*. The pressures inherent in a dynastic office-holding system often affected their attitude and conduct. These pressures are easily discernible in the intrigues surrounding the *présidences à mortier* and the *gens du roi*. Two examples serve to illustrate the position: one in 1738 and the other in 1741. The first of these is related to the death of the first president of another Parisian court, the *Grand Conseil*. There were two candidates to succeed Monsieur de Verthamon: Lamoignon de Blancmesnil and Guillaume-François-Louis Joly de Fleury, the second *avocat général* at the *Parlement*, where his father was *procureur général*. Lamoignon came from an old and distinguished *parlementaire* family, but he was a younger son. As such he could aspire to little more than the post of *avocat général*, which he had exercised from 1707 to 1723 (when his time in the *parquet* overlapped in part with that of Chancellor Daguesseau and of the elder Joly de Fleury). Without the financial resources to buy himself a *présidence à mortier*, he had taken a lease in 1723 on one which belonged to First President Potier de Novion. The lease expired in 1732, but he was allowed to remain in the post until 1736, when Potier de Novion's grandson came of age and decided to take up his duties. That year, however, Lamoignon failed to obtain the first presidency on the death of Portail. He was then already fifty-three years old and his career in the *Parlement* seemed at an end despite his undoubted merits; hence, he had turned his attention to the *Grand Conseil*, a less important court. Unfortunately for him, Cardinal de Fleury did not like him and suspected him, quite erroneously, as Lamoignon's subsequent career amply demonstrated, of holding Jansenist sympathies. Lamoignon did not get the post.

Joly de Fleury's son, the second *avocat général*, stood a better chance: after all, he was Verthamon's heir. Moreover, First President Le Peletier initially encouraged the move, as he wished to be rid of the young man in order to find a place among the *gens du roi* for his own cousin, Le Peletier de Saint-Fargeau. Chancellor Daguesseau's son, Daguesseau de Plainmont, the third *avocat général*, also favoured the move as his colleague's departure from the *parquet* would bring him a step nearer to the rank of *premier avocat*

[49] See J. M. J. Rogister, 'New light on the fall of Chauvelin', *English Historical Review*, lxxxiii (1968), pp. 314–30; and by the same, 'A minister's fall and its implications: the case of Chauvelin (1737–1746)', in *Studies in the French eighteenth century presented to John Lough by his colleagues, pupils and friends*, ed. D.J. Mossop and others (Durham, 1978), pp. 200–17.

général, then held by Gilbert de Voisins. But, according to Daguesseau de Plainmont, the cardinal ruled out young Joly de Fleury as being a *mauvais sujet*. There were also other objections to his appointment. The *procureur général* was asking for three favours at the same time: the first presidency of the *Grand Conseil* for his eldest son; the latter's post as *avocat général* for his second son, Jean-Omer; and Jean-Omer's post as *avocat général* at the *Grand Conseil* for his third son (then one of the *substituts* to the *procureur général*). Le Peletier tried to block these dynastic manoeuvres because of his own intentions concerning Le Peletier de Saint-Fargeau. The situation became more confusing when Gilbert de Voisins wrote angrily to the cardinal saying that he wished to withdraw immediately from the *parquet* so that his own son could be received there before any other newcomer. Gilbert's feelings were understandable; he did not want anyone to join the *parquet* before he left it himself so that, in succeeding him, his son would not find anyone there senior to him except Daguesseau de Plainmont. Cardinal de Fleury was opposed to Gilbert's departure and sought to postpone it. In all this quandary, the cardinal was persuaded to adopt the unusual and expensive course of reimbursing all the presidential offices of the *Grand Conseil* and establishing a commission in their place in order to avoid appointing a successor to Monsieur de Verthamon. These arrangements were made by an edict registered at the *Grand Conseil* on 25 January 1738.[50]

First President Le Peletier was outraged and also worried; he had quarrelled with the cardinal three weeks earlier and he viewed the decision, somewhat unreasonably, as a sinister move directed at the *Parlement*. Joly de Fleury was less apprehensive, but was concerned by a clause in the edict whereby the *Grand Conseil* was required to send copies of the law to the lower jurisdictions of the *Parlement*, the *bailliages* and the *sénéchaussées*. In his view, these courts had to register only laws that were sent to them by the *procureur général* of the *Parlement*. To safeguard the position of the *Parlement* and the prerogatives of his office, Joly de Fleury issued a circular to the lower jurisdictions forbidding them to register anything except upon his instructions. But, apart from this move, he remained passive for the rest of the year in order to repair his dynastic fences. So too did Gilbert de Voisins, who was still in negotiations with Cardinal de Fleury and Chancellor

---

[50] These details come from the autograph memoirs of H. F. Daguesseau de Plainmont (1713–41), the third *avocat général*; these are entitled 'Recueil des affaires Les plus Remarquables qui se traittent à nos assemblées soit Générales, soit Particulières' (hereafter referred to as Daguesseau de Plainmont, 'Mémoires'): Bibliothèque de la Société de Port Royal, Paris, Collection Le Paige (hereafter BPR, LP), 17, pp. 1151–74. On the *Grand Conseil* at this time see François Bluche, *Les Magistrats du Grand Conseil au xviiie siècle, 1690–1791* (Annales littéraires de l'Université de Besançon, lxxxii, Paris, 1966), pp. 24–6, 91 (entry under Jean-Omer Joly de Fleury) and 145 (entry under François-Michel de Verthamon).

Daguesseau to hand over his office to his son. In controversial cases that came up before the *Parlement* during that year (like that of the *Filles du Calvaire*), the *gens du roi* were not prepared to give the lead. By contrast, the disgruntled first president had reached a stage where he was prepared simply to follow the wishes of the majority in the *Parlement*.[51]

Gilbert de Voisins finally left the *parquet* in 1739 and his son became an *avocat général*. Joly de Fleury's eldest son thereby became *premier avocat général*. The *procureur général*'s patience seemed to be rewarded, for in December 1740, the King granted him the favour that his eldest son would succeed him as *procureur général* (that is, he would have what was called the *survivance* of his father). He could hope that when he eventually retired, his second son, Jean-Omer, would succeed the first as *avocat général*. By July 1741, it was clear that Daguesseau de Plainmont, then second *avocat général*, was dying. D'Ormesson de Noyseau, who was the chancellor's nephew, asked for the post. D'Ormesson was at the *Grand Conseil*, where he was junior in age and standing to Jean-Omer. The *procureur général* accordingly asked that the post should be given to Jean-Omer on the grounds that D'Ormesson would have to wait only until the *premier avocat général* succeeded his father as *procureur général* in order to take his place in the *parquet*. But the chancellor used all his influence on behalf of his nephew, and, despite Cardinal de Fleury's reluctance, D'Ormesson de Noyseau was given the promise of the post. Whereupon Joly de Fleury offered to resign, so that both Jean-Omer and D'Ormesson could become *avocats généraux* at the same time with the first having precedence over the second. The King and Cardinal de Fleury would not accept this solution, but the King did agree to his request that Jean-Omer should have the next vacant place in the *parquet*, adding in his own hand on the *bon*: 'Pourvu que mon procureur général serve encor [*sic*] deux ans dans sa place.' Joly de Fleury had to accept the arrangment, but was flattered by the personal compliment implicit in the condition set by the King. Daguesseau de Plainmont died on 29 September – a promising young man who had already started to write his memoirs – and D'Ormesson de Noyseau succeeded him. Despite the clash of interests that marked his entry into the *parquet*, he and Jean-Omer Joly de Fleury remained on excellent terms. As for the *procureur général*, he could feel that he had now gone some way towards establishing at least two of his sons permanently as *gens du roi* in the *Parlement*.[52]

[51] BPR, LP 17: Daguesseau de Plainmont, 'Mémoires'.
[52] On these developments see AN, 342 AP 2 ('Mémoires' of J. O. Joly de Fleury), p. 3; see also a letter from Cardinal de Fleury to the *procureur général* of 30 July 1741, reproduced in part in *Autographes et documents historiques* (Librairie de l'Abbaye, Paris, [undated but in the 1970s], no. 218, p. 14, lot no. 63, where 'chancelier' is wrongly transcribed as 'chevalier'. The *procureur général* sent a letter of condolence to the chancellor on the death of Daguesseau de Plainmont: the chancellor was clearly moved by it and his reply of 30 Sept.

The personalities of some of the leading figures in the *Parlement* also need to be taken into consideration. There was that of Guillaume-François Joly de Fleury himself, for instance. He had been *procureur général* since 1717. He was learned in both civil and canon law, and although he did not always wear his erudition lightly, his enormous output in letters, memoirs and treatises – all in his distinctive spidery hand – reveal an alert, resourceful and ingenious mind. That he had personal and dynastic ambitions is undeniable, and both Cardinal de Fleury and Chancellor Daguesseau, who had earlier been his colleague in the *parquet*, treated him with caution. It is said that the cardinal once asked Gilbert de Voisins: 'Peut-on se fier au procureur général?' 'Oui, Monseigneur', was the bright reply, 'si on s'y fie'.[53] That was the secret, for Joly de Fleury liked to be consulted and to display his skills. The historian who studies his writings comes away fascinated by the remarkable and powerful personality that they reveal. He was intensely dynastic, but perhaps his desire to establish his younger sons sprang from the fact that the fortunes of the family had once been gravely compromised. Because of ill-health, he had been destined for the church, and his career had only been made possible and necessary by the premature death of his young brother. Even so, much had then turned on the willingness of his widowed sister-in-law to assist him and to direct her own child towards the Church.[54] He was also able to appreciate the fact that a younger son might be more gifted than an elder brother: this was the case with his own offspring. He was not a rich man, and he had needed to implore the Duc de Bourbon, the prime minister, in June 1725 for financial assistance to meet his obligations to creditors.[55] His chief passion always

---

1741 indicates the esteem in which he continued to hold Joly de Fleury (Bibliothèque municipale, Amiens, MSS 1152).

[53] Quoted by Louis Guimbaud, *Auget de Montyon, 1733–1820, d'après des documents inédits* (Paris, 1909), p. 42.

[54] For these details, see Bisson de Barthélemy, *Les Joly de Fleury*, pp. 23–4. Guillaume-François Joly de Fleury (1675–1756) was *procureur général* from 1717 to 1746 and is referred to throughout this account as the *procureur général* until that date; after 1746 his eldest son, Guillaume-François-Louis (1710–87), is referred to as the *procureur général*, while his father is simply called Joly de Fleury. The second son, Jean-Omer (1715–1810), was *avocat général* (1746), first *avocat général* (1755) and finally *président à mortier* (1768): he is referred to as Jean-Omer Joly de Fleury to avoid further confusion. A third son, Jean-François (1718–1802), had only a brief career in the *Parlement* and entered the royal administration, where he became *contrôleur général des finances* under Louis XVI (Bisson de Barthélemy errs in making him the eldest son in the genealogical table of the family tree which he gives on p. 319 of his work but then corrects this mistake on p. 31). There are chapters on Guillaume-François and Jean-Omer (with illustrations) in Adolphe Wattinne, *Magistrats célèbres du xviiiᵉ siècle* (Paris, 1941), pp. 181–98 and 199–208.

[55] Cf. former collection of Sir Thomas Phillipps (*apud: Bibliotheca Phillippica, New Series: Sixteenth Part: Catalogue of French, Spanish, Greek & Serbo-Croat Manuscripts with a few Slavonic and Portuguese*, Sotheby Catalogue, London, 1976), 3542/111: f. 13: Joly de Fleury to the Duc de Bourbon, Paris, 25 June 1725, asking for an indemnity to be paid on his *brevet de retenue*.

remained the *Parlement*, its rôle, past, present, and future. He helped to save some of its most valuable records for posterity, and, ultimately, he was happiest in the midst of his impressive collection of books and manuscripts in the house in the rue Hautefeuille.[56] As a young man, the lawyer and polemicist J. N. Moreau often visited him there and charmingly recalled that he had never seen a mirror in the house; perhaps not, but somewhere and in pride of place would have been an impressive portrait by Philippe de Champaigne (now in the National Gallery in Washington) of Joly de Fleury's grandfather, the austere and vulpine Omer Talon, hero of the *Parlement* during the Fronde a century earlier: there possibly was the missing mirror.[57]

It seems appropriate to compare Joly de Fleury with his former colleague and senior partner in the *parquet*, Chancellor Daguesseau. Both men were erudite, though Daguesseau was probably the more gifted of the two and the better stylist. Like some great intellects, however, the chancellor tended to take refuge in a vagueness of thought that is totally absent from the more spontaneous Joly de Fleury. Daguesseau was a cold fish: one of his sons recognised this characteristic and describes him well on a typical occasion: 'Mon père ne dit mot, il parut étonné; il dit seulement que c'était notre affaire, mais que la chose était délicate.'[58] Daguesseau could wield the evasive platitudes of the robe. Between the chancellor and the *procureur général* there was an old, but uneasy, relationship. At best, complicity; at worst, the rapiers were out – on the chancellor's side at least – as in this exchange of letters in March 1735 concerning developments in the *Parlement* that could have been avoided, according to Joly de Fleury, if the *parquet* had been given greater freedom of action:

---

[56] See P.M. Bondois, 'Une réintégration au trésor des chartes en 1736', *Bibliothèque de l'Ecole des Chartes*, lxxxvi (1925), pp. 411–20, and, by the same author, 'Le Procureur général Joly de Fleury et les papiers de Du Cange (1743)', *ibid.*, lxxxix (1928), pp. 81–8. Joly de Fleury also owned the celebrated Dupuy MSS (941 bound volumes) and presented them to the King in 1754; he lent four volumes of these MSS to Durey de Meinières and asked the latter to return them on 27 May 1754; see BN, MS franç. 7573 (Durey de Meinières Papers); Guillaume-François-Louis continued to use the Dupuy volumes after they had become the property of the King: see his letter of 15 Nov. 1784 to Bijot in the Princeton University Library, John Hinsdale Scheide Collection of French Historical Autographs. The house in the rue Hautefeuille was destroyed in the nineteenth century when the boulevard Saint-Germain was built: see the Comte d'Aucourt, *Les Anciens Hôtels de Paris avec une carte gravée des grands hôtels de la rive gauche avant 1789* (Paris, 1880), p. 52.

[57] J. N. Moreau, *Mes souvenirs*, ed. C. Hermelin (Paris, 1898, 1902), 2 vols., i, p. 52; for the portrait of Omer Talon, see *La Peinture française du xviiᵉ siècle dans les collections américaines* (Ministère de la Culture, Editions de la Réunion des Musées nationaux, Paris, 1982), pp. 193 (colour plate) and 234–6 (catalogue entry no. 16); it passed by descent to the De Buttet family who sold it after the Second World War: a copy also exists in Bologna.

[58] BPR, LP 17: Daguesseau de Plainmont, 'Mémoires'; on the chancellor, see also *Lettres inédites du Chancelier Daguesseau*, ed. Rives (Paris, 1823), *passim*, and *Le Chancelier Henri-François D'Aguesseau, Limoges 1668 – Fresnes 1751 : journées d'étude tenues à Limoges à l'occasion du bicentaire de sa mort (octobre 1951)*, ed. G. Rech (Limoges, 1953).

J'ay reçu la lettre que vous m'avés fait l'honneur de m'écrire au sujet de l'arrêt du 1er de ce mois. Il a été entièrement conforme à mes Conclusions. A l'égard du discours vous aviés prévu, Monseigneur, ce que j'auroit à vous répondre: si on n'avoit pas voulu il y a quelques années suspendre le zéle du parquet et exiger qu'on ne fit rien sans ordre, le Parlement ne se seroit pas porté à des dénonciations, si on n'avoit pas voulu exigé la mesme chose du Parlement, les enquêtes n'auroient pas été si vives, et n'auroient pas étably le principe qu'elles sont compétentes de tout ce qu'elles désirent, si on n'avoit pas plusieurs fois insisté à voir et à corrigé [*sic*] les discours des gens du Roy, on auroit cru de son intérest de consulter et de corriger.[59]

The chancellor's reply was devastating:

Pensant comme vous le faites, Monsieur, il n'y avoit qu'à ne me parler de rien, mais ne parler qu'à moy, c'est m'embarrasser sans vous débarrasser: après cela je vous ay dit tout ce qui m'est venu dans l'esprit. C'est à vous de prendre le party que vous jugerés à propos, à vos risques, périls et fortunes. Je comprends vos raisons de Compagnie, et je souhaite qu'il n'arrive aucun inconvénient de tout cecy.[60]

By contrast, First President Le Peletier was a weaker vessel. In his memoirs, Daguesseau de Plainmont vividly described him as follows:

Quand le danger est loin, le P.Pt. fait bonne contenance, il rit, il écoute tout d'un air léger avec un souris gracieux et de complaisance, on dirait qu'il a tout prévu, qu'il va donner remède à tout, ou plutôt qu'il va aller au devant de tout; mais quand le danger s'approche, il ne sait plus où il en est. Le rouge lui monte aux joues, il déplore la situation des esprits; 2 ou 3 lieux communs se présentent à propos, et puis il va par crainte se jetter la tête la première dans toutes les sottises qui peuvent se rencontrer et dont la matière est susceptible.[61]

On this occasion it was the fear of some move at an assembly of the chambers. Le Peletier lived up to Boizot's descriptions of a first president's dilemma: his relations with members of the Government were as tense as those with the rest of the *Parlement*. He and Cardinal de Fleury were united in their desire to eliminate Chauvelin in 1737, but within a year they were at odds concerning a religious dispute. The cardinal is alleged to have accused him to his face of being too compliant to the 'Jansenist party'; 'Le Premier président reprit avec hauteur qu'il n'était ni janseniste, ni moliniste, mais qu'il était magistrat.'[62] In these circumstances, it was perhaps fortunate that, on the Government's side, relations with the *Parlement* were not handled by the cardinal alone: the King naturally had a say, but also

[59] BPR, LP 450, f. 145: Joly de Fleury to Daguesseau, undated [March 1735].
[60] *Ibid.*, f. 146: 'mardi matin'.
[61] BPR, LP 17: Daguesseau de Plainmont, 'Mémoires', pp. 1160–2 (Dec. 1737).
[62] *Ibid.*, p. 1154 (3 Jan. 1738).

the chancellor (as head of the judiciary), the *contrôleur général* (if financial measures were involved), and the minister who had the responsibility for the administration of Paris.

The ministerial and conciliar structure of the French government under the *ancien régime* has been the subject of some notable studies, in particular those by the Comte de Luçay in the last century and by Monsieur Michel Antoine in our own.[63] They serve to emphasise the complexity of the decision-taking process. Normally the chancellor dealt with the *Parlement* in the King's name through the agency of the first president and the *gens du roi*, though orders from the King could be addressed formally to the *Parlement* as well. The minister with responsibility for the Paris *département* despatched the parchment copies of edicts and declarations to the *Parlement* after these had been signed and sealed by the chancellor (and the keeper of the seals if the chancellor did not also hold the seals): he was also entitled to receive reports from the first president and from the *gens du roi* on proceedings in the *Parlement*. Both the chancellor and the minister with the Paris *département* reported back to the King and acted in liaison with one another. If they were dealing with an important issue or crisis, the King would usually refer it to a meeting of the *Conseil des dépêches*, the second of the royal councils (after the *Conseil d'en haut* which dealt with foreign affairs and war), where all the ministers could express an opinion and a decision was taken, normally on a majority basis. The *Conseil des dépêches* met regularly on Saturdays, but extraordinary meetings could be called by the King at any time.[64]

Complications were created by the King's constant movements from one residence to another. When the court moved with monotonous regularity from Versailles to Marly in May, to Compiègne in the summer and to Fontainebleau in the autumn, at least the ministers followed the King. But Louis XV also made frequent trips to his private residences of Choisy and La Muette, and after 1746 to Madame de Pompadour's places at Bellevue and Crécy; few ministers were included in these parties. If a political crisis occurred then, it was not always easy for the chancellor and other ministers to act at once if they needed to refer back to the King. When informed of

[63] Comte de Luçay, *Des origines du pouvoir ministériel en France: les secrétaires d'état depuis leur institution jusqu'à la mort de Louis XV* (Paris, 1881), *passim*, but especially pp. 320–3; and Michel Antoine, *Le Conseil du Roi sous le règne de Louis XV*, *passim*; some useful indications may also be gained from Auguste Dumas, 'L'Action des secrétaires d'état sous l'ancien régime', *Annales de la Faculté de droit d'Aix*, n.s., xlvii (1954), pp. 5–92. For essential biographical details on members of the Government and administration at this time, see Michel Antoine, *Le Gouvernement et l'administration sous Louis XV: Dictionnaire biographique* (Paris, 1978).

[64] Michel Antoine, 'Le Conseil des dépêches sous le règne de Louis XV', *Bibliothèque de l'Ecole des Chartes*, cxi (1953), pp. 158–208, cxii (1954), pp. 126–81; and, by the same author, *Le Conseil du Roi*, *passim*.

developments, the King had a tendency to consult only the ministers who happened to be with him at the time, or else to refer matters back to a special meeting of the *Conseil des dépêches*. With such an *ad hoc* approach to government, it was perhaps inevitable that decisions were sometimes taken without proper consideration to their full implications. Even when matters reached the council table, the prevailing mood could be one of recrimination, saving, of course, the King's august presence.[65]

In the final analysis, it was on the King himself that the whole system turned, not so much in council, where it was his general practice to endorse the view of the majority, but in the day-to-day decisions that were taken by him in consultation with the various ministers, either during their regular audiences in the early evening after he had returned from the hunt, or in his replies in the margin of their respectful letters proffering advice and requesting orders. Again, as far as one can judge, Louis XV usually endorsed the advice he was given. The more one looks at Louis XIV's precepts and practice of government, the more it appears that his successor followed them in deferring to the advice of his ministers. Louis XV's main achievement was that he succeed in maintaining intact the system of government passed on to him by his great-grandfather. He had been inducted into it by the Regent and later by Fleury: he came to know its intricate workings to perfection and watched over its preservation like a hawk. At the same time, it is possible that the Regent and Fleury taught him to look at men and affairs at their own level, from the side, not to say askance, rather than from above. Behind the superb regal façade, the man remained, in Madame de Pompadour's own words, 'indéchiffrable'. He does not seem to have placed his trust in anyone, though Madame de Pompadour may have been closer to him than most. He was also a man of infinite curiosity. For all these reasons he felt a need to have secret informants. The *Secret du Roi* may have started as a means of advancing the cause of the Prince de Conty's candidature to the Polish crown, an instance of what has been described as 'paradiplomacy', but it eventually became one of the King's means of keeping a close check on his ministers of foreign

---

[65] Michel Antoine tends to play down this aspect of the conciliar system in *Le Conseil du Roi*, and also in his article, 'Les Comités de ministres sous le règne de Louis XV', *Revue historique de droit français et étranger*, 4th series, xxix (1951), pp. 213–30. For a different and less flattering account of proceedings in council, see the view of two of its members, the Duc d'Antin and Cardinal de Tencin; D'Antin wrote: '... les véritables affaires se traittent en particulier avec le ministre qui en est chargé: c'est ainsi qu'en usoit le feu roy [Louis XIV], dont les exemples sont respectables: on continue la même méthode. Jamais un ministre n'est instruit de ce qui regarde son confrère'; in his 'Mémoire. Réflexion sur le temps présent', Chantilly, 14 June 1726, quoted in *Autograph letters and historical documents from the collection of Alfred Morrison*, 2nd series (London, 1882–93), i, pp. 63–4; for Tencin's view, see his letter to the Duc de Richelieu of 29 Aug. 1743: 'Quiconque travaille avec le Roi, est maître dans son tripot'; reproduced in 'Autographes et documents: Le Conseil des ministres sous Louis XV', *L'Amateur d'autographes* (1911), pp. 345–8.

affairs. He probably practised a similar system in domestic affairs, but there is less documentary evidence about it than there is for the *Secret du Roi*. Louis XV's natural skills lay in intrigue and negotiation, and his reign was largely spent in these activities wherein he displayed all the devious intelligence of the politically adept. Unlike Louis XIV, he was profoundly unimaginative in political matters, he foresaw difficulties in any course of action, and he allowed his attitude to the *Parlement* to be coloured by a strong, almost atavistic prejudice against it.[66] At times an honest broker was needed between the King and his magistrates. Few were equipped to play the rôle, but one deserves some mention here.

From 1726 to 1749 responsibility for the Paris *département* lay with Jean-Frédéric Phélypeaux, Comte de Maurepas, the minister of marine. Maurepas had a long political career and was principal minister to Louis XVI when he died at an advanced age in 1781 having served the Crown for over fifty years.[67] The Phélypeaux were of robe origin and had been a ministerial family under Louis XIV. Maurepas was the grandson of Chancellor de Pontchartrain (whose saying he was apt to quote: 'Point de parlement, point de monarchie'). Much emphasis is usually placed on Maurepas's flippancy and wit and too little on his legal knowledge, his skill and flexibility in negotiating with leading *parlementaires* (some of whom were related to him). Duclos claimed that, having to make a set of regulations for the colonies, Maurepas showed his draft to Daguesseau. The chancellor, who was a stickler on points of law, looked at it and remarked approvingly: 'On ne peut être plus régulièrement irrégulier.'[68]

Maurepas was also unusually well informed about developments in the *Parlement*. The debates of the *Parlement* were secret, and normally the only details which reached the Government were contained in the regular, but purely formal, accounts of meetings and decisions which the first president and the *procureur général* sent to the chancellor and to the ministers concerned. But who were the 'trouble-makers', what were the highlights of the

---

[66] There is no satisfactory modern biographical study of Louis XV; most current ones, including that by Michel Antoine (Paris, 1990), tend to follow Pierre Gaxotte, *Louis XV* (Paris, 1933, re-edition with illustrations, 1979). The present author is engaged on a new study of the King based on fresh evidence.

[67] No comprehensive study has been written on Maurepas, as most historians have concentrated on his activities as minister of Marine; see Maurice Filion, *Maurepas ministre de Louis XV (1715–1749)* (Montreal, 1967); John C. Rule, 'The Maurepas papers: portrait of a minister', *French Historical Studies*, iv (Spring 1965), pp. 104–5, and, by the same author, 'Jean-Frédéric Phélypeaux, Comte de Pontchartrain [*sic*] et Maurepas: reflections on his life and his papers', *Louisiana History*, vi (1965), pp. 365–77; André Picciola, 'L'Activité littéraire de Maurepas', *Dix-huitième siècle*, iii (1971), pp. 265–96. On his position at court, see Jean Sareil, *Les Tencin: histoire d'une famille au dix-huitième siècle d'après de nombreux documents inédits* (Geneva, 1969), *passim*.

[68] C. P. Duclos, *Œuvres complètes, précédés d'une notice sur sa vie et ses écrits par* [L.S.] *Auger* (Paris, 1820[1]; Geneva, Sladkine reprint, 1968), x, 'Morceaux historiques', p. 254.

debates? Maurepas was able to elicit this information from a variety of sources. As Le Peletier ran into more difficulties with his colleagues, so he became more expansive in his private correspondence with the minister. Successive *lieutenants de police*, Hérault and in particular Feydeau de Marville sent in such information as they had been able to ferret out.[69] And Maurepas also had a spy on the *grand banc* itself, President Talon, an ailing figure whose last reports before his death were written out in his wife's hand. As she was a Chauvelin by birth, a niece of the exiled keeper of the seals, it is possible that Talon's secret activity owed its origins to a desire to alleviate the plight of his wife's uncle by this hidden zeal in the King's seervice.[70]

Maurepas's greatest qualities were his common sense and moderating influence. As early as 1732, when only a young minister of thirty, he had advised the King against taking radical measures towards the *Parlement* in the disputes of that year: he did not think it wise, so he argued in a memorandum, 'de jetter dans le précipice un corps dont le Roy a reçu et peut encore recevoir de grands services'. On that occasion he advocated a policy of working with the *présidents à mortier* to effect a settlement in the crisis.[71] Such a man was a natural conciliator and poured oil on troubled waters.

These instances of the importance of faction, of the pressures of the dynastic office-holding system, and of the rôle of personalities have been drawn entirely from the upper echelons of government and of the *Parlement*. If the evidence were available, one would almost certainly find similar examples at other levels. Even so, the evidence so far adduced adds considerably to our understanding, not only of the complicated workings of the *Parlement* and of the Government, but also of the background to issues and events.

---

[69] *Lettres de M. de Marville, lieutenant général de police, au ministre Maurepas (1742–1747)*, ed. A. de Boislisle (Paris, 1896, 1903, 1905), 3 vols., *passim*; and for a further series of letters which Boislisle had not seen, one should consult Suzanne Pillorget, *Claude-Henri Feydeau de Marville, lieutenant général de police de Paris 1740–1747, suivi d'un choix de lettres inédites* (Paris, 1978), *passim*: the complete set of letters is published in Madame Pillorget's doctoral thesis for the Sorbonne (1975); there are also a few letters in the Collection Tarbé, Bibliothèque municipale, Reims (hereafter BMReims), that have been overlooked by A. de Boislisle and Madame Pillorget.

[70] AN, 257 AP 21 (Maurepas Papers), *dossier* 13 ('pièces diverses'), nos. 26, 36, and 44 (AN numbering of these papers is erratic); cf. with Madame Talon's handwriting in 257 AP 21, 5/4. Françoise-Madeleine Chauvelin (1707–79) married Louis-Denis Talon in 1724. See also Maurepas's effusive letter of thanks to Talon of 16 Dec. 1743 in Archives départementales de la Drôme, Valence (hereafter ADD), Archives de Saint-Vallier (Maurepas Papers), MF *bobine* no. 134: 'Registre de lettres, 1743', f. 152^r. Talon apparently interceded twice with the minister on behalf of his wife's uncle: see Maurepas to Talon, 9 Feb. 1743 and 11 Apr. 1743, ff. 12^r and 35^v.

[71] *Ibid.*, MF *bobine* no. 138: draft of a memoir in the hand of Maurepas, Fontainebleau, 10 Oct. 1732.

2

ISSUES AND INTRIGUES,
1741-1747

Je ne crains point d'asseurer comme un fait notoirement
certain, qu'hors trois ou quatre évêques tolérans et les
appelans, il n'y en a pas un seul qui ne regarde la
Constitution [*Unigenitus*] comme une loy dogmatique de
l'église; et ce qui surprendra V.E. est que plus de la moitié
des gens du Parlement en sont convenus avec moy ...
Cardinal de Fleury to Cardinal Corradini, 9 May 1729

IT IS time to consider the issues themselves and the manner in which they
exacerbated the tensions within the political structure of the Monarchy.
The two chief causes of friction between the Government and the *Parlement*
were the increasing financial demands of the Crown and the enforcement
of the papal bull *Unigenitus* of 1713 in a seemingly endless variety of ways.
Neither issue in itself seriously threatened the stability of the Monarchy. Of
the two, the financial issue was the one which affected the greatest number
of people, but yet it was the religious issue, affecting mainly priests and
persons in holy orders, which caused the greatest stir and eventually raised
fundamental questions about the nature of the Monarchy and the exercise
of power. The chief reason for this paradox may lie in attitudes towards
taxation. As the late Jean Meuvret admirably demonstrated, the mediaeval notion that the King should live off his own resources persisted in the
view, still prevalent in the eighteenth century, that additional taxes considered necessary to meet the King's expenses in war time should be levied
on a purely temporary basis.[1] It is true that by the middle of the century,

---

[1] Jean Meuvret, 'Comment les français du xviie siècle voyaient l'impôt', in *Comment les français
voyaient la France au xviie siècle*, ed. R. Mousnier (Paris, 1955), pp. 59–78. For a useful account
of the financial situation prior to 1741, see J. H. Shennan, 'The political role of the *Parlement*
of Paris under Cardinal de Fleury', *English Historical Review*, lxxxi (1966), pp. 521–6. On the
technical aspects of taxation, see M. Marion, *Les Impôts directs sous l'ancien régime* (Paris,
1910), *passim*.

the financial situation of the State became so desperate that its survival came to depend on the ability of successive *contrôleurs généraux* to perpetuate taxes that were introduced on a temporary basis; but care was taken to preserve appearances and also secrecy: ordinary expenditure could be met only out of extraordinary revenue, but taxes were still being introduced for a limited period and ostensibly to meet the costs of a war. As long as these principles were observed, the King would find *parlementaires*, in the words of one recent historian, 'reserved and suspicious, yet far from rebellious'.[2]

Between 1741 and 1746 the demands of the War of the Austrian Succession forced the Government to introduce a number of short-term financial measures which had to be registered by the *Parlement*.[3] There is unfortunately very little evidence concerning the debates and negotiations that surrounded the re-introduction of the first of these extraordinary levies, the *dixième*, in September 1741; the official records merely indicate that the *Parlement* made remonstrances before it registered the *déclaration*.[4] But the treatment which the *parlementaires* gave to financial measures sent for registration between 1742 and 1746 can be studied in greater depth. In March 1742 there was agitation in the *Parlement* when the Government tried to increase the levy of the *dixième* on owner-occupied houses and on land that was directly exploited by the proprietors; the levy had been fixed by law in 1733 when the *dixième* had last been introduced, and the Government had not brought in any new legislation to increase it (for the *déclaration* of 29 August 1741 which reintroduced the tax had safeguarded the stipulations of 1733). The *parlementaires* recognised that owners who had improved their property since that date ought to pay more tax, but they could not accept that the Government should simply increase the levy without formally producing a new *déclaration*. On 14 March as assembly of the chambers ordered that representations should be made to the King. Representations were a less formal means of pressure on the Government than remonstrances; this fact explains why they had been proposed by the presidents themselves.[5] But these representations met with no success.

At the *rentrée* after the Easter vacation, the *procureur général* normally delivered his first set of *mercuriales*, a critical report on the performance of *parlementaires* in the course of the year with recommendations for improve-

[2] Shennan, 'The political role', p. 526.

[3] M. Marion, *Machault d'Arnouville: étude sur l'histoire du contrôle général des finances de 1749 à 1754* (Paris, 1891), p. 12.

[4] *Les Remontrances du Parlement de Paris au xviiiᵉ siècle*, ed. Jules Flammermont (Paris, 1888–98), 3 vols. (hereafter referred to as Flammermont, *Rems.*), i, pp. 379–83.

[5] *Lettres de M. de Marville, lieutenant général de police, au ministre Maurepas (1742–1747)*, ed. A. de Boislisle (Paris, 1896, 1903, 1905), 3 vols. (hereafter Boislisle, *Lettres de Marville*), i, p. 14: Marville to Maurepas, 14 Mar. 1742. In his reply, Maurepas praised the first president's handling of the situation; see his letter of 14 Mar. 1742 in BN, Cabinet des MSS, Fichier Charavay, 124 (MAR–MAV), entry 242/1997.

ment. The presentation of the *mercuriales* meant that each chamber sent deputies to the *Salle Saint-Louis* (see Figure 1) to discuss the items of the *mercuriales*; these deputies reported back to their chambers and ascertained their views. Thus, for a brief period in the parliamentary year there was in existence an effective mechanism of almost daily liaison between the various chambers. After the King's disappointing reply to the representations made to him by the first president, the *Parlement* clearly had to take further action. Le Peletier would probably have preferred to wait until the deputies had finished their meetings. However it was not possible for him to adopt this course. Whether unintentionally or by design the *procureur général* had ensured that the deputies would be in session until at least the end of the current *Parlement* in September; Joly de Fleury had put forward no fewer than twenty-seven items in his *mercuriales*. The deputies did not require much encouragement to linger over such a formidable agenda, if it gave them the opportunity to concert with each other on the financial question. Consequently Le Peletier thought it prudent to allow the deputies to discuss the line of conduct to be followed by the *Parlement* (in any case, it would have been difficult to prevent them).[6] It seems that an *arrêté* was drafted at their meeting on 5 April. The deputies consulted their chambers and reported to the assembly at the *Salle Saint-Louis* four days later. The text of the *arrêté* does not appear to have survived, which is unfortunate because it would have provided an indication of the feeling in the 2nd and 4th chambers of *enquêtes* and also in the 2nd chamber of *requêtes*, who all supported it. There is some indication, however, that the *arrêté* that was eventually adopted was more moderate; it was proposed by President de Maupeou and supported by the 1st *enquêtes* and 1st *requêtes*. The two remaining chambers of the *enquêtes* (the 3rd and 5th) had reserved their opinion for the assembly of the chambers; they may well have supported Maupeou's proposal when it was adopted by the assembly on 13 April.[7] As the *arrêté* simply called for further representations to be made to the King, the other motion may have been in favour of remonstrances. Le Peletier was fortunate in that Orry, the *contrôleur général*, agreed to introduce a new *déclaration*; otherwise he would naturally have found the situation in the *Parlement* less easy to handle.

The terms of the *déclaration* was discussed privately by Le Peletier with Orry de Fulvy, brother of the *contrôleur général* and an *intendant des finances*. Le Peletier was reluctant to bring Joly de Fleury into these negotiations but could not exclude him without risk. He eventually invited him to a meeting on 18 April. President Talon (who was also present at the meeting) commented in one of his secret reports to Maurepas:

[6] BMReims, MSS, Collection Tarbé, *carton* xvii, no. 5: Marville to Maurepas, 13 Apr. 1742.
[7] *Ibid.*, no. 3: unknown informant in the *Parlement* to Maurepas, 10 [Apr. 1742].

Il est ... très singulier que depuis le commencement de cette affaire, mr le p. président ne luy en ait pas dit un mot. De pareils procédés ne contribuent pas à faire le bien.[8]

According to Talon, Joly de Fleury had indicated to Le Peletier, 'qu'il n'étoit pas insensible au peu d'ouverture qu'il avoit pour luy'. Le Peletier's attitude is nevertheless understandable. Joly de Fleury was trying to build up a following in the *Parlement*; he was in touch with men like Thomé and Severt (both in the *enquêtes*), whom Le Peletier regarded not without justification as agents of Chauvelin; and he coveted Le Peletier's position. The new *déclaration* was registered without much difficulty on 25 April.[9] The importance of the affair is that it demonstrates how issues and parliamentary procedures could be manipulated in the interest of particular groups and individuals. The fact that Le Peletier overcame his difficulties by obtaining a concession from the Government is a measure of the price that had to be paid for a settlement on these occasions.

Later the same year, the relations between the *présidents à mortier* and the government were strained as a result of the King's decision to grant a request made by President Chauvelin, the nephew of the exiled keeper of the seals. The president did not own his office; he leased it, and the office belonged to Le Peletier's son, who had now reached the age of twenty-six, when he could take his seat on the *grand banc*.[10] With the lease at an end, Chauvelin had to surrender his place at a time when there were no *présidences* for sale; his career was threatened. According to Le Peletier, Chauvelin had only himself to blame for his predicament; in 1736 he had taken the unwise step of signing the lease, despite the advice of his friends and relatives, simply in order to escape from the burdens of his post as *avocat général*.[11] Now he asked to be granted the status of an honorary president, a privilege which was normally reserved for first presidents on their retirement. Daguesseau was certainly well disposed towards Chauvelin's request, partly, one suspects, out of a sense of gratitude towards a man whose resignation as *avocat général* had made it possible for the chancellor to place one of his own sons, Daguesseau de Plainmont, in the vacant post.[12]

[8] *Ibid.*, no. 4: [Talon] to Maurepas, 'ce mercredi à midy', 18 Apr. 1742; see also no. 5 (cited in note 6 above); AN, X¹ᴮ 8920 (*Parlement, Conseil secret, Minutes*, Jan. 1742 to Apr. 1743); and Boislisle, *Lettres de Marville*, i, p. 26: Marville to Maurepas, 17 Apr. 1742; i, p. 30: same to same, 19 Apr. 1742.

[9] BMReims, Collection Tarbé, *carton* xvii, no. 6: [Talon] to Maurepas, 23 Apr. [1742]; and Boislisle, *Lettres de Marville*, i, p. 37: Marville to Maurepas, 25 Apr. 1742.

[10] On Chauvelin's status in the *Parlement*, see François Bluche, *Les Magistrats du Parlement de Paris au xviii⁵ siècle, 1715–1771* (Paris, 1960), pp. 58 and 162; E. J. F. Barbier, *Chronique de la régence et du règne de Louis XV (1718–1763), ou Journal de Barbier* (Paris, 1866), 8 vols. (hereafter Barbier, *Journal*), iii, pp. 367–8.

[11] AN, 257 AP 21 (Maurepas Papers), 10/9: Le Peletier to Maurepas, 9 Aug. 1742.

[12] Daguesseau de Plainmont succeeded Chauvelin in 1736 and died in 1741.

At any rate, on 31 July, Daguesseau informed the first president that the request had been granted and gave as the grounds that, as Chauvelin had served for sixteen years in various capacities in the *Parlement*, the King did not wish to condemn him to a life of inactivity at a time when he could still be of use.[13]

Le Peletier immediately protested, and a few days later the King agreed to postpone a decision until he had examined the matter further. Le Peletier lost no time in describing the feelings of the *présidents à mortier* in a letter to the sympathetic Maurepas:

> nul faveur dans m^r Chauvelin ... Mrs les pdts victime [*sic*] de cette indis-crétion s'il obtenoit ce qu'il demande.
>
> les honneurs atachés à leurs charges seroient communiquées à des person-nes qui ne les auroient pas acheptées: de là, diminution infinie pour le prix.
>
> la porte ouverte à une multitude d'honoraires: de là, perte de la considér-ation atachée [*sic*] au petit nombre.
>
> impossibilité dans [*sic*] m^r Chauvelin de faire usage de la grâce qui luy seroit accordée, sans déranger l'ordre observé dans le Parlement.
>
> les honoraires n'ont point de séance à la tournelle; il ne pourroit donc y siéger sans blesser un règlement qui les en exclud.
>
> Auroit-il comme honoraire séance à la grande chambre, avant quatre de ses anciens titulaires? Vous en sentés l'injustice.[14]

In all this there was resentment at the way the chancellor had acted without consulting Le Peletier and the other presidents.

In the midst of the agitation, one of the *zélés*, Le Febvre de Saint-Hilaire,[15] reopened the religious disputes at an assembly of the chambers on 7 August by denouncing a pamphlet written by four doctors of theology and printed with the permission of the *lieutenant général* of Reims.[16] The doctors asserted in their pamphlet, entitled *Cas de conscience*, that a minister of the Church could not receive opponents of *Unigenitus* at the communion table without profaning the body and blood of Jesus Christ.[17] The *parlementaires* handed the publication to the *procureur général* and ordered him to give

---

[13] AN, 257 AP 21 (Maurepas Papers), 10/7: Daguesseau to Le Peletier, 31 July 1742, copy enclosed by Le Peletier with his letter to Maurepas of 31 July 1742.

[14] *Ibid.*, 10/9: Le Peletier to Maurepas, 9 Aug. 1742; see also 10/7, same to same, 31 July 1742.

[15] A. G. C. Le Febvre de Saint-Hilaire, *conseiller*, 5th *enquêtes*, 1738; *conseiller*, 1st *enquêtes*, 1757; *conseiller honoraire* 1763–5; 'homme nouveau' (François Bluche, *L'Origine des magistrats du Parlement de Paris au xviiie siècle (1715–1771): Dictionnaire généalogique in Paris et Ile-de-France: Mémoires publiés par la Fédération des sociétés historiques et archéologiques de Paris et de l'Ile-de-France*, v–vi (1953–4 [1956]), referred to hereafter as Bluche, *L'Origine des magistrats*, p. 254). He had Jansenist sympathies. Some of his MSS are in the BPR.

[16] BPR, LP 514, no. 11: Le Peletier to Daguesseau, 7 Aug. 1742, copy in the hand of L.A. Le Paige.

[17] For a copy of the fifteen-page pamphlet, see AN, Rondonneau AD III 22. On the subject of the *Cas de conscience*, see also Boislisle, *Lettres de Marville*, i, p. 61, note 1, and F. Rocquain, *L'Esprit révolutionnaire avant la Révolution 1715–1789* (Paris, 1878), p. 109.

his conclusions on the 9th. The incident was duly reported to the Cardinal de Fleury and Chancellor Daguesseau, who both decided not to interfere with the debate that would take place that day. Fleury wrote to the chancellor:

> si mrs du Parl. étoient bien intentionés [sic], et que la suppression qu'ils ordoneront [sic] peut-être de cet écrit, fût simple et modérée, sans entrer dans le fond de la question, qui est doctrinal, et nullem'. de la compétence D'un tribunal laïc; ce parti seroit en quelque façon tolérable, mais je ne laisse pas de craindre d'ailleurs que le clergé ne s'élève contre, et que les troubles ne s'excitent de tous les côtés.
> On ne peut trop blâmer l'imprudence De l'auteur de cet écrit, et il méritoit punition. mais le coup est lâché, et j'en apréhende [sic] fort les suites.[18]

The cardinal was expressing a forlorn hope, and with the *présidents à mortier* in high dudgeon over the Chauvelin affair, it was unlikely that moderation would prevail at the assembly of the chambers on 9 August. At that meeting, the *parlementaires* ordered that the *Cas de conscience* should be burned on the grounds that it authorised schism by its proposition concerning the administration of the sacrament.[19] This was no mere condemnation of the pamphlet as contrary to public order, as Fleury had wished. The *lieutenant général de police* of Reims was also summoned to appear before the *Parlement* to explain his conduct. On 13 August the *parlementaires* had their *arrêt* published, a course which had not been taken since 1733.[20]

Le Peletier saw the cardinal in his retreat at Issy on 21 August. He formed the impression that Fleury was well disposed on the Chauvelin affair, but that he would delay a solution on it, thereby placing the first president in an embarrassing position *vis-à-vis* his colleagues on the bench. Le Peletier also felt that Daguesseau was solidly opposed to the decision he wanted. In appealing once again to Maurepas for assistance, Le Peletier hinted at the important rôle which the presidents played in keeping the *Parlement* in order; lest the minister should feel that blackmail was being applied, the first president had doubtless chosen his words with care as he warned of impending dangers:

> on travaille mesme à faire naître pendant cette incertitude des objets de difficultés dans la compagnie, que la scituation de cette affaire nous rend plus embarassantes [sic] par la diminution de notre crédit qui en est une suite.[21]

---

18 BPR, LP 514, no. 11: Fleury to Daguesseau, Issy, 7 Aug. 1742, copy in the hand of Le Paige. On 26 April 1742, an extraordinary meeting of the General Assembly of the clergy of France had voted a grant of twelve million *livres* to the King. Hence Fleury had no wish to cause offence to the clergy after its generous gift.

19 The *arrêt du parlement* is reproduced in Boislisle, *Lettres de Marville*, i, pp. 60–1.

20 *Ibid.*, p. 62: Marville to Fleury, 14 Aug. 1742. The *lieutenant de police* pointed out that *arrêts du parlement* were normally distributed only *à la main*.

21 AN, 257 AP 21 (Maurepas Papers), 10/11: Le Peletier to Maurepas, Paris, 21 Aug. 1742.

Fleury intended to see Daguesseau four days later, and he had probably made up his mind in favour of the presidents. He had discussed with Le Peletier the question of compensation for Chauvelin, now that the cancellation of the *lettres d'honoraires* seemed unavoidable. Le Peletier made the ingenious suggestion that the King should consent to Chauvelin's having the first vacant office of *président à mortier* where the previous incumbent did not leave a son, a brother, or an uncle (on the father's side) who could succeed him. He was thinking of the office held by Chauvelin's ailing brother-in-law, President Talon, and his device was intended to give Chauvelin a prior claim to an office which would probably become vacant before long.[22] Maurepas used his skill with Fleury and Daguesseau, and Le Peletier left Versailles on 25 August with a letter from the minister announcing that the King had suppressed Chauvelin's *lettres d'honoraires*.[23]

At the same time, Maurepas's letter declared that the King had also abolished the practice whereby a magistrate who did not own a presidential office could lease one from its holder. Henceforth the duties of a magisterial office in the *Parlement* were to be exercised only by the holder himself.[24] A practice that had provided men like Chauvelin and Lamoignon de Blancmesnil with an opportunity to exercise presidential office was abruptly brought to an end. Unlike Lamoignon, who remained without office from 1736 to 1746, Chauvelin was fortunate in that a special arrangement had been devised to make his return to the *grand banc* merely a matter of time; indeed as President Talon died in February 1744, Chauvelin was back on the *grand banc* within less than two years.

Le Peletier remained uncertain about the final outcome of the affair for the chancellor still had to inform President Chauvelin of the King's decision. He told Maurepas that there was a plot afoot to grant Chauvelin what were described as 'lettres d'honneur', which would enable him to keep the title and privileges of president without giving him rank or a seat on the *grand banc*. Such letters would also contain the promise of the first presidential office that fell vacant. The letters had to be registered:

> lors de l'enregistrement on se flatte peut-estre de faire proposer par des personnes à sa dévotion (dont on ne manque pas dans la compagnie) que la

---

[22] *Ibid.*, 10/12: Le Peletier to Maurepas, 'ce samedi' (Maurepas note: 25 Aug. 1742); 10/10: same to same, 'ce samedi une heure' (annotated: 25 Aug. 1742).

[23] AN, 257 AP 21 (Maurepas Papers), 10/10. For the text of Maurepas's official letter to Le Peletier of 25 Aug. 1742, see *ibid.*, 5/22; Boislisle used the copy in Maurepas's Letter-book, AN, O¹ 387, p. 213, but unfortunately he omits in his extract the passage whereby Daguesseau was to inform Chauvelin of the favour which the King intended to grant him; *Lettres de Marville*, i. p. 66.

[24] *Ibid.*, note 2.

compagnie elle-mesme demande des lettres d'honoraires. vous sentés le danger dans cette proposition.[25]

Le Peletier's suspicions fell on Joly de Fleury. The *procureur général* was in possession of a plea lodged by the *lieutenant général de police* of Reims indicating that his permission for the publication of the *Cas de conscience* had been extracted from him by the local vicar-general and by one of the authors. Joly de Fleury was trying to get the plea placed before the assembly of the chambers, a course which might result in a decree being passed against the two ecclesiastics. Le Peletier thought the question of Chauvelin's status was linked to the case:

> M^r le p^{eur}. Général fait cheminer de concert avec cette affaire celle du cas de conscience.[26]

Le Peletier thought no action should be taken because the *parlementaires* would find it difficult to execute the *arrêt* on the *Cas de conscience* before the end of the *Parlement* on 7 September. A few days later, the first president admitted that Maurepas's letter of 25 August concerning President Chauvelin had calmed the *parlementaires* and that his fears about the assembly of chambers and its reaction to the plea had been unjustified. His only remaining fear was that the Government might nullify the *arrêt* of 9 August on the *Cas de conscience* before the *Parlement* went on vacation.[27] It too was laid to rest; the Government waited for the *Parlement* to end its sessions on 7 September before it informed Le Peletier that the Chauvelin affair had been finally settled; at the same time it dealt with the matter of the *Cas de conscience*.[28] It seems likely that, in return for deciding in favour of the *présidents à mortier*, the Government obtained their tacit support for an *arrêt du conseil* issued on the *Cas de conscience* on 12 September. Thus, throughout these developments, the Government and the *présidents* had themselves established a connection between both issues and each had sought to exploit it to their own advantage.

The *arrêt de conseil* of 12 September 1742 was a further addition to the already large corpus of laws and regulations relating to *Unigenitus*, and like most of them it was suitably ambiguous in its terms. It quashed the section in the *arrêt du parlement* relating directly to the *Cas de conscience* on the

---

[25] AN, 257 AP 21 (Maurepas Papers), 10/5: Le Peletier to Maurepas, 'ce mardi matin' [28 Aug. 1742].

[26] *Ibid.*

[27] *Ibid.*, 10/13: Le Peletier to Maurepas, 1 Sept. 1742; Boislisle, *Lettres de Marville*, i, p. 70: Marville to Maurepas, 1 Sept. 1742. The *procureur général* proposed that the facts contained in the plea (or *requête d'exoine*, as it was called) should be investigated; this course was then formally proposed by Coste de Champeron and adopted by all present with the exception of the Abbé Pucelle and a few others.

[28] AN, 257 AP 21 (Maurepas Papers), 10/14: Le Peletier to Maurepas, 9 Sept. 1742.

grounds that only the bishops had the right to handle cases concerning religious doctrine. But Daguesseau, who had laboured over the draft, had endeavoured to safeguard most of the other stipulations of the *arrêt du parlement*.[29]

A wider significance was attached by some contemporaries to the Chauvelin affair of 1742. In his journal the Marquis d'Argenson linked the affair to a move at court for the return of the president's uncle, the former keeper of the seals and minister of foreign affairs.[30] The affairs of France were certainly at a low ebb in July–August 1742 following the defection of the King of Prussia. On 24 July, Fleury had written to Cardinal de Tencin broaching the subject of his own retirement and even suggesting that Tencin should succeed him.[31] It was rumoured that the King had already entrusted the Duc de Villeroi with a letter recalling Chauvelin, but that he had confided the scheme to Fleury and it had then been abandoned.[32] The Marquis d'Argenson wrote in his journal that all the plans had suddenly been changed; Chauvelin's erstwhile opponent, the Maréchal de Noailles, was given the command of the Army of Flanders in place of the Duc de Coigny; Bignon, the intendant of Soissons, was appointed intendant of that army over the head of Chauvelin, intendant of Amiens and a cousin of the president. And on the evening of 27 August, it was announced that Cardinal de Tencin and the Comte d'Argenson had been made ministers of state: 'effet de la grande cabale contre M. Chauvelin', so the Marquis d'Argenson concluded in his journal.[33] A few days later, the marquis noted that his brother and Tencin had been made members of the Council only in order to provide Fleury with some further support there in the face of growing opposition from members of a 'King's party' backed by Orry, the *contrôleur général*.[34]

These rumours and statements were not without some foundation.

---

[29] Boislisle, *Lettres de Marville*, i, p. 62, note 1. Two drafts of the *arrêt du conseil*, the first in Daguesseau's hand and the second amended by him, are to be found with subsequent explanatory notes by Le Paige and a printed copy of the *arrêt* in BPR, LP 514, no. 17.

[30] *Journal et mémoires du Marquis d'Argenson*, ed. E. J. B. Rathery (Paris, 1859–67) (hereafter cited as D'Argenson, ed. Rathery), iv, pp. 21–3.

[31] The text of Fleury's letter of 24 July 1742 may be found in C. P. Duclos, *Œuvres complètes, précédés d'une notice sur sa vie et ses écrits par* [L.S.] Auger (Paris, 1820–1; Geneva, Sladkine reprint, 1968), x, p. 231; J. C. de Boisjourdain, *Mélanges historiques, satiriques et anecdotiques* (Paris, 1807), ii, p. 78; M. Boutry, *Un créature du cardinal Dubois: intrigues et missions diplomatiques du cardinal de Tencin* (Paris, 1902), p. 289; and extracts are given by J. Sareil in *Les Tencin: histoire d'une famille au dix-huitième siècle d'après de nombreux documents inédits* (Geneva, 1969), p. 306.

[32] [Mouhy], 'Chronique du règne de Louis XV, 1742–1743', *Revue rétrospective*, v (1834), p. 45. For a study of Mouhy see Evelyn G. Cruickshanks, 'Public opinion in Paris in the 1740's: the reports of the Chevalier de Mouhy', *Bulletin of the Institute of Historical Research*, xxvii (1954), pp. 54–68.

[33] D'Argenson, ed. Rathery, iv, p. 22.

[34] *Ibid.*, pp. 22–4.

Fleury was losing his grip on affairs and needed support in the Council in order to counteract the 'war party' and possibly to safeguard his own position. The appointment of the Comte d'Argenson brought with it the support of the Duc d'Orléans's interest, which had kept the balance in the past between the competing Condé–Chauvelin and Toulouse–Noailles princely factions at court.[35] Tencin's appointment reflected, amongst other things, Fleury's concern that the interests of the clergy were not sufficiently represented in the Council. That concern stemmed partly from the opinion he had formed of the chancellor and which he expressed in a letter to Tencin in August:

> Il est un peu trop serviteur des Parlements et il s'y mêle un peu trop de crainte de se brouiller avec eux. Il devroit pourtant être corrigé de ses ménagements car celui de Paris manque souvent de considération pour lui. Il est absolument livré à M. le Procureur général, qui est beaucoup plus fin que lui, et cherche à s'accréditer à ses dépens.[36]

Daguesseau had not found much favour with Fleury that summer; after all, he had allowed some of the stipulations of the *arrêt du parlement* on the subject of the *Cas de conscience* to go uncensored and he had also used all his influence on behalf of the Chauvelin faction by his support of President Chauvelin. In these activities Daguesseau doubtless had the support of Joly de Fleury.[37] But although there was probably a crisis within the Government in July–August, and developments in the *Parlement* had possibly exacerbated it, one also has to accept that the affair of President Chauvelin's *lettres d'honoraires* and its likely connection with the moves over the *Cas de conscience* can still be explained without reference to that crisis; one can simply take the available evidence at face value.

On a different level, the events of 1742 shed a revealing light on Le Peletier's nervous behaviour at times of crisis; whenever there was trouble, he immediately became restless, and he was quick to cast suspicion on those whom he feared and disliked. Hence, it is not always easy to decide whether his malevolent allegations concerning Joly de Fleury and the Chauvelins were always well founded. What is perhaps more important is that Cardinal de Fleury and Maurepas repeatedly believed them. As Fleury was no

---

[35] On the rôle of these princely factions, see J. M. J. Rogister, 'A minister's fall and its implications: the case of Chauvelin (1737–1746)', in *Studies in the French eighteenth century presented to John Lough by his colleagues, pupils and friends*, ed. D. J. Mossop and others (Durham, 1978), pp. 200–17.

[36] The letter appears, dated simply August 1742, in Duclos, *Œuvres complètes*, x, p. 227; the date of 21 August is given in *Mémoires du Président Hénault écrits par lui-même*, ed. Baron de Vigan (Paris, 1855), p. 315, where the text of the letter is also reproduced by the editor in an appendix.

[37] Joly de Fleury had little objection to the *arrêt du parlement* and claimed he knew of bishops who shared his view: BPR, LP 514, no. 12: Joly de Fleury to Daguesseau, 17 Aug. 1742.

longer particularly well disposed towards Le Peletier by 1742, and Maurepas was a man of sound judgement, there may have been an element of truth in the first president's allegations.

On 1 February 1743 Cardinal de Fleury died and the King lost his mentor. Louis XV had to face up to his own responsibilities. Fleury's demise led to further moves for Chauvelin's recall from exile. A few weeks later Joly de Fleury tried to repeat his performance of the previous year with the *mercuriales*. Le Peletier's suspicions were aroused at once. On 11 April 1743 the first president warned Maurepas of the serious consequences of allowing Joly de Fleury to provide the deputies from the chambers with an opportunity to prolong their sittings from April until September:

> si la situation des affaires oblige le Roy à faire quelques opérations de finances, elles se trouveront naturellement entre les mains de ces députés pour les examiner, ainsi que vous avés veu l'année passée par rapport au dixième. s'il survient d'un autre côté, quelques refus de sacrements, ce sera un moien sûr de les porter tout de suite, à l'assemblée des chambres. Mr. le P[eur] général m'en a donné avis de plus d'une demie douzaine pendant cet hiver, ils paroissoient bien certains dans l'exposé, je luy ay offert de les porter à la grande chambre en m'en fournissant la preuve, il ne cest [sic] pas trouvé une seule ocasion [sic] dans laquelle il ait pu trouver de preuve suffisante pour la grande chambre, ne m'en ayant pas parlé depuis. Mais vous sçavés qu'il en faut bien moins pour les chambres assemblées, et il luy sera aisé par cette voie de parvenir à combat.[38]

A further source of concern for the first president was that Joly de Fleury wanted to renew the regulations concerning *parlementaires* who did not observe residence qualifications. Again Le Peletier sensed danger. There were two *parlementaires* who could not observe the regulations because they were in exile: Carré de Montgeron, for presenting the King with a copy of his book on the miracles of the Jansenist deacon Paris, and, of course, Chauvelin, the former keeper of the seals, who had never relinquished his office of *président à mortier*.[39]

Le Peletier had pointed out to Joly de Fleury the implications of his proposed move, as he explained to Maurepas:

> Je luy fis faire réflexion que ce qu'il feroit sur le défaut de résidence volontaire donneroit lieu de parler de l'absence involontaire de Mr. de Mongeron (Je ne luy parlay point de celle de Mr. Chauvelin qui pourroit bien être leur vray objet). Vous voiés parfaitement que cela y conduit.[40]

---

[38] AN, 257 AP 21 (Maurepas Papers), *dossier* 11, no. 18.

[39] Bluche, *Les Magistrats du Parlement de Paris*, pp. 161, 168.

[40] AN, 257 AP 21 (Maurepas Papers), *dossier* 11, no. 18, quoted in J. M. J. Rogister, 'New light on the fall of Chauvelin', *English Historical Review*, lxxxiii (1968), p. 330, note 4.

As Chauvelin's place of exile had recently been changed to Issoire and then, in March, to Riom, the first president's suspicions were probably well founded. Le Peletier needed the help of Maurepas, his protector, because he felt he could not rely on Daguesseau, who could be influenced by Joly de Fleury.[41] Maurepas told Joly de Fleury that he could take whatever action he thought appropriate as long as he understood that he would bear the responsibility if there were any serious consequences (hinting perhaps, as Le Peletier had suggested, that he might be endangering the career prospects of his second son).[42] The minister's remarks had the desired effect: the *procureur général* announced that he and his colleagues had decided to postpone the *mercuriales* until November.[43]

Despite the assistance he had received from Maurepas, Le Peletier was probably aware that the Government afforded only precarious support and that his position had become increasingly vulnerable. Moreover, he may have known that the Government was planning to introduce new taxes and been alarmed at the prospect of having to guide these measures through the *Parlement*. Besides, he was getting deaf, and his wife was allegedly seeking a separation.[44] On 21 September 1743 he had an audience with the King and asked for his permission to resign. Two days later President de Maupeou, as second president, applied for the post in a letter to Maurepas. Maupeou had been a loyal ally of Le Peletier and enjoyed the protection of Maurepas, who was his kinsman. Both men undoubtedly supported his move.[45] The King appointed him on 26 September.[46] Joly de Fleury complained at once to the chancellor that he had been passed over and tendered his own

[41] AN, 257 AP 21 (Maurepas Papers), 11/19: Le Peletier to Maurepas, 12 Apr. 1743.

[42] *Ibid.*, 11/20: Le Peletier to Maurepas, 19 Apr. 1743. The *mercuriales* would have been delivered on the Wednesday after Quasimodo, i.e. on 24 April in 1743.

[43] *Ibid.*, 11/21: same to same, 20 Apr. 1743.

[44] Bluche, *Les Magistrats du Parlement de Paris*, p. 339; Barbier, *Journal*, iii, pp. 468–9; *Mémoires du Duc de Luynes sur la cour de Louis XV (1753–1758)*, ed. L. Dussieux and E. Soulié (Paris, 1860–5) (hereafter cited as Luynes, *Mém.*), vii, p. 240.

[45] AN, 257 AP 21 (Maurepas Papers), 8/18: Maupeou to Maurepas, 21 Sept. 1743. Although Maupeou claimed that Le Peletier's *démarche* came as a complete surprise to him, his swift action in writing to Maurepas before the news was out strongly indicates that Le Peletier had given him some warning of his intention to resign. It is interesting to note that Maupeou did not think of writing to the chancellor until 26 September (letter to Maurepas: 8/19). Maupeou's *provisions* were sent on 9 October. The previous day Maupeou sent Maurepas Le Peletier's receipt for 200,000 *livres* which Maupeou paid his predecessor for his *brevet de retenue*; the King then presumably sent Maupeou a *brevet de retenue* for a similar amount which would eventually be paid to him by his own successor. Maurepas and Orry also arranged for Maupeou to receive Le Peletier's pension of 20,000 *livres*; for these details, see 8/1 and 2, and ADD, Archives Saint-Vallier (Maurepas Papers), MF *bobine* no. 134: 'Registre de lettres, 1743', f. 122: Maurepas to Maupeou, 8 Oct. 1743; and finally AN, F⁴ (unclassified files on pensions), Maupeou's file. In addition, the new first president retained the pension of 4,000 *livres* that had been given to him as *président à mortier*, the office that he now passed on to his son.

[46] Barbier, *Journal*, iii, p. 470.

Plate 4 First President R.C. de Maupeou, engraving by Petit (1753) after a painting by J. Chevallier (1745)

resignation; Daguesseau endeavoured to soothe his feelings and persuaded him to stay on.[47] Perhaps an opportunity had been missed: whatever his faults, Joly de Fleury had the makings of a first president.

René-Charles de Maupeou, the father of the future chancellor, was then fifty-five years of age. He was impressive in appearance and, when the occasion demanded it, he could speak even to the King, not only with nobility and grandeur but with flashes of inspired improvisation. In per-

---

[47] See a letter from Daguesseau to Joly de Fleury of 2 Oct. 1743 quoted in J. Flammermont, *Le Chancelier Maupeou et les Parlements* (Paris, 1885), p. 6, note 3.

sonal relations he was affable, with 'le tact fin et l'esprit charmant par ses grâces naturelles', in the words of his young colleague in the *Parlement*, Robert de Saint-Vincent.[48] One could pass the time agreeably in his company on a long coach journey talking about the writings of Père Nicole, as Robert de Saint-Vincent did once, or find oneself singing well-remembered songs with him, as did an old intimate friend in his apartment at Versailles many years later, when Maupeou, by then keeper of the seals and 'vice-chancellor', had to interrupt the jollity to get ready for his regular audience with the King.[49] Le Peletier was percipient but inclined to overreact nervously to situations; a peppery man, he had not been popular with *parlementaires* and latterly with members of the Government. Maupeou was less intelligent than his predecessor – indeed, some wags applied to him the Latin tag, *O quanta species! cerebrum non habet*[50] – but he approached the first presidency full of good intentions and with unbounded confidence. He later claimed that he had taken the office only on the condition, which had been accepted by the King, that he would be free to allow an assembly of the chambers whenever the *parlementaires* requested it. He did not want to see a repetition of the events of 1732 and 1737 in this respect, and he relied on his ability to handle his colleagues with a certain *aplomb*.[51] He was a lucky man too. Madame de Pompadour had a soft spot for him (and for his second son, the boisterous Chevalier de Maupeou, who was in the army) even after the events of the 1750s.[52] When, years later, in 1763, he emerged as 'vice-chancellor' from the oblivion to which he had been consigned after his forced retirement from the *Parlement*, she had a hand in the appointment and could still write of him: 'M^r le vice-chancellier est remply de talents, et de bonne volonté'.[53] Yet he had shown little of these qualities in the course of his tenure of the first presidency.

[48] Collection Michel Vinot Préfontaine (Paris), 'Mémoires de P. A. Robert de Saint-Vincent' (typescript copy), pp. 124 and 113.

[49] *Ibid.*, p. 276; and formerly château de Condé-en-Brie (Archives de Sade) on exhibition in 1982: an anonymous note to the Comte de Sade (1701–67), father of the notorious marquis; the note is dated 29 March 1765.

[50] Quoted in M. Gaillard, *Vie ou éloge historique de M. de Malesherbes, suivie de la vie du premier président de Lamoignon, son bisaïeul* (Paris, 1805), p. 19.

[51] AN, 342 AP 2: 'Mémoires' (1746–50) of J. O. Joly de Fleury, p. 41: Maupeou made the claim in the course of an acrimonious discussion with Chancellor Daguesseau on 6 Feb. 1747 in the presence of the *gens du roi* (see below, p. 55).

[52] Madame de Pompadour was interceding with the Comte d'Argenson on behalf of the Chevalier de Maupeou as late as 1752; see Marquis d'Argenson, *Autour d'un ministre de Louis XV: lettres intimes inédites* (Paris, 1923), p. 296. When the chevalier visited England in 1752, George II spoke of her in gracious terms to him: the then British ambassador in Paris, the Earl of Albemarle, duly reported to Sir Thomas Robinson, Secretary of State in the Duke of Newcastle's administration, on 30 July, that the marquise had the most grateful sense of the terms used by the King (*R.H.M.C.*, 3rd Report, ed. Howard H. Peckham, Lansdowne Papers xviii, p. 141, col. 1).

[53] See her letter of 15 Oct. 1763 to an unidentified person (possibly the Duc de Fitz-James) in *Lettres autographes composant la collection de Mme. G. Whitney Hoff* (Paris, 1934), p. 100, no. 307

Over the years he succumbed increasingly to the influence of his elder son, the future chancellor, an intelligent and amoral intriguer for whom it is difficult to feel any sympathy (though several historians have managed to do so in their fervent desire to see in him the last saviour of the French Monarchy). The son lacked his father's distinguished appearance and charm of manner: he had what Sénac de Meilhan described as 'une figure de Juif, un teint olivâtre, des manières de pantalon, un regard faux et perfide'.[54] He exuded false bonhomie, and he had few friends, only cronies. Unlike his father, who was happily married as far as one can tell – indeed, the *première présidente*, a Lamoignon by birth, was of great help to her husband in his new post – the son had been less fortunate in marriage. His wife, Anne-Marguerite-Thérèse de Roncherolles, came from a family of more ancient nobility than his own. He had insisted upon making the match. She was wilful, flighty, witty, and she greatly disliked her husband, 'ce petit homme noir à qui j'ai toujours dit non'. One morning, as he crept into her bedroom, she pretended not to see him and then feigned surprise and slapped his face when he tried to kiss her. Nevertheless, she presumably relented on occasion, because there is no good reason to doubt that he was the father of her three children, although she had a lover at one stage. She spent much of her time in the company of Madame d'Epinay and displayed her acting gifts as Lisette in the first performance of J. J. Rousseau's *L'Engagement téméraire*, playing opposite Madame d'Epinay's rich and eccentric brother-in-law, Lalive de Jully, at the château de La Chevrette in 1748. Her husband stopped her taking any further part in these activities and finally packed her off to the family château at Bruyères (near Arpajon), where she died on 21 April 1752. It was typical of him that he refused to buy any candles for the wake and sold off all her clothes without leaving anything to her servants.[55] His married life had clearly been an unhappy, humiliating, and embarrassing experience for him. It may have left its mark. He was much more at home and at ease in the world of

(3) and in facsimile; also reproduced in the catalogue of a sale of *Précieuse collection d'autographes et de documents historiques* held at the hôtel des Chevau-Légers, Versailles, on 1 December 1981: lot no. 140.

54 [Sénac de Meilhan], *Œuvres philosophiques et littéraires de Mr. de Meilhan* (Hamburg, 1795), 2 vols., ii, p. 275.

55 There has been no thorough study of Chancellor Maupeou since Jules Flammermont, *Le Chancelier de Maupeou*. For a passionately favourable view, see J. de Maupeou, *Le Chancelier de Maupeou* (Paris, 1942), which contains some useful and original material. Maupeou's matrimonial problems are dealt with there on pp. 27–31, and also in Lucien Perey and Gaston Maugras, *Une femme du monde au xviii* siècle: la jeunesse de Madame d'Epinay* (Paris, 1882), pp. 73, 79ff, 106, 128, 361–2; the cultural world of Madame d'Epinay and of her brother-in-law Lalive de Jully, briefly a *parlementaire* and later *introducteur des ambassadeurs* (the son of a rich *fermier général*, he died insane in 1779), is well described in Fausto Nicolini, *La signora d'Epinay e l'abate Galiani* (Bari, 1929) and Barbara Scott, 'La Live de Jully: pioneer of Neo-Classicism', *Apollo*, xcvii, no. 131 (January 1973), pp. 72–7.

intrigue at the *Parlement*. Across the centuries one still gets a feeling of slight unease whenever one reads a letter of his, even on a personal matter, as for instance on the occasion of his recovery from illness in 1748:

> On ne peut être plus sensible que je le suis, Monsieur, à la part que vous avés pris à ma maladie. Recevés-en, je vous prie, mes remerciemens. Je ne doute pas de la joye que vous avés eu de ma convalescence et qu'il n'y ait quelque chose d'encore plus particulier que dans celle de beaucoup d'autres. Vous la devés, je vous assure, aux sentiments que j'aurai toujours pour vous et qui seront toujours distingués par l'amitié et l'attachement avec lequel je serai toute ma vie, Monsieur, votre très humble et tres obéissant serviteur.[56]

Although the first president could also be unctuous at times, he was infinitely more appealing than his son.

The new first president was put to the test within two months of his appointment, when the Government either set up or re-established various taxes and excise duties. No fewer than fourteen edicts and *déclarations* were laid before an assembly of the chambers on 13 December. *Commissaires* were at once appointed to examine them and to make recommendations to the assembly.[57] Maupeou rightly suspected that an attempt would again be made to hinder the Government's operations. The 1st chamber of *enquêtes* began by trying to revive an old dispute about whether *commissaires* ought not to be chosen by the chambers themselves, instead of by the first president, which was the normal practice. Maupeou had appointed Thomé as their *commissaire*, probably as a means of neutralising him. When the *commissaires* met for the first time, Thomé announced that his chamber had instructed him to state that he was attending the meeting only as their nominee. But as soon as he began to speak, Maupeou turned to a neighbour and pretended to be engrossed in conversation until Thomé had finished: it was a good way of avoiding a procedural dispute. The *commissaires* agreed without much difficulty to recommend registration of the eleven edicts that increased inheritance duties and gages and also prolonged the levy of the *4 sols pour livre*, a surtax on all duties.

Contrary to a belief still held by many historians, the *parlementaires* did

---

56 Princeton University Library, John Hinsdale Scheide Collection of French Historical Autographs: signed letter to an unidentified person, 20 Oct. 1748. Maupeou *fils* wrote a bland letter a year earlier to a correspondent who had expressed satisfaction at the first president's recovery from smallpox; BN, n.a.fr. 16253 (Pierre Cornuau's *fiches d'autographes*), no. 1376; on that occasion the son ran the risk of contaminating others by going to court on some intrigue: Maurepas quickly sent him away (see AN, 342 AP 2, 'Mémoires' of J. O. Joly de Fleury, p. 88).

57 Bibliothèque de l'Ordre des avocats à la Cour d'appel de Paris, MSS, Fonds Henri Moulin, *dossier* 12 ('Magistrats, Chanceliers'): Maupeou to Orry, 13 Dec. 1743. For the edicts and *déclarations*, see AN, X^{1A} 8747 (*Parlement: Conseil secret*), ff. 296^v–298^r, 316^r–327^r, and 359–75; and also X^{1B} 8921 (*Minutes*), unnumbered unsigned minutes of the debates, with texts of the new laws, held on 13 and 20 Dec. 1743.

not simply focus their opposition on the financial measures that threatened their interests. They realised that on this occasion the most important edicts before them were the last three which re-established dues on eggs and butter, wood and coal; for these measures seriously hit the largest and poorest sections of the community. Dupré of the 4th *enquêtes* proposed that the assembly should be convened to register the first eleven edicts so as to encourage the *contrôleur général* to negotiate the remainder. This course could hardly meet with the approval of the Government, which took the view that an initial compliance with its demands was an essential precondition of any negotiation. Maupeou pointed out that the *commissaires* were there to examine all the edicts, and he had no difficulty in getting Dupré's proposal rejected by the others. The *commissaires* met again on 16 and 18 December to consider the last three edicts. Only the veteran Abbé Pucelle – the hero of many fights against *Unigenitus* – agitated openly for remonstrances, though an influential cabal of three men, Dupré (4th *enquêtes*), Thomé (1st *enquêtes*) and President Roujault (4th *enquêtes*), tried together with others to achieve the same result by more devious means: their suggestion that the first president should make supplications to the King before the edicts were registered amounted to a resort to remonstrances in the long run.[58] But at the second of these meetings, Severt (*grand'chambre*) and Titon (5th *enquêtes*) argued against this course by saying that a registration of the measures accompanied by supplications would be more agreeable to the King and might elicit concessions from him for that reason. Dupré and Thomé were left in a minority, for all the other deputies of the *enquêtes* and *requêtes* saw the importance of obtaining some reduction of the duties.[59]

Titon again carried his hearers with him at an assembly of the chambers on 20 December. The edicts and *déclarations* were registered with the exception of the last three, on which the *parlementaires* decided to make supplications. Before he left for Versailles Maupeou pressed Maurepas and the chancellor to obtain some concession on the remaining two edicts and one *déclaration*.[60] Daguesseau wrote to Orry the following day:

58 AN, 257 AP 21 (Maurepas Papers), 8/23–4: Maupeou to Maurepas, 'samedi 8 heures' [14 Dec. 1743]; 8/3: same to same, 16 Dec. 1743; 13/26: [Talon, but in the hand of Madame Talon] to Maurepas, 16 Dec. 1743; and ADD, Archives Saint-Vallier, MF *bobine* no. 134, f. 152ʳ: Maurepas to Talon, 16 Dec. 1743.

59 AN, 257 AP 21 (Maurepas Papers), 8/38: Maupeou to Maurepas, 'mercredi, au soir', 18 Dec. 1743; 13/44: Talon/Madame Talon to Maurepas, 17 Dec. 1743; 37: same to same, 18 Dec. 1743; and Suzanne Pillorget, *Claude-Henri Feydeau de Marville, lieutenant général de police de Paris 1740–1747, suivi d'un choix de lettres inédites* (Paris, 1978), pp. 227–9: Marville to Maurepas, 18 Dec. 1743.

60 AN, 257 AP 21 (Maurepas Papers), 8/42: Maupeou to Maurepas, 'vendredi 2 heures et demie', [20 Dec. 1743]: 'nous l'avons emporté sur mrs. pucelle et thomé et pour achever de le [?] confondre et sa cabale aidés-moi à obtenir de Mr. le Contʳ. Général des adoucissements un peu marqués, c'est l'intérêt du roy pour d'autres occasions'.

> Il est bien important d'accoutumer le Parlem^t à une voye aussi respectueuse
> que celle qu'il prend aujourd'huy, et il seroit triste que faute de luy accorder
> quelque adoucissement, sur tout par rapport aux articles qui peuvent exciter
> le murmure de Peuple et les cris des pauvres, il revint au party des Remon-
> trances. Les deux plus grands objets sont le bois et les droits sur les œufs et sur
> le beurre, Personne n'est plus en état que vous de juger jusqu'où l'adouciss-
> ement pourroit être porté à cet égard. Ce qu'il y a de certain est que la plus
> légère diminution fera un très grand effet dans les circonstances présentes.
> aucune de ces réflexions n'eschappera sans doute à votre prudence . . .[61]

Orry agreed to make the desired concessions, chiefly on wood and coal,
butter and eggs; these concessions were embodied in new *déclarations* which
were designed to interpret the edicts.[62] Maupeou was naturally delighted
with the result.[63] The *déclarations* were laid before the *Parlement* on 23
December. In a final attempt to disrupt the arrangements, Thomé and his
followers urged the *parlementaires* to register each *déclaration* at the same time
as the edict which it concerned, so that the public would think that the
edicts had been registered only because the *déclarations* had been granted.
But the majority of their colleagues had a greater regard for the outward
signs of the King's authority than to adopt such a course: they registered
the edicts and the *déclarations* separately.[64]

The first president's system of overcoming opposition to financial
measures in the *Parlement* by obtaining concessions from the Government
was certain to lead in time to friction between him and the *contrôleur général*.
When, in March 1745, Maupeou again tried to obtain concessions on an
edict creating offices in the guilds, he encountered resistance and even
hostility from Orry.[65] On that occasion the King's reply to the supplications of the *Parlement* was not encouraging. The result was that a motion
for the registration of the edict as it stood was defeated by two votes at the
assembly of the chambers on 19 March. The edict was registered with

[61] BN, n.a.fr. 23989 (Collection d'autographes Allard du Chollet), no. 10: Daguesseau to
Orry, 'Samedi matin', [21 Dec. 1743].

[62] There is a rough draft by Maurepas of the procedure that was followed (including the text,
with corrections, of a reply to be made by the King when Maupeou came to announce that
the edicts had been registered): see AN, 257 AP 21 (Maurepas Papers), 8/39. The draft was
adopted (with an inversion of its two phrases) after a formal meeting of the *Conseil des
dépêches* on 21 Dec. 1743: see AN, X^{1B} 8921 (*Minutes*, 23 Dec. 1743).

[63] AN, 257 AP 21 (Maurepas Papers), 8/49: Maupeou to Maurepas, 'Dimanche, au soir', [22
Dec. 1743].

[64] *Ibid.*, 8/40: same to same, 'lundi', [23 Dec. 1743].

[65] *Ibid.*, 8/11: same to same, 15 Mar. 1745; the first president asked Maurepas to remind Orry
'de ce que j'ay eu l'honneur de luy dire que je n'étois pas homme à épargner mes peinnes
[*sic*]. . .' Again, a few months later, Maupeou alluded to his relations with Orry in a letter
to Marville: 'il [Orry] seroit le plus injuste des hommes, s'il n'étoit pas convaincu de mes
bonnes intentions' (Bibliothèque municipale de Rouen, MSS, Collection Duputel (autographes), ii, no. 203: letter of 28 Oct. 1745). On the financial measures of March 1745, see
Boislisle, *Lettres de Marville*, ii, pp. 40–1: Marville to Maurepas, 11 Mar. 1745.

modifications inserted in the *arrêt d'enregistrement*; this course had been proposed by Thomé.[66] Another reason for the outcome of the debate was the part played by President Chauvelin, who had returned to the *grand banc* on President Talon's death in February 1744 in accordance with the arrangement made two years earlier.[67] In his letter to Maurepas reporting the debate of 19 March, Maupeou carefully described the way the president and his cousin, the Abbé Chauvelin, had influenced the other *parlementaires* in the course of giving their opinions:

> ce que j'ay préveu avec vous il y a Longtems vient d'arriver dans cette occasion, c'est un nouveau président qui étoit de nostre advis dans le commancement, qui est revenu à l'autre, qui l'a fait passer, il a un petit bas crochu de cousin frère de l'intendant d'amiens qui se démène comme un diable dans un bénittier pour souffler le feu dans les bancs avec toute l'indécence possible, cependant le dessein de l'un et de l'autre n'étoit pas de faire passer l'advis de thomé, ils voulloient favoriser celuy de M^r. de la fautrière qui étoit infiniement plus dur, et le plus dangereux de touts, ce n'a été que par rage qu'il a abandonné nostre advis pour l'empêcher d'avoir le dessus.[68]

The following year Maupeou implied in a letter to Maurepas that Chauvelin had again created difficulties for him over the registration of edicts creating new *rentes* and establishing a levy of an additional *2 sols pour livre* on the *dixième*:

> Je vous raconteray au 1er Jour la petite tracasserie qu'il y a eue qui vous affermira dans le sentiment que vous aviés quand on a mis certaines personnes dans la compagnie.[69]

In the years that followed, Chauvelin became Maupeou's most dangerous opponent in the *Parlement*, particularly on account of his friendship with Machault, who had succeeded Orry as *contrôleur général* in December 1745. An opponent on the *grand banc* could be a source of serious embarrassment to a first president.

Maupeou was also threatened from a different quarter in the *Parlement*. If he found Chauvelin an increasingly dangerous colleague, he no longer had much to fear from the new president's uncle, the former keeper of the seals. The King had made it a condition of his return from exile that he should

---

[66] AN, 257 AP 21 (Maurepas Papers), 8/15: Maupeou to Maurepas, 19 Mar. 1745.

[67] See above, p. 38. Talon died on 1 Feb. 1744 (Boislisle wrongly gives the date as 1 March, in *Letters de Marville*, i. p. 108, no. 2); see AN, 257 AP 21 (Maurepas Papers), 7/5: Maupeou to Maurepas, 1 Feb. 1744.

[68] *Ibid.*, 8/15. Davy de La Fautrière was a curious man: a Jansenist, freemason, and later, allegedly, an agent of the Comte d'Argenson: see P. Chevallier, 'Les Idées religieuses de Davy de La Fautrière', *Studies on Voltaire and the Eighteenth Century*, lxvii (1969), pp. 229–41.

[69] Cornell University Library, Department of Rare Books, Ithaca, N.Y.: Maurepas Collection, letters of Maupeou to Maurepas (1746–7): letter of 10 Dec. 1746.

sell his *présidence à mortier*.[70] In July 1746 the office was duly sold, at a loss, to Gilbert, the second *avocat général*.[71] It was at this stage that the change had repercussions on Maupeou's position. Joly de Fleury still had the promise of the first vacant post in the *parquet* for his second son, and Gilbert's departure offered him the chance of achieving this family ambition. But the chancellor persuaded the King to go back on the promise made in 1741 on the grounds that it would be wrong to allow three of the four *gens du roi* to come from the same family. According to Jean-Omer Joly de Fleury, the real reason behind this decision was that the chancellor's son, Daguesseau de Fresne, was eager for the vacant post to go to his brother-in-law, Le Bret. The *procureur général* took stock of the situation: he was over seventy years of age, and although the magistracy was to some extent a geronto-cracy, his failure to obtain the first presidency meant that there was no future for him in the *Parlement*. Therefore he decided to resign his office to his eldest son, whose place as *avocat général* would be taken by the second son, Jean-Omer, then *avocat général* at the *Grand Conseil*. The resignation of the *procureur général* was a wise move on his part, especially as he left nothing to chance and was able to protect the position of his family still further by obtaining the right to succeed his successor if the latter predeceased him.[72] These arrangements created problems for the first president. He and the new *procureur général* soon came to dislike each other. As both Le Fèvre d'Ormesson, who now moved up to the place of *premier avocat général*, and Jean-Omer Joly de Fleury, the senior of the two new *avocats généraux* (the other being the unobtrusive Le Bret), were also lukewarm in their feelings towards him, Maupeou soon came to distrust the *parquet*, which was dominated more than ever by the Joly de Fleury clan and its retired

---

[70] Rogister, 'A minister's fall and its implications: the case of Chauvelin', p. 216. In that article the author assembled only circumstantial evidence pointing to the secret terms imposed on Chauvelin as the condition of his return from exile. This hypothesis has now been explicitly confirmed by the memoirs of Jean-Omer Joly de Fleury which became available to him after the article was written; see AN, 342 AP 2, pp. 5–6.

[71] *Ibid.*; Bibliothèque universitaire de Poitiers (hereafter BUP), Archives d'Argenson, série CA, Letters of Jean-Omer Joly de Fleury to the Comte d'Argenson, *dossier* X ('Lettres non datées'): Jean-Omer Joly de Fleury to the Comte d'Argenson, 22 June 1746, enclosing a copy of the *bon* of 1741 from the King promising him the first post of *avocat général* that became vacant. See also Bluche, *Les Magistrats du Parlement de Paris*, p. 168; Barbier, *Journal*, iv, p. 170. Pierre-Paul Gilbert de Voisins (1715–54) was the son of Pierre Gilbert de Voisins (1684–1769), whom he succeeded as *avocat général* in 1739 (see p. 24). As Gilbert de Voisins had the King's preference for the first *présidence à mortier* that became available, Chauvelin was obliged to sell him the office if he wished to return from exile.

[72] AN, 342 AP 2 ('Mémoires' of J. O. Joly de Fleury), pp. 6–7; Paul Bisson de Barthélemy, *Les Joly de Fleury, procureurs généraux au Parlement de Paris au xviii*ᵉ *siècle* (Paris, 1964), pp. 29–30. Guillaume-François Joly de Fleury also obtained a pension of 10,000 *livres* to supplement one of 5,000 *livres* which he already enjoyed. His third son, Jean-François, a future *contrôleur général des finances*, was already in the royal administration as a *maître des requêtes* and president (by commission) of the *Grand Conseil*: he had well-founded expectations of rapidly becoming a provincial intendant.

patriarch. For their part, the *gens du roi* became increasingly prone to criticise the first president, especially in their private correspondence with ministers.

The history of the years from 1741 to 1746 shows that the resistance of the *Parlement* to the financial demands of the Government was the work of a few men who had factional interests but also a concern that was shared by many of their colleagues for the plight of the poorer sections of the community. The opposition of these men became less effective once the Government acceded to the first president's repeated requests to reduce its initial demands. As long as the first president was able to obtain appreciable concessions, the *Parlement* would create no further difficulties over financial measures, at least in time of war. It was a fragile system, constantly endangered by personal intrigues and rivalries and also by changing circumstances at court and in the *Parlement*.

The position was no different where *Unigenitus* was concerned, as the affair of the bishop of Amiens demonstrated in 1747. The long-standing disputes over *Unigenitus* begun in the last years of Louis XIV's reign and continued under the Regency and during the administration of Cardinal de Fleury have already been the subject of several studies and they do not really call for much elaboration here.[73] Louis XIV had asked the Pope to issue a condemnation of a compilation by Father Quesnel republished in 1699 under the title *Le Nouveau Testament en français avec des réflexions morales sur chaque verset*. Quesnel's neo-Augustinian and Jansenist commentary implicitly condemned the 'morale accommodante' of the Jesuits. Louis XIV knew that the French bishops would not be unanimous in condemning Quesnel and so he approached the Pope directly, despite his earlier

[73] See Georges Hardy, *Le Cardinal Fleury et le mouvement janséniste* (Paris, 1925); J. H. Shennan, 'The political role of the *Parlement* of Paris, 1715–23', *The Historical Journal*, viii, 2 (1965), pp. 179–200; and the same author's second article, 'The political role of the *Parlement* of Paris under Cardinal de Fleury', pp. 520–42. For an account that throws more light on the rôle of personalities, see James D. Hardy, *Judicial politics in the Old Régime: the Parlement of Paris during the Regency* (Baton Rouge, La., 1967). The spirit of eighteenth-century Jansenism is captured in Mésenguy's lucid treatise, *La Constitution Unigenitus avec des remarques où l'on fait voir l'opposition de la doctrine des Jésuites, à celle des Saints Pères contenue dans les propositions du Père Quesnel* (s.l., 1743, 12mo); the Jansenist milieux have been studied by A. Gazier, *Histoire générale du mouvement janséniste depuis ses origines jusqu'à nos jours* (Paris, 1922–4), 2 vols.; B. Robert Kreiser, *Miracles, convulsions, and ecclesiastical politics in early eighteenth-century Paris* (Princeton, N.J., 1978); Dale Van Kley, *The Jansenists and the expulsion of the Jesuits from France, 1757–1765* (New Haven, Conn., 1975); Bruno Neveu, 'Port-Royal à l'âge des Lumières: les *Pensées* et les *Anecdotes* de l'Abbé d'Etemare, 1682–1770', '*LIAS*': *Sources and Documents relating to the Early Modern History of Ideas*, iv (1977), pp. 115–53; and J. M. J. Rogister, 'Louis-Adrien Lepaige and the attack on *De l'esprit* and the *Encyclopédie* in 1759', *English Historical Review*, xcii (1977), pp. 522–39. See also Françoise Bontoux, 'Paris janséniste au xviiie siècle: les *Nouvelles ecclésiastiques*', *Paris et Ile-de-France: Mémoires publiés par la Fédération des sociétés historiques et archéologiques de Paris et de l'Ile-de-France*, vii (1955 [1956]), pp. 205–20.

stand against the Papacy on the rights and liberties of the Gallican Church. Rome took its time and in 1713 the decision reached the King in the form of the Bull *Unigenitus*, a muddled condemnation without any qualification of 101 propositions extracted from Quesnel's work. However, not all Quesnel's propositions had been reprehensible; some were even unimpeachable statements of the Church's own true doctrine. The bull was a cumbersome means of eradicating Jansenism. The subsequent disputes brought out the equivocal nature of its legal and religious status, and in that respect *Unigenitus* remained a potential source of discord between the *Parlement* and the clergy of France. On both sides, there were many who remained convinced that to define the bull as a 'jugement de l'église universelle en matière de doctrine' or as a 'loi de l'église et de l'état', as the King had done in a *déclaration* of 1730, was the same as to call it a 'règle de foi': this was the point of the dispute, for a 'règle de foi' was regarded as binding on the faithful. The contestants had thus missed the subtlety of the new definition, which many *parlementaires* chose to ignore anyway because the *déclaration* of 1730 had been registered at a *lit de justice*.[74]

The bishop of Amiens had published an instruction to his diocesan clergy describing the bull as an 'unreformable' judgement of the Church in matters of doctrine and prescribing the conduct that his priests should adopt towards those who rejected that judgement and wished to take communion.[75] In normal circumstances either the Government or the *grand'chambre* of the *Parlement* would have ordered the suppression of the publication as tending to revive religious disputes. Indeed, that was the initial reaction of those chiefly concerned in these matters: the chancellor, Maurepas, the first president, and the *gens du roi*. Consequently, on 7 January the *grand'chambre* passed an *arrêt* suppressing the bishop's publication. However, the circumstances of this case were out of the ordinary. The King took a lively personal interest in the bishop of Amiens, whom he regarded as a saintly figure, and he ordered Daguesseau to find a means of giving him some satisfaction in the light of what had happened at the *Parlement*. Moreover, an assembly of the clergy was about to meet to vote an additional financial contribution to the King, and he did not want to give the episcopate any cause for complaint. Boyer, the former bishop of

---

[74] Shennan also overlooks this point: cf. 'The political role of the *Parlement* of Paris under Cardinal de Fleury', pp. 538–9; though he does note that Cardinal de Fleury tended to avoid referring to the *déclaration* of 1730 after it had failed to win general support. Fleury's strong objection to the use of the phrase *règle de foi* may be seen from his letters to the bishop of Laon in AN, 257 AP 14 (Maurepas Papers), *dossier* 3.

[75] On the affair of the bishop of Amiens see AN, 342 AP 2 ('Mémoires' of J. O. Joly de Fleury), pp. 22–3, 27, 30–69 for the most detailed account; Cornell Maurepas Collection: Maupeou to Maurepas, 25 Jan. 1747; Boislisle, *Lettres de Marville*, iii, p. 152 and note 1; Luynes, *Mém.*, x, pp. 100, 125–8, 137, 391–5.

Plate 5 Avocat général (later President) L. F. Le Fèvre d'Ormesson, painting
by J. S. Duplessis (private collection)

Mirepoix, who had a strong influence on religious policy through his
control of ecclesiastical appointments (the *feuille des bénéfices*), after the
death of Fleury, also left the first president and the *gens du roi* in no doubt
about these pressing concerns of the Monarch.[76]

---

[76] AN, 342 AP 2 ('Mémoires' of J. O. Joly de Fleury), pp. 30 and 46. The chancellor told
   Avocat général d'Ormesson of the King's wishes on 24 Jan.

The outcome of some frantic discussions held separately and then jointly on the same day, 29 January, between the chancellor, the first president and the *gens du roi*, together with Boyer and another leading cleric, the archbishop of Tours, was a scheme designed to dispel any notion that the *arrêt* of the *Parlement* had attacked the bishop's definition of *Unigenitus*.[77] The scheme took the form of a *réquisitoire* delivered by the first *avocat général* before the *grand'chambre* on 1 February. The publication of an issue of the illicit and clandestine Jansenist organ, the *Nouvelles ecclésiastiques*, was made the pretext for the *réquisitoire*, in which, in passing, D'Ormesson reaffirmed the terms of the contentious *déclaration* of 1730 by describing the bull as a *jugement de l'église universelle en matière de doctrine* and a *loi de l'église et de l'état*. The *grand'chambre* then endorsed the *réquisitoire* in a published *arrêt* condemning the *Nouvelles ecclésiastiques*.[78] The matter appeared to be closed. But Thomé and other members of the *enquêtes* indicated their intention of protesting against the terms of the *réquisitoire* before an assembly of the chambers. The chancellor put pressure on the first president. At a stormy meeting between the two men and the *gens du roi* on 6 February, Maupeou gave notice that he would never refuse to grant an assembly of the chambers.[79] When it became clear that he was prepared to allow such an assembly to go as far as to censure the *gens du roi* over the terms of their *réquisitoire*, the chancellor accused him of reneging on the arrangement made on 29 January:

> Dans quels circonstances soufrirés vous qu'on entreprit de donner atteinte à une espèce de Traité fait entre vous-même et le Gouvernement, dans une occasion où tout l'avantage est du côte du parl᷑? Vous savés combien on avoit fait d'efforts pour exciter le Roi à en détruire le 1er. arrêt de la Gde. Chbre.: on avoit déja prévenu plusieurs Evêq[ues]: on se préparoit à metre [*sic*]

[77] *Ibid.*, pp. 34–7. The first president insisted upon having the arrangement in writing; his own copy of it was then endorsed by the King, to whom it was submitted by Bishop Boyer. The arrangement is reproduced on pp. 36–7 of Jean-Omer Joly de Fleury's account.

[78] *Ibid.* D'Ormesson prepared the *réquisitoire* on the basis of a draft sent to him by his uncle, the chancellor. It was printed with the *arrêt* and distributed throughout the jurisdiction of the *Parlement*.

[79] *Ibid.*, p. 41. Maupeou seemed reasonably confident of his ability to handle crises when he wrote to Maurepas:

> ... Je vous entretiendray de la confidence polie que me vient de faire dans l'instant un de Mrs des enquêtes du 1er ordre, son opiniâtreté m'est depuis si longtems connue, que je ne fais aucun doute qu'il ne vienne à bout de son projet. Entre nous, s'il luy réussissoit en tout, le Parlement trouveroit habilement le moyen de servir mr l'évêque D'Amiens et ses adhérants sur les deux ... Cornell Maurepas Collection: incomplete letter of 5 Feb. 1747

Knowing that the former *procureur général* had helped to devise the definitions of 1730, Daguesseau tried to persuade him to use his influence to restrain Thomé and his followers; the irony of the situation was not lost upon Joly de Fleury who elegantly declined to assist but treated his former colleague on the *parquet* to a lengthy and interesting dissertation on the significance of the *déclaration* of 1730: see his letter reproduced on pp. 42–5 of his son's memoirs.

l'ass[emblée] du clergé en mouvement: et la cause d'un seul Evêq[ue] alloit devenir la cause comune [*sic*] de L'Episcopat [*sic*].

C'est dans cete [*sic*] fermentation q[ue] le Roi résiste aux instances les plus vives; qu'il refuse d'interposer son autorité; et qu'il veut bien se reposer sur son parl^t. du soin de finir cette affaire, et d'une manière qui laisse subsister en son entier l'arrêt qu'on attaquoit; en sorte q[ue] l'Ecrit de l'Evêque d'Amiens demeure toujours supprimé.

Il n'y a pas d'exemple que le parl. ait jamais été mieux traité par le Roi: et ce seroit une étrange manière de lui en témoigner sa reconnoissance, q[ue] de chercher à chicaner les G. du. R sur des expressions qui leur ont été Dictées par S.M. même.[80]

Daguesseau told him that the Government would intervene at once if the *Parlement* passed any motion that condemned the use of the terms laid down by the *déclaration* of 1730. He urged Maupeou to reason with Thomé, whom Daguesseau took to be a sensible man who could be persuaded to deter other from taking a dangerous course.[81] But feelings always ran high in the *Parlement* on the question of *Unigenitus*. In the end moderation prevailed, and a move to censure the *gens du roi* was defeated, albeit by only one vote, on 17 February. By sixty-nine votes to sixty-eight the assembled chambers passed an *arrêté* which sought to correct any false impressions that might have been created amongst the public by the *réquisitoire*.[82] The *arrêté* of 17 February omitted all reference to the *déclaration* of 1730 and defined the scope of the bull by simply citing the King's reply to the bishops of 22 July 1731, his replies to the remonstrances of the *Parlement* of 15 May 1733 and 28 June 1738, together with the terms of the *arrêt d'enregistrement* of *Unigenitus* in 1714.[83]

The chancellor's first reaction to the *arrêté* was in the nature of an anticlimax; it was symptomatic of the muddle in high places. He did not have any copies of the important texts that had been cited.[84] With two

[80] BPR, LP 515, no. 18: Daguesseau to Maupeou, 13 Feb. 1747 (copy in the hand of Le Paige). In his note on this letter Le Paige makes two mistakes. Firstly, he claims that it was addressed to Le Peletier, who had retired in 1743; as it is addressed to the first president, the letter must have been sent to Maupeou. Secondly, he states that the sad event to which Daguesseau refers in the opening passage of the letter is the death of his wife; in fact the *chancelière* had died in 1735. But one of the chancellor's sons had been killed at the battle of Lawfelt on 11 February 1747; this event probably explains the passage in the letter. Le Paige had access to Daguesseau's papers after this death; he made painstaking transcriptions of many of them and retained some originals. Despite the errors contained in his note, I have no doubt that this letter existed and that Le Paige's transcription of it is otherwise accurate.

[81] Thomé's family papers contain little on his political activities: see AN, 254 AP 13–14, *passim*.

[82] AN, 342 AP 2 ('Mémoires' of J. O. Joly de Fleury), pp. 52–3.

[83] *Ibid.*, pp. 54–8 for the full text of the *arrêté* and of the documents to which it referred. The replies to the two sets of remonstrances are also reproduced in Flammermont, *Rems.*, i, pp. 313 and 373.

[84] AN, 342 AP 2 ('Mémoires' of J. O. Joly de Fleury), p. 59.

impressive residences, one in Paris, the other in Versailles, secretaries and copyists to hand, the chancellor of France had no complete record of crucial decisions taken in the King's name on matters affecting the relations between Church and State. Daguesseau should not be singled out in this respect; his successor had to make similar admissions about the inadequacy of his records twenty years later. If the political crises of Louis XV's reign had one positive consequence, it was to oblige ministers of the Crown to keep better records. On this occasion it was the *procureur général* who had to send copies of the relevant texts to the chancellor.

After meetings, first, of a *comité* of ministers who made up the *Conseil des dépêches* and then of the *Conseil des dépêches* itself in his presence, the King quashed the decision of the *Parlement* by an *arrêt du conseil* on 21 February: a lengthy restatement of the definitions given by the *déclaration* of 1730 and a further addition to the already bulky corpus of enactments on the subject of *Unigenitus*.[85] A deputation from the *Parlement* was also summoned to Versailles for a royal reprimand.[86] Nothing further was done on either side, an outcome which seems a little strange at first sight. But possibly, although the evidence is lacking, Maurepas and Maupeou had worked out one of those intricate arrangements that, in the years ahead, enabled each side to remain on its original positions. There is more than a hint of such an arrangement in the formalities observed at Versailles and in Paris on 22–23 February. Only a small deputation of the *Parlement* had been summoned to see the King: it was simply an unofficial body.[87] The King's orders were only that his *Parlement* should transcribe his words to the first president in its records and not, therefore, the text of the *arrêt du conseil* itself. On 23 February the assembly of the chambers merely transcribed the first president's account (his *récit*) of the deputation's visit to Versailles and of the form of words exchanged between him and the King; the *parlementaires* were privately given the text of the *arrêt du conseil* afterwards.[88] While the affair of

---

[85] *Ibid.*, pp. 60 and 64–6. See also AN, E 2257, no. 50 (*Minute* of the *arrêt du conseil* of 21 Feb. 1747).

[86] AN, 342 AP 2 ('Mémoires' of J. O. Joly de Fleury), p. 61. The deputation was made up of the first president, two *présidents à mortier* (Molé and Portail), two senior councillors of the *grand'chambre*, and the senior councillor from each chamber of the *enquêtes*: twelve persons in all (including Thomé and Titon); see also Marquis de Lordat, *Un page de Louis XV* (Paris, 1908), p. 392.

[87] AN, 257 AP 21 (Maurepas Papers), 8/17: Maupeou to Maurepas, 21 Feb. 1747. The first president asked the minister, in tones that seem to imply a prior understanding, that he should be allowed to say a few words after the King had expressed his discontent with the *Parlement*, while blithely allowing for the fact that the King might then express further displeasure: 'sauf à luy, s'il est aussi mécontent qu'on le dit à Paris de me tourner le dos ou de me dire qu'il ne le veut pas'. Whether or not the King was influenced by this letter is not known, but he did not turn his back on the first president, and after the latter's speech he uttered the words: 'Je jugerai des sentiments par les actions' ('Mémoires' of J. O. Joly de Fleury, p. 63); this must have caused relief to Maupeou.

[88] *Ibid.*, pp. 62–3.

the bishop of Amiens had clearly demonstrated that, on the question of *Unigenitus*, neither the government nor the *Parlement* was able to compromise because the *déclaration* of 1730 stood between them, neither side wished to force the issue. If the endemic disputes relating to the bull became more serious, the continued uncertainty about the *déclaration* of 1730, and therefore about *Unigenitus* itself, might have to be resolved.

In many ways the clash of personalities was more important than the issues at stake: whether these were financial or religious that clash could envenom them and inflate them out of all proportion. In the affair of the bishop of Amiens, there were some disturbing undertones: a king who singled out a bishop for preferential treatment; a chancellor who was getting old and willing to risk his integrity and who, like Bishop Boyer, was obsessed with a desire not to upset the King or the episcopate on the eve of an important assembly of the clergy; *gens du roi* who were as reluctant to invoke the terms of the *déclaration* of 1730 (with the possible exception of D'Ormesson who may have wished to please his uncle, the chancellor) as they were to be censured by the *Parlement* for having done so; a first president who preferred to handle men rather than issues; a minister, Maurepas, to whom the foibles of the others came as no surprise and who was perhaps waiting to act as the honest broker. Finally, within the *Parlement* itself, there were the *présidents à mortier* to be placated and the principled *zélés* (or intriguing troublemakers, according to the historian's choice of sources) to be accommodated.

The *zélés* had not carried the day, but there were certain lessons to be learned about the nature of their rôle from the events of 1747. To some, like Jean-Omer Joly de Fleury, they were intriguers and troublemakers. His description of President Durey de Meinières was an expression of these feelings:

> Tout s'étoit traité en comité chès le Président de Meynières. Il ... avoit chès luy un recueil de registres du Parlement. Par l'étude qu'il avoit fait de ces registres, il s'étoit acquis assés de réputation; on le regardoit assés généralement comme un garçon appliqué et studieux; mais il n'étoit pas capable de s'élever l'esprit mesme avec le secours des trésors immenses que renferment les registres du Parlement; un esprit de détail, mais étroit, des idées basses et communes, intriguant soit pour les affaires publiques, soit pour les affaires particulières ...

and he concluded:

> Voilà le portrait au naturel de l'homme qui s'érigeoit en cette occasion pour être l'oracle de dix ou douze de ses confrères qui se dispersoient ensuite pour répandre dans le reste de la compagnie les maximes qui pouvoient mener aux partis violents que le comité secret entendait accréditer.[89]

[89] *Ibid.*, p. 52.

The claim of the *avocat général* was exaggerated, as, in ordinary circumstances, the structure of the *Parlement* did not allow the *zélés* to determine the final course of events. Moreover, his view of Durey de Meinières needs to be qualified. Robert de Saint-Vincent, one of the *zélés*, wrote in very different terms about the president, whom he described as:

> l'homme du Parlement le plus instruit des principes du Parlement dont il s'était nourri par l'étude des registres sur lesquels il a travaillé toute sa vie ...
> M. le Président Durey de Mesnières [*sic*] que je ne nommerai jamais sans témoigner mon tendre respect pour son nom et sa mémoire.[90]

The two conflicting views of the character of one man cannot be reconciled, but both direct attention to the reason why Durey de Meinières and others like him were disliked or admired. These men set themselves up as the collective conscience of the *Parlement*, a stand which they based upon a study of its records.

The role of antiquarian studies in the formulation of the arguments advanced by the *Parlement* in the mid-eighteenth century was becoming more important. The roots of this new development probably lay in the previous century with the pioneering work of scholars like Du Cange and Baluze. Within the *Parlement* Durey de Meinières and the former *procureur général* Joly de Fleury were not the only students or collectors of ancient texts: President de Cotte (2nd *requêtes*) possessed copies of the records of the *Parlement* from the time of the mediaeval *Olim* rolls, and Coste de Champeron, a councillor of the *grand'chambre*, owned beautifully bound sets of registers for the period 1364–1553; these men were consulted by others.[91]

---

90 Collection Michel Vinot Préfontaine (Paris), 'Mémoires de P. A. Robert de Saint-Vincent' (typescript copy), pp. 125 and 148. The favourable view of Durey de Meinières was shared by Voltaire and Diderot. Through his friendship with the Comte d'Argental and Madame du Châtelet (see *Les Lettres de la Marquise du Châtelet*, ed. T. Besterman (Geneva, 1958), i, pp. 294, 322 and 361), the president helped Voltaire obtain books, for example. The writer expressed his gratitude to him in a letter from Brussels of 10 Nov. 1743: 'j'ay vu des lettres de vous, monsieur, qui sont des témoignages de votre sensibilité et de votre prudence. Je sens plus que jamais combien il est doux de vous être attaché': *Textes nouveaux de la correspondance de Voltaire: lettres à Voltaire*, ed. V. S. Lublinsky (Leningrad, 1970), p. 165. Diderot, for his part, tells an edifying tale of Durey's patience with an unpleasant *procureur*, indicates that he was on terms of social intimacy with him and gives an endearing portrait of the president in a letter to Sophie Volland of 21 July 1765:

> C'étoit le matin. Il étoit en redingote, en mauvaise perruque ronde, en bas de laine gris, un mouchoir de soye autour du col, ce qui n'était pas propre à sauver sa mauvaise mine ... Il entre dans l'étude sans façon; il s'adresse au procureur, honnêtement, parceque le président de Ménières [*sic*] est l'homme de France le plus doux et le plus honnête, qu'il en a la réputation, et que c'est ainsi que je l'ai vu chez lui et chez moi ... Denis Diderot, *Correspondance*, ed. Georges Roth (Paris, 1959), v (Jan. 1765–Feb. 1766), p. 55

91 Durey de Meinières's collection was dispersed at the beginning of the nineteenth century; parts of it were bought by Boissy d'Anglas and found their way into the Bibliothèque nationale and the Bibliothèque du Sénat. For President de Cotte's collection, see Bodleian Library, Oxford, Mus. Bibl. III 8° 362: *Catalogue des livres rares et précieux et des manuscrits composant la bibliothèque de M.* *** *de Cotte, dont la vente se fera le jeudi 22 Germinal [12 Avril] et*

Plate 6 President (later First President) M. F. Molé, by L. Tocqué (private collection)

Outside the *Parlement* the lawyer Le Paige, the *bailli* of the Temple, was engaged in compiling and copying ancient documents.[92] The activities of men like Durey de Meinières and Le Paige eventually forced the Government to pay greater attention to precedent and to the care and study of ancient records. The affair of the bishop of Amiens seems to have been the first in which the influence of an antiquary had made itself felt within the *Parlement* and been deemed worthy of note by an agent of government.

jours suivans, à six heures très précises de relevée, rue des Bons-Enfans, no. 12 (Paris, An XII [1804]), lots listed on pp. 308–10. For the Coste de Champeron Collection, see the *Catalogue des manuscrits de la Biliothèque royale de Belgique*, ed. J. van den Gheyn, SJ, E. Bacha, and E. Wagemans (Renaix, 1919), x, pp. 94–9; the bound MSS in Brussels are nos. 6878 (2 vols.) and 6879 (31 vols.) in the catalogue and bear the following *ex libris*:

Ex Libris Aegidii Caroli Coste de Champeron in suprema curia senatoris

[92] On Louis-Adrien Le Paige (1712–1802), see Rogister, 'Louis-Adrien Lepaige'.

On the 10 February 1747 the re-marriage of the Dauphin had taken place amid great celebrations. Two days later, Jean-Omer Joly de Fleury, the new *avocat général*, went in the evening to the house of a councillor at the *Parlement* on the Ile de la Cité to watch the firework display from his balcony. There, perhaps even in the darkness of that balcony overlooking the Seine, he joined Madame Chauvelin, the wife of the former keeper of the seals – she had wanted to see the fireworks without being seen herself – and her young, politically minded niece, the widowed Madame Talon. With them, and probably very much under their thumb, was Talon's cousin, President Molé, now, at forty-two, the next in line of seniority to the first president. Naturally Molé and the *avocat général* talked about the forthcoming assembly of the chambers, where Molé would be opening the debate. Joly de Fleury formed a very low opinion of him. Doubtless Molé had no idea that the *avocat général* had already begun to write his memoirs and that their conversation would be recorded with a final comment on Molé's hopes of one day succeeding the first president: 'Dieu garde la compagnie d'un chef si peu digne par ses talents d'une aussi grande place!'[93]

Perhaps this scene is symbolic. After all, many of the events of the preceding years can be seen as a firework display, isolated flares, ominous, frightening, but eventually resolving themselves quietly in the encircling darkness. Then the spectator looks around him and becomes aware of the figures on the balcony. Perhaps though, in the glare of the fireworks, these figures had been momentarily seen as they really were. Within a decade, circumstances were possibly to alter Joly de Fleury's unfavourable view of President Molé, but he may well have remembered that night when a vision of the crises to come and the inadequacy of those in high places might have briefly impinged upon his enjoyment of the celebrations. More than anyone, he was in a position to appreciate the significance of those early events; for he was destined to live through the Revolution, the Terror and much of the Empire, dying at the age of ninety-five in 1810.

[93] AN, 342 AP 2 ('Mémoires' of J. O. Joly de Fleury), p. 49.

3

PRELUDE TO CRISIS: THE
VINGTIÈME AND THE
AFFAIR OF THE *HÔPITAL*
GÉNÉRAL, 1748-1751

On est découragé, mécontent de ses places, et de tout ce
que l'on voit.

Jean-Omer Joly de Fleury (1751)

THE LAST financial measures of the war were introduced by Machault in
March 1748. They consisted of an edict establishing a twelve-year duty on
tallow, candles, stamped paper (needed for notarial acts), and cardboard;
a *déclaration* which in effect obliged holders of feudal *seigneuries* to purchase
the *droits d'échange* on their land if they did not wish others to purchase
them in their place and to enjoy the same seigniorial rights and honours on
that land as they possessed themselves; and finally, a *déclaration* which subjected the transfer of judicial and financial offices and the transaction of
other property that was regarded as real estate to the tax of the *centième
denier* (a payment made on presenting an act of sale or transfer for registration).

Commissaires from each chamber of the *Parlement* examined these
measures and recommended remonstrances, a course which was adopted
by an assembly of the chambers on 19 March.[1] The King announced that
he wanted the remonstrances the next day. The first president hastily prepared a text. In it he pointed out that the duty on tallow would cause dis-
tress over a long period to those craftsmen whose livelihood depended
upon working at home; that the *déclaration* on the *droits d'échange* was vexa-
tious and exposed *seigneurs* who did not purchase the rights of transfer to
the risk of having to share seigniorial rights possibly even with their own
vassals; and that the *déclaration* extending the application of the *centième
denier* would have a grievous effect on the sale of offices and would in par-

[1] AN, 257 AP 21 (Maurepas Papers), 8/21: Maupeou to Maurepas, 16 Mar. 1748; 6/3:
procureur général to Maurepas, 19 Mar. 1748. See also M. Marion, *Machault d'Arnouville: étude
sur l'histoire du contrôle général des finances de 1749 à 1754* (Paris, 1891), pp. 13–14.

ticular make recruitment for the courts more difficult.[2] But the Government made only insignificant concessions on the two *déclarations* and none on the edict.[3] By a majority of fifty-five votes the assembly of the chambers ordered on 21 March that the edict should be registered with a clause that further remonstrances should be made when the war was over. Despite Maupeou's efforts, the *parlementaires* put off consideration of the amended *déclarations* until two days later.[4] The one on the *droits d'échange* was registered with modifications, and it was only by a majority of four that they decided to make supplications instead of *itératives* remonstrances on the *déclaration* concerning the *centième denier*. The King told a deputation that when the *déclaration* was registered he would consider making some further changes to it. The *Parlement* complied with his request, though it again decided that remonstrances would be made at the end of the war. Maupeou ascribed the difficulties that had arisen on this occasion to the haste with which the remonstrances had been demanded and, above all, to the niggardly concessions made by the Government.[5] Machault had clearly shown that he was less inclined than his predecessor to make concessions to weaken the opposition in the *Parlement*. Moreover, he may well have neutralised Maurepas on this occasion by a judicious allocation of extra funds to the navy.[6] The *parlementaires* reacted by resorting directly to remonstrances instead of supplications.

The proclamation of peace in October 1748 brought with it the need to pay off the debts incurred during the war. Machault proposed to suppress the *dixième* of August 1741 and to set up a *caisse des amortissements* to pay off the whole State debt on the proceeds of a new tax, the *vingtième*. In April 1749 Machault confided details of his plan to Maupeou and to the *gens du roi*; they discussed them in turn with the *présidents à mortier* and with the stalwarts of the *grand'chambre*. Their reactions were on the whole favourable to the idea of paying off the State debt. However they thought Machault's plan was too ambitious, and they were concerned to find that the proposed edict did not place a time-limit on the levy of the new tax and that one of its articles seemed to imply that the tax would have to be paid in advance,

---

[2] Marion implies that the remonstrances dwelled particularly on the plight of the *parlementaires* themselves (*Machault d'Arnouville*, p. 13). In fact the relevant passage of the remonstrances refers to the prospect where 'l'on expose *la plupart des tribunaux de la justice* à devenir entièrement déserts' (italics added); see *Les Remontrances du Parlement de Paris au xviii⁰ siècle*, ed. Jules Flammermont (Paris, 1888–98), 3 vols. (hereafter referred to as Flammermont, *Rems.*), i, p. 389.

[3] For these details, see *ibid.*, pp. 389–92.

[4] AN, 257 AP 21 (Maurepas Papers), 8/22: Maupeou to Maurepas, 21 Mar. 1748; 6/5: *procureur général* to Maurepas, 21 Mar. 1748.

[5] *Ibid.*, 8/20: Maupeou to Maurepas, 23 Mar. 1748; 8/24: same to same, 24 Mar. 1748; Flammermont, *Rems.*, i, pp. 394–7.

[6] AN, 257 AP 21 (Maurepas Papers), 6/6: Machault to Maurepas, 14 Mar. 1748.

which was contrary to the King's declared intention, as the first president reminded the controller general. If Machault had limited himself to paying off the debts in stages, the success of the first operation would have led them to accept the continuation of the *vingtième* as a means of paying off the remainder.[7] Jean-Omer Joly de Fleury summed up the opinion of these leading *parlementaires* when he wrote:

> Je crains que la résolution de ne pas limiter le tems ne fasse éprouver de la résistance à l'Edit. on approuve assez généralement le projet de libérer entièrement l'état, et on ne désaprouve [*sic*] pas l'idée de parvenir successivement à une libération entière; mais d'embrasser dès ce premier moment l'exécution générale de la Libération, c'est une opération qui paroit trop étendue et de trop longue durée pour mériter toute la confiance qu'elle devroit avoir. Il paroist que si on avoit fait différentes classes de dettes de l'état, si après ce partage on ne s'étoit proposé d'abord dans l'exécution que de libérer la première classe des debtes, cette première opération qu'il aurait été fort aisée de limiter auroit été du goust de tout le monde et L'extinction des debtes de la première classe finie, le succès de l'opération auroit fait désirer la continuation de L'imposition du vingtièmme pour parvenir à éteindre les debtes de la seconde classe et ainsi succésivement, Je sçay bien que Mr. le Contrôleur général croit qu'il peut y avoir des raisons politiques pour l'illimitation, mais aussi ne craint-on pas que les étrangers ne jugent les debtes plus considérables qu'elles ne le sont peut-être quand ils verront que pour les Eteindre il faut établir une imposition dont on ne peut fixer la durée.[8]

These observations once again help to correct the view that the *parlementaires* were not public-spirited in their attitude towards the financial problems of the Monarchy. Doubtless Machault would have agreed with them had the main purpose of the *vingtième* been to pay off the debts, as they were being led to believe, and not to provide the King with a much needed form of permanent revenue; the *avocat général* must have had some inkling of this intention when he penned the words: 'Mr. le Contrôleur général croit qu'il peut y avoir des raisons politiques pour l'illimitation.' However, on this as on previous occasions, Machault refused to be swayed by their arguments.

Maurepas was no longer there to act as a mediator. He had been dismissed from office on 24 April allegedly for causing offence to Madame de Pompadour. With his departure the Government lost a capable minister whose legal knowledge, foresight, and skill as negotiator were indispensable in its relations with the *Parlement* especially at this time. Maupeou was already on bad terms with Daguesseau and disliked Machault: now he had

---

[7] BUP, Archives d'Argenson, CA 34, file of letters from Maupeou to the Comte d'Argenson: letter of 29 Apr. 1749, with copy enclosed of Maupeou's letter to Machault of the same day.
[8] *Ibid.*, CA 28/I, file of letters from Jean-Omer Joly de Fleury to the Comte d'Argenson (1749): letter of 6 May 1749 (3 p.m.).

lost his friend, protector, and intercessor. The *département* of Paris was given to the minister of war, the Comte d'Argenson; he and *Avocat général* Joly de Fleury knew each other of old (certainly from the days when both men were in the *Grand Conseil*). The first president sensed, perhaps quite rapidly, that his influence at court had begun to wane, while that of the Joly de Fleury clan was increasing. Although at first he made overtures to the new minister and their relations were cordial, his conduct became more circumspect.

Three new financial measures, including the *vingtième*, were presented in the form of edicts for registration on 7 May. The first one was registered the next day; but the *vingtième* and the creation of more *rentes* raised opposition. Given the importance of the *vingtième* in the political and financial history of the last decades of the *ancien régime*, some account should be given of its passage through the *Parlement*. Instead of taking the usual course of handing the texts of the measures over to *commissaires* for examination, the *parlementaires* decided at once to make remonstrances by over a hundred votes to forty-nine. *Commissaires* were then appointed simply to discuss the points that were to be included in the remonstrances. This was also an unusual course to take; it was the normal practice to allow the first president to prepare the remonstrances, once their purpose had been determined by the assembly of the chambers.[9] The *parlementaires* were encouraged in their resistance to the new tax by the impression they had gained from one of the *conseillers honoraires*, Michau de Montaran, who was loudly telling everybody that the Government was prepared to set a time limit on the *vingtième* and even to withdraw the existing tax of the *centième denier*, if there was any opposition. Michau de Montaran was also a *maître de requêtes* in the royal council and was rumoured to have worked on the draft of the *vingtième*. When they heard of these ill-founded rumours, both the Comte d'Argenson and the *procureur général* came to the conclusion that the King might have to hold a *lit de justice* to force the *parlementaires* to register the tax.

The terms of the final *arrêté* were ambiguous; some of the *commissaires*, led by Thomé, interpreted them to mean that the remonstrances were to be on the subject of the establishment of the *vingtième* and of the *rentes*; Salabéry (the *rapporteur*) and the others thought the *arrêté* also referred to the way the new taxes were to be levied. The *grand banc* of the *présidents à mortier* was divided as well on this issue. The dispute had to be referred to the assembly of the chambers which decided on 12 May in favour of the first alternative by 167 votes to 24. Later that day Jean-Omer Joly de Fleury enclosed a list

---

[9] Jean-Omer Joly de Fleury wrote: 'on ne laisse pas de trouver assez singulier que l'on ne se repose pas sur le chef pour rédiger les Remonstrances, quand une fois l'objet est déterminé' (*ibid.*: letter to D'Argenson of 12 May 1749, 2 p.m.).

of the *commissaires* with the daily report which he sent to the Comte d'Argenson, perhaps in the hope that the minister might seek to influence them. Whether he did so is not known, though, according to one of them, Durey de Meinières, both he and Thomé thought they would be imprisoned in the Bastille for proposing remonstrances on the *vingtième*.[10]

The report of the *commissaires* was presented before the assembly of the chambers the next morning. It contained six points that were to form the basis of the remonstrances. These were: the repeated promises made by the King that the *dixième* would be abolished once the war was effectively over ('aussitôt que les armes auroient été posées'); the extent and nature of the impositions and financial aids which the King had already extracted from his subjects in the course of the war; the hope which had been entertained that after such considerable assistance there would be no need for further impositions to pay off war debts; the necessity of placing the immediate relief of the people before the reimbursement of debts that were not yet due for repayment but were described in the edict as the prime motive of the new taxes; the allocation of the new tax (in the singular and therefore a reference to the *vingtième*) which should be reserved for pressing needs, its proceeds not being used as a means of ordering the finances (or 'à des vues d'arrangement', to use the delicate phraseology of the *commissaires*); and finally – a rhetorical point here – the slowing down of agriculture and the danger of seeing a decline in the fixed ordinary revenues of the King if the tax resulted in cultivation being abandoned and commerce weakened.[11]

That evening the Comte d'Argenson hinted in a letter to *Avocat général*

---

[10] *Ibid.*, CA 28/I: Jean-Omer Joly de Fleury to the Comte d'Argenson, letters of 6 May and 12 May (2 p.m.) 1749; *ibid.*, CA 34, Maupeou to the Comte d'Argenson, 12 and 13 May 1749; AN, 342 AP 2 ('Mémoires' of J. O. Joly de Fleury), pp. 149–50; and BN, MS franç. 7573 (Durey de Meinières Papers), f. 115ᵛ: Durey de Meinières to L'Averdy, 20 July 1754, on the times when Durey thought he would be sent to the Bastille; the president claimed that he and Thomé had made enemies of Machault and of the powerful financiers, the Pâris brothers on this occasion. The names of the *commissaires* are as follows: all the *présidents à mortier* with the exception of Potier; for the *grand'chambre*: Pinon (16/8/1704), Montullé (17/3/1706), Severt (5/5/1706), Lambelin (9/6/1706), Tubeuf (28/5/1708), De Blair (30/1/1709), Rulault (8/5/1709), Thomé (4/1/1713), Fieubet (18/1/1713), Langlois (27/8/1718), Bochart (18/8/1724), Macé (1/9/1724), D'Héricourt (19/7/1730), Salabéry (*rapporteur*, entered the *Parlement* 11/5/1720); for the *enquêtes*: Presidents Frémont d'Auneuil (22/8/1730), Frémont du Mazy (13/5/1735), De Fourcy (25/2/1699), Olivier de Sénozan (10/7/1733), Le Clerc (9/8/1735) and *Conseillers* Hénin (31/12/1717), Montholon (5/7/1713), Pelot (28/2/1714), Dupré (28/2/1714) and Titon (22/1/1717); and for the *requêtes*: Presidents Moreau de Nassigny (9/8/1709) and Durey de Meinières (4/5/1731), and *Conseillers* Boutin (31/?/1720) and Chicoineau (5/5/1739). The list is given by chambers and in strict order of seniority by Jean-Omer Joly de Fleury on p. 149 of his memoirs (cf. François Bluche, *L'Origine des magistrats du Parlement de Paris au xviiiᵉ siècle (1715–1771): Dictionnaire généalogique* in *Paris et Ile-de-France: Mémoires publiés par la Fédération des sociétés historiques et archéologiques de Paris et de l'Ile-de-France*, v–vi (Paris, 1953–4 [1956]) for the dates of entry in the *Parlement*). As one might have expected, the *commissaires* who examined the *vingtième* were hardly young.

[11] AN, 342 AP 2 ('Mémoires' of J. O. Joly de Fleury), pp. 150–1.

Plate 7 The Comte d'Argenson, after J. M. Nattier (private collection)

Joly de Fleury that he would like to see him when he came to give his general audience at the Invalides the following day. The *avocat général* went along in eager anticipation: the moment he appeared in the *chambre du conseil* of the Invalides, the minister extricated himself from the throng of military and other hangers-on and led him off to a room where they spoke in private for over an hour.

The character and conduct of the Comte d'Argenson are difficult to analyse. He was the younger of two gifted brothers who had been pupils at the Collège Louis-le-Grand at the same time as Voltaire and the Maréchal de Richelieu.[12] The elder brother, the marquis, was a politically ambitious writer and philosopher who seemed unable to hold on to any official position for long (including that of minister of foreign affairs, from which he had been dismissed in February 1747). The younger D'Argenson was more worldly-wise and the opposite of his brother. Where the marquis was brusque and tactless, the comte was the perfect courtier, attentive, polite, and full of charm. He was a man of close friendships and delicate relationships: with President Hénault and Madame de Deffand (who wrote a perceptive character study of him), with the Comte de Tressan, and with Queen Marie Leczinska herself – a real *amitié amoureuse* here – and her lady-in-waiting, the Duchesse de Villars, an old flame.[13] Cardinal de Tencin, who joined the Government at the same time as the comte, wrote of him: 'D'Argenson est tout propre pour plaire au roi: superficiel et badin.'[14] Louis XV certainly found him agreeable to work with and to listen to in council: without being profound, the comte was an intelligent and efficient minister, and the King had not wavered in his support for him when the military establishment, headed by the Maréchaux de Saxe and de Noailles, had tried to have him removed in July 1747 after the battle of Lawfeld.[15] Was there another, less appealing side to him? Perhaps. He was certainly devious. His brother, whom he helped out of scrapes but who disliked him and envied him his success, averred that he was the model for *Le Méchant* in Gresset's play of that name: a character who spends his time subtly poisoning relationships among his acquaintances and generally

---

[12] There is no full-scale biography of the Comte D'Argenson. On the education at Louis-le-Grand, see Theodore Besterman, *Voltaire* (London, 1969), pp. 31–43.

[13] A small part of his correspondence has been published in a series of volumes by the Marquis d'Argenson (1875–1932) under the following titles: *Correspondance du Comte d'Argenson, ministre de la guerre: lettres de Marie Leczinska et du cercle de la Reine* (Paris, 1922); *Autour d'un ministre de Louis XV: lettres intimes inédites* (Paris, 1923); and *Correspondance du Comte d'Argenson, ministre de la guerre: lettres des maréchaux de France* (Paris, 1924). *Correspondance du Comte d'Argenson ... lettres de Marie Leczinska*, pp. 1–56; Marquis d'Argenson, 'Le Roman de la "Sainte Duchesse", lettres inédites de la Duchesse de Villars au Comte d'Argenson (1738–1741)', *La Revue de France*, iii (1923), pp. 494–527. For Madame du Deffand's portrait of him, see Horace Walpole, *Correspondence*, ed. W. S. Lewis (Oxford, 1939), vol. viii: *Horace Walpole's correspondence with Madame du Deffand*, ed. W. S. Lewis and Warren Hunting Smith, part vi: *Appendices*, pp. 108–9.

[14] Bibliothèque Victor Cousin, Sorbonne, Paris, Papers of the Maréchal de Richelieu (hereafter BVC, RP), xli (catalogue no. 62), no. 68: Tencin to Richelieu, 12 May 1744.

[15] Rohan Butler, *Choiseul*, vol. i: *Father and son, 1719–1754* (Oxford, 1980), p. 695. There are more details on this affair in the comte's unpublished papers in Poitiers.

causing trouble by blackening people behind their backs.[16] It is difficult to check the accuracy of such allegations.

The Comte d'Argenson's appointment to the Paris *département* had also given added edge to his personal feud with the *contrôleur général*. He had been instrumental in securing Machault's nomination in December 1745: both men had old connections with the Orléans household and with the *Grand Conseil*, and one of the minister of war's first acts had been to obtain the appointment of Machault as intendant of the border province of Hainaut, where he had been able to display his abilities during the recent campaigns. The brusque and normally undemonstrative Machault ended his letter of thanks to the Comte d'Argenson for his part in his elevation with the words: 'Je vous embrasse.'[17] But on the very evening of his appointment he made it clear that his gratitude had come to an abrupt end. President Hénault recalled how the Comte d'Argenson, though laid up in bed with gout, had nonetheless invited Machault and his aged father to dinner. Not a word of thanks was uttered by Machault throughout the long, tedious meal. When they were at last alone, Hénault said to D'Argenson: 'Monsieur, voilà un ingrat bien décidé.' The minister merely raised his arms to the heavens and made no reply.[18] Soon, the lack of gratitude turned into hostility. It seems that Machault helped to poison the delicate relationship between D'Argenson and Madame de Pompadour. Although the Comte d'Argenson continued to retain the King's confidence, Madame de Pompadour transferred hers increasingly to the amenable minister of finance. The precise nature of the dispute between the two men is not properly documented, though one possible explanation may lie in a statement made in July 1754 by the former *procureur général* Joly de Fleury that Machault kept cutting the funds of the ministry of war by 4 millions each year, despite the fact that the Comte d'Argenson had an *état*, or authorisation, for the full amount signed by the King. Machault had another *état* also signed by the King for the lesser amount.[19] If this plausible version is

[16] On the relations between the two brothers, see J. M. J. Rogister, 'Missing pages from the Marquis d'Argenson's journal', *Studies on Voltaire and the Eighteenth Century*, cxxvii (1974), pp. 199–221, especially pp. 207–9. Dr Butler argues that the Comte de Stainville (later Duc de Choiseul) was the model for *Le Méchant* (*Choiseul*, i, pp. 718–19). On the whole I favour the Comte d'Argenson as the 'méchant' on the grounds that he was a more notable figure than Stainville at the time and therefore a more obviously recognisable target than the young Stainville: but I have also found some slight evidence that supports Dr Butler's view. That both candidates were indeed 'méchants' is possibly beyond doubt.

[17] BUP, CA 33: Machault to Comte d'Argenson, 6 Dec. 1745, enclosing a copy of his letter to Maurepas of the same day accepting the post of *contrôleur général*; for his correspondence with Maurepas see AN, 257 AP 21 (Maurepas Papers), 6/5 and 4, and Pierre Gaxotte, *Le Siècle de Louis XV* (Paris, 1963), p. 224.

[18] *Mémoires du Président Hénault*, ed. F. Rousseau (Paris, 1911), pp. 205–6.

[19] BVC, RP, xiv (catalogue no. 35), f. 56: letter unsigned, probably from Ysabeau, clerk of the *Parlement*, to the Maréchal de Richelieu, 10 July 1754. Joly de Fleury's remarks were

correct, it tells one more about the King than about the two protagonists, though the Comte d'Argenson was apparently not eager to force the King to make his choice between them – and their *états*.

Such was the man who now discussed the situation in the *Parlement* with the younger Joly de Fleury. The *avocat général* said he thought the first president would allow matters to drag on and would exercise little or no restraint on his colleagues. D'Argenson agreed with him and indicated that he had no high opinion of Maupeou. He revealed that the King was unlikely to modify the edicts and was eager for the affair of the *vingtième* to be settled within the next few days before the *Parlement* went into recess for Whitsun. Accordingly, it was agreed that on the day when they were instructed by the *Parlement* to ask the King when he would receive the remonstrances, the *gens du roi* would leave for Versailles at once in order to be able to report the King's reply the same day. In the meantime, D'Argenson asked Joly de Fleury to supply him with further details not only about the way the remonstrances were received and answered, but also concerning the last *lit de justice*, that of 1732. After making this ominous request, the minister adroitly changed the subject of conversation to the matter of the *avocat général*'s career prospects. Joly de Fleury explained he was not rich (with only the capital to provide an income of 8000 *livres* a year) and that, although he liked his present post, the fact that he was now a widower with a young family on his hands meant that he would prefer less arduous employment. D'Argenson now raised his hopes:

> Il me parla d'une place de conseiller d'état, de celle de Premier Président du Grand Conseil, si on la rétablissoit, car pour les places de Prem[r] Président de Provinces, il ne me conseilla pas d'y penser. Je répondis avec beaucoup de reconnoissance et je remis à l'entretenir de tout cela lorsque L'affaire présente serait terminée.[20]

This meeting had some far-reaching consequences. First, it marked the beginning of an arrangement by which Jean-Omer Joly de Fleury undertook to inform the Comte d'Argenson of the day-to-day developments in the *Parlement*: in person when the minister came to Paris or the *gens du roi* went to court, but also in writing: ten files survive of the reports (sometimes two or three a day) which he sent to D'Argenson over the next eight years of the minister's tenure of office.[21] Were these reports shown in turn to the

---

made in the course of a private conversation with Ysabeau during the negotiations for the return of the *Parlement* (see Chapter 8).

20 BN, Cabinet des MSS, Collection Joly de Fleury (hereafter BN, JF), no. 1450, ff. 40, 41: Comte d'Argenson to Jean-Omer Joly de Fleury, Marly, 13 and 16 May 1749; BUP, CA 28/I: J. O. Joly de Fleury to the Comte d'Argenson, 15 May 1749; and especially AN, 342 AP 2 ('Mémoires' of J. O. Joly de Fleury), pp. 151–2.

21 These letters are now in BUP, CA 28, *dossiers* I–VII (7 May 1749 to 25 Dec. 1755) and CA 29, *dossiers* VIII–X (2 Jan. 1756 to 29 Jan. 1757, together with undated letters). I was

Plate 8 Avocat général (later President) J. O. Joly de Fleury, engraving by
Coqueret after a drawing by Le Moine

King? A single annotation in the royal hand on one of them and a passing
reference in a letter from Madame de Pompadour to the minister would
appear to suggest that they were seen by the King and possibly his mistress;

fortunate in being able to consult the undated letters before they were unwisely separated
from the rest after 1975. In effect the correspondence began a few days earlier, on 7 May.
On 11 May the Comte d'Argenson asked the *avocat général* to address his letters for him to
Charles François Lavechef du Parc (died 1751) who was then *intendant général des postes*: BN,
JF 1450, f. 37: Du Parc to J. O. Joly de Fleury, 11 May 1749. Subsequently, the letters were
addressed openly to the minister, though on occasion they were sent to Mademoiselle
Fournier, who may have been a relative of Fournier, the doctor of both the Comte
d'Argenson and of his friend, President Hénault.

but was this always the case?[22] For his part, the Comte d'Argenson who seldom committed himself on paper, seems to have been unable or unwilling to advance the *avocat général*'s career during the same period. Possibly the able and dedicated Joly de Fleury had made himself indispensable in his post. The most he obtained until he became a *président à mortier* in 1767 was a pension of 6000 *livres* in 1755.[23]

Secondly, this arrangement between D'Argenson and the *avocat général* tended to establish the *gens du roi* as negotiators between the Government and the *Parlement*. As they had a pretext to go to court when the *Parlement* instructed them to ascertain the date on which the King would receive remonstrances (as on this occasion), they would now use their presence there to confer with ministers, perhaps even with the King himself. With feelings of awe and excitement, these men now came to play a more significant part in the ornate ritual surrounding the Monarch. It is hardly surprising, therefore, that Jean-Omer Joly de Fleury devoted a passage in his memoirs to a circumstantial account of their audience with the King on 17 May. There were to be many such occasions in years to come and, as the novelty wore off, so the urge to record them in detail probably waned. The ritual was unchanging and unceasing. Like planets moving round the sun, the King's subjects moved round his person, some nearer, some further away, each according to his place in the solar system. It was Diderot who once wrote: 'Il n'y a dans tout un royaume qu'un homme qui marche, c'est le souverain: tout le reste prend des positions.'[24]

On 17 May, the *gens du roi* left Paris at a quarter to twelve and reached Versailles an hour and a half later, probably after a bumpy and uncomfortable journey. Their first place of call was naturally the chancellery (on the Place d'Armes). There, they were told to go at once to the antechamber of the King's state apartments, the *Œil-de-Bœuf*. On their way on foot through the first courtyard of the palace, they did not omit to write their names down at the Comte d'Argenson's lodgings (in the ministers' wing on the right-hand side), although they knew that he, like the chancellor, was not there but attending the weekly meeting of the *Conseil des dépêches*. They then crossed the second courtyard and entered the palace on the left-hand side. After ascending the marble staircase and going through the King's guard-

---

[22] BUP, CA 28/III: the annotation is on a letter of 13 Aug. 1751 concerning the affair of the *Hôpital général*; see also Marquis d'Argenson, *Autour d'un ministre de Louis XV*, p. 268: Madame de Pompadour to the Comte d'Argenson, 17 May 1749 (quoted below, pp. 76–7). It may be noted that these examples come only from the early years of D'Argenson's tenure of the *département* of Paris.

[23] BN, MS franç. 14432, 'Département de Paris, MDCCLVI', 'Dépenses', p. 75; see also *État nominatif des pensions sur le Trésor Royal imprimé par ordre de l'Assemblée Nationale* (Paris, 1791, 4to), i, p. 68.

[24] Diderot, *Le Neveu de Rameau*, in *Œuvres*, ed. André Billy (Paris, 1951), p. 471.

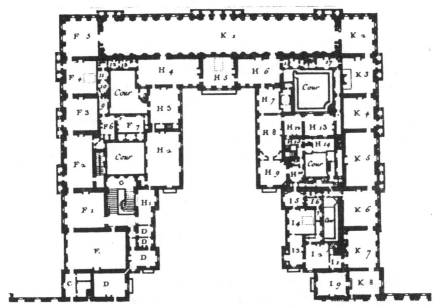

Figure 4 Plan of the first floor of the central part of the Palace of Versailles, *c.* 1755 (detail from J. F. Blondel, *Architecture françoise* (Paris, 1756))

On 17 May 1749 the *gens du roi* arrived by the Queen's staircase (G), crossed the King's guardroom (H 2) and first antechamber (H 3) and waited in the *Salon de l'Œil-de-Bœuf* (H 4). When summoned into the royal presence they crossed the King's state bedroom (H 5) and entered the council chamber (H 6). The room in which they later had a private conference with the chancellor was probably the one (F 13) leading off from the *Œil-de-Bœuf* ('une pièce de communication de l'appartement de la Reine avec celui du Roi, & au dessus de laquelle est contenu le logement du Premier Valet de Chambre de Sa Majesté'). The King's private apartment led off the council chamber (H 7 to H 18). Until 1752 the staircase between H 17 and H 18 led to Madame de Pompadour's apartment on the second floor (above K 3); after 1752 Madame de Pompadour occupied a larger apartment on the ground floor which the King could reach directly by means of a circular staircase accessible from H 13 and visible to the right of H 14.

room and the first antechamber, they reached the crowded *Œil-de-Bœuf* in the central axis of the palace (see Figure 4). The meeting of the council was taking place two rooms away and it lasted until a quarter past three. During their long wait in the *Œil-de-Bœuf*, which they were unable to leave because of the order they had received, the Duc de Gesvres took pity on them and kept them company. At about three o'clock, the Maréchal de Richelieu, the *premier gentilhomme de la chambre* on duty, arrived, an indication that their ballet was about to start. They apologised to him for not having written their names down at his lodgings and invoked the King's order. Then, the adjoining door of the King's state bedroom was opened by one of the ministers, the Comte de Saint-Florentin, who asked if they were there. When they had presented themselves, he went back into the King's state bedroom and immediately afterwards the appropriate minister – the Comte d'Argenson – came to fetch them. Richelieu would normally have accompanied them, but not so on this occasion, for D'Argenson informed him that the council was still formally in session. The four *gens du roi* now entered the King's bedroom, closed the door behind them (as Richelieu was not there to do it) and made their way across the empty room, probably bowing to the royal bed behind its balustrade, to the entrance of the council chamber. The King and his ministers had left their seats at the table and were standing beside it. The *gens du roi* bowed deeply at the door and advanced towards the King, making two further bows on the way. D'Ormesson, as first *avocat général*, asked the King to name the day for the remonstrances. The King's reply was predictably brief: 'à demain une heure après midi; M^r le Premier Président pourra apporter les remontrances avec deux présidents'. The *gens du roi* noticed that Machault was laughing and that the King was also in jovial mood (they knew he was off to have dinner with Madame de Pompadour at La Celle Saint Cloud). That was all they could notice, for it was already time for them to leave the King's presence with the same ritual as before, except that they walked backwards in order to leave the council chamber. They lingered in the *Œil-de-Bœuf*, where they were soon joined by Daguesseau and D'Argenson, who ushered them into a small room occupied by the King's *valet de chambre*. There, behind closed doors, the ministers asked them what the remonstrances contained. They replied that they did not know; the remonstrances had not yet been shown to the *Parlement*. When Daguesseau asked what would happen, D'Argenson observed that it was up to the first president: the King had fixed the day and, having received the remonstrances, he would immediately hold a council and give his reply before going off to Choisy. After having a bite to eat at the chancellery, while their horses were being harnessed, the *gens du roi* returned to Paris as quickly as they could to inform the first president.[25]

If these incidents have been described at some length, it is because they serve to illustrate not simply the part played increasingly by the *gens du roi* as negotiators, but also the contrast between the intricate formality of a royal audience on the one hand and the hasty consultations between certain ministers and *parlementaires* on the other. Etiquette regulated court life down to the most minor details, but beyond the formal contacts between the ministry and the *Parlement*, it was left to individual ministers concerned to establish their own informal links and working arrangements with the *Parlement*. Maurepas had relied on the first presidents: D'Argenson turned instead to the *gens du roi*, at least initially.

---

[25] AN, 342 AP 2 ('Mémoires' of J. O. Joly de Fleury), pp. 154–5.

Finally, the third consequence of D'Argenson's overtures to Jean-Omer Joly de Fleury and his reliance on the *gens du roi* was that it alienated the first president and made him less willing to co-operate with a minister who had chosen not to confide in him. Hitherto the first president had usually prepared the remonstrances within the short space of a few days. But by allowing the *parlementaires* to entrust *commissaires* with the task of planning these remonstrances for him on this occasion, Maupeou had lengthened the process of registration as well as set a new precedent. When confronted merely with the text of an edict, the *commissaires* were able to arrive at some conclusions fairly quickly; when confronted with the task of planning remonstrances, however, they all had different ideas and often needed to refer their disagreements to an assembly of the chambers. At the same time, their participation in the planning of the remonstrances was a limitation on the rôle of the first president. Yet Maupeou's attitude was one of utter detachment; he wrote to the Comte d'Argenson on 12 May:

> ... M^rs les commissaires s'assembleront cet après disné à la chambre de St Louis pour me donner comme à un écolier de réthorique les sujets qu'ils Jugeront à propos que J'amplifie. Je ne manqueray pas de vous informer ce soir de leurs magnifiques Réflexions auxquelles malheureusement je ne seray que trop forcé de me conformer, quoyqu'il arrive.[26]

And again, three days later:

> ... le canevas que l'on m'a donné est enfin rempli, au peu de goût que vous sçavés que j'avois pour l'ouvrage vous ne devés pas douter que je ne me sois bien précisément renfermé dans les limites que l'on m'a prescripts, sans y adjouter du mien.[27]

He still had to show the draft to the *commissaires*: 'c'est un guichet par lequel il faut absolument passer'. But a first president was not powerless to overcome such obstacles and even to curb opposition to his wishes: Maupeou seemed to have given up the struggle. It is also possible that he preferred to shirk the responsibility for the remonstrances, while he lessened his own labour by drawing on the material and ideas provided by erudite *commissaires*. Anyway, the King jolted him out of his dilatoriness and supineness by demanding to have the remonstrances within twenty-four hours. No concessions were made (though the *Conseil des dépêches* discussed the remonstrances for two hours), and the *parlementaires* were ordered to register the edict the next day. After making further supplications they obeyed the order; the *arrêt d'enregistrement* of 19 May stated that the registration was done *du très exprès commandement du roi*.[28] Twelve days

---

[26] See Maupeou's letter of 12 May 1749 quoted in note 10 above.
[27] BUP, CA 34: Maupeou to the Comte d'Argenson, 15 May 1749.
[28] Flammermont, *Rems.*, i, pp. 397–403.

Plate 9 The Marquise (later Duchesse) de Pompadour, by F. Boucher
(National Gallery of Scotland, Edinburgh)

had passed between the time when the edict had been laid before the
assembly of the chambers and the time when it was registered. In his
memoirs Jean-Omer Joly de Fleury concluded his account of the *vingtième*
affair:

> Ainsi finit cette affaire que M^r le Prem^r Président avoit fait traîner en
> longueur soit par pique contre le contrôleur général soit pour marquer aux
> ministres que Mr de Maurepas son amy étant déplacé il ne se presteroit à les
> obliger qu'autant qu'ils rechercheroient son amitié.
>
> On luy sçut mauvais gré à la cour de tous ses retards, et sans l'amitié de m^r
> d'Argenson pour moy qui me mit à Portée de conseiller toutes les voyes de
> douceur, les choses ne se seroient pas passées aussi tranquillement.[29]

The King had also been firm: the day the *gens du roi* came to Versailles
Madame de Pompadour had seized a piece of paper, one on which she had
jotted down the title of a new book, and had told the Comte d'Argenson
that he wanted the affair out of the way within a week and without having
to go to the lengths of holding a *lit de justice*. 'Faites vos réflexions sur cela',

---

[29] AN, 342 AP 2 ('Mémoires' of J. O. Joly de Fleury), p. 161.

she had urged the minister, 'l'avis de l'avocat général serait peut-être bon'.[30]

In religious matters, Cardinal de Fleury's policy had been twofold: to choose moderates as bishops and to restrain those bishops who were or became too zealous in their desire to uphold *Unigenitus*. With his death, the task of presenting candidates to the King for preferment fell on the new holder of the *feuille des bénéfices*, Boyer, the former bishop of Mirepoix, a mediocrity who eventually succeeded in being disliked on all sides in the disputes. The choice of Christophe de Beaumont as archbishop of Paris was but the most significant in a series of bad episcopal appointments made at this time. When Monseigneur de Bellefonds died in July 1746 after barely two months in the post, the favourite candidate to succeed him had been Maurepas's cousin, Frédéric-Jerôme de La Rochefoucauld, archbishop of Bourges, who was then ambassador in Rome and already had a promise of the first available cardinal's hat.[31] Naturally Maurepas had backed him and so had old Cardinal d'Auvergne who, at five in the morning on 1 August 1746, had dashed off a long letter to the minister extolling La Rochefoucauld's qualities and revealing the names (and weaknesses) of the other possible candidates.[32] La Rochefoucauld himself was not keen, as he told Maurepas, to succeed Bellefonds: 'je ne voudrais pas risquer à crever comme mon ancien camarade au bout de deux mois'.[33] But, in any case, the King decided that, although La Rochefoucauld (whom he had known since childhood and liked) would be the right man for the post, he still had a greater need of him in Rome.[34] With the best man out of the running, the King could make only a desperate choice, especially as the merest whiff of Jansenism was sufficient to damn any candidate in his eyes.

---

[30] Marquis d'Argenson, *Autour d'un ministre de Louis XV*, p. 268: letter of 17 May 1749.

[31] Frédéric-Jerôme de Roye de La Rochefoucauld (1701–57), archbishop of Bourges (1729), abbot of Cluny (1747), ambassador extraordinary to the Holy See (1744), cardinal (1747), presided the General Assembly of the clergy of France (1750 and 1755), entrusted with the *feuille des bénéfices* (1755).

[32] Maurepas to La Rochefoucauld, 25 July and 1 Aug. 1746 in *Correspondance de M. de La Rochefoucauld, ambassadeur à Rome 1744–1748* (Nantes, 1871), ed. Baron de Girardot, pp. 216 and 219; ADD, Archives Saint-Vallier (Maurepas Papers), MF *bobine* no. 138, 'Lettres, discours et mémoires sur les affaires du clergé': Cardinal d'Auvergne to Maurepas, 1 Aug. 1746. Henri-Oswald de la Tour d'Auvergne (1671–1747), archbishop of Vienne (1721–43), *premier aumônier du roi* (1732), cardinal (1737); the other candidates he named were the bishop of Langres (Montmorin de Saint-Hérem), supported by the Comte d'Argenson, and the archbishop of Rouen (Saulx-Tavannes), the bishop of Bayeux (Luynes), and the bishop of Amiens (Orléans de la Motte), supported by the Maréchal de Noailles.

[33] AN, 257 AP 26 (Maurepas Papers), no. 85: La Rochefoucauld to Maurepas, 10 Aug. 1746.

[34] *Ibid.*, no. 91[A]: copy forwarded by La Rochefoucauld to Maurepas of a letter of 15 Aug. he had received from the former bishop of Mirepoix. Boyer quoted the King's exact words to him concerning La Rochefoucauld. See also Suzanne Pillorget, *Claude-Henri Feydeau de Marville, lieutenant général de police de Paris 1740–1747, suivi d'un choix de lettres inédites* (Paris, 1978), p. 240.

Plate 10 Christophe de Beaumont, Archbishop of Paris, engraving by R. Gaillard after a painting by J. Chevallier

Beaumont's name finally emerged perhaps because he was an outsider (being of good provincial nobility with few court connections) and was also felt to be sound in doctrine and firm with his flock. Louis XV was markedly unlucky in many of his episcopal appointments, and never more so than on this occasion. Cardinal d'Auvergne, who was the man's predecessor as archbishop of Vienne, had warned that, if appointed, Beaumont would want to do everything himself; but even he had probably not taken the full measure of this stubborn and headstrong priest.[35] To some, the new

---

[35] Letter of 1 Aug. 1746, referred to in note 32 above.

archbishop, who wore his conscience on his sleeve, was a model of piety and Christian charity; to others, he was simply a bigot with a condescending manner towards underlings and social inferiors.[36] He was undoubtedly a trouble maker, even if his intentions were pure and his private life irreproachable. Louis XV's decision not to appoint the sensible and mild La Rochefoucauld to the archbishopric of Paris in 1746 was a fateful one, for the peace and tranquillity of the middle years of his reign were to be marred by Beaumont's activities.

While Maurepas had been in office, Fleury's other policy, that of restraining those bishops who were too zealous in upholding the bull, was adhered to, especially on the question of 'denial of sacraments'. If the *Parlement* was opposed to the practice of denying the sacraments to those who had their doubts about *Unigenitus*, so too was the King. In 1741 Maurepas wrote on his orders to La Fare, the bishop of Laon to warn him about the conduct of one of his priests:

> les règles établies dans son royaume ne permettant pas de refuser à la sainte Table la communion à ceux qui ne sont pas excommuniés ni dénoncés, Elle [Sa Majesté] ne peut que désapprouver [*sic*] la conduite de votre grand vicaire, et qu'ainsi il n'est pas dans le cas d'avoir recours à sa protection.[37]

But with Maurepas's departure, it is possible that zealots like Beaumont felt that a restraining influence on them had been thankfully removed now that the affairs of the clergy were in the hands of a new minister, the Comte de Saint-Florentin (Maurepas's brother-in-law), who needed time to pick up the threads. In June 1749, one of the archbishop's priests, Bouettin, the *curé* of Saint-Etienne du Mont in Paris, refused the sacrament to the dying principal of the Collège de Beauvais, Coffin, and thus began a spate of similar denials of sacraments. The new archbishop was concerned with what he regarded as the misuse of the sacraments in his diocese. When he came to explain his views on this matter to the King some years later, he wrote:

> le diocèse que V.M. a confié à mes soins est celui de tous qui demande le plus d'exactitude. Combien d'étrangers habitent la capitale et combien des gens

---

[36] For a eulogy of Beaumont, see Père E. Régnault, *Christophe de Beaumont* (Paris, 1882), 2 vols., *passim*. For conflicting contemporary opinions about him, see, in his favour, *Mémoires de Charles Claude Flahaut, Comte de la Billarderie d'Angiviller: notes sur les Mémoires de Marmontel publiés d'après le manuscrit*, ed. Louis Bobé (Copenhagen and Paris, 1933), pp. 59–61; and against, *Mémoires du Duc de Choiseul*, ed. F. Calmettes (Paris, 1904), p. 110; AN, 342 AP 2 ('Mémoires' of J. O. Joly de Fleury), p. 162: 'Il [Beaumont] fournit aussi mil [*sic*] preuves de son peu d'esprit, de la petitesse de son qu'il en avoit, et de l'obstination, apanage ordinaire des ignorants et des petits génies'; Collection Michel Vinot Préfontaine (Paris), 'Mémoires de P. A. Robert de Saint-Vincent' (typescript copy), pp. 126–7.

[37] BPR, LP 514, no. 3: Maurepas to the bishop of Laon, 25 Feb. 1741 (copy in the hand of L. A. Le Paige). Fleury also wrote to the *procureur général* of the *Parlement* in similar terms (see AN, 342 AP 2 ('Mémoires' of J. O. Joly de Fleury), pp. 184–5).

sans être approuvés s'immiscent à confesser? Mais ce qui surprendra V.M., c'est que les Laïques portent le sacrilège jusqu'à écouter des malades en confession pour en tirer quelque lucre. Ce n'est pas contre les jansénistes que mes soins s'étendent, ce n'est que sur l'abus des sacrements, et sur la perte évidente de ceux qui se font passer pour ministres des autels et de ceux qui reçoivent en cet état l'Eucharistie . . .[38]

Hence the archbishop had ordered that only authorised priests should hear confession and that a person who wished to obtain the sacraments should first produce a certificate, where it was stated that his confession had been heard by one of these priests. Moreover, the archbishop ordered that a confession certificate should not be issued to any person in holy or religious orders who did not assure an authorised confessor that he submitted to *Unigenitus*.[39] As a result, ecclesiastics who objected to the bull could no longer make a practice of confessing to certain priests who shared their sentiments and of then obtaining the sacraments from their local priests, who themselves might be staunch adherents of the bull. Although the archbishop claimed that his measures were not directed at the so-called Jansenists, he could hardly deny that these measures forced them to submit to *Unigenitus* if they did not wish to be deprived of the sacraments.

Two ministers who were later closely associated with the affairs of the clergy and the *Parlement*, Cardinal de Bernis and the Duc de Choiseul, thought the archbishop's radical device (which had been used before in the diocese) had initially met with the King's personal approval. On the other hand, *Avocat général* Joly de Fleury made a note of a conversation he had with the Comte d'Argenson on 26 July 1749 when the minister told him, 'que le roy étoit bien décidé à ne pas vouloir de refus de cette espèce, ni rien qui troubla l'ordre et la tranquillité publique'. Louis XV's conduct remains enigmatic.[40]

The occasion of the minister's remark was a visit by the *gens du roi* to the court at Compiègne after the Coffin affair had been raised at the *Parlement*.

---

[38] Museum Calvet, Avignon: bibliothèque, MS 2736 ('Mélanges', etc.), f. 135: 'Lettre de Mgr l'archevêque de Paris au Roi, du 20 février 1755'. This document purports to be a copy of a letter, the original of which I have been unable to trace. My reasons for thinking that the letter existed are as follows: in the Comte d'Argenson's Papers at the Archives nationales, 422 AP 1, there is a letter of the same date from Beaumont to the Comte d'Argenson enclosing a letter for the King. The next day, the King wrote to tell D'Argenson that he had failed to persuade the archbishop to change his stand: BVC, RP, xlii (catalogue no. 63), f. 168 (on internal evidence it is clear that the King's letter was addressed to D'Argenson and not to Richelieu). To the coincidence of dates between these three documents has to be added the text of Beaumont's letter to the King which is typical of his style.

[39] Throughout this account *billets de confession* are translated by the words 'confession certificates'.

[40] See *Mémoires et lettres de François-Joachim de Pierre Cardinal de Bernis, 1715–1758*, ed. F. Masson (Paris, 1903), i, p. 317; *Mémoires du Duc de Choiseul*, p. 111; and AN, 342 AP 2 ('Mémoires' of J. O. Joly de Fleury), p. 172.

It was the first crisis in which the Comte d'Argenson was called upon to act. He summoned the first president and the *gens du roi* to Compiègne, a journey which took seven hours.[41] Although Maupeou was clearly piqued that the *gens du roi* had also been invited, he drew some comfort from the fact that Daguesseau had asked the minister to accompany him when Daguesseau had his audience with the King to discuss the course of action to be taken. The *gens du roi* went to Compiègne on the Saturday, but the first president was not due there until the next morning. In conversation with the *avocat général*, D'Argenson expressed disapproval of Maupeou's late arrival, which made discussions between all concerned difficult, and yet he and the King had been responsible for ordering Maupeou to come on the Sunday.[42] Probably, where the first president and the *gens du roi* were concerned, the King and the Comte d'Argenson were practising a policy of 'divide and rule'.

What happened at Compiègne on the morning of 27 July needs to be described in detail as it provides a fair account on the workings of the royal government. The *gens du roi* had seen the chancellor the previous evening and took a firm line with him, as they had been privately advised to do by D'Ormesson's father, a senior councillor of state and the chancellor's brother-in-law. Now, they were already waiting in the Comte d'Argenson's antechamber when the first president arrived. Maupeou saw the minister alone for about an hour. Meanwhile the *gens du roi* were joined by one of the chancellor's sons, Daguesseau de Fresne, a councillor of state: he had his father's draft of the reply the King was to make to the first president. When Maupeou left (without even a glance at the *gens du roi*), Daguesseau de Fresne went in to give the draft to the minister. Afterwards it was the turn of the *gens du roi* to see D'Argenson: as with the chancellor beforehand, they dwelled upon the dangers of repeating the events of 1732, when the *parlementaires* had resigned in protest. D'Argenson then left to see the King. The *gens du roi* followed him shortly afterwards to watch the King going to chapel. When the King returned, the royal bedroom and the adjoining council chamber were cleared of the usual throng of courtiers, and the first president and the *gens du roi* were introduced through the bedroom into the council chamber with what was by now a familiar ritual to them.

The first president made an impressive speech and when it was over, the King pointedly turned to the *gens du roi* and asked them whether they had anything to add. D'Ormesson spoke a few words, and the King then said he would have the matter examined by the *Conseil des dépêches* and told them to withdraw into his bedroom. One was not allowed to sit in the King's bedroom, so, as his gout was troubling him, the first president went to sit

[41] *Ibid.*, p. 171.
[42] *Ibid.*, p. 173 and BUP, CA 34: Maupeou to the Comte d'Argenson, 24 July 1749.

down in the next room. The *gens du roi* were left in the company of Lebel, the King's *premier valet de chambre*. Richelieu took their minds off the matter in hand by pointing out to them that someone had managed to steal four inches of gold braid from the *bonnegrâce* of the royal bed though it was always supposed to be guarded by a *valet de chambre*. An hour passed, and the *parlementaires* were summoned back into the royal presence. Louis XV, who was short-sighted, held a paper immediately in front of his eyes and read out his reply. Maupeou said he would faithfully report it to the *Parlement*. The King folded the paper and handed it to him. The first president asked incongruously if it was in his handwriting: No, replied the King.[43]

They went back into the bedroom, and while those members of the *Conseil des dépêches* who were not also members of the *Conseil d'état* were leaving the council chamber, for the King was about to hold a meeting of that council, the first president, the *gens du roi*, the chancellor and the Comte d'Argenson huddled together in the recess of a window, where the first president once more read out the King's reply to them. It was in Saint-Florentin's handwriting. There was a phrase (reproduced here in italics) which the *parlementaires* did not like in the following passage:

> Je vous charge et vous ordonne de dire de ma part à mon parlement *que je me réserve la connaissance de la matière dont il s'agit* et qu'il attende que je lui fasse savoir mes intentions sur ce sujet pour s'y conformer avec le respect et la soumission qui lui sont dus.[44]

In Jean-Omer Joly de Fleury's view, the phrase amounted to an *évocation* by the King of a case pending at the *Parlement*: it could only create trouble there. He suggested *suspendre toutes poursuites*: Maupeou proposed *surçeoir*. Daguesseau promptly said that he found *surçeoir* more offensive than *réserver*, but he suggested to the Comte d'Argenson that they should both go back to the King. There was no time to lose, for the meeting of the *Conseil d'état* was about to start. Richelieu joined the remaining *parlementaires*, presumably to ask them to leave the bedroom, and Maupeou explained to him why they were waiting. Daguesseau and D'Argenson must have obtained the King's consent to make changes, for they returned fifteen minutes later bearing a text of the reply, now in D'Argenson's handwriting. The offending phrase had been struck out and instead the passage read:

> Je vous ordonne et vous charge de dire de ma part à mon parlement *qu'il suspende toutes poursuites sur la matière dont il s'agit*.[45]

[43] AN, 342 AP 2 ('Mémoires' of J. O. Joly de Fleury), pp. 174–7.   [44] *Ibid.*, p. 177.
[45] *Ibid.*, pp. 177–9; BUP, CA 17: Daguesseau to the Comte d'Argenson, 'Lundy à deux heures', [28 July 1749] and the enclosure in D'Argenson's hand which is the minister's own copy of the reply with the corrections made afterwards. The reply is printed in Flammermont, *Rems.*, i, p. 417 (note).

After dining with the Comte d'Argenson, the *gens du roi* returned to Paris. Although they did not get back until two in the morning, the relief which they felt must have helped to alleviate their weariness and the discomfort of the journey home.

Indeed, they and the first president had cause for satisfaction. The King had implicitly recognised the competence of the *Parlement* in the matter of denial of sacraments. Moreover, in this instance the case remained pending before the *Parlement* until such time as the King introduced the measures which he proposed to take. The *Avocat général* Joly de Fleury unhesitatingly ascribed the successful outcome of the affair to the Comte d'Argenson.[46] On 29 July the *Parlement* agreed to suspend its proceedings in the Coffin case, thereby setting a precedent which was adhered to until March 1752.[47]

Of growing concern both to the Government and to the *gens du roi* was Maupeou's handling of situations that arose in the *Parlement*. This concern was first seriously felt concerning the affair of the *Hôpital général*. The *Hôpital général* was an administration that grouped together nine institutions in Paris which looked after foundlings, lunatics, female prisoners, the sick and the destitute; in 1751 it provided food for over twelve thousand people (including staff).[48] It was administered by a woman, the *supérieure* of the largest institution, the *Salpêtrière*, under the supervision of a board presided over by the archbishop and composed partly of the town's judicial and civic dignitaries (the first presidents of the three royal courts, the *procureur général* of the *Parlement*, the *lieutenant général* of police, and the *prévôt des marchands*) known as the *chefs*, and partly of administrators appointed by the King.[49]

The *Hôpital général* was a place of stark contrasts. Jansenism permeated the atmosphere at every level. Yet at the *Salpêtrière*, for instance, the *supérieures* and *officières*, who were secular persons adopting the style of religious sisters, combined the punctilious observance and enforcement of a long round of religious duties in public with the regular indulgence of every vice in private (from sexual liaisons to beating the inmates). Meanwhile, the poor, the hungry, the mad, and the sick looked on. The archbishop

[46] AN, 342 AP 2 ('Mémoires' of J. O. Joly de Fleury), p. 184.
[47] BUP, CA 34: Maupeou to the Comte d'Argenson, 29 July 1749; CA 17: Daguesseau to the same, 'mardy à six heures du soir', [29 July 1749].
[48] BS, MS 800, f. 205 (Rolland d'Erceville's journal): report of the special *commissaires* of the *Parlement* appointed to investigate the affairs of the *Hôpital général* on 24 May 1751.
[49] On the organisation of the *Hôpital général* and on the events of 1749–51 see H. Légier Desgranges, *Du jansénisme à la Révolution: Madame de Moysan et l'extravagante affaire de l'Hôpital général, 1749–1758* (Paris, 1954). This is a tendentious work by a passionate exponent of the anti-*parlementaire* cause: it needs to be used in conjunction with documents in the Archives d'Argenson and in the Bibliothèque du Sénat. For lists of the *chefs* and administrators, see Légier Desgranges, *Du jansénisme à la Révolution*, pp. 153–4.

made his own predictable contribution to the tensions within this amazing institution by introducing confession certificates through the agency of the rector, a renegade Jansenist from the Cévennes. The *supérieure* could not stand the situation any longer and when she resigned at Easter 1749, the administrators thought of replacing her by Sœur Saint-Michel, who had been the chief *officière* of the penitential wing of the *Salpêtrière*, the *maison de force*, for the past thirty years and was, by the standards of the day and the traditions of the establishment, eminently suitable for the post. But the archbishop wanted to give it to an outsider, Madame de Moysan, an urbane and self-possessed woman who had little in common with her Jansenist rival, Sœur Saint-Michel, austere in approach but willing to turn a blind eye to the less edifying practices of her charges. At a meeting of the administrators on 12 July (attended by six *chefs* and sixteen administrators), the *chefs* including Maupeou and Joly de Fleury voted for her out of deference to the archbishop's wishes, but Madame de Moysan did not obtain the majority of the votes of those present (she lost by nine votes to twelve). Although it had been the practice for decisions in the board to be taken on the basis of a majority among all the administrators, the archbishop now chose to draw a distinction between the *chefs* and the others. He told the opponents of Madame de Moysan that their votes did not count anyway and declared her duly elected. Twelve of the sixteen ordinary administrators thereupon refused to serve on the board any more.[50]

A rift began to appear in the ranks of the *chefs* at the beginning of August when the archbishop tried to persuade the board to nominate four new administrators to fill some of the vacant places. It was clear that he wanted a clean sweep at the *Hôpital général*. He had the active support of Lamoignon de Blancmesnil and of the latter's nephew, Nicolaï (the first presidents of the *Cour des aides* and of the *Chambre des comptes*), but he no longer had Maupeou and Joly de Fleury behind him. Maupeou thought every attempt should be made to induce the former administrators to withdraw their resignations and that some compromise solution should be found. It was a sensible attitude to take, although it was hardly consistent with his earlier support for Madame de Moysan. The first president had previously warned the Comte d'Argenson that the matter of the resignation of the administrators could have repercussions at the *Parlement*.[51] The Government became very concerned at this prospect. On 17 August Maupeou

[50] *Ibid.*, pp. 156–60.
[51] BUP, CA 34: Maupeou to the Comte d'Argenson, 21 July 1749, 'à midi': 'la défection de plusieurs administrateurs de l'hospital général dont vous estes vraysemblablement instruit par mr l'archevêque et la conduite qu'ils tiennent dans le public annonce de reste l'envie qu'on a de remuer et d'échauffer les esprits de Mrs du Parlement'. See also another, more alarming, letter later the same day.

had a meeting with Daguesseau at the chancellor's request. Daguesseau showed him a *lettre de cachet* and a letter signed by D'Argenson suspending all debate at the *Parlement* on the matter; it was the prospect of 1732 and 1737 all over again. Maupeou outlined his views very clearly. Even if the affair came up at the *Parlement*, he thought it quite wrong for the Government to intervene. If he were given the letters, he would have no other option but to use them in full knowledge that nothing roused the *Parlement* more quickly than an attempt to remove its freedom of debate. He made some impression on the chancellor, and Daguesseau quoted to the Comte d'Argenson his apt phrase about the *Parlement*:

> Il [the *Parlement*] aime mieux voir casser ses arrests que de se voir privé du pouvoir d'en rendre, et il faut advouer que l'expérience du passé confirme cette réflexion de M. Le P. Président.[52]

Maupeou told him that, if there were any serious trouble, the King could always put the affairs of the *Hôpital général* in order by means of a new law after consulting the *chefs*. Maupeou said as much in writing to the Comte d'Argenson.[53] All this advice was sensible enough.

On 30 August the chancellor assembled the seven *chefs* to effect a solution. Beaumont again had the support of Lamoignon de Blancmesnil and Nicolaï, but Maupeou and Joly de Fleury appear to have carried the day with their insistence on the reinstatement of the administrators who had resigned. Although Beaumont and his two allies had antagonised the chancellor a few days previously by descending upon him in an attempt to force his hand, they had more success with the King, whom they went to see the morning after the chancellor's conference: in the evening the King spoke to Daguesseau and D'Argenson and it was decided that the whole affair would be brought up at the *Conseil des dépêches* the following Saturday.[54] When the news of the King's intention leaked out, the question of the *Hôpital général* was raised at the *grand'chambre* of the *Parlement*, surprisingly enough by one of its more senior members, Gilbert, a *président à mortier*. The *gens du roi* were asked to present a report on 5 September, the day the *Parlement* was due to start the vacation.[55] Daguesseau roundly accused Maupeou of not having told his colleagues that the affair was already under consideration by the King in order to deter them from

---

[52] *Ibid.*, CA 17: Daguesseau to the Comte d'Argenson, Paris, 17 Aug. 1749.

[53] *Ibid.*, CA 34: Maupeou to the Comte d'Argenson, undated, enclosing a copy of the chancellor's letter to him of 16 Aug. 1749.

[54] Légier Desgranges, *Du jansénisme à la Révolution*, pp. 229–32; BUP, CA 28/I: Jean-Omer Joly de Fleury to the Comte d'Argenson, 30 Aug. 1749 (3 p.m.); CA 34: Maupeou to the same, 3 Aug. [Sept.?] 1749; and AN, 342 AP 2 ('Mémoires' of J. O. Joly de Fleury), pp. 192–5.

[55] Légier Desgranges, *Du jansénisme à la Révolution*, p. 258.

raising it at the *grand'chambre*.[56] Maupeou was naturally sensitive to such criticism: only an engagement at the *Parlement* prevented him from calling at once upon the chancellor, so he stated tartly in his reply, 'moins pour vous justifier ma conduite que pour vous représenter qu'il auroit été de votre sagesse d'attendre que vous en fussiés bien informé avant de la blâmer'. He added that the King had a better opinion of his zeal than to think him guilty of what he called 'un tel excès d'embécillité'. It was at Maupeou's suggestion that the members of the *grand'chambre* had decided to postpone receiving a report from the *gens du roi* until the *Parlement* reconvened in November. The first president felt he had done everything that could reasonably be expected of him.[57]

At the *Conseil des dépêches*, it was decided to confirm Madame de Moysan in her post, to appoint three new administrators and to solicit suggestions through the chancellor for a new set of regulations concerning the *Hôpital général*.[58] As the former bishop of Mirepoix had mistakenly told everyone that the posts of the seventeen remaining administrators had been declared vacant, Daguesseau and D'Argenson delayed the issuing of the *arrêt du conseil* embodying the decisions until these had been further discussed and clarified at another meeting of the council on 8 September.[59]

Maupeou was furious at the turn of events. His proposals had been spurned in favour of an *arrêt du conseil* which, as first president of the *Parlement*, he could not recognise. He let it be known that he would have nothing to do with the *bureau* of the *Hôpital général* or with any administrators who might be appointed. In a final flourish, Maupeou announced that if his presence were required in any part of the *Hôpital général* during the autumn,

> que l'on donnast, par exemple, quelque paire de soufflets à la Moysan et qu'il y eust révolte, il iroit parce qu'il estoit persuadé que sa robe, plustost que celle de M. l'Archevêque, appaiseroit le tumulte.[60]

On that note he went off to the country when the sessions of the *Parlement* came to an end.

[56] BUP, CA 34: Maupeou to the Comte d'Argenson, 4 Aug. [Sept.?] 1749 enclosing copies of his correspondence with Daguesseau of 3–4 Sept.; CA 17: Daguesseau to D'Argenson, 4 Sept. 1749. Daguesseau also wrote along the same lines to the *procureur général* (Légier Desgranges, *Du jansénisme à la Révolution*, p. 239).

[57] BUP, CA 34: Maupeou to the Comte d'Argenson, 5 Sept. 1749 with a copy of Maupeou's reply to the chancellor of the previous day. Upon receipt of Maupeou's letter, Daguesseau wrote him what the first president described as 'une lettre des plus tendres'; but Maupeou observed to D'Argenson: 'entre vous et moy c'est la seconde en 5 mois qu'il m'a fait l'honneur de m'écrire dans ce goût-là'.

[58] Légier Desgranges, *Du jansénisme à la Révolution*, p. 240.

[59] BUP, CA 17: Daguesseau to the Comte d'Argenson, letters of 'samedy, 5 heures' and 'samedy au soir'.

[60] Légier Desgranges, *Du jansénisme à la Révolution*, p. 242.

The first president's conduct had been an unnerving compound of common sense, personal resentment and general irresponsibility. Towards the end of the vacation Daguesseau confided to the *procureur général* that he did not know how to deal with Maupeou over the new draft *déclaration* for the *Hôpital général*:

> Sa conduite a été si incertaine et si singulière dans l'affaire présente qu'il est à craindre que si on le consulte sur le projet, il ne fasse une response qui y ressemble. En tout cas, j'aimerois mieux qu'il le reçut par vous que le luy envoyer moy-même directement parce que vous seriez en état de luy faire les Réflexions nécessaires.[61]

After quoting this letter in his memoirs, *Avocat général* Joly de Fleury added his own crushing verdict:

> On voit par cette lettre L'imbécillité du P. Président qui dans la vue de faire sa cour vouloit ne prendre aucun party et par cette mauvaise finesse, il a perdu le peu de crédit qu'il avoit acquis par son air de hauteur qui luy avoit tenu lieu juscque là de mérite.

Is there any evidence that can be set against these harsh judgements? It seems not, for the opinion of his enemies has been preserved while his papers, and those of his more famous son, have disappeared. Yet one has a sneaking sympathy for a man who had witnessed the failure of successive government attempts to intervene in parliamentary debates and the embarrassment in which they placed a first president, and who claimed, moreover, to have made it a condition of his own appointment that he would not be expected to curtail debates in the manner of 1732 and 1737. If one added to these considerations the slights that he received at regular intervals from Daguesseau and, in a more insidious way, from D'Argenson and the *gens du roi*, then it is hardly surprising that Maupeou should have preferred to wrap himself up in the full dignity of his magisterial robe.

During the vacation Lamoignon de Blancmesnil prepared the draft of a *déclaration* embodying the changes that he and the archbishop wished to make in the administration of the *Hôpital général*.[62] Both men had the support of the Comte d'Argenson, possibly an indication that the King was in favour of Beaumont's designs. At Fontainebleau on 5 November the chancellor communicated the draft to the *procureur général* for his comments and also asked him to prepare a text of his own. Maupeou and Joly de Fleury found Lamoignon's draft unacceptable and submitted their own to

---

[61] AN, 342 AP 2 ('Mémoires' of J. O. Joly de Fleury), p. 105 [205]: copy of Daguesseau's letter to the *procureur général* of 23 Oct. 1749.
[62] AN, 422 AP 1 (Comte d'Argenson's Papers): Beaumont to the Comte d'Argenson, 13 Oct. 1749.

Daguesseau a few days later.[63] Daguesseau made some amendments and communicated it to Beaumont for his approval.[64] The proposed *déclaration* was on the whole favourable to the archbishop, though less radical than the one prepared by Lamoignon.[65] But Daguesseau was possibly mindful of the tensions that now existed between the various protagonists in the affair, and he preferred to delay matters; the *déclaration* had not yet been sent to the *Parlement* when he resigned the chancellorship a year later. Despite his attempts to pour oil on troubled waters, worse feuds were to follow.

That autumn of 1749 Machault decided to prolong the levy of the *4 sols pour livre*, which was a surcharge on all duties.[66] D'Argenson sent the *déclaration* to the *procureur général* on 12 November in time for the *rentrée* of the *Parlement*. The history of the tax was unlikely to induce the *Parlement* to register it without difficulty. The *4 sols pour livre* had been registered at a *lit de justice* in September 1732. In January 1738 the *parlementaires* prolonged the levy with a clause in the *arrêté* that the King should be humbly asked to relieve his people of this burden as soon as he could. They had again been called upon to prolong it in December 1743, when the same clause was again added to the registration.[67]

With this history in mind the *procureur général* was understandably reluctant to appear before the *Parlement* with another request for its prolongation, especially after the trouble concerning the *vingtième*. He accordingly wrote to Machault on 22 November, pointing out that the *gens du roi* would feel obliged to recommend supplications if they presented the *déclaration* for registration; he did not wish to take such a risk without mentioning the matter to him first. Machault did not reply to the letter. As the *procureur général* anticipated opposition in the *Parlement* to the *déclaration*, he did not take steps to present it for registration. Four months later, in March 1750, Machault wrote to tell him that the delay in registering the *déclaration* seriously prejudiced the work of the *fermes des domaines* and asked him to hasten the business. In a pique Joly de Fleury only replied to this letter a fortnight later and simply referred Machault to his letter of 22 November. Machault wrote back testily on 22 April saying that he did not think the *Parlement* had to wait for his reply before going ahead with its supplications.[68] The *pro-*

[63] BUP, CA 28/I: Jean-Omer Joly de Fleury to the Comte d'Argenson, letters of 5 and 15 Nov. 1749.
[64] *Ibid.*, same to same, letters of 18, 22 Nov. and 5 Dec. 1749.   [65] BS, MS 800, f. 67.
[66] On the *4 sols pour livre*, see M. Marion, *Dictionnaire des institutions de la France aux xviie et xviiie siècles* (Paris, 1923, reprint, 1968), pp. 511–12; and J. F. Bosher, *The single duty project: a study of the movement for a French customs union in the eighteenth century* (London, 1964), pp. 7–8.
[67] See p. 47 above.
[68] On this incident, see BUP, CA 28/II: Jean-Omer Joly de Fleury to the Comte d'Argenson, 5 May 1750.

cureur général then irritated the first president by placing the *déclaration* before the assembly of the chambers barely two days after bringing it to his notice. In these circumstances the assembly on 30 April set aside the recommendation for supplications and decided to make remonstrances. Four days later Machault wrote another stiff letter, this time to Maupeou, on the need to hurry the work of the *commissaires* so that the *déclaration* could go through the necessary formalities without further delay. In his reply Maupeou put the blame on Joly de Fleury and announced that the remonstrances would not be ready before the end of the following week.[69] In fact the remonstrances were not presented to the King until a month later, on 7 June.

Machault made no concession on the *4 sols pour livre*. However, he promised to suppress the levy of the *centième denier* on the transfer of venal offices from 1 January 1751. He made this concession, which benefited *parlementaires* as well as other officeholders, only because at that time he needed the co-operation of the *Parlement* in his forthcoming struggle with the clergy. The King's reply containing the promise was made on 2 August; on 20 August a *déclaration* ordering the clergy to declare its income was placed before the *Parlement*, which registered it the next day without much difficulty.[70] But on the whole, Machault's relations with the *Parlement* were bad, and the growing hostility between him and Maupeou made them worse and eventually contributed to the crisis of 1752–3. For his part, the first president must have been particularly concerned about the close links between the *contrôleur général* and President Chauvelin which began to manifest themselves at this time. Chauvelin had worked with Machault on the draft of the *déclaration* of 17 August on the clergy; it was thought privately that even the president's uncle, the disgraced former keeper of the seals, had also been consulted.[71]

On 27 November 1750 the aged Daguesseau resigned the chancellorship, and the choice of his successor had serious consequences. The King did not want to appoint someone from the *Parlement* ('ils sont trop pointilleux', he observed to Saint-Florentin) and did not want to lose Machault at the *contrôle général* for the time being. He offered the post to D'Ormesson, the dean of the royal council. D'Ormesson declined on grounds of ill-health.[72] To everyone's surprise the final choice fell on Lamoignon de Blancmesnil,

69 *Ibid.*, CA 34: Maupeou to the Comte d'Argenson, 6 May 1750, with copies enclosed of Maupeou's correspondence with Machault.

70 Flammermont, *Rems.*, i, pp. 403–14; Marion, *Machault d'Arnouville*, pp. 253–6; BUP, CA 28/II: Jean-Omer Joly de Fleury to the Comte d'Argenson, letters of 18, 19, and 20 Aug. 1750; CA 34: Maupeou to the Comte d'Argenson, letters of 20 and 21 Aug. 1750.

71 *Ibid.*: Jean-Omer Joly de Fleury to the Comte d'Argenson, 20 Aug. 1750.

72 See Louis XV's letter to Saint-Florentin of 28 Nov. 1750, Saint-Florentin's reply to D'Ormesson, and the draft of the latter's reply printed in Wladimir d'Ormesson, 'Un chancelier de France sous Louis XV', *Revue de Paris* (Nov. 1967), pp. 1–7.

Plate 11 Chancellor de Lamoignon, by N. de Largillière (private collection)

the first president of the *Cour des aides*. Unlike his predecessor, the new chancellor was not entrusted with the seals, which were given to Machault. These arrangements were doubtless a source of further disappointment to Maupeou, who had entertained forlorn hopes of succeeding Daguesseau and was not on good terms with Machault; after November 1750 the first president seems to have become even less effective than before in directing events in the *Parlement*.[73]

[73] M. Gaillard, *Vie ou éloge historique de M. de Malesherbes, suivie de la vie du premier président de Lamoignon, son bisaïeul* (Paris, 1805), pp. 18–22. Gaillard gained his information from Malesherbes, who was the son of the new chancellor.

The personality of the new chancellor was also a complicating factor. As we have seen, Lamoignon had left the *Parlement* in 1736 because he could not obtain a *présidence à mortier* to replace the one that had been on lease to him since 1723. He was without office for ten years, though he was twice mentioned (in 1736 and in 1743) as a candidate for the first presidency; after his unsuccessful efforts to fall back on a post in the *Grand Conseil*, he eventually became first president of the *Cour des aides* in 1746. His luckless career in the *Parlement* certainly had an influence on his attitude towards his former colleagues. On religious and legal questions he seldom shared the opinions that were held by many *parlementaires*; it was perhaps this independence of judgement expressed in a direct, forthright manner which appealed to the King.[74] Behind a bluff, rotund exterior, the new chancellor was a hard-working plodder of firm principles and of no very great intelligence or imagination: he rose early and usually completed the copious paperwork of his office in his crabbed handwriting by seven o'clock in the morning. But the *gens du roi* found this former *avocat général* cantankerous and lacking in finesse: it is a fact that after 1751 the King's official replies to the *Parlement* in which Lamoignon had a hand were often terse and occasionally offensive, unnecessarily so at times. It is not surprising that his appointment did not arouse any enthusiasm in the *Parlement*, where it was felt, moreover, that a Lamoignon ought not to have accepted the chancellorship without the seals.[75] The *parlementaires* had an opportunity to interfere with the arrangements. Machault's letters patent of appointment made a significant reference to the post of keeper of the seals as a 'charge', though he merely held it by commission. The *parlementaires* realised that, if they registered the letters patent as they stood, Machault would have the right to preside over the *Parlement*: this was a right reserved to the chancellor. Therefore they took care to register the letters patent with the saving clause, 'sans néanmoins que lesdites lettres puissent attribuer dans l'administration de la justice le pouvoir et autorité appartenant essentiellement au seul état, office, et dignité de chancelier de France'.[76]

Daguesseau was over eighty when he resigned; Lamoignon was a mere sixty-eight years of age when he succeeded him. The new man was expected to be more active than his predecessor, and there would obviously be fewer opportunities for the minister with the Paris *département* to determine the Government's relations with the *Parlement*, as Maurepas and, to a lesser extent, D'Argenson had done. Maupeou became less assiduous in

---

[74] *Ibid.*, pp. 22–3.
[75] BS, MS 800 ('Journal du Président de Meinières'), f. 24: comment on the debate of 22 Dec. 1750.
[76] *Ibid.*, f. 26 (debate of 29 Dec. 1750). Durey de Meinières observed (f. 24) that Machault's friends in the *Parlement* were angry with Lamoignon for having accepted the chancellorship without the seals and thereby preventing Machault from obtaining it as well.

sending the Comte d'Argenson reports on developments in the *Parlement* after February 1751, and on 7 May Maupeou wrote to explain that he had for some time been sending reports only to the new chancellor, 'dans la veue de vous en sauver l'importunité' (certainly, only three letters of his to D'Argenson survive for the period from May 1751 to the minister's fall in February 1757).[77] Perhaps Maupeou felt that, as the *gens du roi* already had the minister's ear, he could obtain his information from them. On the other hand, there is the disturbing possibility that Maupeou and the Comte d'Argenson began to act in collusion with each other through their joint hostility towards Machault. For obvious reasons, there is little hard evidence to substantiate an accusation which was made by contemporaries at this time and especially during the crisis of 1753-4. In any case, whether the first president became increasingly aloof from the minister or whether he was in collusion with him, the consequences were surely the same: an avenue of conciliation between the Government and the *Parlement* had been closed. As for the *gens du roi*, and *Avocat général* Joly de Fleury in particular, they continued to keep the Comte d'Argenson informed and to appeal for his support in various moves, not always very successfully. Were they aware of his growing links with the archbishop of Paris from whom he was also receiving private letters, and if these letters, like their own, were sometimes being shown to the secretive King, were they conscious of simply being pawns in a royal game? As for the chancellor, neither they, nor the first president, had much time for him, though they were punctilious in sending him regular reports of what passed in the *Parlement*: the *gens du roi* had little patience with a man whom they came to regard as a muddler.

Another consequence of Lamoignon's appointment was that it strengthened the hand of the archbishop of Paris and thereby helped to precipitate a serious conflict between the Government and the *Parlement* over the *Hôpital général*. The new chancellor promptly exhumed his discarded draft *déclaration* and sent it to the *gens du roi* on 2 April 1751 for registration at the *Parlement*. As even Lamoignon admitted that the *déclaration* would have to be modified in the course of registration, the *gens du roi* had less hesitation in presenting it to the assembly of the chambers on 23 April. *Commissaires* were appointed to examine it on 5 May. At the same time, the *Parlement* decided

---

[77] It is perhaps unwise to argue from the basis of lack of evidence, but it does seem as if Maupeou ceased to send regular detailed reports to the Comte d'Argenson after February 1751; only a few letters survive for the rest of 1751, and there are none after 1752; BUP, CA 34. It is possible, though not certain, that the King's decision to fix by *arrêt du conseil* the exact responsibilities of the new chancellor and of the keeper of the seals also had repercussions on the co-operation that had hitherto existed between members of the Government responsible for the affairs of the *Parlement*; and also between them and the first president. For the text of the *arrêt du conseil* of 11 December 1750, see Comte de Luçay, *Des origines du pouvoir ministériel en France: les secrétaires d'état depuis leur institution jusqu'à la mort de Louis XV* (Paris, 1881), pp. 320 (note 2) to 323.

to send two special *commissaires* (Thomé and Montholon) to investigate the affairs of the *Hôpital général* and report in time for the meeting of 5 May. Jean-Omer Joly de Fleury told the Comte d'Argenson that there was no cause for alarm at these decisions.[78] On 5 May the special *commissaires* announced that their investigations were not yet completed, and so the meeting of the *commissaires* was postponed until 17 May.[79] When the *commissaires* did meet they decided to continue their discussion on 24 May. There was a possibility that the affair of the *Hôpital général* would be settled without too much trouble. But the favourable dispositions of the *parlementaires* rapidly changed when they were suddenly called upon to register a further set of financial measures, this time an edict creating *rentes viagères* and floating a loan.

The *parlementaires* were incensed because they had been led to believe in 1749 that the resources of the *vingtième* would be sufficient to pay off the Government's debts. The state of the royal finances was always kept secret. But an intelligent *parlementaire* could easily arrive at some disturbing conclusions about them. He could safely assume that since 1749 the *vingtième* ought to have produced at least thirty million *livres*; the King was known to have borrowed a further fifty millions. Yet within two years of obtaining these eighty millions, the King was trying to procure an additional sum of fifty millions in time of peace. The *parlementaires* were understandably alarmed at the situation and doubtless mused on what would happen if war should again break out. As Jean-Omer Joly de Fleury observed to the Comte d'Argenson:

> ce n'est pas que le parlement veuille entrer dans le détail de l'administration de l'Etat; il connoist trop les bornes de son devoir pour en avoir même l'idée, mais on raisonne avec le public sur des opérations connues de tout le monde et à portée d'être jugées par tous les membres qui le composent.[80]

Parlementaires did not like to see an increase in the Government's debts, especially at a time when they believed that the existing debts were being paid off. In their opinion loans were a burden on the State and invariably led to fresh taxation. They also felt that *rentes* (life annuities) were a dangerous inducement to people to divert money needed for the establishment of their families in the hope of an early and profitable return on their investment (it should be said that the magistrates themselves did not always resist this temptation). At the end of their debate on 18 May the *parlementaires* had the usual choice between registration followed by supplications or remonstrances; they chose the second course. The King then

---

[78] BUP, CA 28/III: Jean-Omer Joly de Fleury to the Comte d'Argenson, letters of 23 and 26 Apr. 1751.
[79] BS, MS 800, f. 72 (debate of 5 May).   [80] BUP, CA 28/III: letter of 23 May 1751.

demanded to have the remonstrances within two days so that he could order the *Parlement* to register the edict without further delay. On this occasion, however, the *parlementaires* also resorted to further, or *itératives*, remonstrances, followed on 28 May, after the King had repeated his order to register the edict, by supplications asking him to fix a time limit for the *vingtième*.

The King could drive the *parlementaires* into a corner very quickly by allowing them no time to linger over these flimsy procedural devices. In the course of the heated debate that followed his reply to the supplications, some *parlementaires* felt prompted to raise the question of the limits of the resistance that the *Parlement* was entitled to make. Many *parlementaires* probably sympathised with the view expressed by Drouyn de Vandeuil:

> que lorsque le souverain exigeait un acte contraire au bien de l'état l'obéis-
> sance primitive empêchait absolument d'y consentir, sans qu'il fût permis
> d'obéir à ses ordres réitérés.[81]

The majority, however, preferred to qualify that statement, as President Gilbert did when he declared that their conscience did not require the *parlementaires* to take their resistance to such lengths unless the matter concerned what he called 'l'intérêt entier de tout l'Etat, *de summa rerum*', and as long as such resistance did not entail the destruction of *la compagnie*.[82] Nevertheless, the edict was registered on 29 May by only twelve votes. Jean-Omer Joly de Fleury wrote to the Comte d'Argenson:

> Je crois qu'il faut renoncer de Longtems et tant que le 20ème durera à des
> opérations de cette espèce. on conservera la mémoire de cette résistance, et il
> est à craindre qu'on ne se portât à une fermeté peut-être inébranlable.[83]

Certainly, it was more than three years before the *contrôleur général* presented further financial measures for registration.

The *arrêt d'enregistrement* of 29 May also stated that further supplications would be made. The King could now afford to keep the *parlementaires* waiting for a fortnight before he received the deputation. A reply was then read by the chancellor which accused the *Parlement* of seeking to interfere in matters that were not within its competence and of casting doubt on the King's intention to pay off the debts.[84] Drouyn de Vandeuil commented at the assembly of the chambers on 19 June that:

[81] Flammermont, *Rems.*, i, p. 453; BS, MS 800, ff. 180–2 (Lambert's account): debate of 29 May 1751.
[82] Flammermont, *Rems.*, i, p. 453.
[83] BUP, CA 28/III: letter of 29 May 1751; BS, MS 800, f. 177 (Lambert's account): debate of 29 May 1751; f. 210 (Rolland d'Erceville's account): debate of 29 May 1751.
[84] Flammermont, *Rems.*, i, pp. 453–6.

... la réponse faite par Mr. le Chancelier étoit le dernier coup que l'on vouloit porter au parlement, qu'on vouloit le réduire à n'avoir plus d'autre droit à l'égard des Edits qui seroient apportez que celuy de les enregistrer purement et simplement, qu'on vouloit nous interdire l'examen de ce qui pourroit les avoir précédés, des objets auxquels ils seroient destinés, des inconvéniens qu'ils pourroient produire, que c'étoit nous réduire à l'Etat où seroient en matière ordinaire des juges obligé [*sic*] de prononcer sans connoissance de causes.[85]

The whole affair had left the *parlementaires* discontented, and their mood certainly affected their attitude towards the question of the *Hôpital général*.[86]

On 7 July the *commissaires* completed their examination of the *déclaration* on the *Hôpital général* and went on to consider the terms of a possible *arrêt d'enregistrement*.[87] An assembly of the chambers was held to register the *déclaration* on 20 July. A long list of saving clauses had been prepared on each article of the *déclaration*. The *rapporteur* asked the *parlementaires* whether they wanted to register the *déclaration* with modifications or whether they simply wished to beg the King to withdraw it. Robert de Saint-Vincent, one of the *zélés*, advocated the second course. But the *présidents à mortier* had assured everyone that they understood that the King only wanted the *déclaration* registered and would overlook the modifications. These assurances led the majority to vote for the registration with the modifications.[88] For the same reason they also decided to list the modifications in a separate *arrêt* to which the *arrêt d'enregistrement* would merely refer; it was argued that they would be showing greater respect for the King if they were discreet about the modifications. They were therefore shocked to learn on the morning of 22 July that the first president had received an *arrêt du conseil* quashing all the modifications and ordering that the *déclaration* should be executed as if it had been registered purely and simply.[89]

The Government's move was ill advised. In the first place, it ruled out any possibility of a compromise solution that could be negotiated by the *gens du roi*. Secondly, although it suppressed the modifications, the *arrêt du conseil* deemed the *déclaration* registered. The Government had not perceived the legal implications of the *arrêt du conseil* or the repercussions that they could have on the continuing dispute with the clergy over the *déclaration* of 17 August 1750 which sought to elicit a statement of the

---

[85] BS, MS 800, ff. 184–5 (Rolland d'Erceville's account): debate of 19 June 1751.

[86] BUP, CA 28/III: Jean-Omer Joly de Fleury to the Comte d'Argenson, 30 May 1751.

[87] *Ibid.*, same to same, 8 July 1751.

[88] By ninety-six votes to forty-five according to Rolland d'Erceville (BS, MS 800, f. 217); by seventy-six votes to forty-five according to Jean-Omer Joly de Fleury (BUP, CA 28/III: letter to the Comte d'Argenson, 20 July 1751).

[89] BS, MS 800, f. 220[v] (Rolland d'Erceville's account): note for 22 July 1751.

Church's wealth. Moreover, even if the *parlementaires* took the unlikely course of recognising the suppression of the modifications they could argue that the *déclaration* had also been abolished. Instead, the *parlementaires* took the view that as they had no formal knowledge of the *arrêt du conseil*, which had not been notified to them in the accustomed way by letters patent, they were free to continue to execute their own decisions. It was the stand that they usually adopted in such cases.[90] Those who had to execute the decisions were placed in a difficult situation; as Jean-Omer Joly de Fleury explained to the Comte d'Argenson:

> Ceux qui doivent exécuter se trouvent arrestés dans L'Exécution par cet arrest du Conseil, il [*sic*] ne peuvent faire autre chose qu'instruire le Parlement qui leur a enjoint d'exécuter, de la manière dont ils ont été arrestés dans cette même exécution.[91]

It was not the duty of the first president or of the *procureur général* to show an *arrêt du conseil* to the *Parlement*, unless he had received an order from the King to do so. The *parlementaires* could make his position even more difficult by investigating if their decisions had been carried out.

The first president and the *procureur général* left a meeting of the *bureau* of the *Hôpital général* on 31 July because Beaumont insisted upon reading out the *arrêt du conseil*. Two days later the clerk of the *Hôpital général* was summoned to the *Parlement* and ordered to transcribe the *déclaration* and its modifications in his register. Maupeou and Joly de Fleury were themselves summoned to Compiègne, where the King told them that he wanted the *déclaration* to be registered as it stood. The *Parlement* sent a deputation to explain the legal position. After listening to the first president's speech, the King replied that he did not recognise that the *Parlement* had a right to alter a law on the pretext of inserting modifications. Nevertheless, he tacitly conceded the point about the need to notify his intentions concerning the *déclaration* to the *Parlement* in a more formal manner; he caused *lettres de jussion* (a form of letters patent) to be sent ordering a registration *purement et simplement*. The *Parlement* delayed the registration by deciding to make remonstrances, which were presented to the King on 30 August.[92] The *gens du roi* negotiated with the chancellor and with one or two *parlementaires*. On 4 September Jean-Omer Joly de Fleury told D'Argenson that the *Parlement* would probably register the *déclaration* if a few concessions were made; he suggested that these could be discreetly contained in a further set of *lettres de jussion*.[93] But the King's reply of 6 September caused offence at the *Par-*

[90] BUP, CA 28/III: Jean-Omer Joly de Fleury to the Comte d'Argenson, 22 July 1751.

[91] *Ibid.*, same to same, 1 Aug. 1751.   [92] Flammermont, *Rems.*, i, pp. 465–76.

[93] BUP, CA 28/III: Jean-Omer Joly de Fleury to the Comte d'Argenson, letters of 30 Aug., 3 and 4 Sept. 1751; BS, MS 800, f. 241 (Rolland d'Erceville's account): debate of 31 Aug. 1751.

lement, and the text of the new *lettres de jussion* bore no resemblance to what the *gens du roi* had recommended. The *parlementaires* were surprised; they postponed their debate until after the long vacation, taking steps to ensure that the vacation chamber would not be able to register the *déclaration* in their absence. They went off to chant a *Te Deum* for the birth of the Duc de Bourgogne and then left for the country.[94]

The Government had decided to put an end to the dispute by more radical means. On 20 November, four days before the debate was due to be resumed, the *greffier* of the *Parlement* received a *lettre de cachet* ordering him to place the most recent registers before the King. The next day, the first president and other leading *parlementaires* accompanied him to Versailles, where the *minutes* of the *arrêts* and *arrêtés* relating to the affair of the *Hôpital général* were removed in the presence of the King. The act of registration of the *déclaration* was then struck out.[95] The removal of the records of the *Parlement* was certain to lead to a protest. At the same time, however, the *parlementaires* could draw some consolation from the fact that the *déclaration* of 24 March 1751 on the *Hôpital général* had been annulled as well as its modifications by the striking out of the *arrêt d'enregistrement*. But what made it impossible for the *parlementaires* to accept the solution of 21 November was that the King forbade them to hold a debate on the matter. Their right of debate was what *parlementaires* held to be most sacred. Jean-Omer Joly de Fleury wrote:

> Si La Compagnie se soumet sans se plaindre à la défense de délibérer, elle se croit perdue sans ressource, parce que Ils regardent la délibération comme L'âme de toutes les compagnies: et que sans cette faculté ils ne peuvent être en état de continuer leurs fonctions.[96]

Insofar as any crisis in the relations between the Government and the *Parlement* may be described as typical (for each crisis was made up of different ingredients), that of November 1751 was typical. For that reason it is particularly illuminating to follow its development in detail, especially as the evidence is unusually plentiful. The first president's position was unenviable in the circumstances; if he allowed a debate (even for the purpose of registering his account of what had happened at Versailles) he contravened the King's orders; if he refused one, he precipitated a crisis in

---

94 BUP, CA 28/III: Jean-Omer Joly de Fleury to the Comte d'Argenson, 6 Sept. 1751 (11 a.m.); BS, MS 800, ff. 244–5 (Rolland d'Erceville's account): debates of 6 and 7 Sept.
95 For Durey de Meinières's account of what took place at the *Parlement* from 20 November until the resumption of service in December, see Flammermont, *Rems.*, i, pp. 651–713. In the same volume see also pp. 477–9.
96 BUP, CA 28/III: Jean-Omer Joly de Fleury to the Comte d'Argenson, 21 Nov. 1751 (9 p.m.).

the *Parlement* like that of 1732 or 1737. The *gens du roi* again tried to mediate. The *procureur général* wrote to the chancellor on 23 November pointing out that if the ban on the debate at the *Parlement* were relaxed to allow the registration of Maupeou's account, then it might be possible to get the *parlementaires* to pass an *arrêté* acceptable to the Government. Could not the chancellor discuss it with him? Lamoignon was non-committal in his reply but told him to come to Versailles that evening, and also sent copies of the correspondence to the King at Bellevue.[97] Joly de Fleury arrived at seven o'clock on a miserable night. He and Lamoignon talked for almost three hours. The chancellor argued that the *Parlement* could perfectly well register the first president's account without reopening the debate which the King had forbidden. They got nowhere, and at last a reply from Bellevue put an end to all further discussion. The King had shown the chancellor's letter to the few ministers who were with him (including the Comte d'Argenson) and had decided that the position should remain unchanged.[98] It was too late for the *procureur général* to return, so he spent the night at Versailles and left for Paris at 5.30 the next morning full of foreboding for the day's events.

As things turned out, the first president was spared an embarrassing choice. When Maupeou finished his report to the assembly of the chambers on that morning, the *doyen* read out a statement, which had been agreed to beforehand by the *enquêtes*:

> Monsieur, la compagnie vous déclare qu'elle pense que les défenses de délibérer étant une interdiction de toutes fonctions, elle ne peut et n'entend continuer aucun service.[99]

In 1732 the *grand'chambre* had wavered; in 1751 it was in full accord with the *enquêtes*. When, four days later, the *parlementaires* received *lettres de cachet* ordering them to go to the *Palais* the next morning to attend to their duties, they went but did not resume their service.[100] Jean-Omer Joly de Fleury blamed the first president for the turn which events had taken; he even told him to his face,

> combien dans tout cecy il s'étoit comporté avec l'affectation d'un Homme

---

[97] FL, Rosanbo MSS: 1/1/5–6: *procureur général* to Lamoignon, 23 Nov. 1751 with copy of chancellor's reply; Lamoignon to Louis XV, 23 Nov. 1751 and the King's reply in the margin; BUP, CA 30: Lamoignon to the Comte d'Argenson, 'le mercredi matin', 24 Nov. 1751, 3 pp.; *ibid.*, CA 28/III: Jean-Omer Joly de Fleury to the Comte d'Argenson: 23 (two letters), 24 (noon and 4 p.m.) and 25 Nov. 1751.

[98] FL, Rosanbo MSS: 1/1/5: the King's reply dated 23 Nov., 'au soir'. The King asked Lamoignon to inform the other ministers, Machault, Rouillé and Saint-Contest, if they were at Versailles.

[99] Flammermont, *Rems.*, i, pp. 479–80.　　[100] *Ibid.*

Livré sans mesure aux volontés d'une compagnie du gouvernement de laquelle il est chargé.[101]

But Maupeou was in an impossible position; unable or unwilling to rely on the Government on the one hand, and threatened with losing the confidence of his colleagues on the other. On 1 December the King sent letters patent ordering the *parlementaires* to resume their duties. After lengthy debates they decided to register the letters patent. The first serious crisis between the *Parlement* and the Government since 1732 had ended in a manner humiliating to the magistrates and to the first president in particular. Its full effects had yet to be felt.

Some attempt has been made to examine the events from 1737 to 1751 in order to discover whether they reveal any significant developments in the relations between the Crown and *Parlement*. The history of the years immediately preceding the great crises of the 1750s naturally reflects the continued importance of religious and financial issues as a source of conflict. It illustrates, in the light of contemporary notions, the attitude of the *parlementaires* to questions of finance, an attitude which was public-spirited, even if it failed to move the Government. The rôle played by personalities and factions has now emerged much more clearly; it often exacerbated the disputes on religion and finance and encouraged the use of procedural devices as means of political action. Over these years not so much the ability as the willingness of the first president to control the *Parlement* when an issue arose was seriously eroded. Le Peletier and Maupeou had come to depend upon being able to persuade the Government to lower its financial demands or to overlook a move made by the *Parlement* on the religious question. But from 1745 onwards Maupeou had found the Government less willing to co-operate in this manner. His insistence often led to friction between him and Daguesseau or Machault. Because he was increasingly unable to obtain concessions, the first president did little to prevent the *Parlement* from resorting more readily to remonstrances in the place of supplications. As he could not rely on the support of the Government, particularly after the fall of Maurepas, he clearly felt a need to be especially considerate in his treatment of obstructive elements within the *Parlement*, if only in order to reduce the influence there of serious rivals like President Chauvelin, who had close links with the controller general. In turn this attitude further estranged him from ministers. These feelings came to a head after the governmental changes of

---

101 BUP, CA 28/III: Jean-Omer Joly de Fleury to the Comte d'Argenson, 30 Nov. 1751 (9 p.m.). In another letter of 1 Dec. (1 p.m.) he complained that Maupeou had reverted to his 'système de complaisance aveugle pour son fils et pour les testes échauffées de la Compagnie', and he added: 'Je crois que cet homme devient fol.'

1749–50 and led directly to the first important crisis in the relations between the King and the *Parlement* since that of 1732. The seriousness of that crisis is measured by the fact that the King had asked the Chancellor to suggest contingency arrangements for the administration of justice should the *Parlement* cease its service. While making some tentative proposals involving the initial use of councillors of state to deal with criminal cases while the search for new judges was put in hand, Lamoignon had warned about the dangers of striking a blow at the *Parlement*: 'un coup violent qui révoltera le public et qui forcera ceux qui composent le parlement d'abbandonner [*sic*] l'administration de la justice sans pouvoir les engager d'y rentrer'.[102] The affair of the *Hôpital général* left behind it much smouldering resentment on all sides. It is difficult not to attach great significance to the developments that had taken place in the period from 1737 to 1751; it is only in their light that the subsequent and more dramatic crises can be properly understood.

[102] See Lamoignon's 'Réflexions sur le Parlement' of November 1751 published as an appendix in Antonella Alimento, 'Politica ed amministrazione: alcune riflessioni sulla Monarchia francese d'ancien régime', *Rivista storica italiana*, xcvi (1984), pp. 637–79; the quotation comes from p. 678.

4

DENIAL OF SACRAMENTS:
THE CONFLICT OF 1752

Avouons-le si nous n'avons pas le pouvoir d'agir par nous
même [*sic*] le Roy dont nous implorons l'autorité ne l'a
pas non plus car sa puissance dont il nous a confié une
portion pour rendre la justice en son nom et maintenir la
police n'est qu'une puissance Temporelle et séculière.
President Durey de Meinières at an assembly of the chambers,
February 1751

IN MARCH 1752 Father Bouettin, the *curé* of Saint-Etienne-du-Mont in
Paris, informed a dying priest called Lemerre that he could not administer
the last sacraments to him. This incident was the first in a sequence of
events that culminated a year later in the exile of the *Parlement* of Paris. It
marked the beginning of a political crisis that affected the Monarchy for
over five years during which the rights of the King, the delegated authority
of the *Parlement*, and the privileges of the Clergy of France were all called in
question. A fresh attempt to study the events of those five years in terms of
the political and legal framework of the *ancien régime* may help to explain
how ministers, *parlementaires*, and ecclesiastics of the middle years of Louis
XV's reign grappled with seemingly insoluble problems which were largely
inherited from the previous reign.[1]

---

[1] On the conflict over confession certificates and denial of sacraments, see the following works:
Soulavie, *Mémoires du Maréchal de Richelieu pour servir à l'histoire de Louis XIV, de la Régence, de
Louis XV et des quatorze premières années du règne de Louis XVI* (London, Marseille and Paris,
1790–3), 9 vols., viii, pp. 241–73; F. Rocquain, 'Les Refus de sacrements', *Revue Historique*, xv
(1877), pp. 370–420; E. Régnault, *Christophe de Beaumont, archevêque de Paris, 1703–1781* (Paris,
1882), i, pp. 200ff; M. Marion, *Machault d'Arnouville: étude sur l'histoire du contrôle général des
finances de 1749 à 1754* (Paris, 1891), pp. 330–62; J. Flammermont, ed., *Remontrances du Parlement de Paris au xviii᷎ siècle* (Paris, 1888–98) (hereafter Flammermont, *Rems.*), i, pp. 414–614;
E. Glasson, *Le Parlement de Paris, son rôle politique depuis le règne de Charles VII jusqu'à la
Révolution* (Paris, 1901), ii, pp. 180ff; L. Cahen, *Les Querelles religieuses et parlementaires sous
Louis XV* (Paris, 1913), *passim*; P. Godard, *La Querelle des refus de sacrements 1730–1765* (Evreux
and Paris, 1937), pp. 233–52; J. H. Shennan, *The Parlement of Paris* (London, 1968), p. 309;

Bouettin later explained why he could not administer the sacraments to Lemerre: the dying man could not produce a confession certificate, he refused to give the name of his confessor and he did not submit to the bull *Unigenitus*. Bouettin added that the archbishop forbad him to administer the sacraments on this occasion. The *curé* knew that Lemerre did not submit to the bull, so he refused even to hear his confession.[2]

When Beaumont revived the use of confession certificates in his diocese, the *Parlement* had not taken strong action from the outset against priests who obeyed his instructions, although it regarded the archbishop's practice as an abuse and a scandal.[3] In July 1749, the *parlementaires* readily obeyed the King's order that they should suspend proceedings against Bouettin, who on that occasion had denied the sacraments to the dying principal of the Collège de Beauvais.[4] Moreover, Beaumont's example had been followed by other bishops. By March 1750 six cases of refusing to administer the sacraments had come before the *Parlement*.[5] And in each case the *gens du roi* were ordered to inform the King and to find out his intentions. But the King did not make his intentions known; he and his advisers (especially the aged Daguesseau) seemed reluctant to tackle a question that was too closely connected with the position of *Unigenitus* and the division between the lay and the spiritual powers to be easily solved. In a letter to the Comte d'Argenson in March 1750 *Avocat général* Joly de Fleury discreetly urged the Government to allow the *Parlement* to go through with its proceedings, and he wrote of the desirable effect – from the Government's point of view – that such a decision might have upon the clergy, which at that time was opposed to the *vingtième*. The General Assembly of the clergy was due to meet in May, and Joly de Fleury knew that it was expected to oppose the government's attempt to levy the new tax on the Church's income:

> ... Le clergé craindra, et ses craintes, suivant les vues que le roy peut avoir pour le 20ème, peuvent produire une docilité proportionnée à la douceur que l'on mettroit dans la suite de L'instruction [des procès]. Il est plusieurs magistrats dans la Compagnie susceptibles d'entrer dans ces vues ...[6]

and J. Egret, *Louis XV et l'opposition parlementaire 1715–1774* (Paris, 1970), pp. 56–67. Some of these works are outdated.

[2] Flammermont, *Rems.*, i, p. 483; see also Bouettin's letter of 3 Apr. 1752 to the former bishop of Mirepoix (who had the *feuille des bénéfices*) printed in *Mémoires du Duc de Luynes sur la Cour de Louis XV (1735–1758)*, ed. L. Dussieux and E. Soulié (Paris, 1860–5) (hereafter cited as Luynes, *Mém.*), xi, pp. 473–4.

[3] Cf. Flammermont, *Rems.*, i, pp. 362–73.

[4] *Ibid.*, i, p. 417 (note 1). See also Chapter 3 above, pp. 79–83.

[5] BUP, Archives d'Argenson, CA 27/II: Jean-Omer Joly de Fleury to the Comte d'Argenson, 28 March 1750.

[6] *Ibid.*, letter of 20 March 1750 (3 p.m.); Marion, *Machault d'Arnouville*, pp. 250–1. Under the circumstances the King was still in a position to force the clergy to declare their wealth, and a law to that effect was sent to the *Parlement* for registration in August 1750.

But the Government resisted the temptation to use the *Parlement* against the clergy in this way.

In December 1750 Bouettin denied the sacraments to a dying councillor of the *Châtelet*.[7] The *Parlement* called the *curé* to account, and he again explained that he had acted on the archbishop's orders. The magistrates found his reply arrogant and he spent the night in the *Conciergerie*.[8] The following day they fined him and ordered his release.[9] The *Parlement* twice invited the archbishop to arrange for the sacraments to be administered to the dying man, but met with no success. It then had recourse to the King. On 2 January 1751 the King severely rebuked the *parlementaires* for their treatment of Bouettin.[10] The royal reply, which marked an inauspicious beginning to Lamoignon's tenure of the chancellorship, naturally vexed them. Although the councillor of the *Châtelet* received the sacrament, the *Parlement* decided to make remonstrances. The main points of these were decided by *commissaires* drawn from each chamber. Durey de Meinières went to their meeting on 4 January with material to go into the remonstrances. Although two of the *présidents à mortier*, Molé and Le Peletier de Rosanbo, took exception to what they regarded as an attack on the first president's right to draw up the remonstrances, Durey de Meinières's action was defended by the first president himself and by Presidents de Maupeou and Gilbert.[11] The first president then prepared his draft and showed it to the four *commissaires* who had provided him with material for the task.[12] These men (Thomé, Davy de La Fautrière, President Durey de Meinières, and the Abbé Chauvelin) tactfully pointed out that his text was feeble and badly argued. Maupeou allowed them to revise it,[13] and the remonstrances were presented to the King on 4 March.[14] The position of the *Parlement* was stated in very mild terms. The remonstrances declared that the procedure concerning the 'external' administration of the sacraments was laid down by the recognized canons of the Church and that any innovation capable of causing scandal and disorder called for the attention of the *Parlement*. The practice of denying the sacraments to those who failed to produce confession certificates was deemed to be an innovation of

---

[7] Flammermont, *Rems.*, i, pp. 414–15.   [8] *Ibid.*, p. 416.

[9] President Durey de Meinières noted and deplored the eagerness of a number of his colleagues to release Bouettin; they were afraid that the King might order his release; see BS, MS 800 ('Journal du Président de Meinières'), f. 33ᵛ: entry for 30 Dec. 1750.

[10] Flammermont, *Rems.*, i, p. 417.   [11] BS, MS 800, f. 46ᵛ.

[12] *Ibid.*, f. 52ʳ; on the work of the four *commissaires*, see f. 47ᵛ *et seq.*

[13] *Ibid.*, f. 53ʳ.

[14] *Ibid.*, f. 55ʳ. The first president had seemed in no hurry to present the remonstrances until pressed by the Abbé Chauvelin (f. 54ᵛ). According to Durey de Meinières, the abbé was accused by his powerful relatives of having jeopardised the chances of a settlement of the dispute over confession certificates by his action (ff. 54ᵛ–55ʳ).

this nature.[15] No reply was given to these remonstrances until a year later.[16]

The *zélés* in the *Parlement* had often deplored the continued recourse to the King in cases of denial of sacraments. They wished to proceed directly against priests like Bouettin. President Durey de Meinières tried to persuade the moderates to adopt this course; he argued his case before the assembled chambers in February 1751:

> Avouons-le, si nous n'avons pas le pouvoir d'agir par nous même [*sic*] le Roy dont nous implorons l'autorité ne l'a pas non plus car sa puissance dont il nous a confié une portion pour rendre la justice en son nom et maintenir la police n'est qu'une puissance Temporelle et séculière. Ainsi inutilement nous adressons nous au souverain, notre propre démarche est en quelque façon une reconnoissance de notre impuissance.[17]

Although the argument was unanswerable, the *zélés* had little success. Most *parlementaires* did not wish to offend the Monarch and preferred to take the line of least resistance. Durey de Meinières frequently indicated in his journals that the majority tended to follow the lead given by the *présidents à mortier* and by the *grand'chambre*; a man like President Molé could usually count on almost the total support of the *grand'chambre*.[18] The attitude of many *parlementaires* changed, however, in the course of the dispute over the *Hôpital général*, which left behind much frustration and resentment at the end of the year. Hence three months later, when Bouettin told Lemerre that he could not receive the sacraments, the probability was that the *Parlement* would treat the matter with greater severity than it had done in the past.

It has not perhaps been noted before that the Lemerre affair had a recent princely parallel. The Duc d'Orléans, son of the Regent, had died on 4 February. He had been a recluse with Jansenist sympathies, living in the abbey of Sainte-Geneviève (where he commissioned the painter Jean Restout, also a Jansenist, to decorate the cupola of the renowned library suitably with an apotheosis of St Augustine of Hippo). Robert de Saint-Vincent claimed in his memoirs that the archbishop of Paris had personally refused the prince the last sacraments. The Duc d'Orléans protested in a dignified manner against the archbishop's behaviour, which he deemed improper and illegal, but as he wished to avoid all publicity, he

---

[15] Flammermont, *Rems.*, i, pp. 419–43.   [16] *Ibid.*, p. 496.   [17] BS, MS 800, f. 38ʳ.
[18] See above, Chapter 1, p. 18 for his witty description of the conduct of members of the *grand'chambre* at meetings of *commissaires*; and other instances given in BS, MS 800: f. 37ʳ, f. 39ʳ, and f. 40ʳ.

received the sacraments instead from one of his chaplains inside the abbey church. Lemerre had been a member of the prince's council.[19]

On 23 March Bouettin was ordered to appear before the *Parlement* the same day,[20] and the archbishop was invited to attend the hearing in his capacity as a peer.[21] Beaumont declined the invitation and informed the *Parlement* that the *curé* had acted in accordance with his instructions. At the hearing Bouettin said that he could not administer the sacraments to Lemerre, or even hear the confession of a man who did not submit to *Unigenitus*. It was not before midnight that the *parlementaires* agreed on the terms of an *arrêt*: Bouettin was ordered not to repeat the offence on pain of his temporalities being seized; he was directed to treat his parishioners charitably; and he was again fined. By the same *arrêt* the archbishop was bound over to see to it that similar scandals did not occur in his diocese in future and invited to arrange for Lemerre to receive the sacraments within twenty-four hours. The *arrêt* did not require that the *gens du roi* should inform the King of what had taken place.[22]

When the details of the *arrêt* were known at Versailles the first president and two other presidents were told to attend upon the King on 26 March. An *arrêt du conseil*[23] which quashed the *Parlement*'s decision and evoked the case was read out to them by Paulmy in the presence of the King and of the other members of the *Conseil des dépêches*.[24] 'Monsieur', the King said to the first president, 'je suis fort mécontent de mon parlement; j'en excepte les gens sages'.[25] The *Parlement* was restless the next day when it heard Maupeou's

---

[19] Collection Michel Vinot Préfontaine, Paris: 'Mémoires de P. A. Robert de Saint-Vincent' (typescript copy), pp. 138–41; according to this account the *Parlement* alluded to these events in its remonstrances of May 1752; there is indeed a passage in them which would be consistent with this view: cf. Flammermont, *Rems.*, i, p. 494, first paragraph. On Restout's work for the duke at Sainte-Geneviève, see Pierre Rosenberg and Antoine Schnapper (eds.), *Musée des Beaux-Arts de Rouen, juin–septembre 1970: Jean Restout (1692–1768)* (s.l., 1970), pp. 20 and 190 (no. 20).

[20] Archives départementales de la Gironde, Bordeaux (hereafter ADG), MS 104(J): 'Mémoire, contenant un fragment du Journal historique de ce qui s'est passé au Parlement de Paris à l'occasion des refus de sacrements, depuis le jeudi 23 mars 1752, jusques et compris le mardi 2 mai suivant, dressé par M. l'abbé Moreau, Conseiller-Clerc en la cour, depuis Evêque succésivement de Vence et de Mâcon', pp. 1–4. The Abbé Moreau relates that it was Blondeau (2nd chamber of *enquêtes*) who denounced Bouettin before the court. Blondeau had seen the first president at the *buvette* and asked him to call an assembly of the chambers. Maupeou told him to see the *procureur général*. In the absence of the *procureur général*, Blondeau and his colleagues forced the first president to call the assembly. The *procureur général* was then summoned in haste from a memorial service for the Duc d'Orléans at Sainte-Geneviève.

[21] Flammermont, *Rems.*, i, pp. 482–3. The archbishops of Paris were dukes-peer of Saint-Cloud, but sat in the *Parlement* as *conseillers d'honneur nés*.

[22] *Ibid.*, p. 483.

[23] For the *minute* of the *arrêt du conseil* of 26 Mar. 1752, see AN, E 2317, n. 88.

[24] ADG, MS 104(J), p. 14. Paulmy read the *arrêt* in the absence of his uncle the Comte d'Argenson. A meeting of the *Conseil des dépêches* had just taken place.

[25] Flammermont, *Rems.*, i, p. 484.

account of what had taken place. Moreover, a councillor at the 2nd chamber of *enquêtes* revealed that Lemerre had been unsuccessful in a second attempt to persuade Bouettin to give him the sacrament.[26] But the moderates again prevailed, and after a lengthy debate the *Parlement* decided to adopt a proposal from the *gens du roi*, who offered to give the King an account of Lemerre's plight.[27] The *gens du roi* reached Versailles late in the evening and were unable to see the King.[28] As they were due to report to the *Parlement* early the next morning, the chancellor wrote to the King at once. In his letter[29] Lamoignon suggested that he should be allowed to tell them that the King was pleased with the result of the debate and would take prompt measures to provide for Lemerre's needs. The King readily approved the suggestion.[30] His reply was well received by the *parlementaires*, who ordered the *gens du roi* to report to them later that day on the execution of his instructions.[31] In his journal the Marquis d'Argenson accused Lamoignon of having neglected to make arrangements for Lemerre to receive the sacraments until the morning of 28 March, although he had received the King's instructions the night before.[32] But Lamoignon's letter to the King and the latter's reply establish that Louis XV omitted to give precise orders to that effect on the night of 27 March. The King probably repaired the omission the next morning, but it was he and not the chancellor who was responsible for the delay that proved fatal to Lemerre's chances of receiving the last rites. A Capuchin who was sent to offer his services to the unfortunate man arrived too late. The *gens du roi* reported to the *Parlement* that Lemerre died before he could receive the sacrament.

The *parlementaires* were annoyed and they decided to continue the proceedings instituted against Bouettin. They ordered his arrest, though a cautious *avocat général* refused to give any *conclusions*.[33] Bouettin may have been given advance warning of this move by Jean-Omer Joly de Fleury.[34] He went into hiding; the *huissier* of the *Parlement* was unable to apprehend him and took care not to report to the assembly of the chambers until 3

[26] ADG, MS 104(J), p. 16ᵛ.   [27] Flammermont, *Rems.*, i, p. 484.

[28] E. J. F. Barbier, *Chronique de la régence et du règne de Louis XV (1718–1763), ou Journal de Barbier* (Paris, 1866), 8 vols. (hereafter Barbier, *Journal*), v, p. 182.

[29] FL, Rosanbo MSS, 1/2/9: Lamoignon to Louis XV, 27 March 1752.

[30] *Ibid.* The King's reply is in the margin; it was written at midnight.

[31] Barbier, *Journal*, v, pp. 184–5.

[32] *Journal et mémoires du Marquis d'Argenson*, ed. E. J. B. Rathery (Paris, 1859–67) (hereafter D'Argenson, ed. Rathery), vii, p. 184; cf. Barbier, *Journal*, v, p. 190.

[33] Flammermont, *Rems.*, i, p. 485.

[34] See a marginal note by President Durey de Meinières in BS, MS 800, f. 274: 'on prétend que M de Fleury de la Mousse, advt général, le fit avertir'. There is no trace of Jean-Omer Joly de Fleury's intervention in his correspondence with the Comte d'Argenson; cf. BUP, CA 28/IV.

a.m. The *parlementaires* were due to adjourn later that morning for the Easter vacation, and they postponed their debate to 10 April.[35]

The King had not observed the established procedure when he quashed the criminal proceedings that were being taken against Bouettin; for an *arrêt du conseil* that was merely read out to the first president did not legally bind the *Parlement*.[36] Beaumont was aware of this fact. He knew that so long as the *Parlement* was not ordered by means of letters patent to register an *arrêt du conseil*, the magistrates would merely suspend judicial proceedings and not suppress them altogether.[37] As steps now had to be taken to protect Bouettin from the full rigours of the law, the complaisant chancellor had allowed the archbishop to send him a draft of an *arrêt du conseil* before a meeting of the *Conseil des dépêches* on 4 April.[38] Beaumont enclosed with it a draft of letters patent[39] and tried to overcome the doubts that Lamoignon probably had about their use:

> le Roy est bien disposé, vous le savés; il a pleine confiance en vous; le succès est donc entre vos mains, et c'est ce qui me fait espérer qu'il sera tel que je le désire pour le bien de l'église.[40]

Beaumont and Boyer, the former bishop of Mirepoix, who held the *feuille des bénéfices*, had conferred with the King the day before the archbishop wrote to the chancellor.[41] A majority of the members of the *Conseil des dépêches*, however, may have been of the opinion that it was undesirable and unnecessary to send letters patent to the *Parlement* on this occasion. After all, it was safe to assume that, under the strong influence of the moderates, the *Parlement* would again proceed no further against Bouettin if the King were to notify the first president of another *arrêt du conseil*. On the other hand, the same result might not be achieved without a conflict if letters patent were used, for the King would probably have to force the *parlementaires* to register them. The first view prevailed; the decision to arrest Bouettin was quashed by an *arrêt du conseil*.[42] No use was made of letters patent as a means of formally notifying the *arrêt du conseil* to the *Parlement*:

---

[35] Flammermont, *Rems.*, i, p. 485.

[36] *Ibid.*, p. 499. Some ministers were certainly of the opinion that the King could evoke cases from the *Parlement* without sending letters patent. There is a fuller discussion of the question of evocations on pp. 214–15.

[37] FL, Rosanbo MSS, 2/2/9: Beaumont to Lamoignon, 4 Apr. 1752.

[38] The *Conseil des dépêches* met on 30 and/or 31 March (cf. Luynes, *Mém.*, xi, pp. 474, 478) and on 4 April (D'Argenson, ed. Rathery, vii, p. 183). The *arrêt du conseil* was dated 4 April. Although the date of a royal *arrêt* is not necessarily a reliable guide (see p. 117 below), the evidence suggests that this particular *arrêt du conseil* was adopted on that date. The Council met again on 9 April (Luynes, *Mém.*, xi, pp. 485, 487), but it was probably to consider new cases of denial of sacraments.

[39] FL, Rosanbo MSS, 2/2/10 and 11.   [40] *Ibid.*, 2/2/9: letter of 4 Apr. 1752.

[41] D'Argenson, ed, Rathery, vii, pp. 182–3.

[42] AN, E 2317, no. 103: *minute* of the *arrêt du conseil*.

'on assure même que M. Le Garde des Sceaux a refusé de les sceller'; this interesting detail was supplied to Lord Hardwicke's son, Philip Yorke, by a secret informant, Bousquet de Colomiers (whose reliable 'nouvelles à la main' were forwarded to England by Dr John Jeffreys). Such a stand would have been consistent with Machault's beliefs; there were precedents for his conduct.[43] On 9 April the King told the first president to inform *parlementaires* that he had quashed their *arrêt* and that he forbad them to continue their proceedings.[44]

The Government's equivocal action served its purpose. It also gave the *présidents à mortier* and other moderates an opening: they could recommend that the *Parlement* should make remonstrances. A course that purported to enlighten the Monarch was one which the *zélés* had no choice but to support, though they were probably more concerned about fresh denials of sacraments which had come to their notice.[45] The remonstrances were planned once again by *commissaires* from all the chambers and hastily drawn up by the first president: they were presented to the King on 15 April.[46] They laid stress on the threat of schism as well as on the danger to public order created by what were described as illegitimate attempts to enforce obedience to *Unigenitus* by means of denials of sacraments.[47] The King referred the question of his reply to a committee of ministers, which sat for four hours, and a text was finally adopted at a meeting of the *Conseil des dépêches*.[48] In this lengthy document which he handed to the first president on 17 April, the King announced that he was taking steps to

[43] British Library (Hereafter BL), Add. MSS 35,445 (Hardwicke Papers), f. 219: 'Nouvelles à la main', 19 Apr. 1752; the reasons for the identification of Bousquet (or Bosquet) de Colomiers as Philip Yorke's informant are given in Appendix A (pp. 267–8). There was a precedent for Machault's alleged refusal to seal the letters patent: that of Chancellor Daguesseau in July 1720, when, in consequence, the Regent himself had to seal the *déclaration* transferring the *Parlement* to Pontoise; AN, 342 AP 2: Memoirs of G. F. Joly de Fleury, the former *procureur général*, ff. 127–8. On the use of the seals, see Auguste Dumas, 'L'Action des secrétaires d'état sous l'ancien régime', *Annales de la Faculté de Droit d'Aix*, n.s., xlvii (1954), pp. 9–15.

[44] Flammermont, *Rems.*, i, p. 485.

[45] In particular, there was the distressing case of Bruslay, the former *curé* of Mussy-L'Evêque (diocese of Langres); see Flammermont, *Rems.*, i, pp. 486–7.

[46] *Ibid.*, pp. 487–8.   [47] *Ibid.*, pp. 488–96.

[48] The *comité*, presided over by Lamoignon, was attended by Machault, Saint-Florentin, D'Argenson, Rouillé, Saint-Contest, and the Duc de Béthune (Luynes, *Mém.*, xi, p. 489). Noailles, Saint-Séverin and Puyzieulx were not present. The meeting of the *Conseil des dépêches* took place on the evening of 16 April. Philip Yorke's informant claims that Machault, Noailles and Saint-Séverin 'ont totallement [*sic*] déterminé la Réponse du Roy aux Remontrances du Parlement, malgré l'évêque de Mirepoix qui avec son parti a fait faire à M. de dauphin la fausse démarche de demander au Roy sa protection pour l'arch-evêque de Paris dans cette affaire'. He states, possibly erroneously, that Saint-Séverin had even refused to attend the meeting of the Council (it is unlikely that a minister would behave in that way towards the King), though Saint-Séverin was certainly absent from the *comité*. For these details, see BL, Add. MSS 35,445, f. 222: 'Nouvelles à la main', 23 Apr. 1752.

remove Bouettin from Saint-Etienne-du-Mont and censured his conduct.[49] It seems that the reply originally contained the words (in italics): 'J'ai pris des mesures *de concert avec l'archevêque de Paris* pour retirer le curé de Saint-Etienne-du-Mont d'une paroisse, etc.' The chancellor had been ordered to write to the archbishop to ask him to effect Bouettin's removal, but Beaumont had demurred and the reference to him was then removed from the text of the King's reply.[50] Finally, the King implied that denials of sacraments fell within the cognisance of the *Parlement*, though he still wished cases arising from them to be referred directly to him:

> Mon intention n'a jamais été d'ôter à mon parlement toute connaissance de la matière dont il s'agit; et si je lui ai ordonné comme je le fais encore, de me rendre compte des dénonciations qui lui seront faites sur de pareilles objets, ce n'a été et ce n'est que pour me mettre en état de juger par moi-même des voies qu'il conviendra d'employer dans chaque circonstance, la procédure ordinaire n'étant pas toujours la plus propre par son état à maintenir le bon ordre et la paix qui est le but que je me propose et dans lequel mon parlement doit chercher à concourir avec moi.[51]

The King's reply was favourably received at the *Parlement*. All the same, the *parlementaires* were not eager to refer each case of denial of sacraments to him. His intention was clearly to punish priests like Bouettin by removing them temporarily from their parishes, and the *parlementaires* were apprehensive lest it should appear as if these priests were being protected from the law by the use of *lettres de cachet*. Consequently, although they suspended their judicial proceedings against Bouettin (and others), they decided to issue a regulation in the form of an *arrêt de règlement*, which would keep priests in check until such time when the King saw fit to make a new law.[52] Their *arrêt de règlement* of 18 April contained an important clause about denial of sacraments:

> La Cour, toutes chambres assemblées ... fait défense à tous ecclésiastiques de faire aucuns actes tendant au schisme, notamment de faire aucun refus public des sacrements, sous prétexte de défaut de représentation d'un billet de confession ou de déclaration du nom du confesseur ou d'acceptation de la Bulle Unigenitus, leur enjoint de se conformer dans l'administration extérieure des sacrements aux canons et règlements autorisés dans le

---

[49] Flammermont, *Rems.*, i, pp. 496–7.
[50] ADG, MS 104(J): 'Mémoire, etc.' of the Abbé Moreau (whose family had connections with the Comte d'Argenson), p. 15; Collection Michel Vinot Préfontaine, Paris: 'Mémoires de P. A. Robert de Saint-Vincent' (typescript copy), p. 128. The Marquis d'Argenson tends to confirm these accounts: he noted that the first president was kept waiting while the King awaited a courrier from Beaumont: D'Argenson, ed. Rathery, vii, p. 201.
[51] Flammermont, *Rems.*, i, p. 497.
[52] *Ibid.*, p. 498. On the subject of *arrêts de règlement* see G. Deteix, *Les Arrêts de règlement du Parlement de Paris* (Paris, 1930).

Royaume ... à peine contre les contrevenants d'être poursuivis comme perturbateurs du repos public et punis suivant la rigueur des ordonnances ...[53]

The *Parlement* sent copies of the *arrêt de règlement* to the *bailliages* and *sénéchaussées* within its jurisdiction and also had it printed and placarded.[54] It was the *Parlement*'s most important pronouncement on the question of denial of sacraments and became the basis for its judicial proceedings over the next two years.

The *arrêt de règlement* was the subject of discussion at several *comités* and meetings of the *Conseil des dépêches*. A majority in the *Conseil des dépêches* on 19 April probably advised the King to allow it to stand (at least for the time being),[55] and the *arrêt de règlement* even appeared in the official *Gazette de France* three days later.[56] Moreover, it seems that the King and the Comte d'Argenson took swift action to prevent the archbishop from publishing a pastoral letter that was directed against the new regulation.[57] Nevertheless, Beaumont saw the King on 23 April and put pressure on the Government; he had the support of the chancellor, who strongly disapproved of the *arrêt de règlement*.[58] The Government decided to make some gesture that would reassure Beaumont and other bishops. The members of the *Conseil des dépêches* devised an *arrêt du conseil* in which it was stated that the administration of the sacraments was a purely spiritual matter.[59] But the *arrêt du conseil* (of 29 April) cannot have afforded Beaumont much satisfaction; for it neither quashed the *arrêt de règlement* nor made mention of what the

[53] Flammermont, *Rems.*, i, p. 498.
[54] *Ibid.*, p. 499. It was the responsibility of the *procureur général* to notify the lower jurisdictions of the decisions of the *Parlement*.
[55] The *Conseil des dépêches* met at Choisy; FL, Rosanbo MSS, 1/2/13; Luynes, *Mém.*, xi, p. 490; Barbier, *Journal*, v, p. 211.
[56] *Gazette de France*, p. 203; cf. D'Argenson, ed. Rathery,, vii, p. 208. Philip Yorke's informant noted that the secretaries of state had sent each other the proofs of the *Gazette de France* and that none had taken it upon themselves to give the item their approval. 'Cependant', he added, 'elle a été Renvoyée aux [*sic*] compositeur de la Gazette': BL, Add. MSS 35,445, f. 227: 'Nouvelles à la main', 30 Apr. 1752.
[57] BN, MS franç. 22092 (Anisson-Duperron Collection, xxxii), f. 222 for the text of the archbishop's proposed *mandement* of 22 April; and f. 224 for the King's intervention; see also, BL, Add. MSS 35,445, f. 227; Barbier, *Journal*, v, p. 212; and n. 108 below.
[58] Luynes, *Mém.*, xi, p. 495. On 24 April the archbishop sent Lamoignon a memorandum on the *arrêt de règlement* and, in a covering letter, expressed the hope that the chancellor would give fresh proof of his love for religion; FL, Tocqueville MSS, 1/8; for Lamoignon's hostile comments on the *arrêt de règlement*, see *pièce* 7 of the same *dossier*.
[59] This decision was probably taken by the *Conseil des dépêches* on 23 April after the King had seen the archbishop. As a result a *comité* met on 26 (Luynes, *Mém.*, xi, p. 496) and 28 April (FL, Rosanbo MSS, 1/2/15: Lamoignon to Louis XV, 28 Apr. 1752) to draft an *arrêt de conseil*, which was adopted by the King at the *Conseil des dépêches* on 29 April; for the *minute* of this *arrêt de conseil* see AN, E 2317, no. 127: it generally followed the terms of the *arrêt de conseil* of 6 Sept. 1740.

Parlement had done.[60] This limp document was forwarded to the bishops, and, in his covering letter, Saint-Florentin told them to make only prudent use of 'précautions qui, quoique dictées par le zèle et la piété, alarment souvent les consciences ou servent de prétexte pour soulever les esprits':[61] an obvious allusion to confession certificates.

On 3 May the chambers were assembled to hear an accusation made against the *curé* of Saint-Jean-en-Grève, who claimed he was authorised by the archbishop to circulate a petition among *curés* in Paris which supported the use of confession certificates.[62] As it was illegal to circulate petitions that might provoke people or which presupposed the existence of an association of private persons (and *curés* were private persons),[63] the *Parlement* immediately ordered a preliminary investigation.[64] The chancellor happened to be in Paris and he wrote off at once to the King at Marly.[65] The King probably realised that the inquiry could lead to proceedings being taken against the archbishop and he acted swiftly: he suggested that the first president, the *procureur général* and a few other *parlementaires* should be told to bring him the results of the investigation the next day, and he sent Machault to Paris to discuss the plan with Lamoignon.[66] At 4 a.m. the first president learned that he and others had to be at Marly later that day.[67] The assembled chambers were due to consider the results of the investigation at 10 a.m. Maupeou knew that the *Parlement* would accuse him of dereliction of duty if he were a party to the removal of legal documents. As he was probably afraid lest the King should confiscate the results of the investigation, he sent word to the *parlementaires* that the assembly of the chambers would take place at 8 a.m.[68] The documents were read out and formally consigned to the records so that only copies could be taken to the King. The *gens du roi* wished to avoid giving their *conclusions* on the results of the inquiry before the first president returned from Marly, but they were forced to give them when the assembled chambers threatened to remain *in deliberatis*.[69] By then ordering the offending priest to appear before them with his petition, the *parlementaires* adroitly set their judicial proceedings in motion before the first president left. The King had also

[60] Luynes, *Mém.*, xii, p. 5; Barbier, *Journal*, iii, p. 377. In their subsequent report to the next General Assembly of the clergy of France in 1755, the *agents généraux* commented that the *arrêt de conseil* 'ne prononçoit qu'indirectement la nullité de celuy que le Parlement avoit rendu le 18 avril ...': AN, G^{8*} 789, f. 26^v.

[61] AN, O¹ 396 (Saint-Florentin's letter-book), p. 115, no. 852: Saint-Florentin to the archbishops and bishops of France, 30 Apr. 1752; cf. Luynes, *Mém.*, xii, pp. 5–6.

[62] Flammermont, *Rems.*, i, p. 499.

[63] BUP, CA 28/IV: Jean-Omer Joly de Fleury to the Comte d'Argenson, 29 Apr. 1752.

[64] Flammermont, *Rems.*, i, p. 499.   [65] FL, Rosanbo MSS, 1/2/18: letter of 3 May 1752.

[66] *Ibid.* The King's reply is in the margin.   [67] Luynes, *Mém.*, xii, p. 270.

[68] *Ibid.*, for evidence that the first president changed the time of the meeting.

[69] *Ibid.*

summoned the archbishop; it was said later that Beaumont had at first told the King and the chancellor that the petition existed only in the speeches of the *parlementaires*.[70] After the *Conseil des dépêches* had examined the results of the *Parlement*'s investigation the King said to the first president that he did not wish the proceedings to continue.[71]

The *parlementaires* were indignant because the King had shown that it was still his intention to interfere with their judicial proceedings. On 5 May they passed an *arrêté* ordering that a deputation should be sent to the King and that it should point out to him that, in the circumstances,

> ... les voies d'autorité par lesquelles ledit seigneur Roi paraît vouloir d'une seule parole ou par quelque acte étranger à l'ordre judiciaire annuler les arrêts du premier tribunal de sa justice souveraine serait le coup le plus fatal qu'il pût porter à la constitution de son état et du plus pernicieux exemple contre ses intérêts et ceux de sa postérité ...[72]

The *arrêté* further ordered that the deputation should draw his attention to the threat of schism, 'pour lequel', it said, 'l'archevêque de Paris ose se déclarer ouvertement'. It also stated that if the King persisted in destroying or suspending the measures taken by the *Parlement*, its members would humbly seek his permission to discontinue their duties. And it declared that, in the meantime, the chambers should remain assembled; thus the ordinary administration of justice was suspended. Of these three final provisions of the *arrêté*, the first two had been passed by eighty-one votes to seventy-eight, and the third had been opposed by only sixteen *parlementaires*.[73] The King refused to receive the deputation unless his judges resumed the administration of justice; but his judges did not yield at once to this condition. The *gens du roi* were left to act as intermediaries, for the first president was apparently making no attempt to break the deadlock. They privately urged the *parlementaires* to fulfil the King's condition, and they had the support of President Molé, who carried some influence as second president.[74] The crucial decisions were taken behind closed doors at the assembly of the chambers held on 8 May.

Unbeknown to most of those present that day, the Comte d'Argenson had a newly acquired secret informant in their midst: Titon, the *doyen* of the

---

[70] *Ibid.*; see also Barbier, *Journal*, v, p. 217; and BL, Add. MSS 35,445, f. 245ᵛ: 'Nouvelles à la main', 21 May 1752.

[71] Flammermont, *Rems.*, i, p. 499.   [72] *Ibid.*, pp. 500–1.

[73] BUP, CA, *dossier* no. 54: letters of J. B. M. Titon to the Comte d'Argenson (with some of the latter's first secretary, Dupin): no. 33, 'ce vendredy 2. heures' [5 May 1752], for the various *avis* proposed and the voting figures.

[74] *Ibid.*, CA 28/IV: Jean-Omer Joly de Fleury to the Comte d'Argenson, 8 May 1752 (noon): '... Mʳ Molé se plaint avec amertume et raison ce me semble que Mr le Premʳ Président n'a pas assemblé hier chez luy les Présidents pour prendre quelque résolution, et entendre et Résoudre les difficultés'.

Plate 12 J. B. M. Titon, Councillor at the *Parlement,* anonymous engraving
after a painting by J. F. de Troy

5th chamber of the *enquêtes.* The two men had known each other since their
schooldays at Louis-le-Grand where, in that hot-house of puberty, Titon
had perhaps developed the complex and slightly unnatural feelings which
bound him, with little hope of reciprocity, to the Comte d'Argenson.
Through this lapsed Jansenist, now a debauchee and short of money, the
minister, and presumably also the King, knew how the voting went in the
assembly of the chambers, and were in a position to act accordingly.[75]

[75] On Titon, see Appendix A, 'Note on the Comte d'Argenson's informants', pp. 259–68
below.

The *parlementaires* first of all ordered that four *curés* who had been asked to sign the petition should be summoned to give their account; as this decision did not strictly amount to a preliminary investigation, the *parlementaires* had not disobeyed the King's prohibition.[76] According to Titon, the result of their enquiries dampened their ardour, for the *curés* revealed in their statements that confession certificates had been in use in their parishes for between thirteen and forty-five years. By 116 votes to 45 the assembly of the chambers merely ordered the *gens du roi* to give their conclusions on these statements the following day.[77] The outcome was that the *gens du roi* were sent to inform the King of the decision to suspend the clause in the *arrêté* of 5 May which ordered that the chambers should remain assembled.[78]

The King agreed to receive the deputation on 14 May. The first president gave him the signed statements of the *curés*. But the *avocat général* had been unable to dissuade Maupeou from reading out the text of the *arrêté* of 5 May, which was a strong indictment of the Government's interference with judicial proceedings.[79] The King was in a difficult position. If he gave a favourable reply to the deputation he would be endorsing the *arrêté*; whereas if he gave an unfavourable reply, or even no reply at all, the *parlementaires* would probably cease to perform their duties. On the face of it, the King's reply did not give satisfaction to the *parlementaires*. He blamed their conduct and again forbad them to continue their proceedings. He said that, although he disapproved of the attempt to circulate a petition, the document itself contained nothing reprehensible.[80] He announced that, on the advice of a commission of prelates and magistrates which would be set up without delay, he would take 'les mesures les plus convenables pour faire cesser entièrement tout trouble et toute division'. And he added:

> Mon parlement doit, par la conduite la plus sage et la plus mesurée et par la circonspection de ses démarches, ne rien faire qui puisse m'obliger à retenir l'autorité que je lui confie, et qui soit capable d'apporter quelque obstacle à l'exécution des mes volontés.[81]

The *parlementaires* did not abandon their duties. They found a way out of their difficulty by registering not the King's reply but merely the first

---

[76] BUP, CA 28/IV: Jean-Omer Joly de Fleury to the Comte d'Argenson, second letter of 8 May 1752 (12.45 p.m.). The voting had been ninety-six to sixty-four according to Titon: CA 54, no. 32, report to the Comte d'Argenson 'Du 8' [May 1752], 12.30 p.m.

[77] BUP, CA 54: [Titon] to the Comte d'Argenson: no. 9, 'Ce 8 sept heures du soir', [8 May 1752].

[78] Flammermont, *Rems.*, i, pp. 501–2.

[79] BUP, CA 28/IVB: Jean-Omer Joly de Fleury to the Comte d'Argenson, 12 May 1752.

[80] Philip Yorke's informant claims that the King expressed his disapproval of the attempt in a letter to the archbishop on 12 May: BL, Add. MSS 35,445, f. 245ᵛ: 21 May 1752.

[81] Flammermont, *Rems.*, i, p. 503.

president's account of what had taken place at Marly.[82] Even the King appears to have connived at this arrangement, which enabled the *parlementaires* to keep to their *arrêts* and *arrêtés* in spite of his reply. There are certainly signs that the Government had come to some understanding with leading *parlementaires*, though the details are by no means clear, particularly where they concern the first president. Two days before the deputation went to Marly, *Avocat général* Joly de Fleury had supplied the Comte d'Argenson with a note on a case where a deputation had been asked to leave the King's presence while the council discussed the terms of a reply.[83] This procedure was certainly followed on 14 May, if one is to judge from the first president's account.[84] Moreover, in his account, Maupeou also stated that after the reply had been read out to the deputies he had asked the King to let him have it in writing. His request had been granted, and he gives the impression, which is possibly misleading, that he was handed the text while his colleagues were still in the room.[85] But he was called back to speak to the King after the deputation had left the royal presence: he says only that this meeting lasted two minutes. On the other hand, Philip Yorke's informant reported that the King had called in the first president in order to give him the written reply, and that the *Parlement* had subsequently registered Maupeou's account, and not the reply itself, because the other members of the deputation had not been present at the private meeting.[86] As the terms of the *arrêté* itself had not escaped the attention of the informant, it seems difficult to doubt the accuracy of his report. At any rate, the deputies were probably well disposed to an arrangement: they had partaken of a lavish buffet at Marly, and the first president dined them on their return to Paris.[87] Several months later, the Marquis d'Argenson gleaned some details about what was said at that brief meeting between the King and the first president on 14 May; the King had apparently told Maupeou: 'allez de votre chemin, je paraîtrai fâché, et j'en serai bien aise'.[88] D'Argenson's information was probably correct.

In the course of the affair the *gens du roi* also seem to have come to a new arrangement with the Government, for they began to employ different

---

[82] The *arrêté* of 15 May is inaccurately reproduced by Flammermont, (*Rems.*, i, p. 503). In the appropriate register of the *conseil secret* of the *Parlement* it runs: 'surquoy La Matière mise en délibération La cour a arresté qu'il sera fait registre du Récit fait par Monsieur Le premier Président, sans néanmouns par la cour se départir de l'exécution de ses précédens arrests et arrestés': AN, X^{1A} 8486, f. 125^r (see also the *minute* of the *arrêté* signed by Maupeou in the *liasse* for May 1752 in AN, X^{1B} 8929).

[83] See note 79 above.   [84] AN, X^{1A} 8486, ff. 122^r–124^r.

[85] *Ibid.*, f. 124^v: 'aprèsquoy Luy Premier Président L'ayant supplié de luy faire donner sa réponse par écrit, Il [le Roi] La luy avoit accordé [*sic*]'.

[86] BL, Add. MSS 35,445, f. 248: 28 May 1752.

[87] AN, X^{1A} 8486, f. 121^r, ^{v}; Barbier, *Journal*, v, p. 235.

[88] D'Argenson, ed. Rathery, vii, p. 340.

tactics. Hitherto they had avoided bringing matters like denials of sacraments to the notice of the *Parlement* and had tried to delay judicial proceedings. As a result, the *zélés* had taken the initiative from the *gens du roi*, and the assembly of the chambers had taken it from the *grand'chambre*, which had previously dealt with these delicate cases. This subject had long been a bone of contention between the *gens du roi* and the Government.[89] But after the crisis of May 1752, the *gens du roi* were allowed to forestall the *zélés* on occasion, though they always had to obtain the King's permission beforehand.[90] On 31 May, for instance, their action enabled the *grand'-chambre* to dispatch two cases before they could be raised at an assembly of the chambers: the first concerned the *lieutenant général* of Meaux, who had failed to give due publicity to the *arrêt de règlement*, and the second related to the illicit publication of two pamphlets, one by the archbishop of Sens (a prolix and long-standing opponent of the *Parlement* on matters affecting *Unigenitus*), the other by supporters of the *Parlement*.[91] However, the *gens du roi* were never allowed sufficient freedom, and consequently the *grand'-chambre* did not regain the initiative over the assembly of the chambers.

From May to the middle of August the *parlementaires* acted circumspectly as regards denials of sacraments. They referred each new case to the King and suspended their proceedings on his orders. But he did not prevent them from instituting those proceedings, which were not suspended until the stage of a *décret d'ajournement personnel* or even of a *décret de prise de corps* had been reached.

Decrees of this nature in criminal proceedings were passed on the accused by a court wishing to question them about the accusations made against them or even to have them arrested. There were three categories of decrees which represented different stages in a criminal prosecution. In each case the decree was given on the *conclusions* of the *procureur général*. The *décret d'assigné pour être ouï* was like a writ served upon a person requiring him to answer a charge before a court. The *décret d'ajournement personnel* was more serious; the accused was required to present himself before the court at a certain date to answer the charge and could not be released afterwards until the *procureur général* had given his opinion. Finally, the *décret de prise de corps* was used to arrest and imprison the accused if an officer of the court

---

[89] See the acrimonious correspondence between *Procureur général* Joly de Fleury and Chancellor Daguesseau over the incident concerning the *Instruction pastorale* of the archbishop of Cambrai, in March 1735, quoted above, Chapter 1, pp. 26–7.

[90] BN, JF 2482, f. 113; Saint-Florentin to the *procureur général*, 16 May 1752.

[91] BUP, CA 28/IV: Jean-Omer Joly de Fleury to the Comte d'Argenson, 31 May 1752 (1 p.m.): '... vous voyés, Monsieur, qu'en nous laissant un peu agir suivant nos mouvements nous ne négligerons rien pour resaisir la grande chambre où toutes ces matières doivent être naturellement portées, et delà [*sic*] il en naîtra un grand bien que vous devés sentir mieux que personne'.

succeeded in apprehending him. If an *assigné* did not appear before the court, the judge would convert his decree into one of *ajournement personnel*; similarly, an *ajourné* who did not appear on the day would be arrested under a *décret de prise de corps*. An ecclesiastic on whom a decree either of *ajournement personnel* or of *prise de corps* had been passed was not allowed to exercise his duties; if he was merely an *assigné* this rule did not apply.[92]

Because the Comte d'Argenson affected to disengage himself to some extent from the affairs of the *Parlement*, the *gens du roi* had to deal mainly with the chancellor. Lamoignon was over-cautious: on 29 May he told them that he did not want an *ajourné*, the *curé* of Saint-Jean-en-Grève (Paris), to attend the summons of the *Parlement*, though he was warned that the *curé*'s arrest might be ordered if he failed to appear. The *gens du roi* did not serve the decree of *ajournement personnel* on the *curé* until the evening of 5 June. The *curé* then helpfully went into hiding, but a week later it proved necessary for the chancellor to afford him the dubious protection of an *arrêt du conseil*. Having summoned him, Lamoignon extracted his consent to the legal figment that it had been issued at his request and he then backdated the *arrêt du conseil* to 6 June.[93] Such were the desperate devices to which the Government was prepared to resort.

By setting up a commission, the King had again helped the moderates to retain their influence over the *Parlement*; for they successfully appealed to their colleagues to wait for the results of the commission and for the King's final decision. And when the members of the commission were named at the end of May, the *parlementaires* had the satisfaction of noting that the body was composed equally of prelates and magistrates (a denomination that comprised councillors of state) and included a respected *parlementaire* in the person of Guillaume-François Joly de Fleury, the former *procureur général*.

Beaumont was naturally irritated at the turn of events; for the *arrêt de règlement* had not been quashed, and priests who faced proceedings before the *Parlement* were merely ordered by the Government to absent themselves from their parishes. Bouettin, for instance, had not reappeared at Saint-Etienne-du-Mont. Some parishes, like Saint-Jean-en-Grève, were beginning to suffer from a dearth of priests. Moreover, a few days after the deputation had been to Marly, there appeared an illicit edition of the first president's speech to the King; and the archbishop felt that the accusations

---

[92] J.-B. Dénisart, *Collection de décisions nouvelles et de notions relatives à la jurisprudence actuelle* (4th edn, Paris, 1763), i, pp. 390–4.

[93] BUP, CA 28/IV: Jean-Omer Joly de Fleury to the Comte d'Argenson, 31 May 1752 (1 p.m.); CA, 30: Lamoignon to the Comte d'Argenson, 'A Paris le dimanche une heure après midy' [11 June 1752]; AN, E 2317, for the *minute* of the *arrêt du conseil* of 6 June 1752.

that were made against him in the *arrêté* of 5 May could not remain unanswered now that they were in print.[94] Since April, he had held private meetings with a number of bishops. These bishops had been joined by others who had come to Paris for the memorial service for the Duc d'Orléans, and the meetings had continued at the archbishop's palace.[95] The *gens du roi* raised the matter with the chancellor when they saw him on 29 May, as they were worried about the effect that these meetings would have on the *Parlement*. They reminded him that the clergy 'n'étoit pas un corps, mais un ordre', and that 'les corps seuls dans L'Etat pouvoient s'assembler sans permission'. Lamoignon hotly disagreed with them and implied to the *gens du roi* that he approved of the assembly of bishops; 'et qu'il y avoit lieu de Présumer que le roy le leur avoit permis'.[96] It appeared that without the knowledge of his ministers the King had indeed given the archbishop a verbal permission to hold these meetings.[97] Perhaps Beaumont had persuaded the Comte d'Argenson, and through him, the King, that, without such meetings, which exercised a restraining influence, the bishops would have spoken out with what he later described as 'toute la force que les conjonctures exigeoient'.[98] All the same, it is surprising that the King should have allowed them to continue after 14 May when he could more prudently have told the bishops to await the outcome of the commission.

With the King's permission the bishops held their first formal meeting on 24 May. Beaumont later claimed that he had called the assembly, but the bishops had been formally invited to attend by the permanent officers of the clergy of France, the *agents généraux du clergé*.[99] The archbishop arranged

[94] AN, 422 AP 1 (Comte d'Argenson's Papers): Beaumont to the Comte d'Argenson, 22 May 1752.

[95] Bousquet de Colomiers, Philip Yorke's informant, records the first meetings of bishops at the house of La Taste, bishop of Bethléem, and later at Beaumont's palace, where they become a daily occurrence: BL, Add. MSS 35,445, f. 215ʳ (13 Apr. 1752), and f. 225ʳ (27 Apr. 1752). There is no trace of the early meetings in the papers of La Taste: cf. BN, MS franç. 19667-8. Several memorial services were held for the Duc d'Orléans, but the most important took place at Notre-Dame on 13 May. When it was over, several bishops went back to Beaumont's palace to confer: D'Argenson, ed. Rathery, vii, pp. 95, 188, and 233.

[96] BUP, CA 28/IV: Jean-Omer Joly de Fleury to the Comte d'Argenson, 31 May 1752 (1 p.m.). The view expressed by the *gens du roi* had also been that of Chancellor Daguesseau: see G. Rech, 'D'Aguesseau et le Jansénisme', in *Le Chancelier Henri-François D'Aguesseau, Limoges 1668-Fresnes 1751: journées d'étude tenues à Limoges à l'occasion du bicentenaire de sa mort (octobre 1951)*, ed. G. Rech (Limoges, 1953), p. 129. It was based on Justinian and the *Digest*, bk 1, 'de colleg. & corp': see the English translation by William Strahan of Domat's *The Civil Law in its Natural Order; together with the Publick Law* (London, 1722), ii, pp. 309-10.

[97] BN, JF 1683, f. 8: undated note in the hand of the *procureur général*. There is no trace of the King's permission having been given through the normal ministerial channels, i.e. through D'Argenson or Saint-Florentin. The *gens du roi* called on Saint-Florentin on 29 May (Barbier, *Journal*, v, p. 241); it is possible that they discussed the matter with him.

[98] AN, 422 AP 1: Beaumont to the Comte d' Argenson, 18 July [1752].

[99] *Ibid.*, letter of 26 May 1752; AN, G⁸* 796: 'Procès verbal de l'assemblée de Messeigneurs les Archevêques et Evêques, tenue à Paris dans l'Archevêché, en L'année 1752', f. 1. On the

first to leave the room on the pretext of another engagement, and in his absence the bishops resolved to send the King a letter of protest about the *arrêté* that accused the archbishop of supporting schism. Beaumont then rejoined the meeting and proposed that the bishops should write to the King, asking him to quash the *arrêt de règlement*; his proposal was unanimously adopted. The task of drawing up both letters was entrusted to the archbishops of Aix and Sens and the bishops of Langres, Carcassonne and Troyes. These prelates privately consulted with Beaumont before then submitted their drafts to the others on 6 June. The letters were signed five days later: the first (which Beaumont did not of course sign) bore nineteen signatures and the second twenty-one.[100] A deputation led by the archbishop of Aix solemnly presented them to the King on 20 June.[101] He received the letters graciously, though he told the deputation that they were not to be either published or copied by the bishops to whom they might be sent.[102] He wished to prevent the letters from coming to the notice of the *Parlement* in the form of illicit pamphlets. But some of the bishops were probably indiscreet, and a *parlementaire* or Jansenist faction was doubtless on the alert; for an edition of the first letter appeared a month later. The King promptly suppressed it in order to forestall its possible suppression by the *Parlement*: the *arrêt du conseil* described the work as an *imprimé*, 'sans titre, mais qui paraît être une Lettre écrite au Roi par dix-neuf évêques'. It amused the public to think that the King ought to know whether or not he had received a letter from the nineteen bishops. Nevertheless, the King (and the *Parlement*) had several precedents for suppressing clandestine editions of letters which had been addressed to him.[103]

two *agents généraux du clergé* and their duties, see the entry in M. Marion, *Dictionnaire des institutions de la France aux xvii* et xviii* siècles* (Paris, 1923, reprint, 1968), p. 7, and Louis S. Greenbaum, *Talleyrand, statesman, priest: the agent general of the clergy and the church of France at the end of the old régime* (Washington, D.C., 1970), *passim*.

100 AN, 422 AP 1: letter quoted in note 99 above; AN, G⁸* 796, ff. 1–2, f. 3ʳ. For authenticated texts of the two letters, see G⁸* 796, ff. 7–10 (concerning Beaumont) and ff. 11–34 (concerning the *arrêt de règlement*). The second letter is printed in [Mouffle d'Angerville], *Vie privée de Louis XV; ou principaux évenemens, particularités et anecdotes de son règne* (London, 1781), ii, pp. 378–403; it was signed by the archbishops of Paris, Cambrai, Aix, Sens and Toulouse, and by the bishops of Langres, Meaux, Bayeux, Metz, Carcassonne, Bethléem, Cahors, Troyes, Dijon, Perpignan, Tréguier, Avranches, Chartres, Apt, the former bishop of Orange and the bishop of Nitrie (*in partibus infidelis*).

101 Luynes, *Mém.*, xii, pp. 47–9; and AN, G⁸* 796, ff. 3ᵛ–4ᵛ.

102 M. Picot, *Mémoires pour servir à l'histoire ecclésiastique pendant le dix-huitième siècle* (Paris, 3rd edn, 1853–7), iii, p. 215; and AN, G⁸* 796, f. 35ʳ: *agents généraux* to the archbishops and bishops of France, 24 June 1752 (*et seq.*).

103 BUP, CA 28/IV: Jean-Omer Joly de Fleury to the Comte d'Argenson, letters of 14 and 19 July 1752; FL, Tocqueville MSS, 9/35, for the text of the *arrêt de conseil* of 25 July 1752; Barbier, *Journal*, v, p. 260–1. There is a fuller discussion of the question of illicit publications and their suppression on pp. 232–3.

The bishops in Paris ordered the *agents généraux* to send copies of the letters to the rest of the French episcopate. The two agents did not ask the bishops to adhere to the letters but simply to acknowledge receipt of them. Beaumont and his friends, however, must have been heartened by the response: within a few weeks sixty-one bishops had written in support of the letters.[104] The agents had written to the whole episcopate, including the *clergé étranger* like the archbishops of Cambrai and Besançon, the bishops of Metz, Toul, Verdun, Strasbourg and Saint-Dié. The term Clergy of France, however, was reserved for the 121 archbishops and bishops whose sees had formed part of the French Monarchy in 1561. The support for Beaumont within this body may be reckoned at seventy-eight (it being noted that three of the original signatories of the letter to the King were not members of the clergy of France).[105] The *agents généraux* were therefore acting on behalf of over two-thirds of its members when they decided to petition the King in a formal *requête* calling for the annulment of the *arrêt de règlement* and of the *arrêté* of 5 May.[106] Beaumont's cause had become that of the bishops of France. The *agents généraux* handed their *requête* to the Comte de Saint-Florentin at Compiègne on 15 July.[107] And three days later, in a timely move, Beaumont warned the Government of what the bishops had in store if the King did not grant their requests; he wrote to the Comte d'Argenson:

> Nous devons sans doute attendre de Sa bonté une réponse favorable, mais si des raisons de prudence et de sagesse que je respecterai toujours empêcher-aient Sa Majesté d'employer son autorité pour faire rendre aux décisions de L'Eglise la soumission qui leur est due, et pour assurer la Liberté du saint ministère, nous ne pourrions nous empêcher, d'agir pour la conservation du sacré dépôt que Dieu nous a confié, et alors nous retomberions dans les inconvénients que nous avons craints et que nous voulions éviter en nous addressant au roy.

Beaumont thereby implied that he and other bishops might issues pastoral letters that required the faithful to disobey the ruling of the *Parlement*, though he promised D'Argenson that he would not issue his own without having first shown it to the King.[108] As might be expected, the King and the *Conseil des dépêches* were in no great haste to reach a decision on the *requête* of the *agents généraux*; Saint-Florentin was ordered to send the document to the *gens du roi* for an opinion and to give them until the end of

---

[104] AN, G⁸* 796, f. 35ʳ: *agents généraux* to the archbishops and bishops of France, 24 June 1752 (*et seq.*); for their replies see ff. 37–70. Picot's figure of sixty-one appears to be correct (*Mémoires pour servir à l'histoire ecclésiastique*, iii, p. 216).
[105] *Ibid.*   [106] AN, G⁸* 789: 'Minute du rapport d'agence de 1750 à 1755', f. 26ᵛ.
[107] FL, Tocqueville MSS, 10/11: the *requête* bore the signatures of the two *agents généraux*, the Abbé de Coriolis and the Abbé de Castries; Luynes, *Mém.*, xii, p. 73.
[108] AN, 422 AP 1: letter of 18 July 1752.

August to produce it in writing.[109] After all, as long as the commission was in session, the King could delay his decision, the bishops would postpone their pastoral letters, and the *Parlement* would suspend its proceedings. In the art of procrastination Louis XV needed no encouragement.

[109] AN, O¹ 396, p. 229, no. 1039: Saint-Florentin to *Procureur général* Joly de Fleury, 22 July 1752. The Tuscan minister, the Marquis de Stainville, informed the Emperor of the presentation of the *requête* in these terms:

> Les évêques ont retranché quelques articles de leur requête, et se sont contentés de demander que l'arrêt du Parlement fût cassé, ainsi que tous les arrêtes et Décrets d'ajournemens personnels contre les curés rendus en conséquence. On ne sçait encore ce que le Roy y aura répondu, mais il paraît qu'il est fort difficile de leur accorder leur demande après avoir laissé subsister si longtemps tous ces différens actes.

> Archivio di Stato (hereafter AS), Florence: Segretaria Ministreo Esteri, no. 2296 (Francia 1750–1758: Carteggio col il Marchese Stainville no. 4), no. 96: letter of 25 June 1752.

5

A DECISION FOR THE KING

Je n'aime pas plus l'authorité des prestres en temps qu'ils
veulent sortir de leurs bornes mistiques, mais je veut
qu'on rende à dieu ce qui est [à] dieu, et à ceesar [*sic*] ce
qui est à ceasar [*sic*]. Hors ceasar [*sic*] ne tient que de dieu
ce qui est à ceesar [*sic*], mais il ne le laschera à personne
sur la terre françoise.

Louis XV to the Maréchal de Richelieu, 11 May 1753

THE COMMISSION was presided by Cardinal de La Rochefoucauld, archbishop of Bourges. This mild and gentlemanly figure had returned from his
Roman embassy in 1748 and while taking the waters at Plombières later
that year had agreed with three other leading bishops (including the
pro-Jansenist Fitz-James of Soissons) on an unofficial policy of ignoring
Unigenitus. He had recently led the assembly of the clergy of France through
the turmoil created by Machault's attempts to impose the *vingtième*.[1] The
other prelates on the commission were Cardinal de Soubise, the archbishop
of Rouen, and the bishop-duke of Laon. The lay *commissaires* were Joly de
Fleury (the former *procureur général*), and three senior councillors of state:
Trudaine, Bidé de La Grandville, and Castanier d'Auriac. Armand de
Rohan-Soubise was the brother of Louis XV's friend, the Prince de
Soubise. He had succeeded an uncle as bishop of Strasbourg, and in his
short life he became a cardinal and also Grand Almoner of France.
According to the Marquis d'Argenson, the cardinal's health had been
ruined from youth, 'par la luxure et par les liqueurs'.[2] D'Alembert later
managed to produce an eulogy of this prelate who was a member of the

---

[1] For details concerning the formation of the commission see FL, Rosanbo MSS, 1/2/20–8;
AN, o¹ 396, p. 116, no. 855: Saint-Florentin to Cardinal de La Rochefoucauld, 7 May 1752;
and BN, JF 1496, f. 2.

[2] *Journal et mémoires du Marquis d'Argenson*, ed. E. J. B. Rathery (Paris, 1859–67) (hereafter
D'Argenson, ed. Rathery), ix, p. 235.

Plate 13 Cardinal F. J. de La Rochefoucauld, by J. M. Nattier (private collection)

French Academy. Nicolas-Charles de Saulx-Tavannes, of an old Burgundian family and a nephew of Chancellor Daguesseau, had been bishop-count of Châlons and therefore a peer of France before being translated to the archbishopric of Rouen in 1733. While at Châlons he secured the submission of his clergy to *Unigenitus* through means that forced the grudging admiration of even the clandestine *Nouvelles ecclésiastiques*, which claimed that one *curé* 'se laissa gagner par une tabatière dont le généraux prélat lui fit présent'.[3] The career of the third cleric, Jean-François-Joseph de Rochechouart Faudoas, bishop-duke of Laon and peer of France, seemed to follow the pattern of that of Saulx-Tavannes, whom he later succeeded as Grand Almoner to the Queen. He became ambassador to the Holy See in 1757 and later a cardinal.

Of the three councillors of state appointed to serve on the commission, Trudaine, a kinsman of the Joly de Fleury family, was the only one who had begun his career in the *Parlement* of Paris. He was an intendant of finances and a close collaborator of Machault. Trudaine was highly esteemed by the King.[4] Bidé de la Grandville (usually known as De La Grandville, perhaps on account of his unfortunate surname) was an old lawyer who, after a lifetime of service in provincial intendancies, found himself regularly in receipt of the royal commission to preside over that fifth wheel of the French judicial system, the *Grand Conseil*.[5] Castanier d'Auriac came originally from the *Parlement* of Toulouse and, like Bidé de La Grandville, he had been a president of the *Grand Conseil*; his chief attribute was that he was the chancellor's son-in-law.[6]

On 7 June Lamoignon had sent La Rochefoucauld a list of the six points on which the King sought the advice of the commission. They show that complexity of the question of confession certificates and denial of sacraments:

   1°. la nécessité ou utilité des billets de confession, et s'il convient de les approuver ou de les supprimer.

   2°. l'usage qu'on doit faire des billets de confession supposé qu'ils soyent conservés en déterminant autant que faire se pourra les cas dans lesquels on doit les exiger.

   3°. la conduitte que doivent tenir les ministres de l'église à l'esgard de ceux qui refusent de présenter des billets de confession, et s'ils doivent estre privés des sacrements lors qu'ils se présentent à la sainte table ou lors qu'ils sont au lit de la mort.

   4°. La différence qu'on peut proposer à ce sujet entre les diocèses dans lesquels les billets de confession sont autorisés par des rituels ou des

---

[3] L. Pingaud, *Les Saulx-Tavanes. Etudes sur l'ancienne société française: lettres et documents inédits* (Paris, 1876), p. 264.

[4] Michel Antoine, *Le Gouvernement et l'administration sous Louis XV: Dictionnaire biographique* (Paris, 1978), p. 239.

[5] *Ibid.*, p. 38; and F. Bluche, *Les Magistrats du Grand Conseil au xviii*e *siècle 1690–1791*, (Annales littéraires de l'Université de Besançon, lxxxii, Paris, 1966), pp. 54–5.

[6] Antoine, *Le Gouvernement*, p. 60; Bluche, *Les Magistrats du Grand Conseil*, p. 62.

statuts synodaux et ceux dans lesquels ils ne sont establis que par un simple usage.

5°.   les voies qu'il faut prendre soit pour supprimer soit pour authoriser les billets de confession.

Enfin l'intention de S.M. estant de chercher les moyens de conserver l'union et la concorde entre le sacerdoce et l'empire, elle attend du zèle de mrs. les commissaires pour son service et pour leur amour de la religion que sans aucun esprit de prévention ils donneront leur advis sur la compétence des tribunaux auxquels il appartient de connoistre de la matière dont il s'agit à l'effet d'empêcher les entreprises respectives des deux puissances.[7]

The *commissaires* met once a week, and they usually discussed these controversial points in a manner typical of the *ancien régime*: the object was to floor one's opponent by quoting every known legal or theological precedent that was in favour of one's argument (with a memory that unremittingly spanned the centuries). Soubise and Joly de Fleury frequently confronted each other in this manner, and their reading of copious *mémoires* on each point took up several meetings. The former *procureur général* had met his match in the cardinal, who probably had a team of scholarly clerks busily working for him. On one occasion he had to refute Soubise's interpretation of two hundred texts; 'la lecture que je fis hier de mon mémoire', he informed the minister Rouillé, 'dura trois heures et demy: cela est assés fort pour une poitrine délicate et un individu qui est près de 77 ans'.[8] Still, this exchange came at the end of July, and by then the *commissaires* were in a position to give their opinion on the first five points. Joly de Fleury was eager for them to give it. But La Rochefoucauld wanted the *commissaires* to go on to discuss the sixth point in order that they should be able to give their opinion on all the points at the same time. The sixth point was important because the other five turned on it; for if the commission decided that question of confession certificates and denials of sacraments did not fall within the cognisance of the royal courts, a decision on the other points was in effect unnecessary. Joly de Fleury suspected the prelates of trying to force the commission into deciding that the lay courts, and therefore the King, were not competent to pronounce upon these matters. Moreover, Soubise, a man of vehement character, wanted the commission wound up as soon as possible; he was saying quite openly that the bishops were only

[7] FL, Rosanbo Mss, 1/2/29: copy in Lamoignon's hand; reproduced in Michel Antoine, *Le Conseil du Roi sous le règne de Louis XV* (Geneva and Paris, 1970), p. 165, note 205.

[8] BPR, LP 21, p. 647: Joly de Fleury to Rouillé, 30 July 1752; cf. BN, JF 1493, f. 5; same to same, 24 July 1752 (draft/copy): 'Je ne laisseray sans réponse un mémoire de deux heures de lecture qui tend à un despotisme absolu au préjudice de l'autorité du roy.'

waiting for that moment to make fresh moves.[9] But the King was not so eager as the cardinal for the meetings of the commission to end, and he probably indicated as much to La Rochefoucauld when he received him on 26 July; La Rochefoucauld left Compiègne also with the impression that the Government were contemplating a new law.[10] For his part, Joly de Fleury did his best to protract the meetings by means of procedural ploys and seemingly endless feats of erudition. There were already clear signs, however, that the *commissaires* would not be unanimous in their opinion on the points submitted to them.

Some people felt that the situation called for a new law, and Rouillé, the minister of marine, was one of them.[11] Because he was a former *parlementaire* he had close links with Joly de Fleury, and he sent him the draft of a *déclaration* with the request for his comments.[12] Rouillé outlined his purpose in a letter to Joly de Fleury on 19 July:

> il seroit inutile de se proposer de satisfaire les deux partis, et il seroit dangereux de donner guain de cause à l'un ou à l'autre: l'on ne peut donc que se proposer de présenter un plan qui puisse convenir dans les deux partis aux gens raisonables [*sic*] qui aiment et respectent la rellgion [*sic*], qui sont attachés au Roy, et qui sont zélés pour le bien et la tranquillité du Royaume. Il y en a plusieurs dans le clergé et dans le Parlement avec lesquels on pourra négocier, lorsque le Projet sera dressé, et qu'il aura été approuvé, par le Roy, à qui je n'ay pas encore eu l'honneur d'en parler.[13]

When he received Joly de Fleury's comments Rouillé communicated his plan to the King: Louis XV had a receptive mind and he adopted it at once.

Rouillé's draft contained references to the *déclaration* of 1730 and to its definition of *Unigenitus* as a 'jugement de l'église universelle en matière de doctrine'. Joly de Fleury remarked that regrettably neither of these references would get through the *Parlement* when the law came to be registered. He wrote:

---

[9] *Ibid.*

[10] *Mémoires du Duc de Luynes sur la cour de Louis XV (1735–1758)*, ed. L. Dussieux and E. Soulié (Paris, 1860–5) (hereafter quoted as Luynes, *Mém.*), xii, p. 78 and D'Argenson, ed. Rathery, vii, pp. 268–9 for details concerning La Rochefoucauld's visit to Compiègne. Luynes recorded that the cardinal, who saw the King at his own request, had come to give an account of the progress of the commission; D'Argenson noted that La Rochefoucauld's private meeting with the King, who saw him for fifteen minutes in the relative privacy of his *cabinet des perruques*, created a stir at court. For the cardinal's 'hunch' concerning the Government's intentions see BPR, LP 21, p. 69: Joly de Fleury to Rouillé, 3 Aug. 1752.

[11] For Rouillé's career, see Michel Antoine, *Le Gouvernement*, p. 221.

[12] BN, JF 1493, f. 91: Rouillé to Joly de Fleury, 14 July [1752], Compiègne; f. 2: same to same, 19 July [1752]. It is not clear when these negotiations began; as early as 2 April 1752 Joly de Fleury had sent Rouillé a memoir on denial of sacraments: BPR, LP 21, p. 289.

[13] BN, JF 1493, f. 2.

j'en suis fâché car cette Déclaration et ces termes n'avoient mérité l'impro-
bation de Mr Gilbert ny de moy, qui avons eu beaucoup de part à cette
Déclaration; mais l'usage qu'on a fait de ces expressions en les regardans
comme synonymes à la *règle de foy*, ont reveillé l'attention relativement
surtout à une Déclaration registrée dans un Lit de Justice.[14]

It had also been Cardinal de Fleury's view that the terms 'jugement de
l'église universelle en matière de doctrine' were not synonymous with a
règle de foi.[15] However, the contestants in the religious disputes had
thought differently. The problem was now that the clergy was certain to
insist upon references to the contentious *déclaration* of 1730 and to its
equally controversial definition of *Unigenitus*. Joly de Fleury offered to
prepare a draft that avoided these difficulties, and his offer was accepted.
On 29 July he submitted a text in which he cleverly paraphrased previous
déclarations and Rouillé's version.[16] The next day he gave the minister the
impression that the meetings of the commission could barely last out
another week.[17] Rouillé saw the King on 1 August and was authorised to
invite Joly de Fleury to discuss the question of a new *déclaration* with La
Rochefoucauld and eventually with Saulx-Tavannes, the archbishop of
Rouen.[18] Joly de Fleury asked that, on certain important points concerning the *déclaration*, the King should make his wishes known to the
prelates before the discussions began; in particular, he hoped that the
King would declare himself entitled to decide these points.[19] But it was

[14] *Ibid.*, f. 4: Joly de Fleury to Rouillé, 20 July 1752 (draft/copy); original emphasis. In 1730
Gilbert de Voisins was an *avocat général* and therefore a colleague of Joly de Fleury.

[15] AN, 257 AP 14 (Maurepas Papers): Correspondence of Cardinal de Fleury with the bishop
of Laon, III, Undated letters: Fleury to La Fare, the bishop of Laon:

> Vous traittés la constitution de règle de foy qui n'a été regardé [*sic*] que comme un
> jugement dogmatique de l'Eglise universelle par presque tous les évêques, et par le concile
> d'Embrun que comme *circa fidem* appartenant à la foy. En vérité vous allez nous exciter de
> nouveaux troubles et de nouvelles questions. C'est absolument vouloir mettre le feu partout
> et soulever les évêques les uns contre les autres. A quoi aboutiroit cette règle de foy qui
> seroit contredit [*sic*] et ne suffit-il pas que ce soit un jugement dogmatique?

Unfortunately this point is missed by J. H. Shennan in 'The political role of the *Parlement* of
Paris under Cardinal de Fleury', *English Historical Review*, lxxxi (1966), pp. 520–42.

[16] BPR, LP 21, p. 651: Joly de Fleury to Rouillé, 29 July 1752; for Joly de Fleury's draft see
BN, JF 1493, f. 59 *et seq.* (holograph) and ff. 302–8 (copy including the preamble). There is
a copy of Rouillé's text, revised in the light of Joly de Fleury's comments, on ff. 22–8. It is
interesting to note that Joly de Fleury consulted with the Abbé Guéret (1678–1758), *curé* of
Saint-Paul, who was a doctor of the Sorbonne and an eminent theologian; cf. BN, JF 1493,
f. 10.

[17] BPR, LP 21, p. 647: letter of 31 July 1752; see also BN, JF 1493, f. 96: Rouillé to Joly de
Fleury, 31 July [1752], Compiègne.

[18] BN, JF 1493, f. 101: Rouillé to Joly de Fleury, 1 Aug. 1752. Rouillé noted on his draft that
the letter had been approved by the King and read out to Machault before it was sent off:
BPR, LP 21, p. 47.

[19] BPR, LP 21, p. 51: Joly de Fleury to Rouillé, 1 Aug. 1752; and BN, JF 1493, f. 103: same
to same, 2 Aug. 1752 (draft/copy).

not the King's intention to adopt this course, as Rouillé explained to Joly de Fleury:

> . . . *je ne croy pas qu'il convienne de faire entendre comme vous le proposés à M. le Cal de la Rochefoucault de la part du Roy qu'elle peut être son intention* sur les quatres articles dont vous faittes mention, parceque si le Roy s'en expliquoit précisément, touttes les questions se trouveroient décidées par son autorité, et il ne pourroit plus être question de négociation, ou du moins elle n'auroit plus pour objet que la rédaction et l'exéution de la loy.[20]

The King wished to be impartial. Nevertheless, by not fixing a common ground for the negotiations, he seriously weakened their chances of success.

The King hoped that a *déclaration* could be sent to the *Parlement* before the start of the vacation on 7 September, and that it would make a decision on the *requête* of the *agents généraux* unnecessary.[21] But the discussions between La Rochefoucauld and Joly de Fleury did not begin until 22 August partly because of the horror and confusion created at court when the Dauphin caught smallpox and partly because of the King's own delay in writing to the cardinal.[22] Joly de Fleury sounded La Rochefoucauld as to the advisability of a new law and then steered the discussion to the main points of his own draft, of which he showed him only an extract. Though generally sympathetic to the plan, the cardinal had grave doubts about its chances of success, but he copied down the main points of the draft in order to discuss them with the archbishop of Rouen.[23] After the meeting of the commission on 26 August he asked Joly de Fleury to receive them both the next day. But La Rochefoucauld was not well and took himself off the the country instead, leaving the courtly Saulx-Tavannes to hold his own in face of the prolix and erudite Joly de Fleury. Saulx-Tavannes voiced the objections that other bishops might have to the proposals.[24] Although they were moderate, well intentioned and conciliatory, the two prelates were not

---

[20] BN, JF 1493, f. 107ᵛ: Rouillé to Joly de Fleury, 4 Aug. 1752. The passage in italics is underlined in the original.

[21] Rouillé to Joly de Fleury (see note 18 above).

[22] BN, JF 1493, f. 134: Joly de Fleury to Rouillé, 22 Aug. 1752 (draft/copy). Rouillé gave the King the draft of a letter for the cardinal on 9 August: in it the King said that he was convinced of the need for a new law and that La Rochefoucauld was to discuss various drafts with Joly de Fleury (BPR, LP 21, p. 89). But the King did not send it off until 18 or 19 August; see BN, JF 1493, ff. 131–2: Rouillé to Joly de Fleury, 18 Aug. 1752; and La Rochefoucauld's reply to the King in BPR, LP 21, p. 115: letter of 20 Aug. The King's delay caused the cardinal some embarrassment: he had been told unofficially on 8 August that the King contemplated a *déclaration*, and he suspected that it was the King's intention that he discuss the matter with Joly de Fleury. But he could make no *démarche* until he heard from the King, and so he and Joly de Fleury had to exchange knowing glances in the meantime.

[23] Joly de Fleury to Rouillé (see note 22 above); and BN, JF 1493, ff. 135–8: 'Ce que j'ay dit à Mr Le Cal de la Rochefoucault le 22 Août 1752' (in the hand of Joly de Fleury).

[24] BPR, LP 21, p. 127: Joly de Fleury to Rouillé, 28 Aug. 1752.

Table 3 *Cases of* refus de sacrements *outstanding at the* Parlement

First brought to attention of Parlement	Persons refused the sacraments	Parish (Diocese)
17 May 1752	Barbe Dufossé	Abbeville (Amiens)
	Marie Dupuis, Anne Blanchard, Marie-Anne Coutilleur, Philippe Branche, Marie-Philippe Branche, Nicolle Piquet	Joigny (Sens)
	Jean Drouet	Loos (Sens)
6 June 1752	Reine Auget	Chanvres (Sens)
	Sr Allot	Aulray (Amiens)
16 June 1752	Jean Fourd	Monsaujon (Langres)
	Anne Gauthier, Barbe Chillon	Tonnère (Langres)
30 June 1752	Dlle Moreau	Saint-Hilaire, Sens (Sens)
	several parishioners	Le Plessis-Rozainvilliers (Amiens)

Source: AN, L 20, no. 5: 'Table et fait Général Concernant les Refus de Sacremens'; this list is possibly in the hand of Louis Adrien Le Paige.

prepared to go against the wishes of a majority of the episcopate. It was clear that the clergy's objections had to be discussed more fully and that a new law would not be ready before the *Parlement* broke up for the vacation on 7 September.

The existence of the commission had led the *Parlement* and the clergy to exercise some restraint for much of the summer. The *gens du roi* were able to get away with reporting back to the assembly of the chambers that they had not yet completed their investigations and proceedings in nine outstanding cases of denial of sacraments (see Table 3).[25] Only in the case of the *grand vicaire* and two *portes-dieu* of Saint-Etienne-du-Mont who allowed a priest who had accepted *Unigenitus* to die without the sacrament did the *Parlement* pass sentence, and even then leniently and *in absentia*. (See Table 4 for a breakdown of the voting figures in the debate of 19 August.)[26] The only serious incidents occurred shortly before the magistrates were due to begin their holidays. They arose in consequence of an *arrêt du conseil* of 23 August which quashed proceedings taken by the officers of the *bailliage* of Tours against the *curé* of Saint-Pierre-le-Puellier. The *curé* had refused to give the last rites to a dying priest. The lay courts could not order a priest to administer the sacraments: they could only order him to put an end to the

25 BUP, Archives d'Argenson, CA 59: [Titon] to the Comte d'Argenson, undated letters, no. 11: '18 [Aug. 1752] vendredi'.
26 BUP, CA 28/IV: Jean-Omer Joly de Fleury to the Comte d'Argenson, 18 and 19 Aug. 1752; CA 59: [Titon] to the Comte d'Argenson, undated letters, no. 8, '19 août, samedy' [1752].

Table 4 *Opinions expressed at the assembly of the chambers on 19 August 1752 with their reduction to form the* arrêt

(In deciding the fate of the *grand vicaire* (Brunet) and of the two *portes-dieu* (Fressinet and Merisset) of Saint-Etienne-du-Mont who had refused the sacrament to Sr Coffin, a priest, the *parlementaires* arrived at the *arrêt* after taking opinions four times.)

No.	Avis	No. of votes	Arrêt
	On Brunet		
	Conclusions des gens du roi: à le blâmer, et à 10 livres d'amende		
1	à l'avis des conclusions	44	
2	au même avis, et à imprimer, publier, et afficher l'arrêt et après le jugement des trois	?	
3	à le bannir et 10 livres d'amende	75	*
4	à le bannir et amende honorable sèche et 200 livres envers le roi	1	
	On Fressinet		
	Conclusions: admonesté et 3 livres d'aumône		
1	à l'avis des conclusions	27	
2	à le blâmer et 10 livres d'amende	85	*
3	à le blâmer et 3 livres d'amende	1	
4	à le bannir 3 ans et 10 livres d'amende	26	
	On Merisset		
	Conclusions: à être ordonné par la cour ce qu'elle verra être à faire par raison		
1	à l'avis des conclusions	0	
2	au plus informé dans les 6 mois	49	
3	au blâme	31	
4	à l'admonition et à 3 livres d'aumône	45	*
5	au plus ample informé dans les 3 mois	2	
	On the printing of the *arrêt*		
1	lu, publié et affiché	1	
2	avis à l'imprimer et afficher	m.n.†	*
3	avis que non	1	
4	avis à imprimer, publier, et afficher	1	
5	avis à envoyer des copies	2	

Source: BUP, CA 59: [Titon] to the Comte d'Argenson, undated letters, no. 8, '19 août, samedy' [1752].
* Opinion that prevailed and formed the *arrêt*; figures not available.
† *Maximo numero*; total figure not given.

'public scandal' and thus force him indirectly into administering the sacraments. The officers of the *bailliage* had to enforce the *arrêt de règlement* of 18 April, but they lacked the legal finesse of their superiors in Paris; they had bluntly ordered the *curé* to administer the sacraments and, upon his refusal, they had simply suspended him. The *arrêt du conseil* did not just quash these indelicate proceedings, but also passed judgement in a peremptory, though confused, manner on the whole question of denial of sacraments.[27] This strange pronouncement, which was known to be the chancellor's handiwork, may have been intended only to silence a lower court: Rouillé later made an oblique reference to its not having 'succeeded'.[28] The fact remained that the *arrêt du conseil* was completely at variance with the King's professed intention of reserving his judgement on the issue of denial of sacraments. *Avocat général* Joly de Fleury complained vehemently to the Comte d'Argenson:

> que le conseil du roy prenne la résolution de casser la procédure de tours [*sic*], je crois qu'il n'y a rien de mieux, soit parce que les Juges ont fait ce que le parlement même croit ne pas être en droit de faire en ordonnant d'administrer [les sacrements], soit parceque le prestre refusé est dans une vilaine posture qui a même indisposé fort le général du parlement contre luy.
>
> Mais que celuy qui rédige en cette matière les décisions respectables du conseil décide par un seul mot ce qui [*sic*] depuis 6. mois le roy évite de décider, et des questions auxquelles plus habiles que luy trouvent des difficultés du premier ordre, en vérité, monsieur, c'est un Phénomène pour lequel notre langue n'a pas encor [*sic*] de nom.[29]

Moreover, because it appeared in print, the *arrêt du conseil* seemed calculated to give offence to the *parlementaires*, and they reacted accordingly. On 29 August they decided to ask the King to prorogue the *Parlement*, a request that was refused a few days later.[30] In their irritation they ordered the burning of a recent clandestine edition of the bishops' second letter to the King on 20 August, though the same edition had already been suppressed by an *arrêt du conseil* three days before; and they condemned the terms of the letter as much as its illicit publication.[31] *Avocat général* Joly de

---

27 *Ibid.*: [Titon] to the Comte d'Argenson, undated letters, no. 11: 'vendredy 18' [Aug. 1752]; AN, E 2313, for the *minute* of the *arrêt du conseil* of 23 Aug. 1752; and Luynes, *Mém.*, xii, p. 163 (on the Tours affair).

28 BN, JF 1493, f. 146: letter to Joly de Fleury, 31 Aug. [1752].

29 BUP, CA 28/IV: letter of 28 Aug. 1752. President Ogier (a former *parlementaire* who acted as an intermediary between Rouillé and Joly de Fleury in the negotiations over the new law) also judged the Government's action severely: 'on n'a jamais plus complèttement [*sic*] jugé sans connoissance de cause, puisqu'on Décide la peine trop forte sans avoir vu les informations': letter to Joly de Fleury in BN, JF 1493, f. 143ᵛ, Aug. 1752.

30 *Les Remontrances du Parlement de Paris au xviiiᵉ siècle*, ed. Jules Flammermont (Paris, 1888–98), 3 vols. (hereafter referred to as Flammermont, *Rems.*), i, p. 505; BUP, CA 28/IV: Jean-Omer Joly de Fleury to the Comte d'Argenson, 28 and 29 Aug. 1752. Durey de Meinières told Ogier that the *Parlement* had asked for a prorogation because rumours of a *déclaration* had caused disquiet: BN, JF 1493, f. 147: Ogier to Joly de Fleury, 31 Aug. 1752. Fears in the *Parlement* about the *déclaration* had probably been increased by the appearance of the *arrêt du conseil*. The Government would have granted the request for a prorogation if it had wanted a *déclaration* to be registered before the start of the vacation. The *Parlement* registered the usual commission setting up a vacation chamber, on 1 September.

31 BN, JF 1683, ff. 8 *et seq.* (note in the hand of the *procureur général*); BN, JF 1482, f. 148: undated and unsigned letter from D'Ormesson to the *procureur général* or to Jean-Omer Joly de Fleury; for the text of the *arrêt* of the *Parlement* of 30 August, see Luynes, *Mém.*, xii, p. 213.

Fleury deplored this measure and told the Comte d'Argenson that it compromised the King's authority.[32] Then, on 1 September, the *parlementaires* took up the question of the proceedings at Tours, where the zeal of the officers of the *bailliage* had been cut short by the *arrêt du conseil*, which those officers had been made to transcribe in their records. The *gens du roi* were now in possession of the documents in the case and of a *procès-verbal* relating to the transcription, and they recommended to the *Parlement* that remonstrances should be made about the *arrêt du conseil*. But the *parlementaires* brushed aside this recommendation and evoked the case in order to handle it themselves.[33] They then ordered the arrest of the *curé*.

These measures alarmed the archbishop of Paris. Beaumont was still hoping to bring out a spirited pastoral instruction before the *Parlement* went on holiday. His text had been ready since at least the middle of July.[34] At the beginning of August there was a rumour that the archbishop had made arrangements with two printers, though, in any case, he had a press of his own.[35] The Dauphin's illness had intervened, though his recovery gave the archbishop an opportunity to issue a pastoral instruction on 27 August, when a *Te Deum* was held at Notre-Dame. A few days before the service the *procureur général* voiced his fears to the Comte de Saint-Florentin. The minister reassured him:

> ... je suis persuadé que M. l'archevêque de Paris a trop de prudence pour que son mandement ne soit pas mesuré ainsi qu'il doit l'estre Et qu'il y risque rien qui s'écarte de l'objet qui y donne lieu.[36]

Saint-Florentin's prediction proved correct, for Beaumont's pastoral instruction on that occasion was uncontroversial.[37] Perhaps the Government had already taken steps to prevent the archbishop from publishing the pastoral instruction on which his heart was set. According to one document, this instruction contained a stipulation that those who refused to regard *Unigenitus* as a rule of faith would be excommunicated, 'nonobstant tous actes de tribunaux Laïcs à ce contraires'. The archbishop also regarded as null and void 'tous les jugements Laïcs qui peuvent troubler

---

The bishop's second letter appeared in print on 26 August: E. J. F. Barbier, *Chronique de la régence et du règne de Louis XV (1718–1763), ou Journal de Barbier* (Paris, 1866), 8 vols. (hereafter Barbier, *Journal*), v, p. 278. The chancellor hastily obtained the King's permission to suppress the edition; see FL, Rosanbo MSS, 1/2/31: Lamoignon to Louis XV, with the King's reply in the margin; and AN, E 2318, f. 268 for the *minute* of the *arrêt du conseil* of 27 August.

[32] BUP, CA 28/IV: Jean-Omer Joly de Fleury to the Comte d'Argenson, 1 Sept. 1752.

[33] *Ibid.*

[34] See p. 110 above and letter referred to in Chapter 4, note 108.

[35] BUP, CA 28/IV: Jean-Omer Joly de Fleury to the Comte d'Argenson, 29 July and 1 Aug. 1752.

[36] AN, O¹ 396, f. 271, no. 1116: Saint-Florentin to the *procureur général*, 24 Aug. 1752, copy.

[37] Barbier, *Journal*, v, p. 275.

notre juridiction spirituelle'.[38] Be that as it may, Beaumont submitted the text of a pastoral instruction to the King, possibly on 29 August when he had a fairly long audience.[39] The King had not returned it. On 2 September the archbishop wanted to go to Versailles the next day to retrieve it and to protest, on behalf of his fellow bishops, against the terms used by the *Parlement* in its *arrêt* ordering the clandestine edition of their letter to be burned. When he consulted D'Argenson about his intention, the minister curtly told him not to come.[40]

The Government had already decided to quash the two recent decisions of the *Parlement* and *arrêts du conseil* for that purpose were issued on 3 September.[41] When asked before the assembled chambers whether they had executed the *arrêt* of 1 September (concerning the Tours affair), the *gens du roi* hinted at the obstacles in their path. *Avocat général* Joly de Fleury wrote:

> Nous avons fait connoître que nous avions des ordres de n'en rien faire, et dès ce moment on a été peu curieux d'en venir à l'Explication. Je vois qu'on glissera peut-être pardessus.[42]

Once again, the impending vacation made it impossible for the *Parlement* to take any further action immediately. The *parlementaires* decided to hold an important debate on 29 November, when they intended to consider what their *arrêté* of 6 September ominously described as

> les mesures necessaires à prendre pour obvier aux principes que l'on voudroit introduire et aux conséquences des actes qui s'en sont ensuivis contre l'indépendance de la couronne et l'autorité du roi sur tous ses sujets, tant ecclésiastiques que laïques, de quelque qualité et condition qu'ils soient et conserver avec honneur dans les sièges royaux inférieurs l'administration de la justice et les maximes par lesquels ils ont contribué à soutenir l'autorité royale par celle des lois dans les temps où elle a été le plus violemment attaquée . . .[43]

The same *arrêté* gave those *parlementaires* who were appointed to the vacation chamber the awkward task of having to execute the *arrêts* of the *Parlement* by taking 'whatever steps their zeal might suggest to them'; for these

---

[38] AN, L 20, no. 4: 'Dispositif du mandement de l'archevêque de Paris du 22 août 1752 dont la planche fut rompue par ordre du Roy'. The entry in the AN catalogue claims that this item comes from the Joly de Fleury papers.

[39] Luynes, *Mém.*, xii, p. 131.

[40] AN, 422 AP 1 (Comte d'Argenson's Papers): Beaumont to the Comte d'Argenson, 2 Sept. 1752, with d'Argenson's note of his reply.

[41] According to Philip Yorke's informant, Bousquet de Colomiers, a *comité* met first under the chairmanship of the chancellor on 31 August; on that occasion Lamoignon was criticised by the ministers for the *arrêt du conseil* in the Tours affair: BL, Add. MSS 35,445, f. 310: 10 Sept. 1752. The decision to quash the *arrêts* of the *Parlement* was probably reached at a meeting of the council at Choisy on 2 September; cf. BUP, CA 28/IV: Jean-Omer Joly de Fleury to the Comte d'Argenson, 2 Sept. 1752.

[42] *Ibid.*: same to same, 4 Sept. 1752, 'après midy'.

[43] Flammermont, *Rems.*, i, pp. 505–6.

arrêts (especially the *arrêt de règlement*) remained binding upon those who were subject to the jurisdiction of the *Parlement*. In effect, the *Parlement* had given the Government three months in which to produce a new law.

The *parlementaires* dispersed to the country, but the commission continued to meet. Joly de Fleury had succeeded in dragging out its proceedings. He continued to read out lengthy *mémoires* that seemed calculated to provoke Cardinal de Soubise to make frequent interruptions, during which Trudaine came to Joly de Fleury's help with discursive rejoinders. He completed the reading of a final *mémoire* on 13 September. The *commissaires* needed another meeting to discuss it and to reach a decision on the six points: Saturday, 13 September was out because Castanier d'Auriac had not attended previous meetings and was still laid up with gout; and nothing could be arranged for the following week because Saulx-Tavannes had to be in Rouen. The *commissaires* agreed that Cardinal de La Rochefoucauld should report to the King and state that, as they had not been told how they were to draft their decision on the six points, they believed that they ought not to put it in writing for the time being.[44] The King knew that their decision could not be unanimous and he did not press them for it at a time when it might have adverse effects. Moreover, he did not want the decision to affect Joly de Fleury's negotiations with the two prelates on the subject of the proposed *déclaration*.

La Rochefoucauld and Saulx-Tavannes were now in possession of the full text of Joly de Fleury's draft *déclaration*, for which they showed little enthusiasm when they discussed it at some length with him on 11 September. Their main objections concerned articles 1, 8 and 10. Over article 1, which gave a definition of *Unigenitus*, they questioned the statement that the bull had been accepted by the French clergy subject to the pastoral instruction of 1714 and to the official interpretation of the bull given at the General Assembly of the Clergy of France held in 1720. They did not deny that it was the close connection between the bull and these two pronouncements that had finally induced Cardinal de Noailles and other recalcitrant bishops to accept *Unigenitus*. Nor did they deny that a person was entitled to regard the bull solely in the light of those pronouncements. But they maintained that *Unigenitus* had been accepted as it stood and that its link with the pronouncements had always been purely tacit.

In a strict sense they were right. It was true that, out of deference to the Pope, the bishops had not openly qualified their acceptance of the bull at the extraordinary assembly of the bishops in 1714. However, many bishops had accepted *Unigenitus* only because they were allowed to relate it to the

---

[44] BN, JF 1493, f. 159: Joly de Fleury to Rouillé, 10 Sept. 1752 (draft/copy); and same to same, 13 Sept. 1752 (9 p.m.).

pastoral instruction and later to the *Explications* of 1720. The pastoral instruction was the outcome of negotiations begun in October 1713. On 22 January 1714 a commission headed by Cardinal de Rohan had proposed to the bishops that the assembly should adopt five resolutions: the first three contained a straightforward acceptance of *Unigenitus*, and the last two stipulated that a pastoral instruction should be drawn up which would be published by each bishop for the guidance of his flock. The *commissaires* had implied that these proposals would serve to link the bull tacitly to the interpretation of it which would be provided by the pastoral instruction. Cardinal de Noailles, archbishop of Paris, was one of nine bishops who had moved that the acceptance of the bull be deferred until the pastoral instruction had been approved. But the commission's proposals had been adopted, and so later was the draft of the pastoral instruction. The nine bishops had refused to sign the *procès-verbal* of the assembly's meetings. By appealing to a future General Council of the Church they were able to suspend the effects of the bull. In 1717 the Regent had asked the Pope to interpret *Unigenitus*, but the Pope refused. Consequently the French bishops had drawn up the *Explications* of 1720; these were not recognised by the Pope but they led Noailles and the other recalcitrant bishops to submit to *Unigenitus*; as Daguesseau observed, this new body of doctrine 'fait entendre d'une manière fort douce à quoi se réduit l'effet de l'acceptation'. Both Joly de Fleury and Daguesseau recognised that the bishops' acceptance of *Unigenitus* was only tacitly linked to the pastoral instruction and to the *Explications*. Moreover, the Pope's unwillingness to sanction the latter remained a complicating factor.[45]

Despite the legal and ecclesiastical position, Joly de Fleury was understandably vexed, however, that La Rochefoucauld and Saulx-Tavannes were not prepared to remove all controversy by countenancing a new law that defined *Unigenitus* in the sense in which they themselves, together with other moderates in the clergy and the *Parlement*, understood it. In the same first article of his draft Joly de Fleury had omitted all reference to the *déclaration* of 1730 and to its definition of *Unigenitus* as a *jugement de l'église universelle en matière de doctrine*: and the article forbad the use of the term *règle de foi* with reference to the bull. But, as Rouillé had anticipated, the two

---

[45] For these details, see Joly de Fleury's historical account: BN, JF 1493, f. 173; his unpublished memoirs for the years 1716–20: AN, 342 AP 2, ff. 81–90, 109–10, 136–45; and G. Rech, 'D'Aguesseau et le Jansénisme', in *Le Chancelier Henri-François D'Aguesseau, Limoges 1668–Fresnes 1751: journées d'étude tenues à Limoges à l'occasion du bicentenaire de sa mort (octobre 1951)*, ed. G. Rech (Limoges, 1953), pp. 124–9. The accounts in A. Le Roy, *La France et Rome de 1700 à 1715* (Paris, 1892), pp. 458–548; J. H. Shennan, 'The political role of the *Parlement* of Paris, 1715–23', *The Historical Journal*, viii, 2 (1965), pp. 179–200; and James D. Hardy, *Judicial politics in the Old Régime: the Parlement of Paris during the Regency* (Baton Rouge, La., 1967), pp. 51–70, 148–62, are unsatisfactory.

prelates wanted to see a mention of the 1730 *déclaration*, a reference to at least one of its two definitions of the bull – *loy de l'église et de l'état* – and the omission of the clause about *règle de foy*. They also raised difficulties over article 8, which circumscribed denial of sacraments, on the ground of its being a vindication of the *arrêt de règlement*, and they asked that it should contain a reference to articles 30 and 34 of an edict of 1695 which set down the rights of ecclesiastical jurisdictions.[46] On article 10, which circumscribed the use of confession certificates, Le Rochefoucauld and Saulx-Tavannes argued that the commission had not yet come to a decision on the matter and expressed their own doubts about whether the King had the right to prescribe to bishops and priests how to administer the sacraments.

Joly de Fleury sent a full report of his discussions to Rouillé, adding the following comment:

> Rien n'est plus aimable que les deux Prélats; ils veulent le bien; ils sentent toutes les suites de la division présente; ils redoutent le schisme; ils en aperçoivent toutes les conséquences; mais ils sont Evêques, ils ont des Collègues; Je ne cesse de leur dire qu'il n'y a aucun bruit dans leur [*sic*] Dyocèse [*sic*]; qu'il ne s'agit que d'autoriser par l'autorité du Roy, la conduite qu'ils tiennent eux mêmes; qu'il ne s'agit point de ce que pensent les autres, mais de ce qu'ils pensent sur l'objet actuel ... malgré ce que je puis dire sur chaque article, sur chaque difficulté; on avance toujours pour objection l'inutilité, le peu de succès, l'archevêque de Paris qu'on n'approuve pas cependant, mais sans presqu'aucune espérance de le ramener.[47]

To his son, the *avocat général*, he expressed concern lest the prelates should wish the King to consult the archbishop of Paris; the archbishop could be expected to raise insurmountable objections over the draft *déclaration*. The *avocat général* discussed this prospect with his brother-in-law, Saint-Contest, the minister of foreign affairs, who was staying with him in the country. He tried to reassure his father:

> L'Idée de Consulter l'archevêque parût à mon beaufrère inconcevable; quoy parceque le roy veut bien consultés [*sic*] Deux Prélats impartiaux sur les veues d'une semblable déclaration, le Clergé prétendra que L'archevêque de Paris doit L'estre également; Si c'est comme archevêque de Paris, jamais son siège ne luy donne cette prérogative, si c'est comme ayant à sa suite d'autres Evêques dont il gouverne les suffrages, le roy ne doit pas reconnoistre un concert de ce genre qui sent L'esprit de Cabale et voilà tout.[48]

---

[46] For the text of articles 30 and 34 of the edict of April 1695, see *Recueil général des anciennes lois françaises depuis l'an 420 jusqu'à la Révolution de 1789*, ed. F. A. Isambert *et al.* (Paris, 1821–33), XX, pp. 252–3.

[47] BN, JF 1493, f. 162: Joly de Fleury to Rouillé, 12 Sept. 1752 (draft/copy); see also f. 164: same to same, 13 Sept. 1752 (draft/copy); and ff. 168–82: a draft of his *mémoire* on the discussions.

[48] *Ibid.*, ff. 204–5: Jean-Omer Joly de Fleury to his father, 16 Sept. 1752 from Epône.

The King moved to Fontainebleau on 26 September after a pleasant round of parties at Choisy and at Madame de Pompadour's place at Crécy.[49] Rouillé placed before him the report on the discussions and a final draft of the *déclaration*, to which Joly de Fleury had made some of the amendments requested by La Rochefoucauld and Saulx-Tavannes. The King knew that any new law would have to be drafted formally by the chancellor. It is possible that he had been reluctant to approach Lamoignon on the matter, probably because the chancellor had shown himself to be fairly unaccommodating.[50] But on 3 October, Rouillé went to Lamoignon's country-house at Malesherbes on orders from the King to show him the draft and to sound him on his views about it.[51] Lamoignon's initial reaction to the draft was seemingly favourable. But while he deplored the practice of denying the sacrament to those who declined to submit to *Unigenitus* or failed to produce confession certificates, he doubted whether the King was entitled to decide these questions. Rouillé left the draft with him, and they probably intended to discuss the matter again after Lamoignong had seen the King at Fontainebleau.[52] Valuable time was lost in these belated consultations.

The Tours affair again threatened to bring matters to a head between the *Parlement* and the archbishop of Tours. Despite informal assurances given to President de Novion (who presided over the vacation chamber) by the chancellor, the *curé* of Saint-Pierre-le Puellier had been allowed to resume his duties in the parish.[53] The chamber ordered his arrest on 27 September. But the *gens du roi* were in no hurry to acquaint the officers of the *bailliage* of this decision, and their delay enabled the archbishop of Tours, Rosset de Fleury, to whisk the *curé* off to safety in his own coach.[54] On 30 September, the decision of the vacation chamber was quashed by an *arrêt du conseil*, which Saint-Florentin had hurriedly obtained from Lamoignon, who was in the country. The King personally insisted that the new *arrêt du conseil* should include a reference to the earlier and controversial one

---

[49] Luynes, *Mém.*, xii, p. 161; BN, n.a.fr. 23621, f. 149.

[50] Cf. Lamoignon's views on the draft of a *déclaration* which was probably communicated to him in early September; FL, Tocqueville MSS, 9/71.

[51] *Ibid.*, 9/61: Rouillé to Lamoignon, 2 Oct. 1752. Rouillé proposed that his brother-in-law Pallu, a councillor of state, should accompany him: Pallu had possibly assisted him in preparing drafts of the *déclaration*.

[52] BN, JF 1493, f. 232: Rouillé to Joly de Fleury, 3 Oct. [1752]. Two days after his meeting with Rouillé Lamoignon received a formal request for his opinion on a number of points concerning a possible *déclaration*: FL, Tocqueville MSS, 9/61: 'Mémoire que j'ay reçu le Jeudy 5 8bre 1752'. It appears that Lamoignon moved to Fontainebleau around 8 October: D'Argenson, ed. Rathery, vii, p. 320.

[53] For the assurances given to Potier de Novion by Lamoignon, see BUP, CA 28/IV: Jean-Omer Joly de Fleury to the Comte d'Argenson, 28 Sept. 1752; and also D'Argenson, ed. Rathery, vii, p. 319.

[54] *Ibid.*, p. 318.

of 23 August.[55] At a meeting on 3 October the vacation chamber prudently referred the question of the misconduct of the *curé* to a full assembly of the *Parlement*. The *gens du roi* had explained their dilatoriness by referring to the *arrêt du conseil*, which, they said, called for remonstrances: 'tant sur le fond que sur la forme'. The vacation chamber made difficulties but was content to remind the *gens du roi* of an edict of 1493 concerning the duties of their office.[56] Someone, however, expressed fears that the example of the *curé* might be followed by the other priests whose cases were pending before the *Parlement*. Consequently the vacation chamber issued an *arrêt* to remind those priests that the law did not allow them to exercise their duties.[57]

Beaumont protested against the decision, and his letter to the Comte d'Argenson read once more like an ultimatum:

> ... vous sçavés, monsieur, que c'est par respect pour le roy que j'ay demeuré jusqu'icy dans le silence, mais que les choses sont poussées si loin, que ma conscience ne me permettroit plus de le garder, si Le roy ne jugeoit pas à propos d'employer incessamment son autorité pour réprimer les entreprises du parlement, et que je serois obligé de supplier sa majesté de me rendre la parole que je luy ay donné au sujet de la publication de mon mandement.

Moreover, Beaumont had sensed what was taking place at court, and he warned the minister that the episcopate would not be satisfied with a law that was prepared by Joly de Fleury, whom he regarded as a prop of Jansenism.[58] The archbishop's attitude could have a decisive influence at a time when, according to one well-informed observer, the bishops did not know whether or not they should state their position before the new law appeared.[59] Beaumont was again persuaded not to issue his pastoral letter. There are signs, however, that the King now felt it necessary to seek his opinion on points that appeared to be connected with a possible *déclaration*.[60]

55 AN, O¹ 396, f. 305, no. 1190: Saint-Florentin to Lamoignon, 28 Sept. 1752 (copy); AN, E 2313, pp. 517–20: for the *minute* of the *arrêt du conseil* of 30 September.
56 BS, MS 800, ff. 250 *et seq.*: 'Récit de Mr. le Président de Novion'.
57 D'Argenson, ed. Rathery, vii, p. 317. The contemporary legal authority, Dénisart, cited the *arrêt* of 3 October 1752 as setting a legal precedent; for while it reaffirmed the law concerning ecclesiastics who continued to exercise their duties while under decrees of *ajournement personnel* or of *prise de corps*, it also declared null and void all acts performed by such ecclesiastics: see *Collection de décisions nouvelles et de notions relatives à la jurisprudence actuelle* (4th edn, Paris, 1763), i, p. 390 (no. 5).
58 AN, 422 AP 1: letter of 8 Oct. 1752.
59 BN, n.a.fr. 23619 (Collection Bauffremont: Loménie de Brienne Papers), f. 63, no. 122: Abbé de Villevieille to Abbé de Brienne, 11 Oct. 1752. The Abbé de Villevieille, abbot of the Cistercian house at Valence (Poitiers) since 1744 and later a canon of the cathedral of Albi, was a close friend of Loménie de Brienne, the future principal minister and cardinal. His revenues from Valence amounted to 2,300 *livres*. He later acted as informant to Gualterio, who was sent to France to replace Durini as papal nuncio in 1754.
60 AN, 422 AP 1: Beaumont to the Comte d'Argenson, 11 Oct. 1752. In this letter Beaumont denied that he had said in a previous communication, unfortunately missing, that the

The commission resumed its labours on 7 October. But Trudaine failed to appear; he remained at Montigny, his country-house, and later claimed that La Rochefoucauld's notification of the meeting had not reached him in time. In a letter to Joly de Fleury written a few days later, however, he made the curious statement that the King had not been concerned at his absence. It seems that Trudaine also did not attend the last meeting of the commission on 14 October.[61] It may be that he stayed away in order to delay a decision on the six points: he was certainly of the opinion that the King should settle the matter without awaiting the advice of the *commissaires*.[62] If so, his mysterious absences did not prevent La Rochefoucauld from asking the other *commissaires* for their verdict. At the first meeting, the four prelates outvoted the three magistrates on the first five points. On one of the points Bidé de La Grandville tended to share the opinion of the four prelates. Joly de Fleury thought Trudaine's presence would have resulted in an evenly split vote.[63] At the second meeting the voting on the sixth point was probably the same as before. La Rochefoucauld had already received the summons from Fontainebleau; he saw the King there on 20 October and probably gave him an account of the result.[64]

It is difficult to piece together the sequence of events that took place at Fontainebleau in the last fortnight of October. It seems that Lamoignon submitted his own draft of the *déclaration* around 16 October and that a modified version of it was handed over to Cardinal de La Rochefoucauld by the King.[65] But Joly de Fleury's draft was still under consideration on

bishops could pronounce on what he calls 'les intérêts civils', a remark which seems to imply that he had been asked for his views on a matter connected with the *déclaration*.

[61] BN, JF 1495, f. 9: Trudaine to Joly de Fleury, 11 Oct. 1752, Montigny; f. 5; Joly de Fleury to Trudaine, undated (but, on internal evidence, written between 7 and 10 October), copy/draft. La Rochefoucauld wanted to hold the last meeting on 14 October, before the first meeting of the council at Fontainebleau; Trudaine was apparently still at Montigny that day.

[62] *Ibid.*: Trudaine to Joly de Fleury, 14 Oct. 1752, Montigny.

[63] *Ibid.* 1493, f. 233: Joly de Fleury to Rouillé, 7 Oct. [1752], copy/draft.

[64] BN, n.a.fr. 23619, f. 164, no. 125: Villevieille to Loménie de Brienne, 20 Oct. 1752 (copy); Luynes, *Mém.*, xii, p. 174. The cardinal reached Fontainebleau on 17 or 18 October: BN, JF 1493, f. 252: Ogier to Joly de Fleury, 21 Oct. 1752 (postscript). Bousquet de Colomiers wrote on 27 October that the *commissaires* had made their report to the King: BL, Add. MSS 35,445, f. 337. Shortly afterwards Philip Yorke's informant was sent to the Bastille (see Appendix A).

[65] FL, Tocqueville MSS, 9/63: 'Nouveau projet rectifié, 1752' (and for earlier drafts in Lamoignon's hand: *ibid.*, 9/69); FL, Rosanbo MSS, 1/2/34: Lamoignon to the King, 5 Nov. 1752. On 16 October Rouillé had an important conversation with an unnamed person on the subject of the proposed *déclaration*, and he told Ogier to send a report of it to Joly de Fleury. From internal evidence it seems that the unnamed person was probably the chancellor and that some of the points made by him in the course of the conversation had already been overruled by the King, to whom he had just submitted his draft of the *déclaration*: BN, JF 1493, f. 249: Rouillé to Joly de Fleury, 17 Oct. 1752, and ff. 247-9; Ogier to Joly de Fleury, same date. Rumours were circulating about the possible removal of Lamoignon at this time; cf. D'Argenson, ed. Rathery, vii, pp. 319-20, 328 and 330.

24–25 October, when the chancellor presided over meetings of a committee of ministers where the four prelates of the commission haggled with Rouillé over its main points.[66] The prelates were probably backed by the chancellor when they again objected to the inclusion of a comprehensive definition of *Unigenitus* in the first article and cavilled about the King's right to lay down the law on confession certificates and denial of sacraments.[67] Whatever their own convictions might be, the prelates had chosen to stand by an episcopate that was under the influence of Beaumont and his followers. The disheartened Rouillé wrote to Joly de Fleury:

> Vous apprendrés, monsieur, que nos conférences avec les quatre Prélats n'ont pas produit l'effet que j'aurois désiré. Je suis persuadé qu'on se seroit aisément concilié si tout le clergé pensoit comm'eux mais je voy qu'on ne parviendra à aucune conciliation si mr l'arche. n'y veut pas concourir.[68]

Because no agreement was reached, the King decided to abandon Joly de Fleury's draft in favour of a revised version of Lamoignon's draft. He asked the prelates to attempt to persuade Beaumont into joining the commission before La Rochefoucauld formally submitted the new draft to the *commissaires* for their opinion.[69] The King foresaw that Beaumont would make difficulties and that the opinion of the *commissaires* would again not be unanimous, so he decided to proceed at the same time with the examination of *requête* of the *agents généraux* which was still in the hands of the *gens du roi*.[70] Du Four de Villeneuve, a *maître de requêtes*, was given the task of presenting a report on it before the *Conseil des dépêches*, and Trudaine, Gilbert de Voisins, Bidé de La Grandville, and Castanier d'Auriac were instructed to assist him.[71] The King wished the opinion of the *commissaires* on the draft *déclaration* and the report on the *requête* to be ready by 17

---

[66] BN, JF 1493, f. 256: Rouillé to Joly de Fleury, 25 Oct. 1752. The meeting was probably one of the *comités particuliers* (as opposed to the *comités généraux*) described by M. Antoine in 'Les Comités de ministres sous le règne de Louis XV', *Revue historique de droit français et étranger*, 4th series, xxix (1951), pp. 213–14.

[67] BN, JF 1493, f. 256: Rouillé to Joly de Fleury, 25 Oct. 1752; see also BN, n.a.fr. 23619, f. 65, no. 127: Villevieille to Loménie de Brienne, 1 Nov. 1752 (copy).

[68] BN, JF 1493, f. 262: Rouillé to Joly de Fleury, 28 Oct. 1752.

[69] FL, Rosanbo MSS, 1/2/34: Lamoignon to the King, 5 Nov. 1752; with the King's reply in the margin.

[70] BN, JF 1493, f. 262: Rouillé to Joly de Fleury, 28 Oct. 1752. The chancellor asked the *procureur général* to return the *requête* with the written opinion of the *gens du roi*; FL, Tocqueville MSS, 10/12 and 15: Lamoignon to the *procureur général*, 27 and 30 Oct. 1752. The *procureur général* complied with this request on 2 November (*ibid.*, 10/16); the opinion of the *gens du roi* was a copious document of 185 pages.

[71] For the procedure observed at the council, see Michel Antoine, 'Le Conseil des dépêches sous le règne de Louis XV', *Bibliothèque de l'Ecole des Chartes*, cxii (1954), p. 196. Du Four de Villeneuve is described as an 'homme juste et légal' in a curious list of councillors of state for 1779; see Tony Sauvel, 'Note sur les "Portraits" des membres du conseil du Roi (1662 et 1779)', *Revue historique de droit français et étranger*, 4th series, xlviii (1970), p. 252.

November[72] so that he could reach a decision before the *Parlement* held its debate twelve days later.

On 4 November the four prelates had dinner with the archbishop of Paris at Conflans, his country seat, and they invited him on behalf of the King to join the commission. Beaumont was probably faced with a difficult choice, as the well-informed Abbé de Villevieille indicated in a letter about the discussions:

> Il y a 2ux réponses à faire, l'une d'accepter, L'autre de ne vouloir en être qu'avec les 19. ou 22. Evêques qui ont signé la lettre au Roy; on agita la question contradictoirement, on ne prit aucun parti, les difficultés pour et contre ont arrêté, on se décidera au plutôt.[73]

The bishop of Laon offered to stand down to allow Beaumont to join the commission without upsetting the parity between ecclesiastics and magistrates.[74] The archbishop explained his position to the King in a private audience at Versailles on 10 November, and Louis XV did not insist on his joining the commission.[75] It is possible, however, that Beaumont undertook to abide by the recommendations of the commission, especially as he may have known that the four prelates had taken a firm stand over Joly de Fleury's draft *déclaration*.

The new text was shown to the *commissaires* on 9 November.[76] It represented a compromise between the views of Lamoignon and the prelates on the one hand and those of Joly de Fleury on the other. Lamoignon had carried one important point: the comprehensive definition of *Unigenitus* had been relegated to the preamble of the law. Lamoignon had a first been willing to forbid the use of the term *règle de foi* to describe *Unigenitus*, but in the final draft of article 3 he merely stated that the bull was not to be given 'd'autre titre et dénomination que celles que l'Eglise luy a données'.[77] In article 7 Lamoignon reaffirmed the edict of 1695 on ecclesiastical jurisdiction and interpreted its thirty-fourth article as meaning that all cases

---

[72] BN, JF 1496, f. 10: Joly de Fleury to Rouillé, 16 Nov. 1752 (copy/draft); FL, Tocqueville MSS, 10/47: Bidé de La Grandville to Lamoignon, 7 Nov. 1752.

[73] BN, n.a.fr. 23619, ff. 65–6, no. 129: Villevieille to Loménie de Brienne, 6 Nov. 1752 (copy).

[74] FL, Tocqueville MSS, 10/39; Bishop of Laon to Lamoignon, 9 Nov. 1752.

[75] FL, Rosanbo MSS, 1/2/34: Lamoignon to the King, 5 Nov. 1752, with the King's reply of 6 Nov. in the margin. The meticulous Luynes noted that the audience lasted thirty-four minutes; Luynes, *Mém.*, xii, p. 184.

[76] AN, K 698 (Gilbert de Voisins Papers), no. 154: copy of the final text; BN, JF 1496, f. 5: Joly de Fleury to Rouillé, 9 Nov. 1752 (draft/copy); FL, Tocqueville MSS, 10/48: Bidé de La Grandville to Lamoignon, 9 Nov. 1752: Joly de Fleury claimed to have no prior knowledge of the final text, though he failed to convince Bidé de La Grandville. The King had possibly delayed showing the draft to Joly de Fleury in an attempt to lure the archbishop of Paris into the commission with an assurance that the text had not yet been shown to the former *procureur général*; cf. the curious rôle of the Maréchal de Noailles on this occasion: BN, JF 1496, ff. 2–3.

[77] Cf. his first draft and his final draft: FL, Tocqueville MSS, 9/69, p. 2 and 9/63, p. 3.

arising from denial of sacraments with the exception of *cas privilégié*, which were crimes committed by ecclesiastics, and cases in breach of the laws of the Kingdom resulting in an *appel comme d'abus*, should go before the ecclesiastical courts.[78] A further proviso, which had probably not originated with the chancellor, had been added:

> sans préjudice à nos cours et juges de pourvoir par les autres voyes qu'ils estimeront convenables à la réparation du scandale et trouble à l'ordre et tranquillité publique qui auroit pu être causé à l'occasion dusd[it] refus.[79]

This important and wise proviso left the *Parlement* free to treat denial of sacraments as a breach of the peace. The chancellor had felt that, on the question of confession certificates, the King should be guided by the opinion of the *commissaires*, and in his draft of article 11 he had contented himself with directing the bishops to ensure that these certificates were used only in accordance with 'the rules of charity and prudence'.[80] But the opinion of the *commissaires* had not been unanimous and other influences had prevailed upon the King. In the final text, article 11 was borrowed from Joly de Fleury's draft and it ordered, though in measured terms, that the sick, if they were unable to produce confession certificates, should not be deprived of the sacraments.[81] The last article of the draft *déclaration* quashed all proceedings that had been taken over denial of sacraments: its necessity had been felt by Joly de Fleury as well as by the prelates.[82]

Cardinal de La Rochefoucauld called the first meeting of the *commissaires* to examine the draft on 9 November, but Trudaine again failed to appear and so it had to be postponed. The *commissaires* finally discussed the *déclaration* at length on 13, 14 and 15 November.[83] Bidé de La Grandville thought the articles on *Unigenitus* still threw doubt upon the *déclarations* of 1720 and 1730 and might occasion further controversy. Moreover, he drew

---

[78] AN, K 698, no. 154; *Recueil général des anciennes lois françaises*, ed. F. A. Isambert *et al.*, xx, pp. 252–3 for the text of the relevant articles of the edict of 1695; J. B. Dénisart, *Collection de décisions* (7th edn, Paris, 1771), i, p. 389, no. 1: 'on nomme *cas privilégié* [non seulement les crimes commis par les ecclésiastiques promus aux ordres sâcrés, qui méritent d'être punis de peines afflictives ou infamantes, mais encore tous les crimes qui peuvent faire infliger quelque peine, de la nature de celles qu'il n'est pas au pouvoir des juges d'église de prononcer]'; square brackets in original.

[79] AN, K 698, no. 154; it was added by Lamoignon to his final draft and appears as an amendment in another copy of the *déclaration* in his papers: FL, Tocqueville MSS, 9/63, p. 8 and 9/70, p. 3.

[80] FL, Tocqueville MSS, 9/63, p. 12; cf. BN, JF 1493, ff. 247–9: Ogier to Joly de Fleury, 17 Oct. 1752, item no. 5.

[81] AN, K 698, no. 154; see also the note attached to article 11 in FL, Tocqueville MSS, 9/70, p. 4; cf. BN, JF 1493, ff. 306–7 (article 10).

[82] AN, K 698, no. 154: article 12; it follows Lamoignon's text: FL, Tocqueville MSS, 9/63, p. 13; cf. article 11 in Joly de Fleury's draft *déclaration*: BN, JF 1493, ff. 308 *et seq.*

[83] FL, Rosanbo MSS, 1/2/34: Lamoignon to the King, 5 Nov. 1752; 1/2/35: same to same, 14 Nov. 1752 (copy); BN, JF 1496, f. 10; Joly de Fleury to Rouillé, 16 Nov. 1752 (draft/copy).

attention to the loophole in article 7 and he aptly remarked that it was difficult to interpret the edict of 1695 in a manner that left no possibility of dispute between lay and ecclesiastical courts. He thought the article on confession certificates might create problems; in the country, for instance, where it might be used to obtain the sacraments by those wishing to avoid confessions.[84] The prelates supported him and they repeated the clergy's point of view.[85] Although Joly de Fleury and Gilbert de Voisins (who replaced the gout-ridden Castanier d'Auriac) were not satisfied with the *déclaration*, they argued strongly in its favour.[86] They were unable to win the elusive Trudaine over to their side. Trudaine supported them when they claimed that the rights of the lay courts were not sufficiently established in article 7 and when they asserted that the King could pronounce on confession certificates. However, he no longer felt that the King should make such a pronouncement, and he now argued that the *déclaration* was useless, even dangerous, and that other means should be used to meet the situation.[87] La Rochefoucauld briskly wound up the discussions by asking the *commissaires* whether or not they were in favour of the *déclaration*: only two, Joly de Fleury and Gilbert de Voisins, were in favour.[88] The cardinal duly reported the result to the King on 17 November.[89] The King shelved the *déclaration* and fell back upon the expedient of an *arrêt du conseil* that would deal with the *requête* presented by the *agents généraux*.

Trudaine's attitude had probably reflected a quick shift in court or ministerial politics about which little is known. Before La Rochefoucauld wrote to notify him of the first meeting of the *commissaires*, Trudaine had written unconcernedly to Dufour de Villeneuve that he did not intend to be in Paris before 13 November and did not think the report on the *requête* could be presented to the royal council four days later. Bidé de La Grandville was puzzled by his conduct: 'car vous ne doutez pas', he confided to the chancellor, 'qu'il ne soit mieux informé que nous, et il me paroist étonnant que le Roy, paroissant avoir à cœur qu'on expédie si promptement, il paroisse si peu pressé'.[90] Nevertheless, when Trudaine

---

[84] FL, Tocqueville MSS, 10/1 *bis* (a formal report of the opinions expressed on each article of the proposed *déclaration*), pp. 1, 6, 14 and 11.

[85] *Ibid.*, pp. 5, 7 and 14.

[86] *Ibid.*, pp. 1, 3, 6, 8 and 14. Joly de Fleury commented extensively upon the *déclaration* in a document that was handed in with the formal report when the King saw the cardinal on 17 November: it is now in FL, Tocqueville MSS, 10/33 *bis*. He had previously shown his comments to Gilbert de Voisins: AN, K 698, nos. 149–51. For Gilbert de Voisins's comments on the *déclaration*, see *ibid.*, no. 155.

[87] FL, Tocqueville MSS, 101 *bis*, pp. 7, 11 and 14; cf. BPR, LP 21, p. 51: Joly de Fleury to Rouillé, 1 Aug. 1752, and BN, JF 1493, f. 147: Ogier to Joly de Fleury, 31 Aug. 1752.

[88] *Ibid.*, 1496, f. 10: Joly de Fleury to Rouillé, 16 Nov. 1752 (draft/copy).

[89] *Ibid.* There is no record of his audience.

[90] FL, Tocqueville MSS, 10/47: Bidé de La Grandville to Lamoignon, 7 Nov. 1752.

asked for a postponement of the meeting of the council arranged for 17 November, the King only grudgingly agreed to it and insisted that the report should be presented four days later.[91] Trudaine's mysterious conduct may perhaps be linked to rumours that were circulating at the time; the Marquis d'Argenson noted, for instance, that Machault might succeed Lamoignon in the chancellorship and that Trudaine was in line for the post of *contrôleur général*.[92]

As for the decision to shelve the *déclaration* and to proceed instead with a response to the *requête*, it does not seem to have been taken at the meeting of the *Conseil des dépêches* held on 17 November when only measures relating to the *Parlement* were apparently discussed.[93] The next day the King left for Madame de Pompadour's house at Bellevue, taking with him La Roche-foucauld's report. The house party there included the Comte d'Argenson and his nephew and acolyte Paulmy. Machault went to Bellevue on 19 November, probably on business relating to a crisis in Brittany, and returned to Versailles in the evening with the cardinal's report, which, on arrival, he forwarded to Lamoignon on instructions from the King.[94] The crucial decision thus appears to have been taken in the intimate, not to say closed, circle at Bellevue.

The *requête* was debated at Versailles on 21 November at a tense meeting of the *Conseil des dépêches* lasting five hours.[95] In addition to the King, those present were, in descending order of seniority in the council, the Dauphin, the chancellor, the keeper of the seals, the Maréchal de Noailles, Saint-Florentin, D'Argenson, the three *commissaires*, Rouillé, Puyzieulx, Saint-Séverin, Paulmy, and Du Four de Villeneuve as *rapporteur*.[96] When there was a *rapporteur*, he spoke first, and the others then expressed their opinions in ascending order of seniority.[97] Du Four de Villeneuve explained the four main points of the *requête* and then read out the text of an *arrêt du conseil* which he had prepared with the help of the three *commissaires*.[98] The *agents*

91 FL, Rosanbo MSS, 1/2/35: Lamoignon to the King, 14 Nov. 1752 (copy); 1/2/36: Louis XV to Lamoignon, 14 Nov. [1752], 'au soir', Choisy; 1/2/37: Lamoignon to Trudaine, 13 Nov. 1752 (draft/copy); and 1/2/38: Trudaine to Lamoignon, undated reply to the chancellor's letter.

92 D'Argenson, ed. Rathery, vii, pp. 328–9, 342.

93 FL, Rosanbo MSS, 1/2/36: Louis XV to Lamoignon, 14 Nov. [1752], 'au soir', Choisy.

94 FL, Tocqueville MSS, 10/unnumbered: Lamoignon to the King, 19 Nov. 1752, together with the King's reply from Bellevue and a covering letter to the chancellor from the Comte d'Argenson; 10/1: Machault to Lamoignon, 'dimanche au soir' [19 Nov. 1752].

95 BN, n.a.fr. 23619, f. 67, no. 133: Villevieille to Loménie de Brienne, 23 Nov. 1752 (copy).

96 AN, K 698, no. 140: '1752: conseil des dépêches' (note in the hand of Gilbert de Voisins).

97 M. Antoine, 'Le Conseil des dépêches', pp. 203–5; and the same author's *Le Conseil du Roi sous le règne de Louis XV*, pp. 124–7.

98 The only known account of his report is the summary in the hand of Gilbert de Voisins in AN, K 698, no. 140. The arrêt du conseil of 21 November 1752 is reproduced with misleading inaccuracies in Luynes, *Mém.*, xii, pp. 300–1 and in E. De Heeckeren, *Correspondance de Benoît XIV* (Paris, 1912), ii, p. 548 (Appendix 3). Flammermont gives an inade-

généraux asked first in their *requête* that the King should quash the *arrêt de règlement* of 18 April on the ground of its encroaching on ecclesiastical authority, basing their claim on what seemed at first sight to be an imposing series of laws. But their legal position was weak.[99] Du Four de Villeneuve exploded it and proposed that the *arrêt de règlement* should be quashed on other grounds, viz:

> comme rendu par entreprise sur le pouvoir qui appartient à S.M. Seule de donner des Lois et des règles géneralles à ses sujets, et notamment comme tendant à Etablir qu'il n'y a aucun cas où le refus public des sacrements puisse être autorisé sur le fondement de refus de soumission à la bulle Unigenitus.[100]

Secondly, the *agents généraux* asked the King to quash the *arrêts* and proceedings that had arisen in consequence of the *arrêt de règlement*. But Du Four de Villeneuve argued that these *arrêts* and proceedings concerned only private individuals who were always at liberty to seek redress before another branch of the royal council, the *Conseil des parties*.[101] And the *arrêt du conseil* accordingly put the *agents généraux* out of court 'for the time being'.[102] It put them similarly out of court over their third request, which was for the suppression of certain *arrêtés* of the *Parlement*, especially that of 5 May concerning Beaumont.[103] Du Four de Villeneuve pointed out that these *arrêtés* were secret decisions, which were therefore beyond the official cognisance of the *agents généraux*.[104] Finally, the *agents généraux* asked the King to reaffirm article 34 of the 1695 edict, which treated cases involving the administration of the sacraments as non-criminal actions that should be tried in the ecclesiastical courts.[105] However, they did not refer to any criminal actions that might arise. This omission had not escaped Du Four de Villeneuve, who argued that, if the administration or the denial of the sacraments should occasion a *cas privilégié*, a royal court was entitled to institute criminal proceedings against an ecclesiastic.[106] Hence, while the *arrêt du conseil* reaffirmed article 34 of the 1695 edict, it made allowance for these criminal proceedings.[107] It also summarised the complicated procedure followed when an ecclesiastic committed a criminal office: a royal

quate summary of its stipulations: *Rems.*, ii, p. 506. It is therefore necessary to refer to the *minute* in AN, E 2312, no. 120 *bis*, or to the certified copy preserved by the *agents généraux* in AN, G⁸* 796, ff. 120 *et seq.*

99 Cf. the pencil notes made by Gilbert de Voisins in the margin of his copy of the report: AN, K 698, no. 140.

100 AN, G⁸* 796, f. 121ᵛ.   101 AN, K 698, no. 140.

102 Du Four de Villeneuve's arguments are summarised by Gilbert de Voisins in an account of his own contribution to the debate; *ibid.*, no 144: 'Idée de mon opinion au conseil des dépêches du 21. novembre 1752', etc.

103 *Ibid.*, no. 140.   104 *Ibid.*, no. 144.   105 *Ibid.*, no. 140.   106 *Ibid.*, no. 144.

107 AN, G⁸* 796, f. 121. This part of the *arrêt du conseil* is accurately reproduced in Luynes, *Mem.*, xii, p. 301.

court tried the *cas privilégié*, but an ecclesiastical court was allowed to take part in the preliminary investigations if it claimed that the *cas privilégié* also involved a *délit commun* (an offence committed against the discipline of the Church); the two courts then gave their sentences separately.[108]

In the course of the debate the proposed *arrêt du conseil* was chiefly attacked by the Comte d'Argenson, his nephew Paulmy, and Bidé de La Grandville.[109] Their objections, of which no record apparently survives, may be inferred from the accounts left by Rouillé and Gilbert de Voisins of their own opinions. They appear to have been aimed mainly at the two most important provisions of the *arrêt du conseil*, namely the stipulation about criminal proceedings and the terms in which the *arrêt de règlement* was quashed.[110] It was pointed out that because the stipulation did not clearly distinguish between what were the *cas privilégiés* and what were the *délits communs*, an ecclesiastic who denied a person the sacrament could still be prosecuted by the *Parlement* on the pretext that his action constituted a *cas privilégié*. In 1731 the Comte d'Argenson had himself been a *commissaire* appearing before the *Conseil des dépêches*. On that occasion his task had been to examine the practical implications of an *arrêt du conseil* reaffirming the King's right to fix the limits between the spiritual and the temporal power in the State. His view then was that the clergy had a jurisdiction which it could exercise in an 'external' manner by means of sentences and decrees and that its judgements implied a right of constraint. But he had not listed the instances when the jurisdiction applied: he had found what he called a 'caractère d'équivoque' in article 34 of the 1695 edict which left, in his words, 'à chacune des deux puissances ses prétentions et ses droits'.[111] Perhaps D'Argenson still held those views in 1752; if so, he may well have argued that existing legislation was too difficult to interpret. Moreover, he

---

[108] *Ibid*. See also Dénisart, *Collection de décisions*, i, p. 389: '*cas privilégié*', nos. 2 and 3; and AN, K 698, no. 144. The procedure was laid down in a law of 1678.

[109] BN, n.a.fr. 23619, f. 68, no. 135: Villevieille to Loménie de Brienne, [Nov. 1752], copy; C. F. Durini (the Papal nuncio) to Cardinal Valenti (Secretary of State), 11 Dec. 1752, in *Curiosità storiche e diplomatiche del secolo decimottavo; corrispondenza segrete di grandi personaggi*, ed. Felice Calvi (Milan, 1878), pp. 255–6.

[110] CF. AN, K 698, no. 144; and BPR, LP 517, no. 60: 'Avis de M. Rouillé' (Rouillé's own account of the opinion he expressed at the meeting). Concerning the attitude of the Comte d'Argenson, some indication of it may be gained from an interesting account left by Joly de Fleury of a conversation between his son, the *procureur général*, and the minister which took place a fortnight after the meeting of the council. The subject was the attitude of the bishops. 'M D [Argenson] n'a pas osé douter expressément de l'autorité du Roy; il s'est retranché sur la crainte que 30 Ev[êques] ne se révoltent; sur quoy il [le procureur général] a répondu: en voilà déjà cent qui ne feront rien, mais prenons la liste des trente aut[res]: nous allons les nous réduire à ou 6, 7 ou 8 au plus'; BN, JF 1497, f. 119: Joly de Fleury to Rouillé, 6 Dec. 1752.

[111] Bibliothèque de l'Arsenal, Paris, MS 3053: 'Portefeuille de M. de Paulmy', ff. 297, 300, 343ʳ, 357–359ʳ, 360ᵛ, 361ʳ, 362ᵛ; notes and drafts of the Comte d'Argenson on the *arrêt du conseil* of 10 March 1731 and on articles 30, 34, 37, 40 and 41 of the edict of 1695.

or others present at the meeeting on 21 November were able to show that
the ground on which Du Four de Villeneuve proposed to quash the *arrêt du
règlement* was couched in ambiguous terms; for although the proposed *arrêt
du conseil* ruled that the sacraments could legitimately be denied – and then
only in some cases (a further reservation that later did not escape the
attention of the astute Pope Benedict XIV) – to those who openly rejected
Unigenitus, it did not state that the sacraments could legitimately be denied
to those who failed to produce confession certificates.[112]

Rouillé recognised these objections and answered them at the meeting
with characteristic bluntness:

> il seroit à désirer que l'on pust expliqué [*sic*] quels sont les cas seulement
> privilégiés qui doivent donner lieu à une procédure criminelle car tant que
> guerre durera entre les magistrats et le clergé on prendra toujours la voie
> criminelle, quand on devroit se pourvoir seulement à fin civile. Mais cette
> distinction à faire dans une loy de délit commun et du cas privilégié est bien
> difficile à faire.

In his opinion the ambiguous clause in the *arrêt du conseil* presented no
problem:

> on crains, sire, que de cette clause on n'en puisse induire que les parlements
> sont autorisés à poursuivre tous les refus de sacrements pour déffaut de billets
> de confession. A cet egard, si V. Mté. me permet d'en dire mon sentiment, je
> seray plus hardy et je croy que c'est une raison de plus pour laisser subsister
> cette clause.[113]

The best defence of the *arrêt du conseil* probably came from Gilbert de
Voisins, who explained the complicated legal position sensibly and know-
ledgeably.[114] He differed from Du Four de Villeneuve only about putting
the *agents généraux* out of court 'for the time being' on the question of the
suppression of the judicial proceedings and secret *arrêtés* of the *Parlement*,
and he eventually succeeded in having them put out of court altogether.
But Saint-Florentin, Noailles, and Machault were undoubtedly the most
important advocates of the *arrêt du conseil*.[115] It was adopted by the King
because it met with the approval of a majority of those present. The King

---

112 Benedict XIV to Cardinal de Tencin, 20 Dec. 1752, printed in *Le lettere di Benedetto XIV al
Cardinale de Tencin dai testi originali*, ed. E. Morelli (Roma, 1965), ii, pp. 533-4.

113 BPR, LP 517, no. 60: 'Avis de M. Rouillé'. It was not royal policy to set limits to the
application of *cas privilégiés*; see M. Marion, *Dictionnaire des institutions de la France aux xvii*[e]* et
xviii*[e]* siècles* (Paris, 1923, reprint, 1968), p. 73. Dénisart listed cases, which generally
involved sexual offences. One is interested to learn, for instance, that 'le simple concubi-
nage des prêtres ne forme qu'un délit commun; mais si le commerce est adultérin, c'est un
cas privilégié': *Collection de décisions*, i, p. 391, no. 17.

114 AN, K 698, no. 144: *passim*, for Gilbert de Voisins's account of his opinion.

115 The evidence is circumstantial; see BN, JF 1496, f. 3: Joly de Fleury to Rouillé, Nov. 1752
(copy/draft); f. 16: Rouillé to Joly de Fleury, 17 Nov. 1752.

had his own misgivings, which he expressed at the close of the meeting. 'Le Clergé', he asked, 'sera-t-il content?'[116]

The King certainly tried to reassure Cardinal de Tencin, the archbishop of Lyons, with whom he kept up a close correspondence since the cardinal's retirement from the council the previous year. He had no success, but his line of argument may perhaps be discerned, despite the cardinal's evident disagreement, in a letter which Tencin wrote to the Maréchal de Richelieu shortly afterwards:

> Le pauvre Prince est bien trompé. Je lui avoit écrit contre l'arrêt du Conseil du 21 9bre, et il me répond que je l'entens aussi mal que mes confrères; qu'il a dit au Parlement qu'il n'appartient qu'à lui (Roi) de faire des Règlemens dans son Royaume, bien entendu, me dit-il, que c'est dans les matières qui ne sont pas toutes spirituelles, ou pour mieux dire sous entendu, car vous sçavés, ajoute-t-il, qu'il n'est pas possible de séparer les deux Puissances. Tout ceci est un peu embrouillé. Il ne répond rien sur les autres réflexions que je lui avois faites. Mon intention est de répliquer. Mais je n'entrerai point dans une discussion dont il ne peut pas être capable, qui seroit inutile, et ne serviroit peut-être qu'à l'indisposer contre moi ...[117]

In taking the sensible view that one could not entirely separate the spiritual and the temporal powers, the King was simply echoing the opinion already expressed by the Comte d'Argenson himself and also by Joly de Fleury, the former *procureur général*, over twenty years previously, when the Government had tried, without much success, to fix the limits of the two powers; by an *arrêt du conseil* of 10 March 1731 the King had reaffirmed his right to fix those limits but had not exercised it.[118] The legal texts were vague, and the legislator had willingly sought refuge in ambiguity.

The clergy was certainly not pleased with the *arrêt du conseil*, and the *agents généraux*, who, as suppliants, were entitled to arrange for it to be printed, chose not to exercise their right.[119] The Government accordingly decided against sending a copy of the *arrêt du conseil* to each bishop with a

---

[116] BN, n.a.fr. 23619, f. 68, no. 135: Villevieille to Loménie de Brienne, [Nov. 1752], copy.

[117] BVC, RP, xliii (catalogue no. 64), f. 189: Tencin to Richelieu, 24 Dec. 1752.

[118] For the text of the *arrêt du conseil* of 10 March 1731, see Léon Mention, *Documents relatifs aux rapports du clergé avec la royauté* (Paris, 1903), ii, p. 71 (note 1). Joly de Fleury had thought it preferable on this occasion for the King to remain silent concerning the principles which should determine the limits of the two powers: 'principes qui, gravés dans le cœur des français, produisent souvent des conséquences différentes, suivant que l'on est affecté: on substitue ses préjugés au zèle de la Religion': Bibliothèque municipale, Grenoble, MS 94, 'Traité sur les Limites des deux Puissances, fait en 1731 par M. Joly de Fleury, Procureur Général', f. 40ʳ.

[119] FL, Tocqueville MSS, 10/50: Bidé de La Grandville to Lamoignon, 24 Nov. 1752; BN, n.a.fr. 23619, f. 68, no. 134: Villevieille to Loménie de Brienne, 29 Nov. 1752 (copy); AS, Florence: Segretaria Ministero Esteri, no. 2296 (Francia, no. 4), no. 104: Stainville to Francis I, 3 Dec. 1752.

covering letter from the chancellor.[120] The attitude of the *Parlement* depended on the outcome of the meeting that was due to take place on 29 November. The *parlementaires* were not expected to look favourably on an *arrêt du conseil* that was merely interpreted by many people as an annulment of their *arrêt de règlement*. But Joly de Fleury, the *avocat général*, remained hopeful; he wrote to the Comte d'Argenson:

> Le Parlement dans son mécontentement sera modéré. Cette compagnie vit dans le Principe que ses arrests de Règlement ne sont jamais que provisoires, et ne prétend pas qu'on doive donner la communion publiquement à un homme qui publiquement criera contre la Constitution [*Unigenitus*].

Although he continued to press for a new law, the *avocat général* found comfort in the *arrêt du conseil*, which, as he told the minister, safeguarded important points of law, gave tacit approval to the prosecution of priests who denied sacraments over confession certificates, and allowed a censure of the archbishop of Paris to remain on record. He confidently expected the *Parlement* to appoint *commissaires* to examine the position, 'et par là', he concluded, 'il sera possible de s'entendre'.[121]

A legal historian has claimed that, with the exception of the 'Law of Silence' of 1754, royal jurisprudence

> ne subit aucune modification, en ce sens que le roi interprète de façon constante l'édit de 1695 et les déclarations de 1720 et de 1730 de manière favorable à la compétence des officialités et des évêques, déniant systématiquement à ses juges le droit de pourvoir à l'administration des sacrements de quelque façon que ce soit, et ne tint aucun compte de leurs contentions juridiques plus ingénieuses que solides.[122]

This view is misleading in the light of the *arrêt du conseil* of 21 November 1752.

---

[120] When Saint-Florentin sent a copy of the *arrêt du conseil* to the *agents généraux* he made no comment upon it in his covering letter to the Abbé de Coriolis; AN, O¹ 396, f. 351, no. 1278: 22 Nov. 1752 (copy). A day or so later, however, the chancellor showed Bidé de La Grandville the draft of a letter he proposed to send to the bishops. Bidé de La Grandville threw cold water on the idea, pointing out that it might irritate the bishops and arouse the suspicions of the *Parlement*. His opinion probably influenced Lamoignon and the King: FL, Tocqueville MSS, 10/51 and 51 *bis*.

[121] BUP, CA 28/IV: letter of 23 Nov. 1752.

[122] P. Godard, *La Querelle des refus de sacrements 1730–1765* (Evreux and Paris, 1937), p. 209.

6

◇◇◇

THE CRISIS OF 1753

J'ay toujours ouï-dire que l'autorité des Roys se conserve
surtout par le respect que les sujets ont pour elle et par la
persuasion où ils sont qu'on ne peut former aucun doute
sur le pouvoir qu'ils s'atribuent [*sic*], et que si on com-
mence une fois à en critiquer l'exercice, on ne manquera
jamais de raisons apparentes pour troubler tout gouvernement. Mais ceux qui raisonnent ainsi adjoutent [*sic*]
aussi que ce préjugé si précieux ne peut subsister long-
temps que par la prudence et la modération des ministres
auxquels les Roys confient leur autorité ...
Chevalier d'Aydie to the Bailli de Froullay, 18 January 1753

THE RENTRÉE of the *Parlement* had taken place on 13 November. On that
occasion the fifty-one *parlementaires* who had troubled themselves to go to
the *Palais* unwittingly averted a major crisis by putting off to 29 November
the discussion of the report of an inquiry concerning two cases of denial of
sacraments which had been forwarded to the *Parlement* by the officers of the
Châtelet. It was a decision some of them had cause to regret when they
learned that the previous day the Government had tried, though unsuccessfully, to prevent a copy of the report from being sent to the *Parlement*
and had tampered with the records of the *Châtelet*.[1]

By twelve votes to nine the officers of the *Châtelet* had decided to refer the
two cases of denial of sacraments to the *Parlement*. On the night of 12–13
November Berryer, the *lieutenant général de police*, received a *lettre de cachet*
from the Comte d'Argenson ordering him to call an extraordinary meeting
of the *Châtelet* the next morning for the purpose of registering an *arrêt du
conseil*. At this meeting three more *lettres de cachet* were produced to compel
the other officers of the court to comply with the Government's wishes.

---

[1] BS, MS 800. f. 259: 'Récit de Mr. le Président de Novion' (with marginal comments by
President Durey de Meinières).

However, when the clerk was asked to produce the authenticated copy of the judicial report of the inquiry (what was known as the *grosse de l'information*), he revealed that it had already been sent off to the *greffe* of the *Parlement*; he had dispatched it the night before (possibly because someone had leaked the Government's planned coup). Nevertheless, the clerk was made to transcribe the *arrêt du conseil* in the records of the *Châtelet*; it quashed the proceedings there on the flimsy pretext that the *lieutenant particulier* of the *Châtelet* had no right to call a meeting of the court in the absence of the *lieutenant civil* if the *lieutenant général de police* was available. The minutes of that meeting were also removed by Berryer.[2]

At the debate on 29 November President Molé had little difficulty in convincing the *parlementaires* that the matters contained in their *arrêté* of 6 September were too important to be discussed simply at an assembly of the chambers; his proposal, that *commissaires* should be appointed 'pour aviser au parti à prendre', was unanimously adopted. A *procès-verbal* of the events at the *Châtelet* was then read out, and the *parlementaires* decided to submit the whole affair to the *gens du roi*, who were told to present a report on 1 December.[3] The *gens du roi* skilfully handled the situation; D'Ormesson gave the assembled chambers an exhaustive account of the state of progress in over a dozen cases that were pending and brought up the *Châtelet* affair only at the very end; 'afin d'engager à ne placer cet objet que le dernier dans l'ordre de la délibération ou au moins le faire tomber dans le travail des commissaires', as his colleague Joly de Fleury explained to the Comte d'Argenson.[4] The ruse succeeded; the matter was referred to the *commissaires*, though only after a long debate. The Abbé Chauvelin and other *zélés* had tried in vain to persuade the *parlementaires* to annul the proceedings begun by the *Châtelet*, arguing that these proceedings involved a peer in the person of the archbishop (whose name was mentioned in the report of the inquiry); hence they had also failed to persuade them to call the peers and to initiate their own judicial proceedings.[5] Despite these tangible results, the moderates were still apprehensive; on 2 December President Molé saw the *procureur général* and urged him to do his utmost to get the King to bring out a new law.[6]

---

[2] For these details see *ibid.*, ff. 260 and 268 (debates of 13 Nov. and 2 Dec. at the *Parlement*.
[3] *Ibid.*, f. 261.
[4] *Ibid.*, ff. 262-3; BN, JF 2482, f. 217; BUP, Archives d'Argenson, CA 28/IV: letter of 1 Dec. 1752.
[5] BS, MS 800, ff. 264-9 (debates of 1-2 Dec. 1752). The first president's report of the debate on 2 December is not in the chancellor's papers: it came up in a sale but no details of its contents were given in the sale catalogue; see Charavay, *Lettres autographes et documents historiques*, bulletin no. 749 (June 1973), p. 41, lot 35609 (5): Maupeou to Lamoignon, Paris, 2 Dec. 1752, s.a.l. 1/2 p. in-fol.
[6] BN, JF 1497, f. 123: Joly de Fleury to Rouillé, 3 Dec. 1752, draft. The former *procureur général* also reported his son's meeting with Molé to the Maréchal de Noailles (*ibid*). Molé

The thirty-eight *commissaires* were drawn from each chamber, and they met only twice, on 4 and 11 December, before their meetings were interrupted.[7] A majority of them felt that the proceedings at the *Châtelet* should be annulled.[8] But they were not unanimous as to the course that the *Parlement* should follow in the light of the *arrêt du conseil* of 21 November; at the close of the second meeting, at which just over half of those present had time to express their opinions, there were, according to one *commissaire*, Revol (from the 1st chamber of the *enquêtes*), 'autant d'avis différents qu'il avoit eu d'opinion'.[9] Revol probably expressed the general view when he said that the *arrêt du conseil* appeared to indicate the King's support for the *Parlement*; in an account of his opinion he wrote:

> Il ne paraît en effet guères douteux que sans l'effort du party contraire, nous aurions eu une déclaration dont le dispositif auroit décidé pour nous, Quoyque peut-être il eut pu se trouver dans le préambule des expressions un peu trop honorables pour la Bulle mais qui néantmoins eussent vraysemblablement évité La pierre d'achoppement, c'est à dire la Qualification de Loy de l'état et de l'église. après tout, Quel a été le fruit des efforts combinés du ministre qui nous est contraire joint aux Evêques schismatiques et aux jésuites? nous venons de le voir dans le résultat de cette déliberation du Conseil dont l'opération a été substituée à l'émission d'une déclaration. Quest [*sic*] ce que ce résultat? Un arrêt sur Requête si peu avantageux pour les impétrants malgré l'atteinte portée à l'arrêt du 18 avril 1752, qu'ils n'osent le présenter au public. Que faut-il donc à ceux que cet arrêt favorise plus en leur adjugeant la compétence qu'il ne les flétrit par une prétendue cassation si foiblement motivée, toujours cachée? il leur faut un degré d'approbation de plus qui les mette à portée de jouir encore d'une plus grande autorité sur la matière présente.[10]

In seeking this greater measure of royal approval, the *parlementaires* faced a difficult choice. If they asked the King to issue a *déclaration*, they weakened their own position, though many probably believed that a *déclaration* was the best solution to the dispute. On the other hand, if they decided to prosecute the archbishop, some of them probably felt they would have to obtain the King's permission to call the peers; they could not entertain much hope of obtaining it. But if they continued to prosecute ordinary priests and to spare the bishops, they risked losing the support of 'public opinion', which might soon prove sympathetic to the priests as scapegoats

---

had been to Versailles on 30 Nov (see BUP, CA 28/IV: Jean-Omer Joly de Fleury to the Comte d'Argenson, 30 Nov. 1752); it is possible that he had also raised the matter there.
[7] BS MS 800, f. 273; BPR, LP 42 (Revol Papers), p. 207.
[8] *Ibid.* In this 'Mémoire sur la démarche la plus utile que le Parlement puisse faire dans le moment présent sans manquer à la dignité de la Compagnie et à La nécessité de ses devoirs', Revol also states that the Abbé Chauvelin had now changed his mind about the validity of the *Châlelet* proceedings.
[9] *Ibid.*   [10] *Ibid.*, pp. 208ʳ, 208ᵛ.

and was, in any case, more concerned with the price of grain and with the *vingtième*.[11] The *arrêt du conseil* had indeed placed the *parlementaires* in a quandary, from which they emerged only because a new turn of events interrupted their inconclusive debates and forced them to take decisive action.

On 12 December the *parlementaires* heard that the sacrament had been denied to two nuns of the Community of Sainte-Agathe in Paris.[12] They immediately ordered an inquiry, sending ushers in search of the *curé* of Saint-Médard and his two *vicaires*, who were the priests involved in the affair. As usual on these occasions, the *curé* was not to be found. The *vicaires* told the assembled chambers that the *curé*, in refusing to administer the sacrament to the nuns, had acted on orders from the archbishop.[13] If both nuns had died in these circumstances, the crisis would probably have blown over. But one of them, Sœur Perpétue, was still alive and clamouring for the sacrament. Hence the *parlementaires* had to act at once. By now the *gens du roi* were expert in the use of delaying tactics; they cautiously recommended that the archbishop should be invited 'dans le jour de pourvoir au besoins spirituels de la malade qui sont pressants'. Although the final *arrêté* was more strongly worded, it was still in the nature of an invitation: ' ... l'archevêque de Paris sera invité dans le jour par un secrétaire de la cour de faire cesser le scandale et de pourvoir à L'état de la malade par L'administration des Sacremens ...'[14] The next morning, when the court was told that the archbishop had refused, the *gens du roi* gently went a stage further by proposing that the *Parlement* should again invite the archbishop, this time 'to end the scandal'; the proposal was adopted. Once more the archbishop refused. The *gens du roi* now proposed that the *Parlement* should resort to the King. In the tense debate that

---

[11] *Ibid.*, pp. 209^r,^{v}–210^r. Revol claims that the Abbé de Vougny threatened at any moment to raise the matter of the price of grain at an assembly of the chambers. His colleagues apparently succeeded in restraining him.

[12] *Les Remontrances du Parlement de Paris au xviiie siècle*, ed. Jules Flammermont (Paris, 1888–98), 3 vols. (hereafter Flammermont, *Rems.*), i, p. 506. See also BN, JF 1497, f. 117: Joly de Fleury to Rouillé, 9 Dec. 1752; f. 113: same to same, 12 Dec. 1752 (drafts); BS, MS 800, ff. 273–7 (for details of the debate). The Filles de Sainte-Agathe were a community that followed the rule of the Cistercians. When Beaumont suppressed it in 1753, the community sold its house in the rue de l'Arbalète. It was bought by one Sieur de Monchalon, who opened what the geographer Jaillot described as 'une Pension distinguée, dans laquelle on éleve les jeunes gens avec autant de soin & d'attention, que les Filles de Ste Agathe en avoient pour les pensionnaires dont on leur confioit l'éducation': see Jaillot, *Recherches critiques historiques et topographiques sur la ville de Paris*, (Paris, 1775), iv (2), p. 13.

[13] BS, MS 800, f. 276.

[14] *Ibid.*, f. 277. Beaumont probably discussed the *arrêté* with the King later the same evening; see *Mémoires de Duc de Luynes sur la cour de Louis XV (1735–1758)*, ed. L. Dussieux and E. Soulié (Paris, 1860–5) (hereafter cited as Luynes, *Mém.*), xii, p. 202. Louis XV then left for Choisy: AS, Florence: Segretaria Ministero Esteri, no. 2296, Francia: no. 105, Stainville to Francis I, Paris, 10 Dec. 1752.

followed, Molé tried in vain to persuade his colleagues to take this course. A motion by the Abbé Chauvelin was passed instead, by ninety-eight votes to about thirty-four; the *Parlement* ordered the archbishop to end the scandal within a day on pain of having his temporalities seized, and it also decided that the peers would be invited to take their places at a meeting on 18 December. The first president was given the unenviable task of 'inviting' the King to attend that meeting.[15] The moderates had momentarily lost control of the assembly. The implications of the new crisis were perceived at once; Bidé de La Grandville wrote to the Chancellor:

> Il est bien affligeant, Monseigneur, que le nouveau refus dans la paroisse de St. Médard soit venu troubler les projets de tranquillité que la commission du parlement sembloit adopter, nous voylà aux grands événements.[16]

Everything turned upon the Government. The *gens du roi* assumed that it would be guided by the terms of the *arrêt du conseil*. An inquiry had shown that the *curé* had denied Sœur Perpétue the sacrament for failing to produce a confession certificate and not for refusing to submit to the bull, though she had made a disparaging comment – which she later withdrew – about *Unigenitus* in her conversation with him. Hence the *gens du roi* thought the action of the *Parlement* in taking up her case did not contravene the terms of the *arrêt du conseil*. Jean-Omer Joly de Fleury explained the position to two of the ministers on 14 December: Saint-Contest accepted his account of what had taken place, and D'Argenson did not question its accuracy. As the *avocat général* realised that the King could not allow the peers to be summoned, he insisted in his conversations with the ministers upon the need for the King to condemn the archbishop's conduct as a concession to the *Parlement*.[17] As for the first president, he took an easy way out of his difficulties: he simply wrote to the chancellor asking for the King's orders. The King decided to call a meeting of the *Conseil des dépêches* at Versailles the following day; the first president was told to come on 16 December.[18] On the morning of 15 December the *Parlement* had no alternative but to order that the archbishop's temporalities should be seized: the motion, which was proposed by a resigned President Molé, was adopted by all but four of those present.[19] The *gens du roi* had proposed that the court make another approach to the archbishop, but they cannot have entertained any

---

[15] Flammermont, *Rems.*, i, p. 507; BUP, CA 28/IV: Jean-Omer Joly de Fleury to the Comte d'Argenson, 13 Dec. [1752]; BS, MS 800, ff. 278–84.

[16] FL., Tocqueville MSS, 10/53: letter of 13 Dec. 1752.

[17] BN, JF 1497, f. 109: Jean-Omer Joly de Fleury to his father, 14 Dec. 1752. D'Argenson asked the *avocat général* to supply him with details concerning the rights of the peerage; BUP, CA 28/IV: Jean-Omer Joly de Fleury to the Comte d'Argenson, 17 Dec. 1752.

[18] FL, 1/2/40: Lamoignon to the King, 14 Dec. 1752 (10 a.m.). The King's reply of the same day was dated from Choisy at noon; it is in the margin of the letter.

[19] BS, MS 800, f. 285.

hopes of this course being adopted. Titon supported it in the assembly, arguing that the seizure of the archbishop's temporalities presented difficulties for a reason that was, as he put it, 'plus claire de sentir que d'exprimer', but only three others were of his opinion.[20]

There remained the matter of what was to be done about the two curates of Saint-Médard and about the spiritual needs of Sœur Perpétue. President Molé succeeded in separating the question of the two curates from that of Sœur Perpétue. On the first, he pointed out the dilemma of these priests, caught between the demands of their ecclesiastical superior and the need to obey the law, in order to persuade his colleagues to limit themselves to a *décret d'assigné pour être ouï* against them. The majority decided to give the curates the rest of the morning to attend to the spiritual needs of Sœur Perpétue.[21] When the *Parlement* reconvened in the afternoon it was announced that the curates had fled and the nun had still not received the sacrament. President Molé, supported by President Gilbert, adopted the *conclusions* of the *gens du roi* that the curates should receive a *décret d'ajournement personnel*, the next stage up from a *décret d'assigné pour être ouï*. The court was now beyond such delicacy and simply ordered their arrest. Then it went on to consider the steps it could take to assist Sœur Perpétue. After a tense debate that lasted until 7.30 in the evening the magistrates adopted a barely modified version of the *conclusions* left by the *gens du roi*: they ordered that the most senior priest of the parish of Saint-Médard, or, failing him, the former incumbents of that parish, would be obliged, 'sous telle peine qu'il appartiendra, de faire cesser le scandale dans demain huit heurs du matin en procurant à la malade les secours spirituels par l'administration des sacrements'.[22] By this turn of phrase the *parlementaires* were not, in their view, transgressing the limits of the temporal power by explicitly ordering priests to administer the sacrament, but remained within their legal entitlement to halt any public scandal, albeit through a precise injunction to the priests to administer the sacrament in a particular instance.

In the course of that afternoon's debate there was, according to Titon, a plot to secure the passage of an *avis* which aimed at implementing an offer made by one of the clerks in the *Parlement*, the Abbé Boucher, the *chantre* of the church of Saint-Honoré, who had previously offered to give the sacrament himself to Sœur Perpétue; if adopted, this *avis* would have led to an *arrêt* ordering Boucher to collect the Holy Sacrament from Saint-Honoré, 'et de se transporter dans la maison de Ste. Agathe pour y procurer à la malade les secours spirituels par l'administration des sacrements'. This would have been a dramatic step, as it meant that the

[20] *Ibid.*   [21] *Ibid.*, f. 286.   [22] *Ibid.*, ff. 287–94.

Parlement was openly ordering a priest to administer the sacrament. The first president intervened at once. As Titon secretly informed the Comte d'Argenson:

> Mr le premier président avec cette éloquence noble et mâle que tout le monde luy connoist fait [*sic*] sentir en interrompant l'inconvénient de cet avis, et a beaucoup ébranlé un très grand nombre de Mrs qui avoient dessein de le proposer; plusieurs des anciens des enquêtes ont aussi parlé contre et sentent qu'il était opposé aux règles.[23]

Even a modified version of the *avis* failed to get more than one vote.

That same evening the King returned from Choisy for a meeting of the council. The outcome was an *arrêt du conseil* evoking the case and granting the archbishop replevin of his temporalities. As Beaumont was now the object of judicial proceedings, and as Sœur Perpétue's case undoubtedly presented complications, the Government had probably taken the safest course. News then came that the bishops were planning to descend upon Versailles the next day. D'Argenson wrote at once to Beaumont urging him to dissuade them from taking this step and warning him of possible royal displeasure. Around midnight Beaumont returned a disappointing reply: he said he was powerless to stop the bishops, claiming that several of them, including Cardinal de La Rochefoucauld, had already left for Versailles.[24] The next morning twenty-seven bishops assembled in the palace and deputed La Rochefoucauld and Soubise to voice their fears to the King at his *lever*. As the two prelates (wearing their surplices for greater effect) bore down upon the royal apartments they encountered Saint-Florentin in the *galerie des glaces*. After a tart exchange of words, they succeeded in gaining access to the King's presence. Louis XV expressed surprise at the conduct of the bishops and listened, scarlet-faced, as La Rochefoucauld implored him to halt the activities of the *Parlement*. His only reply was to inform them of the decision he had taken the previous day. Afterwards, in the words of the historian Soulavie, 'le cardinal de Soubise fit bien boire et bien manger les vingt-sept évêques, et chacun s'en retourna sans que la monarchie fût renversée'.[25] The clergy's *démarche* had been ill advised and quite unnecessary.

Fresh from his encounter with the prelates the King saw the first president and notified his wishes to him in the manner of a personal rebuff,

---

[23] BUP, CA 59: Titon to the Comte d'Argenson, 15 Dec. 1752, 'de relevée'.

[24] AN, 422 AP 1 (Comte d'Argenson's Papers): Beaumont to the Comte d'Argenson, 'vendredi au soir'; internal evidence strongly indicates that this letter was written on 15 Dec. 1752.

[25] Luynes, *Mém.*, xii, pp. 205–6; Soulavie, *Mémoires du Maréchal de Richelieu pour servir à l'histoire de Louis XIV, de la Régence, de Louis XV et des quatorze premières années du règne de Louis XVI* (London, Marseille and Paris, 1790–3), 9 vols., viii, pp. 250–2. Soulavie's sources are usually reliable; he gives a text of the King's reply to the cardinals.

which was unfair as well as unwise. As the former *procureur général* observed afterwards to his friend Rouillé:

> Ce qu'il y a de singulier c'est que le moment de samedy étoit celuy où l'on ne devoit pas être mécontent du Premier président et mesme du Parlement; il avoit à la séance du Parlement la veille empêche de passé [*sic*] un Arrêt qui eut co[mmis] l'abbé Boucher, conseiller au Parlement ... pour administrer la malade, et qui auroit produit une procession innombrable de gens derrière le saint sacrement depuis st.honoré jusqu'à st.agathe.[26]

The King told Maupeou that he forbade the calling of the peers and proceeded to give him a sealed parcel with strict instructions to open it only in the presence of the assembled chambers. In addition to the *arrêt du conseil* which granted the archbishop replevin of his temporalities, the parcel contained two *lettres de cachet*, the first ordering the first president to read out and to 'notify' the *arrêt du conseil* to the *Parlement*, and the second ordering the *parlementaires* to hear him out and to abide by the King's decision.[27] It was not the usual practice for the first president (or, for that matter, the *procureur général*) to produce *arrêts du conseil* at the *Parlement* unless, as in this case, he was formally ordered to do so by means of a *lettre de cachet*. It was always doubtful, however, whether *parlementaires* would consider themselves bound by an *arrêt du conseil* brought to their notice in this informal manner and without letters patent calling for its registration.[28]

The Government's device was calculated to sow division between the first president and the *enquêtes* in a time-worn manner; according to President Rolland d'Erceville (who left an account of these events) the King had adopted it at the instigation of Machault. The decision to give the parcel to Maupeou had probably been endorsed by a majority of the members of the council; the Comte d'Argenson privately admitted this fact to the first president at Trianon the following week, when Maupeou protested to him about the decision.[29] The keeper of the seals may have

[26] Luynes, *Mém.*, xii, p. 207; BN, JF 1497, f. 108: Joly de Fleury to Rouillé, 18 Dec. 1752 (draft).

[27] Luynes, *Mém.*, xii, p. 208.

[28] Cf. BUP, CA 28/III: Jean-Omer Joly de Fleury to the Comte d'Argenson, 1 Aug. 1751. At the time of the affair of the *Hôpital général*, the *avocat général* had commented on a similar situation in these words: 'Se croiront-ils [les parlementaires] liés par la connaissance qu'ils auront alors de l'arrest du Conseil? Vous connoissés assés, Monsieur, les compagnies, et les Principes pour sentir que jamais on ne pourra les amener là, et à raisonner, homme de loy, on ne peut les blâmer'.

[29] Archives du Ministères des Affaires Etrangères, Paris (hereafter AAE), Mémoires et Documents (hereafter MD), France 1344, ff. 28off: 'Mémoire du Président Rolland' (a copy made for the Maréchal de Richelieu). Another copy, where certain passages are omitted and where the author has toned down some of his statements, exists in the Lamoignon Collection: BN, MS franç. 8496. For the details about Machault's intrigue, see f. 290 of the Richelieu copy and pp. 20–1 of the Lamoignon copy; and *Journal et mémoires du marquis d'Argenson*, ed. E J. B. Rathery (Paris, 1859–67) hereafter D'Argenson, ed

wanted to take advantage of the turn of events to bring about the resignation of the first president, whom he greatly disliked, and his replacement
by his own friend and acolyte, President Chauvelin.[30] If that was his plan,
it seriously underestimated Maupeou's resilience and experience of the
Parlement. The first president's account of his audience with the King
certainly indisposed his hearers, and many of them hastily and wrongly
assumed that the *arrêt du conseil* contained a stipulation prohibiting all
further debate on the case.[31] They interrupted Maupeou's reading and left
the *grand'chambre* amid general pandemonium; in the evening the King
wrote to the Comte D'Argenson:

> vous devés avoir reçu des nouvelles du parlement, le brouha a été très grand,
> et tout le monde s'en est allé à ce que l'on dit. il faudra voir s'ils rentreronts
> lundi matin.[32]

According to Rolland d'Erceville the week-end was taken up in attempts to
avert a split between the first president, who was naturally supported by
the *grand'chambre*, and the *enquêtes*. These attempts proved successful: on
Monday the meeting was resumed.[33] The first president had been able to
convince the *enquêtes* that the King's orders had been the work of those
whom he referred to as 'les ennemis de la compagnie'.[34] They recognised
his predicament; he retained their confidence. Nevertheless, the whole
incident had significantly increased his dependence upon them.

There were now two new aspects to the crisis: the rights of the peerage
and the matter of the validity of *arrêts du conseil* that were notified to the
Parlement without letters patent. To the *parlementaires* these delicate questions had become as important as the proceedings against the archbishop
and the spiritual needs of Sœur Perpétue. At their meeting on 18 December
they decided not to call the peers; instead they sent the *gens du roi* to
Versailles with a request for the King to hear a deputation.[35] The request
was granted without difficulty. At Versailles the *gens du roi* also saw

Rathery), vii, p. 376. There are some useful details in the memoirs of P. A. Robert de
Saint-Vincent (Michel Vinot Préfontaine Collection, Paris; typescript), p. 145.

[30] On the hostility between Machault and Maupeou, see Chapter 3, p. 89.

[31] BN, JF 1497, f. 108: Joly de Fleury to Rouillé, 18 Dec. 1752; JF 2192, ff. 152–3: 'Maison de
Sainte-Agathe' (note on the events of 10–19 December in the hand of J. O. Joly de Fleury).

[32] BVC, RP, xlii (catalogue no. 63), no. 180. I believe this letter is addressed to D'Argenson;
it is in a volume of autographs that came from the Feuillet de Conches collection, and,
unlike the Richelieu papers, it bears no mark of the inventory of those papers done at the
time of the Revolution.

[33] BN, MS franç. 8496, p. 19.

[34] *Suite des Nouvelles Ecclésiastiques*, 27 Mar. 1753, p. 50: details concerning events of 18 Dec.
1752. Flammermont gives the erroneous impression that the first president was caught
unawares by the request that the debate should be resumed (*Rems.*, i, p. 508).

[35] E. J. F. Barbier, *Chronique de la régence et du règne de Louis XV (1718–1763), ou Journal de
Barbier* (Paris, 1866), 8 vols. (hereafter Barbier, *Journal*), v, pp. 314–15.

Machault, and Jean-Omer Joly de Fleury retailed the meeting to the Comte d'Argenson:

> nous avons trouvé hier mr le garde des sceaux fort peiné de ce que le roy ne pouvoit pas faire par arrest du conseil ce qu'il vouloit: c'est un vice si l'on veut, mais ce vice est dans la constitution de L'Etat, il n'y a qu'à la réformer par les voyes ordinaires, si le roy peut croire ce point intérrésant [*sic*] pour son autorité; mais vous sentés qu'il pourroit être dangereux pour l'autorité du roy que cette nouvelle voye fût introduite dans les Parlements.[36]

His last comment is as cryptic as it is interesting; it is perhaps an allusion to the extent of the opposition that could be expected from the *Parlement* if the King attempted to introduce a law extending the scope of *arrêts du conseil*.

The King saw the deputation at Trianon on 20 December. In his speech the first president said that the ban on the convocation of the peers was an attack upon the rights of the peerage and added, in a thinly veiled reference to the *arrêt du conseil*, that the laws forbade the *Parlement* to recognise 'les ordres qui ne sont pas revêtus du sceau de V.M. et des marques anciennes et respectables de votre autorité'. The Government maintained its original stand.[37] Moreover, the King's reply contained a phrase that caused great offence at the *Parlement*: 'Quant à vos formes, je ne refuserai jamais de vous entendre; expliquez-vous avec mon chancelier qui m'en rendra compte.'[38] The *Parlement* recognised no intermediary between itself and the sovereign. When the chambers met to consider the reply they decided to reconvene the peers for 29 December and to make further representations to the King. The Abbé Chauvelin, who had proposed the motion, had been given to understand that the peers might respond favourably to a second invitation. The King's ban had caused a stir amongst them, and several had already met at the residence of the Duc d'Orléans to discuss their position. But the peers feared the King's wrath and made no move; consequently the *parlementaires* decided not to send out the invitations.[39] Moreover, the King implied to the *gens du roi* that he would hear the representations of the *Parlement* only if his order forbidding the convocation of the peers continued to be observed.[40] In the debate on 29 December President Molé urged that the *parlementaires* should suspend their discussion about the rights of the peerage in order that their representations should be heard, and his view prevailed by a large majority. The next day the *gens du roi* announced that the King would again receive a deputation, on 3 January.[41]

[36] BUP, CA 28/IV: letter of 19 Dec. 1752.   [37] Flammermont, *Rems.*, i, p. 509.
[38] *Ibid.*, i, p. 510; BUP, CA 28/IV: Jean-Omer Joly de Fleury to the Comte d'Argenson, 22 Dec. 1752.
[39] BS, MS 800, ff. 304–5 (including a note in the hand of Durey de Meinières); D'Argenson, ed. Rathery, vii, p. 362.
[40] BS, MS 800, f. 307.   [41] *Ibid.*, f. 309. This extract is in the hand of L'Averdy.

There remained the question of Sœur Perpétue, who had been at the point of death for over a fortnight. On 16 December the King had written to the Comte d'Argenson:

comme nous avons donné guain de cause à m^r. l'arch. dans cette affaire cy, et que j'ay évoqué cette affaire cy à moy, il faut que vous lui mandiés de ma part qu'il fasse tout ce qu'il sera en lui pour que la malade puisse être administrée.[42]

But the archbishop was not a man to put gratitude before principle. He maintained that Sœur Perpétue was still opposed to *Unigenitus*, and he wrote to D'Argenson the next day:

Vous comprenés bien, Monsieur, qu'il n'est pas possible de la faire administrer tandis qu'elle restera dans les mêmes sentiments, que je ne pourrois le faire sans exposer le sacrement à la plus évidente profanation et sans devenir moi-même complice d'un sacrilège. D'ailleurs je n'ay rien négligé pour la ramener à la soumission . . .[43]

Paulmy had then been sent to the archbishop's palace ostensibly to take written statements from the parties concerned in the case, which was now deemed to be before the council.[44] It is possible, however, that his mission resulted in the statement that Sœur Perpétue made before a notary and notified to the *Parlement*; she declared that she no longer required the assistance of the *parlementaires*, for she was now well enough to receive communion in church.[45] As the Government did not allow priests to refuse the sacraments at the altar to persons who had not been either excommunicated or publicly denounced, she would have had no further difficulty in obtaining the sacrament.[46] However, on 23 December the Government

---

[42] Letter quoted in note 32 above. As Jean-Omer Joly de Fleury admitted to the Comte d'Argenson, the King probably did not have the authority to command that the sacraments should be administered to Sœur Perpétue (see his letter of 17 Dec. 1752 mentioned in note 17 above).

[43] AN, 422 Ap 1: letter of 17 Dec. [1752]. Luynes claims that on this occasion the archbishop, who had forbidden that the sacraments be administered to Sœur Perpétue, had at first sent two Capuchins to persuade her to submit to the bull; the Superior of the community would not let them see her. Beaumont then sent his *grand pénitancier*, who almost got Perpétue to admit that she had not made the disparaging comment about *Unigenitus* which had been attributed to her. See Luynes, *Mém.*, xii, pp. 210–11.

[44] D'Argenson, ed. Rathery, vii, pp. 363, 367–8 (from this last entry it would appear that Paulmy went on 17 Dec.). There was now some urgency in the case, for the parishioners of Saint-Médard had staged a 'tumulte populaire' when no masses had been held on Sunday (*ibid.*, p. 362).

[45] Cf. Barbier, *Journal*, v, p. 316.

[46] In an important letter of 25 Feb. 1741 to the bishop of Laon, Maurepas had stated the law on this matter: '. . . Sa Majesté m'ordonne de vs faire savoir, que les règles établies dans son royaume ne permettant pas de refuser à la Ste Table la communion à ceux qui ne sont pas excommunié [*sic*], ni dénoncés, Elle ne peut que désapprouver la conduite de vt grand-vicaire; et qu'ainsi il n'est pas dans le cas d'avoir recours à sa protection'. See BPR, LP 514, f. 3 (copy in Le Paige's hand).

took more drastic measures; the community of Sainte-Agathe was suppressed by an *arrêt du conseil*, and orders were given for Sœur Perpétue to be transferred to another religious house. Her removal was a barbaric affair; she died the next day.[47] On the face of it these measures had been taken at the archbishop's request,[48] but they were probably taken because the *Parlement* had refused to register her statement or because she had feigned or suffered a relapse and changed her mind.[49]

The forced removal of Sœur Perpétue naturally angered the *parlementaires*. President Molé proposed that strong representations should be made about it to the King on the occasion of the deputation.[50] The first president was given the delicate task of raising a matter that concerned the use of *lettres de cachet*.[51] He acquitted himself of it as best he could at the end of his speech. After a meeting of the council, the King read out a reply that made almost no concession to the *Parlement*. Then he rounded upon the first president, saying: 'Quant aux ordres particuliers que je juge à propos de donner, je ne croyais pas, Monsieur, que vous eussiez osé m'en parler.' This undeserved rebuff left the first president speechless. According to Rolland d'Erceville, Maupeou saw clearly that another attempt was being made to undermine his position.[52] Although the immediate crisis was over, this new factor decisively influenced the subsequent course of events.

The King's reply was communicated the next day, 4 January, to the assembled chambers. The *parlementaires* resolved upon making remonstrances, and *commissaires* were appointed to prepare a plan. Dubois (an honorary president of the 1st chamber of *enquêtes*) proposed that a deputation be sent to explain to the King that Maupeou had acted only in accordance with his duty when he had spoken of 'ordres particuliers'.[53] But Maupeou rejected the suggestion, saying:

[47] BS, LP 514, f. 3 (note in the hand of Durey de Meinières).

[48] It was to the archbishop that the Comte d'Argenson sent the *arrêt du conseil* suppressing the Community and the orders for the removal of Sœur Perpétue (on 23 December). Berryer, the *lieutenant général de police*, was instructed to concert with the archbishop over the execution of these measures; see AN O¹, 203.

[49] Soulavie claims (*Mémoires du Maréchal de Richelieu*, viii, p. 254) that the police had decided that Perpétue was only a 'petite coquine' who feigned illness in order to give the *Parlement* more time to act. Her last moments were certainly protracted; however, the intervention of the police brought about her death.

[50] BS, MS 800, f. 308 (debate of 29 Dec. 1752).

[51] At this period the *Parlement* made an issue of *lettres de cachet* only in cases where they had been misused (mainly cases concerned with the religious disputes); see F. Olivier-Martin, 'Les Lettres de cachet et les cours souveraines au xviiième siècle', *Revue historique de droit français et étranger*, 4th series, iv (1925), pp. 508–9.

[52] Flammermont, *Rems.*, i, pp. 511–12; BS, MS 800, f. 309; BN, MS franç. 8496, p. 21.

[53] BS MS 800, f. 310 (debate of 4 January); BN, MS franç. 8496, pp. 21–2; BUP, CA 28/V: Jean-Omer Joly de Fleury to the Comte d'Argenson, 4 Jan. 1753.

qu'il croioit avoir rempli son devoir et n'avoir besoin de justification ni dans l'esprit du Roy ni dans celuy de la compagnie ni dans celuy de public; et que Mrs. luy feroient beaucoup de peine s'ils n'entroient point à cet égard dans sa façon de penser.[54]

The *commissaires* were therefore left to decide whether the 'ordres particuliers' should be mentioned in the remonstrances. But at their meeting on 9 January, the *présidents à mortier* and the *commissaires* from the *grand'chambre* disagreed with the majority of the other *commissaires*, who wanted to include the matter in the remonstrances. Maupeou informed them that if 'ordres particuliers' were mentioned, he would not draw up the remonstrances. He agreed to hold an assembly of the chambers to decide the issue.[55]

The assembly took place on 11 January, and it provides an interesting illustration of what has been called 'judicial politics'.[56] The *parlementaires* knew that if they decided to include the matter of 'ordres particuliers' in the remonstrances, they would also have to decide who should draw them up. Opening the debate, President Molé proposed that 'ordres particuliers' should not be mentioned at this stage and that the *commissaires* should be told to concentrate on the other items that were to form the basis of the remonstrances. His view was certain to have the support of the *grand'chambre* and of the moderates elsewhere. But President Gilbert broke the presidential ranks by fatally amending Molé's proposal with the suggestion that the decision about 'ordres particuliers' should be referred back to the *commissaires*, his argument being that the *arrêté* of 4 January gave the *commissaires* full powers to decide the issue subject to the eventual approval of the assembly. When it was his turn to speak, President Turgot declared that he did not think President Gilbert's motion was in order. He maintained that, as a divergence of views had arisen among the *commissaires*, it was up to the assembly to take the decision; he proposed that 'ordres particuliers' be included in the remonstrances. Naturally he drew much support from the *enquêtes* and *requêtes*. At the close of the first round of the procedure, Molé's *avis* mustered only eighteen supporters, who now had simply to choose between the *avis* of President Gilbert and of President Turgot; no further opinions could be expressed. They, and probably the

---

[54] BS, MS 800, f. 311.

[55] BS MS 800, f. 312 (debate in the first chamber of *enquêtes* on 9 January). It was at this debate on the subject of the disagreement amongst the *commissaires* that L'Averdy made the moving plea: 'après ce que le Roi a dit au P. Presid'., quiconque ne dit pas au Roy, Oui Sire, nous osons vous parler parceque il est de notre devoir de le faire ainsi que du bien de l'état, manque au devoir de sa place et à la patrie' (*ibid.*, f.313). The assembly of the chambers was convened at the request of the 2nd and 5th chambers of the *enquêtes*.

[56] This analysis of the debate is based on a comparison of the notes left by Durey de Meinières (BS, MS 800, ff. 313–16) with the memoirs of Rolland d'Erceville (AAE, MD, France 1344) and of Robert de Saint-Vincent (Michel Vinot Préfontaine Collection, Paris; typescript, pp. 144–6).

majority of those present, would undoubtedly have chosen President Gilbert's *avis*, but for the intervention of one of their number, President de Maupeou, the first president's son. After Presidents Molé, Potier de Novion, Le Peletier, and Chauvelin had all opted for President Gilbert, President de Maupeou broke the conventions of the *Parlement* by expressing a second opinion.[57] He declared:

> qu'il s'agissoit d'avoir une décision et qu'ainsi l'avis de ne point parler des ordres du Roy ne prévalant pas il revenoit à l'avis de Mr Le Présidt. Turgot.[58]

The effect of these remarks was that most of Molé's remaining followers also went over to President Turgot, whose motion was thereby narrowly carried by sixty-five votes to sixty-three.

It is difficult to resist the view that President de Maupeou's purpose had been to rally support for President Turgot's motion from among the stalwarts of the *grand'chambre*, men who normally looked to the first president for guidance and now felt they had that guidance from the lips of his son. Rolland d'Erceville (1st chamber of the *requêtes*) studied these events closely and left two varying accounts of them. According to one version, the first president, in an attempt to scotch President Molé's motion, had originally instigated President Gilbert to propose an *avis* that could then subsequently be defeated through the combined efforts of another acolyte, President Turgot, and of President de Maupeou. If this plausible interpretation is correct, then the first president's cynical manipulation of the procedure at the *Parlement* would indicate that, despite his earlier protestations to the contrary, he was eager for the *parlementaires* to vindicate his conduct in their remonstrances, whilst appearing to take no part in them himself.[59] In this way he hoped, perhaps, to make it clear to the King and to Machault that he possessed the full confidence of the *Parlement*. His success cannot have been complete on 11 January, for the discussion of the question of who was to draft the remonstrances in his place had been postponed to another assembly. Moreover, the decision reached left misgivings in the minds of many *parlementaires*, and Jean-Omer Joly de Fleury thought the matter of 'ordres particuliers' would probably be passed over lightly in the remonstrances.[60] Nevertheless, apart from what it reveals about the ways in which the system of expressing opinions in the *Parlement* could be manipulated, the debate of 11 January shows the extent to which

---

[57] On these conventions see Dury de Meinières's account of the events of November 1751, in Flammermont, *Rems.*, i, p. 702.
[58] BS MS 800, f. 316.   [59] BN, MS franç. 8496, f. 25.
[60] BUP, CA 28/V/1: Jean-Omer Joly de Fleury to the Comte d'Argenson, 16 Jan. 1753; see also BN, JF 1497, f. 97: G.F. Joly de Fleury to Rouillé, 12 Jan. 1753 (copy/draft): 'Il faut voir si dans les assemblées des commissaires on ne fera pas de nouvelles réflexions.'

the turn of events and the worsening personal tensions within the upper echelons of the State had succeeded in breaking the usually monolithic structure of the *grand banc* and of the *grand'chambre* as a whole.

The *commissaires* were unable to decide between two drafts of the items that were to be included in the remonstrances; one was couched in general terms and was the work of Davy de La Fautrière, a friend and agent of the Comte d'Argenson; the other was a more detailed draft prepared by the pugnacious Abbé Chauvelin. The question was referred back to each chamber, and soon there were nine drafts instead of two. According to Rolland d'Erceville, intrigues were rife:

> Les créatures des ministres se flattaient que MM. des requêtes et des enquêtes ne parviendraient jamais à se concilier, ou que du moins ils y emploieraient beaucoup de temps, pendant lequel on pourrait peut-être parvenir à diviser la compagnie ou à faire naître quelque nouvelle affaire qui fit perdre de vue celle des remontrances.[61]

To thwart these schemes the chambers of *enquêtes* and *requêtes* each secretly appointed a deputy to settle the matter. The seven deputies met at the house of President Frémont du Mazy (of the 2nd chamber of the *enquêtes*), and their informal discussions produced a single draft.[62] The assembly of the chambers adopted it on 25 January.[63] The plan contained twenty-one points, which nevertheless failed to state the point of view of the *Parlement* in an adequate manner; as Jean-Omer Joly de Fleury wrote to his father:

> Je vois que ce qu'il falloit dire n'y est pas, c'est à dire, Démontrer que la Religion et L'église sont dans L'Etat: prouver comment les Principes de la Religion, du culte qu'elle prescrit et du gouvernement de L'Eglise s'allient avec ceux de L'autorité temporelle et enquoy il luy sont subordonnés . . .[64]

It was at the same assembly that, despite attempts made by President Chauvelin and other agents of Machault to force the first president to draw up the remonstrances, Maupeou formally imposed his refusal; four men were appointed to do the task in his place: the Abbé du Trousset d'Héricourt (the *rapporteur*), Boutin (the *doyen* of the 1st chamber of the *requêtes*),

[61] M. Marion, 'La Rédaction des Grandes remontrances de 1753', *Annales de la Faculté des lettres de Bordeaux* (1893), p. 139. Marion's article (pp. 132-52) was based extensively on the version of Rolland d'Erceville's memoir in the BN, Collection Lamoignon, MS franç. 8496.

[62] Flammermont, *Rems.*, i, p. 512; BS, MS 800, f. 318 (debate of 18 Jan. 1753 at the 1st chamber of *enquêtes*). The *commissaires* of the 5th *enquêtes* accepted the draft only after further changes had been made to it. On 23 Jan., the 2nd *enquêtes* made a formal protest about the delay of the *commissaires* in deciding upon a draft.

[63] Flammermont, *Rems.*, i, p. 512.

[64] BN, JF 1497, f. 148: letter of 26 Jan. [1753]; he wrote in almost identical terms to the Comte d'Argenson: BUP, CA 28/V/7: letter of 26 Jan. 1753. For the text of the twenty-two articles see Flammermont, *Rems.*, i, pp. 513-15. A copy of them in the hand of Robert de Saint-Vincent (*commissaire* from 5th *enquêtes*) is in BPR, LP 517, no. 86.

Revol (1st chamber of the *enquêtes*), and Rolland de Challerange (4th chamber of the *enquêtes*).[65]

In the course of the weeks that followed the *Parlement* had to deal with about half a dozen cases of denials of sacraments. On several occasions the Government, using *arrêts du conseil*, halted the judicial proceedings at the stage when they involved the bishops themselves. The *arrêt du conseil* which gave the archbishop of Paris replevin of his temporalities had not been issued at his request but by royal command. The King had personally handed it to the first president on 15 December. Beaumont somehow obtained the assistance of an usher of the royal council and tried to serve the *arrêt du conseil* on the *procureur général* of the *Parlement*. On 20 January the usher delivered a letter from the archbishop informing the *procureur général* that he was obliged to serve the *arrêt* on him. Joly de Fleury told the usher that he would reply to the letter. When the usher then asked him how he should execute the task he had been given and which was mentioned in the letter, the *procureur général* told him that he had nothing to prescribe, and the usher left. The *procureur général* and his brother, who reported the incident to the Comte d'Argenson, were at a loss to understand the archbishop's move:

> à quoy bon cette signification de la part de Mr l'archevêque d'un arrest qui n'est pas accordé sur sa requête et qui est déjà dans les mains de Mr. le Procureur général?[66]

In a sybilline reply to the archbishop the *procureur général* expressed regret at being unable to comment on his letter or to answer it as he would wish.

Three days later, as he was leaving early in the morning for the *Palais* with his brother, the *procureur général* was once more approached by an usher of the council who asked his permission to serve an *arrêt du conseil* on him. Again Joly de Fleury said that he had nothing to prescribe to him. According to the *avocat général*:

> L'huissier est resté dans la perplexité et voulait présenter à mon frère la signification. Je me suis tué de luy faire entendre qu'il n'était pas d'usage de faire à Mr le Procureur général des significations parlant à sa personne. La perplexité de l'huissier, l'heure qui nous pressait pour le palais nous ont fait monter en carosse et laisser un secrétaire pour être témoin de la conduite de l'huissier.
>
> L'huissier est sorti sans rien laisser. Une heure après il est revenu, et le suisse à qui il a laissé la signification l'a heureusement aporté [*sic*] au palais à temps.[67]

---

[65] Marion, 'La Rédaction des Grandes remontrances', pp. 139–40.
[66] BUP, CA 28/V/4: Jean-Omer Joly de Fleury to the Comte d'Argenson, Paris, 20 Jan. 1753.
[67] *Ibid.*, 28/V/5: same to same, 23 Jan. 1753, 2.30 p.m.

The apparent fumbling on the part of the ushers of the council probably reflected the hesitant attempts and uncertain steps being taken by certain ministers to obtain greater recognition for the decisions of the royal council in judicial matters which were normally reserved to the *Parlement*.

The *gens du roi* informed the assembly of the chambers that morning of the notification of the second *arrêt du conseil*. As the *arrêt* contained an *evocation* to the council of a case of denial of sacraments they advised the *Parlement* to include it in its forthcoming remonstrances.[68] It was an advantage of the remonstrances that they could be used to cover a multitude of sins. In this respect they were a godsend to the *gens du roi*.

On 24 January it was the turn of the chief clerk of the *Parlement* to announce to the assembly that he had been served with an *arrêt du conseil* quashing a decision of the court taken the previous day in a case of denial of sacraments at Orléans.[69] The debate was put off for two days but its outcome was an *arrêt* which was one of the most subtle to be issued by the *Parlement*[70] and, as such, deserves to be quoted in full:

Du 26 janvier 1753

La Cour, toutes les chambres assemblées, en délibérant sur le compte rendu par le greffier en chef le 24 du présent mois, n'ayant pas cru devoir se faire représenter la signification dont il a parlé, a ordonné et ordonne que la délibération demeurera continuée à mardi dix heures et que cependant les gens du roy se retireront incessamment par devers le Roy à l'effet de supplier qu'il luy plaise soutenir son autorité dans la personne de ses principaux officiers et dans la dignité du Premier tribunal de sa Justice royale en leur accordant au sujet de la signification dont il s'agit la satisfaction que ledit seigneur Roy voulût bien accorder en 1716 et 1751 par la suppression de l'original et de la copie de significations semblables.

Comme aussi de représenter audit seigneur Roy que sa justice et sa bonté donnent à son Parlement lieu de croire que ledit seigneur Roy daignera donner tels ordres qu'il ne soit plus fait à l'avenir des entreprises si contraires à la dignité de la première compagnie du royaume et à l'autorité dudit seigneur Roy. Pour le compte rendu par les gens du Roy mardy dix heures aux chambres assemblées être ordonné ce qu'il appartiendra.[71]

Without falling into the trap of recognising the validity of *arrêts du conseil* by requiring the clerk to produce the one he had received, the *Parlement* had realised that the wheel should not be used to crush a butterfly. It did not want to provoke an immediate confrontation with the Government.

In sending a copy of the *arrêté* of 26 January to the King at Choisy the chancellor added the comment:

[68] *Ibid.*   [69] *Ibid.*, 28/V/6: same to same, Paris, 24 Jan. 1753.
[70] *Ibid.*, 28/V/7: same to same, Paris, 26 Jan. 1753.
[71] *Ibid.*, 28/V/8: copy in the hand of Jean-Omer Joly de Fleury.

Votre Majesté jugera peut-estre en le lisant qu'il n'est pas nécessaire qu'elle assemble son conseil des dépêches avant son retour à Versailles.[72]

Louis XV replied at once: 'Il est inutile comme vous le pensiés bien que vous veniés ici; l'arresté du parlement ne me paroist pas aussi outré que je l'aurais cru.'[73] It is not clear that he had perceived its full subtlety.

Although the Government's repeated interference with judicial processes filled them with indignation, the *parlementaires* did not wish to jeopardise by any intemperate action the chances of success which their remonstrances might have. Nevertheless, the issue of the validity of *arrêts du conseil* used to halt proceedings or to evoke cases to the royal council had been raised anew.[74] It was a potentially dangerous issue which was always present like a *leitmotiv* throughout all the subsequent disputes.

The Government, for its part, had no earnest desire to force the issue. It was more interested in playing for time, for the question of a *déclaration* was again under discussion. Rouillé and Ogier discussed the terms of a new draft with the former *procureur général* Joly de Fleury. In a separate move, which was doubtless also instigated by the King, Lamoignon and Bidé de La Grandville sounded La Rochefoucauld once more on the by now familiar and vexed questions of the competence of the ecclesiastical courts and the administration of the sacraments.[75] But, as Bidé de La Grandville noted with some regret, 'les principes sur lesquels le conseil a agi jusqu'à présent, et les inspirations de l'ancien procureur général sont très éloignées de ce que pense M. le cardinal de la Rochefoucaut'.[76] For his part Joly de Fleury was disillusioned with La Rochefoucauld and Saulx-Tavannes, whom he now regarded as 'des pouilles mouillées'.[77] The King's cousin – and acolyte in that exercise in 'paradiplomacy' known as the *Secret du Roi* – the Prince de Conty entered the lists at this stage with a draft *déclaration*, which was probably the work of Murard (4th chamber of the *enquêtes*), his adviser, or of L. A. Le Paige, the *bailli* of the Temple, the prince's residence as *grand prieur* of the Order of Malta. Rouillé showed the

[72] Fl, Rosanbo MSS, 1/2/43: Lamoignon to Louis XV, 26 Jan. 1753.

[73] *Ibid.*, 1/2/44: Louis XV to Lamoignon, Choisy, 26 Jan. 1753.

[74] There is a fuller discussion of the question in Chapter 7. For the previous history of evocations to the royal council, see Albert N. Hamscher, *The Conseil Privé and the Parlements in the age of Louis XIV: a study in French absolutism* (Philadelphia, Transactions of the American Philosophical Society, lxxvii (2), 1987), especially pp. 113–23.

[75] For the negotiation between Rouillé, Ogier and G. F. Joly de Fleury, see BPR, LP 21, pp. 157ff; BN, JF 1497, f. 92 and 1493, ff. 143ff (text of Joly de Fleury's new draft); on the negotiations between Lamoignon, Bidé de La Grandville and La Rochefoucauld, see FL, Tocqueville MSS, 10/58 and 59.

[76] *Ibid.*, 10/58: letter of 27 Jan. 1753 to Lamoignon.

[77] BN, JF 1497, f. 122: G. F. Joly de Fleury to the Maréchal de Noailles, 5 Dec. 1752 (copy/draft).

prince's draft to Joly de Fleury without telling him whom it was from; the former *procureur général* was allowed to discuss it with Gilbert de Voisins. The prince's draft *déclaration* prescribed a rule of silence on the subject of *Unigenitus*; the time was not yet ripe for a solution of this nature to be adopted.[78] Everyone was willing to help; no one had found an acceptable remedy. At the same time, there was an indication of a significant and onimous change in the Government's attitude towards the *parlementaires*; Rouillé was now also seeking Joly de Fleury's advice on the means of re-establishing discipline within the *Parlement*.[79]

The uneasy truce was temporarily broken on 21 February, when the *Parlement* passed a *décret d'assigné pour être ouï* on the bishop of Orléans following a case of denial of sacraments in a religious house at Orléans itself.[80] The *parlementaires* had ignored an evocation of the case to the royal council obtained by the bishop, and also a recommendation by the *gens du roi* that the evocation should be regarded as a matter to be included in the remonstrances. From Versailles the chancellor quickly sent word to the King at Trianon (and indeed, on his short journey through the grounds of the palace, the hasty messenger took such a sharp turning at the *bassin de Neptune* that he was thrown from his horse).[81] At its meeting the next day the *Conseil des dépêches* took two decisions. The first was to quash the proceedings against the bishop by an *arrêt du conseil*, which was served on the *greffier* of the *Parlement*. The second was more important; the King ordered that letters patent suspending proceedings in all cases of denial of sacraments until further notice should be sent to the *Parlement* to be registered, 'sous peine de désobéissance'.[82] This decision probably owed a great deal to the King's growing impatience with his judges. The Marquis d'Argenson learned that when the King was told of the decree taken against the bishop:

> il devint rouge de colère et ne se possédait pas. Il tint conseil et ordonna avec un grand air de fâcherie à M. de Machault de sceller les lettres patentes, ce qui a mortifié ledit Machault.[83]

It is not clear whether there was at this time a difference of opinion within the *Conseil des dépêches* concerning the validity in judicial proceedings of *arrêts du conseil* that were not accompanied by letters patent and regis-

---

[78] On the Prince de Conty's scheme see BN, JF 1493, ff. 309ff, 329ff; JF 1494, ff. 51, 67, 215, and 227; and BPR, LP21, ff. 671ff.

[79] Cf. BPR, LP 21, p. 159: Ogier to [Rouillé], 24 Jan. 1753.

[80] BUP, CA 28/V/14: Jean-Omer Joly de Fleury to the Comte d'Argenson, 21 Feb. 1753; and Luynes, *Mém.*, xii, p. 362.

[81] Luynes, *Mém.*, xii, p. 363.

[82] Flammermont, *Rems.*, i, p. 516; BS, MS 800, f. 351 (debate of 23 Feb. 1753).

[83] D'Argenson, ed. Rathery, vii, pp. 414–15. The King later described his growing impatience with the *Parlement* in a letter to the Maréchal de Richelieu: see Appendix B.

tered at the *Parlement*. It has already been noted that Machault thought *arrêts du conseil* were sufficient on their own, and it is therefore tempting to assume that the Comte d'Argenson took the opposite view. D'Argenson was also possibly eager to force the issue with the *Parlement*; Machault was perhaps not keen to antagonise the magistrates whose support he might need for the registration of financial measures. On this occasion, however, as the letters patent again safeguarded the judicial position of the *Parlement*, one can hardly view them, as some contemporaries did, as a triumph for the clerical party. Even so, it is unlikely that the Government seriously expected the *parlementaires* to register the letters patent without delay or difficulty. But as long as the *parlementaires* observed the tenor of the letters patent, a majority in the council was probably not inclined to force the issue of their registration; the King could wait until the remonstrances were ready before he took further steps in that direction. Nevertheless, the council had considered the strong measures that might have to be taken if the *parlementaires* did not tacitly observe the letters patent or decided to force the issue themselves by immediately refusing to register them.[84]

The *gens du roi* received the letters patent on 23 February in the morning. They found them badly drafted. No reason was given for their having been issued; the suspension of proceedings in cases of denials of sacraments was unlimited in time; even *informations* (or judicial inquiries) were banned, as the letters patent referred to proceedings as a whole. Jean-Omer Joly de Fleury pointed out these drawbacks to the Comte d'Argenson:

> La conséquence enfin qui en résulte [est] que tant qu'elle [la surséance] durera, il peut y avoir des refus injustes sans qu'il y ait des voies ouvertes pour s'en plaindre. Voilà, Monsieur, ce qui agite et consterne les esprits.[85]

It was the task of the *gens du roi* to lay letters patent before the *grand'chambre* only: but they disagreed among themselves about the *conclusions* they were to give. Jean-Omer Joly de Fleury and his brother, the *procureur général*, wanted to recommend registration followed by remonstrances; however, D'Ormesson, the first *avocat général*, stuck out for remonstrances only. The brothers, though vexed at his attitude, nevertheless adopted his view after discussing the alternatives with the *présidents à mortier* and other leading *parlementaires*. As Jean-Omer Joly de Fleury admitted to the Comte d'Argenson:

> ... Il a paru demeurer pour constant que nous révolterions en proposant d'enregistrer sauf à faire ensuite des Remontrances, et que nous donnerions par la vivacité qui résulteroit contre nous de cet avis, une occasion presque certaine à quelque extrémité fâcheuse.[86]

---

[84] FL, Tocqueville MSS, 10/60: Bidé de La Grandville to Lamoignon, 24 Feb. 1753.
[85] BUP, CA 28/V/17: letter of 23 Feb. 1753.
[86] *Ibid.*

The *grand'chambre* was not willing to take upon itself the responsibility of dealing with the letters patent and it briskly summoned the other chambers for an assembly. Even so, the prudence of the *gens du roi* was rewarded; for the assembly adopted the course that they proposed: the letters patent simply became another item for the remonstrances.[87] In such a case the *Parlement* was entitled to defer registration.

It now remained to be seen whether the *parlementaires* would observe the letters patent all the same. At the assembly on 23 February which he had presided over in the absence of the first president, now conveniently laid up with the gout, President Le Peletier de Rozambo said, when refusing to allow a debate on a motion that entertained the possibility of further proceedings being taken in the Orléans affair, that he was afraid to contravene the King's orders. His attitude had caused an outburst of indignation, as one eyewitness described:

> tout [*sic*] mrs. se sont recriés que c'étoit donc vouloir faire exécuter à la compagnie des lettres patentes qu'elle avoit refuser d'enregistrer, quelques uns de mrs ont dit que m. le pt. peltier vouloit donc renouveller la dispute que L'on avoit eu pendent [*sic*] 3 semaines en 1737 avec m. son père et sur laquelle il avoit été obligé de céder: d'autres ont dit que mrs les pts faisoient partie de la compagnie aussy [bien] que ses autres membres et qu'ils devoient se conformer à ses délibérations.
>
> mrs les présidents disoient qu'il y avoit une assemblée de chambres indiquée à mardy, que mrs. feroient ce qu'ils jugeroient à propos, mais que de délibérer sur le champ sur la proposition de M. Douet c'étoit peut-être s'exposer au Reproche d'avoir manqué au Respect deu au Roy.
>
> Mrs. répondoient qu'aucun membre de la compagnie n'étoit capable de manquer au Respect deu [*sic*] au Roy, et qu'il étoit étonnant qu'on voulût imputer à la compagnie une façon de penser si éloignée de la sienne.
>
> Mr. le pt. lepeltier a proposé pour terminer un point si important de délibérer s'il y avoit Lieu de délibérer sur la proposition faite par M. Douet.
>
> Mrs. ont dit que cette tournure ne convenoit pas, que l'on devoit délibérer sur la proposition en elle-même, que le droit de délibérer étoit de l'essence de la compagnie; d'autres ont dit que sur des lettres patentes aussi fâcheuses mrs avoient eu la modération de ne pas demeurer assemblés et que mrs. les pts. par leur Résistance alloient forcer La compagnie de demeurer assemblées [*sic*].[88]

But as soon as the tactless Le Peletier and his colleagues gave way on what

---

[87] Flammermont, *Rems.*, i, p. 516; BS, MS 800, ff. 351ff (debate of 23 Feb. 1753).

[88] BS, MS 800, f. 354; on the events of 1737 involving Le Peletier's father, see Chapter 1, p. 21; J. M. J. Rogister, 'New light on the fall of Chauvelin', *English Historical Review*, lxxxxiii (1968), pp. 314–30; and by the same, 'A minister's fall and its implications: the case of Chauvelin (1737–1746)', in *Studies in the French eighteenth century presented to John Lough by colleagues, pupils and friends*, ed. D. J. Mossop and others (Durham, 1978), pp. 200–17.

was an important point of principle, the *parlementaires* were satisfied; Douet's motion was not in fact passed.[89]

Monsignor Durini, the Papal nuncio, a peppery Milanese who was a staunch supporter of *Unigenitus* in all its manifestations, reported the King's initial reaction to Cardinal Valenti in Rome:

> Riferita al Re questa nuova insolenza dei Parlamentarj, fu in una collera ben grande, a già era portato a dar qualche esempio contro i più temerarj, a che avevano aperto gli avvisi; ma i buoni amici hanno trovato modo di placarlo dandogli ad intendere che bisognava attendere la deliberazione di domani, mentre forse a testa più fresca il Parlamento avrebbe obedito.[90]

The Government probably was waiting for the outcome of the other crucial debate, on 27 February, when the *gens du roi* were to give an account of the various proceedings that were pending. On that occasion D'Ormesson mentioned only the case at Orléans and said that the *gens du roi* were not yet ready to report on the other proceedings. The *parlementaires* agreed to postpone their debate on the Orléans case until after the remonstrances had been drawn up. When the *rapporteur*, the Abbé du Trousset d'Héricourt, was also questioned about the other proceedings, he replied that his labours on the remonstrances gave him little time to work on them; the *parlementaires*, who were unconvinced, pressed the matter no further, though some of them gave him a rough passage.[91] After the debate the *Parlement* adjourned for Lent and did not reassemble until 9 March.[92] A week or so later the *rapporteur* again secured a postponement, this time on a case at Mussy L'Evêque, by saying that the results of the preliminary inquiry had not yet come through.[93]

On 28 March the *parlementaires* learned that Pétard, the priest who had been suspended, had resumed his duties in Tours (as a result of a misunderstanding at Versailles).[94] In the course of the debate even a *zélé* like

---

[89] BS MS 800, f. 355. In a comment on this passage in a colleague's diary President Durey de Meinières observed:

> Il n'y avoit pas de mauvaise volonté pour le compagnie de la part de Mrs. les Présidens, mais un peu de témérité pour eux-mêmes et le déffaut de l'usage de conduire un corps comme le Parlement. Le premier président les a désapprouvé [*sic*] et leur a représenté qu'ils seraient bien plus exposé du costé de la cour s'ils étoient les maîtres d'empescher les délibérations, prétention d'ailleurs qui est intolérable. f. 354

[90] Calvi (ed.), *Curiosità storiche e diplomatiche del secolo decimottavo; corrispondenza segrete di grandi personnagi* (Milan, 1878), p. 258: Durini to Valenti, 26 Feb. 1753.
[91] BS MS 800, f. 356 (debate of 27 Feb. 1753); BUP, CA/V/18: Jean-Omer Joly de Fleury to the Comte d'Argenson, 27 Feb. 1753.
[92] Barbier, *Journal*, v, p. 356.
[93] BS, MS 800, f. 369 (debate of 20 Mar. 1753). The decision to postpone passed by about sixty-five votes to fifty-two.
[94] BS MS 800, f. 370; BPR, LP 21, p. 223: Joly de Fleury to Rouillé, 4 Apr. 1753:

> le Roy a dit à Mr. le Prince de Conty, que c'étoit sans son aveu que les curés de Tours

Lambert (of the 2nd of *enquêtes*), who wished to see Pétard arrested, nevertheless spoke of 'L'inconvénient d'un parti trop décidé dans les circonstances délicates où se trouvoit la compagnie'.[95] But Pétard had committed a serious offence; hence the *Parlement* felt obliged to order that its previous *arrêts* concerning him should now be carried out. The *gens du roi* were asked to report on 6 April on the execution of the decision.[96] They pleaded with the Government to be allowed to send the *arrêt* to the *procureur du roi* at Tours, as they thought, or more likely hoped, that he had been sent a *lettre de cachet* preventing him from enforcing it.[97] But on 31 March the *parlementaires* suddenly questioned their delay and ordered them to send off the *arrêt* at once.[98] It was a delicate situation. But the Government proved accommodating and helped the *gens du roi* out of their difficulty with an *arrêt du conseil* quashing that of the *Parlement*.[99] When the *greffier-en-chef* notified it to the chambers three days later, the *parlementaires* again agreed to postpone discussion until they had finished the remonstrances. As one of them ironically observed, 'la compagnie commençoit à s'accoutumer aux arrests du conseil et aux récits du greffier en chef'.[100]

One of Beaumont's adherents had written to a friend on 8 March:

> nos affaires vont toujours mal, et notre espérance n'est guère humainement que dans les excès du Parlement. Il n'est pas possible qu'enfin ils ne réveillent ce prince qui, jusqu'à présent, a paru si peu sensible aux affronts que lui fait cette compagnie.[101]

But the *parlementaires* had in fact shown great restraint from the time when they had received the letters patent. Otherwise the King would not have waited over two and a half months before ordering them to register the letters patent without further delay.[102]

avoient repris leurs fonctions, que l'archevêque avoit pris cela sous son bonnet, que le Roy étoit furieux contre luy; l'archevêque de Tours dit à qui veut d'entendre que Mr de Saint Florentin luy a dit que les curés pouvoient reprendre leurs fonctions, et m^r. de st florentin le désavoue bien hautement.

95   BS MS 800, f. 372 (debate of 28 Mar. 1753).   96   *Ibid.*
97   BUP, CA 28/V: Jean-Omer Joly de Fleury to the Comte d'Argenson, 30 Mar. 1753.
98   BS MS 800, f. 376.
99   The *gens du roi* were ordered to go to Versailles on 1 April to receive the King's orders; as the *Conseil des dépêches* met that day (Luynes, *Mém.*, xii, p. 400), the decision to quash the *arrêt* of the *Parlement* was probably taken then. There are no details available about this meeting of the council where a few other important matters relating to the *Parlement* were also discussed.
100 BS MS 800, f. 379 (debate of 3 Apr. 1753). The decision was passed by a large majority.
101 Letter of the bishop of Amiens to the Abbé de La Trappe, printed in E. Régnault, *Christophe de Beaumont, archevêque de Paris, 1703–1781* (Paris, 1882), i, p. 244. This was also the view of the papal nuncio; see Calvi, *Curiosità storiche*, p. 262: Durini to Valenti, 12 March 1753.
102 For an illustration of the ambiguous relations between the Government and the *Parlement* at this time see John Rogister, 'Teaching the Gallican Articles: the affair of the *Quaestio theologica* and the Paris Faculty of Theology', *Parliaments, Estates and Representation* ix (1989), pp. 165–74.

The *parlementaires* had suspended their proceedings over the long period from February to April because they were engrossed in the task of preparing the remonstrances that the first president had refused to draft. There were other reasons for the delay in producing a text. The four *commissaires* entrusted with the task had begun their meetings on 25 January. Rolland de Challerange wanted to gain the credit for being the author of the remonstrances, and he offered to present his three other colleagues with a preliminary draft of the first six articles within three days. His text was considered unsatisfactory: hardly a surprising outcome as his piece on the fourth article began with a statement that taxed the credulity of even the most enthusiastic antiquary: 'La France n'oubliera jamais ce qui s'est passé sous Louis le Débonnaire.'[103] Du Trousset d'Héricourt, eager to retrieve the initiative for the moderates, proposed that the four *commissaires* should each produce a draft for a meeting on 17 February. On that occasion Rolland de Challerange brought a revised version of his draft, while Du Trousset d'Héricourt and Revol came with texts based on material supplied by President de Cotte from his celebrated collection of parliamentary records. Boutin pleaded ill health and brought nothing to the meeting. Revol secured the rejection of Rolland de Challerange's version by ensuring that Du Trousset d'Héricourt was given the task of producing a single draft.

This news was greeted with dismay by the *zélés*, as it meant that, despite division in high places, the moderates were still in control of the situation; the remonstrances were going to be drafted by no less a person than the *rapporteur*, a clerk in holy orders known to be favourable to *Unigenitus*. Clément de Feillet, one of the *zélés* and a Jansenist, found a solution to the problem. The *zélés* would secretly prepare their own draft of the remonstrances and then secure its adoption by the official draftsmen as their own work.[104] He recruited Lambert, a gifted young councillor of the 2nd *enquêtes*, to do the task. On 21 February Du Trousset d'Héricourt showed

---

103 Marion, 'La Rédaction des Grandes remontrances', pp. 132–52. As it has been already stated, Marion based his account largely on the BN, Collection Lamoignon version of the memoir by Rolland d'Erceville; this version was also used by Flammermont for his commentary in *Rems.*, i, pp. 515–16. These accounts need to be supplemented by the earlier version (*ante* 21 August 1753) of Rolland d'Erceville's memoir in AEE, MD, France 1344, ff. 28off (used by Soulavie), by the memoirs of Robert de Saint-Vincent, (Collection Michel Vinot Préfontaine, Paris; typescript), and by the diary kept by a *parlementaire* and annotated by Durey de Meinières in BS, SM 800, f. 374 (debate of 30 March 1753).

104 Marion, 'La Rédaction des Grandes remontrances', p. 142; cf. Collection Michel Vinot Préfontaine, Paris: 'Mémoires de P. A. Robert de Saint-Vincent', typescript, p. 147. Robert de Saint-Vincent was cool about Rolland d'Erceville and tends to give himself a more important rôle in the drafting of the remonstrances than Rolland d'Erceville ascribes to him in both versions of his memoir.

his own draft to Lambert and others and later agreed to adopt the amendments which they had proposed. He paraphrased them instead, and when his version was shown to the *commissaires* from all the chambers on 10, 17, and 24 March, it provoked so many criticisms that he decided to give up the task altogether. The *commissaires* fell back on Revol's text but rejected it as badly written, repetitive, and lacking a scholarly apparatus. With Du Trousset d'Héricourt, Revol, and Rolland de Challerange out of the running, and still without a draft from Boutin, the four *commissaires* had failed lamentably in their mission.[105]

The path was now clear for the cabal of *zélés*. The Abbé Chauvelin and President Durey de Meinières persuaded Lambert to produce a text for the first ten articles of the remonstrances, while Chauvelin himself tackled articles 11–14 (on evocations of judicial cases to the royal council) and Robert de Saint-Vincent worked on articles 15–22 with some help from Lambert. As their work progressed they showed the results to Clément and to some experts outside the *Parlement*, including the Abbé Mey, an author and theologian, and possibly the lawyer, Louis-Adrien Le Paige. Lambert's text was accepted, but Chauvelin's was modified by Mey, acting tactfully through Lambert. Robert de Saint-Vincent's section on *lettres de cachet* had been lifted from a book and was accepted, but his text on *Unigenitus* was thought to be feeble; there was time to make only a few corrections to it.[106]

The *zélés* now faced a harder task: that of securing the adoption of their version by the official draftsmen and through them by the assembly of the chambers. Revol was sounded but refused categorically to present Lambert's work as his own. Fortunately for the *zélés*, Boutin and Rolland de Challerange had formed the idea of producing a joint text with outside help and had approached Mey for assistance. Using Mey as their intermediary, the *zélés* were able to manipulate the two men with a view to pressing Lambert's draft on them at the appropriate moment. There was little time to spare before the meeting of the *commissaires* from all the chambers on 28 March. Chauvelin spent the night of 25–26 March redrafting Robert de Saint-Vincent's section on *Unigenitus*: Lambert spent the following night revising that section as well as Robert de Saint-Vincent's passages on *lettres de cachet*. The *zélés* put the finishing touches to the remonstrances on 27 March and spent another night making copies.[107]

Boutin and Rolland de Challerange had obtained little assistance from

[105] Marion, 'La Rédaction des Grandes remontrances', p. 143.
[106] Collection Michel Vinot Préfontaine, 'Mémoires de P. A. Robert de Saint-Vincent', typescript, p. 148.
[107] Marion, 'La Rédaction des Grandes remontrances', p. 146.

Mey and were in a state of panic. They called on him on the evening of 27 March and were greatly relieved when told that Clément would now allow them to see parts of Lambert's work. They obtained a postponement of the assembly of the *commissaires* by twenty-four hours and went off to present Lambert's work as their own to Revol and Du Trousset d'Héricourt. Their two colleagues rejected the text as being too strongly worded. Clément was an able tactician. It seems that he appealed to Boutin's pride by urging him not to allow himself to be browbeaten by Du Trousset d'Héricourt. Besides, he argued, the remonstrances would be adopted anyway. Boutin agreed to present the text at the assembly of the *commissaires* on 29 March.[108] There, after an acrimonious discussion, it was decided that the chambers would be assembled the next day.[109]

The assembly of the chambers of 30 March turned into a confrontation between the divided moderates and the *zélés*. The first president was conveniently laid up with gout for the occasion, and his place was taken by President Molé.[110] As the thirty-eight *commissaires* from the chambers had been divided on the question whether the remonstrances were ready to be shown to the assembly, Molé was able to make that question the object of a preliminary debate. The four *commissaires* took opposite sides. By eighty (or, in one version, seventy-two) votes to fifty-four the *parlementaires* decided that the remonstrances should be read out and discussed. But the moderates (led by Presidents Le Peletier de Rozambo and Gilbert) had a come-back in the debate that followed the reading, which took nine hours. By seventy-one votes to fifty-six they defeated their opponents (including Fermé, the Abbé Chauvelin, Clément de Feillet, and Rolland d'Erceville), who wanted the remonstrances to be adopted at the same meeting; the acceptance of the remonstrances was postponed for another week on the pretext that corrections had to be made.[111] At a noisy meeting on 3 April the four *commissaires* reluctantly undertook not to make substantial changes in the text, which was formally adopted two days later and signed, after another reading, on 9 April.[112]

The *zélés* had succeeded beyond their hopes in securing the acceptance of their draft of the remonstrances by two of the official draftsmen, by the *commissaires*, and by the assembly of the chambers. Towards the end, Rolland de Challerange had second thoughts and tried to make significant changes to the text, but Lambert had silenced him by threatening to reveal

---

[108] *Ibid.*, p. 147. [109] *Ibid.* [110] BS MS 800, f. 374.

[111] *Ibid.*, ff. 374–6; Marion, 'La Rédaction des Grandes remonstrances', p. 150. President Durey de Meinières deserves a place in the history of scholarship for deciding that references should go at the bottom of the page instead of at the end of the work.

[112] BS MS 800, ff. 379–81 (debate of 9 April 1753).

what most *parlementaires* probably already knew: that neither he nor Boutin were the real authors of the remonstrances.[113]

The standard pattern of interpretation of these events was set a century ago by Marcel Marion and it has not changed since. Marion rightly argued that a body like the *Parlement* could not have produced a work of the size and scope of the *Grandes remontrances* without the assistance of dedicated antiquaries, Jansenist theologians, clever lawyers, and, finally, of a gifted twenty-seven-year old councillor with the stamina to spend his days and nights on the task. However, the comparison which Marion drew between the painful birth of the remonstrances and what he saw as the immodest pretensions of the *Parlement* is misleading. So too is his claim that the *Grandes remontrances* marked the establishment of the permanent control of an active minority in the *Parlement* over a weak and hesitant majority.[114] Such an interpretation fails to take account of the special circumstances of the moment created in large part by the conduct of the first president and the ineptitude of the Government. The *Grandes remontrances* of 9 April 1753 have to be seen as an exceptional event because they were drafted in an unusual way in circumstances that were unique.

By their length, their occasional flights of eloquence, and their inclusion of erudite notes and quotations, they formed a stark contrast with previous remonstrances, especially those of July 1752 prepared by the first president. Many of the arguments contained in them were not new but for once they were forcefully expressed. The clergy was accused of seeking independence from all royal authority; of being in revolt against the personal wishes of the King whose peaceable intentions had frequently been expressed in replies preserved in the records of the *Parlement*; and of being in revolt against the King's judicial authority, which was the same as that exercised by the *Parlement*.[115]

The *Grandes remontrances* also came to occupy a particular place in the history of the resistance of the *Parlement* to royal arbitrariness. They made a

---

[113] Marion, 'La Rédaction des Grandes remontrances', p. 150. According to Rolland d'Erceville, the final version of the remonstrances was the work of the following authors: Clauvelin for the section on *Unigenitus* and the expressions of love and respect for the King; Robert de Saint-Vincent (with revisions by Lambert) for the section on *ordres particuliers* (derived from an unidentified book); Mey (with small changes by Lambert) for articles 7-10, except for the section on the competence of the lay courts which was by Lambert. Some of Du Trousset d'Héricourt's ideas had been adopted. In the main, Lambert was the chief contributor (Marion, 'La Rédaction des Grandes remontrances', p. 151). Robert de Saint-Vincent also attributes much of the credit to Lambert, while stating that he was himself responsible for the concluding passages ('Mémoires', p. 150).

[114] Marion, 'La Rédaction des Grandes remontrances', pp. 151-2.

[115] Collection Michel Vinot Préfontaine, 'Mémoires de P. A. Robert de Saint-Vincent', typescript, p. 147.

significant contribution to the revival of the debate on the nature of the
Monarchy and of the Fundamental Laws and thus became a point of
reference. They embodied a powerful argument concerning the nature and
force of law in society and in the political structure of the *ancien régime*.[116]
They included a quotation from a celebrated treatise produced a century
earlier under Government auspices to sustain the claims of Queen Marie-
Thérèse to the Spanish inheritance:

> La loi fondamentale de l'Etat forme une liaison réciproque et éternelle entre
> le Prince et ses descendans, d'une part, et les sujets et leurs descendans, de
> l'autre, par une espèce de contrat qui destine le souverain à régner et les
> peuples à obéir ... engagement solennel dans lequel il se sont donnés les uns
> aux autres pour s'entraider mutuellement.[117]

After this definition of a contractual theory of government, the remonstrances went on to describe the rôle of law:

> Les lois sont le nœud sacré et comme le sceau de cet engagement indissoluble.
> Le Roi, l'Etat et la loi forment un tout inséparable.[118]

As subjects owed obedience to their sovereign, so the sovereign owed
obedience to the law. Hence, royal power ought not to be exercised
arbitrarily but in accordance with the spirit of justice and reason expressed
in the law. The maintenance of the law was, so the *parlementaires* told the
King, 'un dépôt sacré dont les ordonnances "chargent la conscience" de
votre Parlement':

> C'est en votre nom, Sire, que votre Parlement veille à la conservation de
> l'Etat; son autorité n'est autre que la vôtre, mais c'est votre autorité devenue
> inaccessible aux surprises, employée uniquement au bien public, conduite et
> éclairée par les lois. Il en est, Sire, le ministre essentiel.[119]

Too much emphasis should not be placed on the supposed divergence
between these notions and those held in governmental circles. On all sides
in 1753, and as time was to show, there was a considerable measure of
agreement on two points: the first was that the King's sovereign power was
absolute, and the second was that he exercised that sovereign power in such

---

[116] J. M. J. Rogister, 'The crisis of 1753–1754 in France and the debate on the nature of the
Monarchy and of the Fundamental Laws', in *Herrschaftsverträge, Wahlkapitulationen, und
Fundamentalgesetze*, ed. R. Vierhaus (Studies presented to the International Commission
for the History of Representative and Parliamentary Institutions, lix, Göttingen, 1977),
pp. 105–20; and the same author's 'Parlementaires, sovereignty, and legal opposition in
France under Louis XV: an introduction', *Parliaments, Estates and Representations*, vi (1986),
pp. 25–32.

[117] Flammermont, *Rems.*, i, p. 522; for the use made of this passage in the remonstrances by
the *encyclopédistes*, see John Lough, 'The *Encyclopédie* and the Remonstrances of the Paris
Parlement', in *Modern Language Review*, lvi (1961), pp. 393–5.

[118] Flammermont, *Rems.*, i, pp. 525–6.   [119] *Ibid.*, p. 528.

a way that it could be distinguished from despotism and was in accordance with the traditions and customs of the French Monarchy. Between these two agreed points, there was scope for the disagreements as well as for the flexibility of practical politics.[120]

Finally, the *Grandes remontrances* were significant because they subsequently appeared in print.[121] Remonstrances were intended only for the King and were supposed to be a secret between him and his *parlementaires*. Again, the exceptional circumstances of the moment had played their part. Persons outside the *Parlement* had been shown the text, and the collaborative effort expended upon it had led to a proliferation of copies, some of which found their way into the hands of clandestine printers by early May. The religious and constitutional debate was thus given an unprecedented public airing.

The *gens du roi* had gone to Versailles on 7 April to arrange a date for the presentation of the remonstrances. Louis XV gained a short respite by telling them that he wished first to see the *arrêté* of 25 January containing the twenty-two articles. This unusual request worried the *parlementaires*, who felt that the King would get only an inadequate view of the substance of their remonstrances from the text of the articles. They wasted four days trying unsuccessfully to obtain his permission to deliver the *arrêté* through a deputation. The text of the twenty-two articles was given to the King by the *gens du roi* on 15 April.[122] At a meeting of the chambers the next day the *parlementaires*, who were about to adjourn until 3 May for the Easter vacation, decided to send the *gens du roi* again to Versailles to ask the King when he would receive the remonstrances. When the *gens du roi* saw him he told them to come for a reply on 2 May.[123]

The moment of decision had arrived for the King. A majority of his ministers urged that the *Parlement* should be made to register the letters patent without delay; in this respect it is possible that Saint-Florentin had gone over to the side of D'Argenson (which, by some accounts, already included Paulmy, Puyzieulx and Saint-Séverin) and had thus decisively weakened the group led by Machault, Rouillé, and the unpredictable Noailles.[124] But there were two problems. In the first place, a decision to

---

[120] Rogister, 'The Crisis of 1753–1754 in France', pp. 118–19.

[121] Marion, 'La Rédaction des Grandes remontrances', p. 151, note 1.

[122] Barbier, *Journal*, v, p. 367; BS MS 800, ff. 381, 384–5: BUP, CA 28/V: Jean-Omer Joly de Fleury to the Comte d'Argenson, 9 April 1753; FL. Rosanbo MSS, 1/2/11: Lamoignon to the King, 9 April 1753 (with the King's reply of the following day in the margin); BN, JF 309, f. 342: Lamoignon to the *procureur général*, 'mardi', [10 April 1753], 1.30 p.m.; Flammermont, *Rems.*, i, pp. 517–18.

[123] BS MS 800, f. 386; Barbier, *Journal*, v, p. 372.

[124] See Giorgio Renucci, 'Una inedita relazione di Raimondo Cecchetti di Oderzo sulle questioni insorte tra il clero e il parlamento francese nel 1754', *Nuova Rivista Storica*, xlviii (1964), p. 626. Cecchetti, a member of Cardinal Rezzonico's secretariat, accompanied

force the issue over the letters patent would look like a victory for the clergy unless the King made that decision palatable to the *parlementaires* by bringing out a new law on denial of sacraments which made important concessions to their point of view. Early in March the eight lay and ecclesiastical *commissaires* had been recalled and asked to work out the terms of a *déclaration*; but they still could not agree amongst themselves.[125] The *Conseil des dépêches* was also divided on the matter. The final decision rested with the King, who was free to overrule the objections of either side. Louis XV remained impenetrable; on 22 April Rouillé wrote to Joly de Fleury:

> Je suis toujours Monsieur dans l'incertitude de sçavoir si le Roy se portera à donner une déclaration. mon doutte est fondé sur l'opposition des Evesques, la diversité des opinions des commissaires qui ont été chargés d'examiner le question, les sentimens différens, qu'il entend dans son conseil, l'incertitude de l'effet que produira une déclaration dans un tems où les esprits sont aussy échauffés, et surtout les scrupules de S. Mté. et La crainte qu'elle a d'em-piéter sur la jurisdiction Eclésiastique [*sic*] en prescrivant des règles pour ce qui concerne l'administration des sacremens. en suposant [*sic*] vraye cette incertitude que je présume peut être sans fondement . . .[126]

Rouillé had admirably perceived the King's predicament. As Louis XV himself wrote to the Maréchal de Richelieu a few weeks later: 'Je n'aime pas plus l'authorité des prestres en temps qu'ils veulent sortir de leurs bornes mistiques, mais je veut qu'on rende à dieu ce qui est [à] dieu, et à ceesar [*sic*] ce qui est à ceasar [*sic*].'[127] But he probably found it an impossible task to apply these simple notions to the problem of denial of sacraments which was such a complicated legal and political tangle. He hesitated and chose not to decide the issue himself.

The second difficulty concerned the remonstrances; the King would not receive them, probably because they dealt with 'ordres particuliers'.[128] The decision to ask for the twenty-two articles may well have been a compromise between his views and the different opinions expressed in the *Conseil des dépêches*. The King's resolve was further strengthened after the

Mgr Branciforte to France in June 1753 on a mission to present the Pope's traditional gift of swaddling clothes for the King's grandson, the Duc de Bourgogne. Branciforte asked him to keep notes on what he observed during their stay.

[125] FL, Tocqueville MSS, 10/44: Castanier d'Auriac to Lamoignon, 13 Mar. 1753; 10/63: Bidé de La Grandville to Lamoignon, 156 Mar. 1753; 10/69: 'Mémoire sur le projet de déclaration proposée, 15 mars 1753' (by Lamoignon). It is possible that the question of a new law was discussed at the meetings of the *Conseil des dépêches* on 24–25 March; Lamoignon's memoir was probably a report presented to the council at about this time. The *commissaires* were subsequently asked to give their opinions separately in writing (see, BPR, LP 21, p. 223: Joly de Fleury to Rouillé, 4 Apr. 1753).

[126] BN, JF 1494, f. 215.   [127] See Appendix B.

[128] The suggestion that the King should not receive the remonstrances had been expressed by the archbishop as early as 15 January in a letter to the Comte d'Argenson; AN, 422 AP 1.

articles had been examined by the council.[129] The chancellor doubtless presented a report on them which was markedly unfavourable;[130] few of those present at the meeting probably expressed a contrary opinion. Moreover the King wanted to take a firm stand towards the *Parlement* and barely concealed his impatience.[131] On 4 May he made known his decision to the first president in surprisingly moderate terms:

> J'ai examiné avec attention dans mon conseil l'arrêté du 25 janvier dernier qui fixe l'objet de vos remontrances et j'ai reconnu que dans les différants points que vous vous proposez d'y traiter, il y en a plusieurs sur lesquels je vous ai déjà donné mes ordres, d'autres enfin dont la discussion ne pourrait qu'apporter de nouveaux obstacles aux vues que j'ai toujours eues pour le rétablissement et le maintien de la tranquillité. Ces motifs me déterminent à ne point recevoir vos remontrances et à vous ordonner d'enregistrer, sans différer, mes lettres patentes du 22 février dernier.[132]

It is possible that the Government were sanguine enough to think that the *parlementaires* might yet be persuaded to register the letters patent in the belief that their judicial competence had not been called in question.[133] But the decision not to receive the remontrances was a grave mistake; for as it was in contradiction with the King's professed intention, expressed in April and again in December 1752, of always giving the *parlementaires* a fair hearing, it provided them with a plausible excuse to suspend the exercise of

---

[129] The King's resolve was already known to the *gens du roi* on 25 April; see BUP, CA 28/V: Jean-Omer Joly de Fleury to the Comte d'Argenson, 25 Apr. 1753. It is not clear when the twenty-two articles were examined by the council. The chancellor showed the King the draft of a reply to the *Parlement* on 28 April. The King asked to see it again the next day, together with the text of the articles, so that he could examine them more fully before the next meeting of the *Conseil des dépêches*; FL, Rosanbo MSS, 1/2/16: Louis XV to Lamoignon, 28 Apr. [1753], 'au soir'. It is possible that the articles had already been discussed before the King went to Trianon for a few days on 24 April and that the discussion was going to be resumed, as the King's letter to the chancellor implied.

[130] Cf. FL, Tocqueville MSS, 10/68: 'Réflexions sur le projet de remontrances arresté au Parlement le 25 janvier 1753'. This document is Lamoignon's report on the articles; it is entirely in his hand. Each article is quoted in full and commented upon at length (generally in a hostile manner).

[131] See his letter to the Maréchal de Richelieu, in Appendix B. Cecchetti also indicates that the King was convinced of the need to take a firm stand with the *Parlement*; Renucci, 'Una inedita relazione', p. 626.

[132] Flammermont, *Rems.*, i, p. 518.

[133] Jean-Omer Joly de Fleury may well have encouraged this belief when he suggested to the Comte d'Argenson, on 25 April, that the King had a pretext for calling a deputation from the *Parlement*:

> ... ne pourroit-il [the King] pas l'expliquer en improuvant de la manière la plus forte ceux des articles qui ont pour objet les lettres de cachet: après quoy il seroit ce me semble possible de tranquilliser les esprits sur le fond de la matière et sur le maintien de l'autorité du roy. Puisque l'on résiste à L'Idée d'une loy, il faut bien y substituer un espèce d'équivalent. BUP, CA 28/V.

their duties. The decision was also later to be a stumbling-block in all the negotiations that took place after the exile of the *enquêtes*. But it had another, more immediate, effect: the matter of the registration of the letters patent became a trial of strength between the Government and the *Parlement*. The Government accepted that confrontation but had not fully perceived its implications. Maupeou later told a *parlementaire* that he had warned Lamoignon of the unfortunate consequences of the King's decision; but, he admitted, 'toutes mes instances ont été inutiles et je n'ai pu rien obtenir'.[134]

The King's decision was considered at an assembly of the chambers held the next day. The *parlementaires* adopted an *arrêté* stating that, as the *Parlement* was unable to fulfil its most important function, that of making the truth known to the King, the chambers would remain assembled, all other service ceasing, until it pleased the King to listen favourably to their remonstrances. The Government was probably prepared for this move, but was deeply divided about the steps it should take. According to the papal nuncio, at a meeting of the *Conseil des dépêches* held that evening at Versailles, it was decided on the advice of the majority to order the *parlementaires* to resume their duties and to register the letters patent of 23 February. Those in favour of this move were the chancellor, the Duc de Béthune, D'Argenson, Puyzieulx, Saint-Séverin ('il quale parlò con violenza'), and in the end they had rallied Saint-Florentin to their side. Machault, Saint-Contest, and the Maréchal de Noailles had been left in the minority, advocating that the *parlementaires* should be ordered to resume their duties without the requirement to register the letters patent. D'Argenson had apparently made light of their fears that there might be an uprising in the capital.[135] On Monday, 7 May, the *gens du roi* appeared before the assembly of the chambers with letters patent *en forme de jussion*, a legal device enabling the King to order that the previous letters patent should be registered at once and that the *parlementaires* should continue to carry out their ordinary judicial duties.[136] But the *parlementaires* refused to obey; they unanimously passed an *arrêté*, of which the terms had already been decided before the meeting began:

> La Cour, en délibérant sur les lettres patentes en forme de jussion du 5 du présent mois et persistant dans l'arrêté du même jour, a arrêté qu'elle ne peut

[134] BN, MS franç. 8496 (Memoir of Rolland d'Erceville), p. 176. These remarks were made to Nouveau de Chenevières, a young councillor of the 2nd chamber of *requêtes*.

[135] Calvi (ed.), *Curiosità storiche*, pp. 267–8: Durini to Valenti, 14 May 1753.

[136] Flammermont, *Rems.*, i, p. 519; BN, JF 309, f. 362: Comte d'Argenson to the *procureur général*, 6 May 1753; f. 363: 'Lettres patentes en forme de jussion', Versailles, 6 May 1753; f. 357: *conclusions* in the hand of the *procureur général* for registration but with remonstrances; f. 356: the first draft of the *conclusions* by the former *procureur général*.

sans manquer à son devoir et à son serment obtempérer auxdites lettres patentes en forme de jussion.[137]

The preference given to the word 'obtempérer' in place of the word 'obéir' had doubtless satisfied some tender consciences.

There are signs that the Government had not expected this 'act of disobedience'. The same afternoon the King came over to Versailles from Bellevue for a specially convened meeting of the *Conseil des dépêches*.[138] His advisers were again divided on the course of action to be taken. The previous day the Maréchal de Noailles had told the King in one of his occasional fits of bluntness that the division between the clergy and the magistrates was fostered by public knowledge that the Government was divided:

> Les choses sont arrivées à un tel point qu'il est d'une nécessité absolue d'y apporter les plus prompts remèdes. On a osé dire dans votre conseil que cela étoit impossible; mais rien, Sire, ne vous sera impossible lorsque vous le voudrez bien, & que vous le voudrez efficacement.[139]

The King adjourned the meeting in the evening and ordered the members of the council to continue the discussion in his absence as a *comité* under the chairmanship of the chancellor.[140] But it seems that there was still no agreement amongst them the next day when the King again came over from Bellevue to preside over the council. Observers learned that while D'Argenson had pressed for strong measures to uphold the King's authority, Machault had urged that the *Parlement* should be given a last chance to register the letters patent.[141] D'Argenson carried the day, doubtless with a confident assurance that he could maintain order in the capital. The

---

[137] Flammermont, *Rems.*, i, p. 519; BUP, CA 28/V: Jean-Omer Joly de Fleury to the Comte d'Argenson, 7 May, 1753.

[138] For evidence that the King was staying at Bellevue from the evening of 6 to 9 May, see Barbier, *Journal*, v, p. 380. D'Argenson says he left on 5 May (ed. Rathery, viii, p. 8). For the other details see *ibid.*, viii, pp. 16, 20.

[139] C. F. X. Millot, *Mémoires politiques et militaires pour servir à l'histoire de Louis XIV et Louis XV, composées sur les pièces originales recueillies par Adrien-Maurice duc de Noailles, maréchal de France & ministre d'état* (Paris, 1777), vi, p. 321. The Abbé Millot's work was censored by the Duc de Nivernais acting on the orders of the marshal's son, a fact that might explain why Noailles's position is not clearly stated in the extracts that are given; on the censoring of Millot's memoirs of the marshal, see Bibliothèque municipale, Besançon, MSS [P] 652: Millot Papers.

[140] Barbier, *Journal*, v, p. 380; D'Argenson, ed Rathery, viii, p. 17.

[141] That the King attended another meeting of the council at Versailles on 8 May seems to appear from D'Argenson, ed. Rathery, viii, pp. 20–1. For unconfirmed details about the discussions in the council, see *ibid.*, viii, pp. 26, 34; Renucci, 'Une inedita relazione', p. 627 (for Cecchetti's account); and BL, Add. MSS 35,630 (Hardwicke Papers), f. 85ᵛ: Jeffreys to Philip Yorke, 9 May 1753. Paulmy had apparently pressed for a *lit de justice*. Jean-Omer Joly de Fleury reluctantly urged this solution on the Comte d'Argenson in a letter of 10 May: BUP, CA 28/V.

King's gaiety over supper at Bellevue seemed to indicate that he was himself pleased with the result.[142] That night the musketeers patrolled the streets of Paris. In the early hours of the morning they delivered *lettres de cachet* to all the presidents and councillors of the chambers of *enquêtes* and *requêtes*. Each *parlementaire* was ordered to leave Paris within twenty-four hours for the place of exile mentioned in his *lettre de cachet*. The Government also singled out the Abbé Chauvelin and three others for arrest; these men were conveyed to remote fortresses but otherwise suffered little hardship.[143]

It is possible that D'Argenson and other ministers hoped that these measures would lead the *grand'chambre* to register the letters patent.[144] If so, then they overlooked one important factor: the pride of the *présidents à mortier* and councillors who were its members. Later the same morning, the first president had a long conference with the *présidents à mortier*; they decided to stand by their exiled colleagues.[145] Maupeou went to the *grand-chambre* afterwards and told the councillors, in a moving speech, that he presumed it was their wish to abide by the previous decisions of the *Parlement*; the resultant *arrêté* confirmed this opinion.[146] There is evidence to suggest that some, if not all, members of the Government expected that Maupeou would seize the opportunity of the exile of the *enquêtes* and *requêtes* to seek an audience with the King to offer his servises.[147] But Maupeou made no such move. Moreover, the *grand'chambre* did not take advantage of the circumstances to send him to Versailles at the head of a deputation. Jean-Omer Joly de Fleury held the first president responsible for the deadlock; Maupeou, so he alleged, was making no attempt to hold discussions. The *avocat général* thought the Government should try to influence President Gilbert ('qui peut beaucoup') and President de Maupeou; the others would follow their lead or were already well disposed.[148] Instead the *grand'chambre* behaved as if nothing had happened; it ordered the *gens du roi*

---

[142] D'Argenson, ed. Rathery, viii, pp. 20–1.

[143] Barbier, *Journal*, v, pp. 381–3. The confidential letters informing the intendants Blossac and Barentin of the transfer of the *parlementaires* to towns within their administrative jurisdiction were drawn up on 9 May: see AAE, MD, France 1345, ff. 163ff. On the draft the names of those who were to be imprisoned (President Gaultier de Besigny, Chauvelin, President Frémont du Mazy – the brother-in-law of Saint-Contest and of Jean-Omer Joly de Fleury – and Bèze de Lys) are added in the hand of the Comte d'Argenson (f. 172).

[144] Cf. BN, JF 1497, f. 137: Jean-Omer Joly de Fleury probably to his father, 'ce mercredi 11 heures', [9 May 1753].

[145] *Ibid.* See also BUP, CA 28/V: Jean-Omer Joly de Fleury to the Comte d'Argenson, 10 May 1753.

[146] Barbier, *Journal*, v, pp. 384–5.

[147] See a letter of 1 March 1754 from Ysabeau to the Maréchal de Richelieu; BVC, RP, xiv (catalogue no. 35), no. 8. This fact emerged in the course of discussions held, in February 1754, between the *gens du roi* and Machault, Rouillé and Saint-Florentin. D'Ormesson, the first *avocat général*, mentioned it to Ysabeau.

[148] D'Argenson, ed. Rathery, viii, p. 19; BUP, CA 28/V: Jean-Omer Joly de Fleury to the Comte d'Argenson, 10 May 1753.

to investigate two cases of denial of sacraments, and the following day, 10 May, it converted a *décret d'ajournement personnel* into a *décret de prise de corps*.[149]

The Government reacted with another show of force. At 4 a.m. on 11 May, the first president and the other members of the *grand'chambre* received *lettres de cachet* ordering them to go to Pontoise, where the *Parlement* was to be transferred without the *enquêtes* and *requêtes*; as in 1720, they were given forty-eight hours in which to leave. The *avocat général* had told the Comte d'Argenson that it would be useless to transfer the *Parlement* to another town, for the members of the *grand'chambre* would behave no differently. In such an eventuality he doubted whether the subsequent dispersal of the *grand'chambre* which would constitute a suppression of the *Parlement* would be in the interests of the State.[150] The Maréchal de Richelieu had privately warned Maupeou of the measures the day before and appears to have suggested to him that, when a *déclaration* formally transferring the *Parlement* to Pontoise was sent to the *grand'chambre*, it should register it unconditionally so as to free itself, and thus the *Parlement*, from the *arrêtés* of 5 and 7 May.[151] It is not known whether Richelieu – an experienced negotiator whom historians persist in regarding as a mere intriguer – was acting on his own initiative or whether he was acting on behalf of Machault: his negotiations of May 1753 appear to have been directed in part against D'Argenson; in February–March 1754 they were certainly conducted in concert with Machault.[152] In any case, Maupeou had expressed alarm at Richelieu's suggestion. Nevertheless, the two men had made arrangements to keep in touch with each other and to employ the good offices of Etienne-Henri Ysabeau, the discreet and resourceful chief clerk of the *Parlement*, as their intermediary.[153]

On 11 May, when Maupeou received the order to go to Pontoise, he sent Richelieu a letter for the King.[154] In it he asserted that his past conduct had been misrepresented, and he ended:

> Je demande à V. Mté pour toute grâce de ne pas me condamner sans m'entendre, Daignés Sire me faire sçavoir les fautes que l'on m'impute.[155]

Richelieu gave it to the King, possibly with a covering letter saying that he

---

[149] Barbier, *Journal*, v, p. 386.   [150] *Ibid.*, p. 387; BUP, CA 28/V: letter of 10 May 1753.
[151] AAE, MD, France 1344 (Soulavie Papers; these were originally part of the Richelieu Papers), f. 226.
[152] See Chapter 7.   [153] AAE, MD, France 1344, f. 234.
[154] *Ibid.*, f. 223: Maupeou to Richelieu, 11 May 1753. Richelieu later claimed that his correspondence with Maupeou began with this letter (cf. his letters to the first president of 21 and 28 May, ff. 230 and 236). But Maupeou certainly wrote his letter to the King in the light of his conversation with the marshal on 10 May, as he implied in his covering letter.
[155] *Ibid.*, f. 224 (copy in Maupeou's hand).

Plate 14 The Maréchal-Duc de Richelieu in 1753, by L. Tocqué (Musée des Beaux-Arts, Tours)

had been asked to arrange for him to see the remonstrances.[156] In the

---

[156] Cf. the King's first letter to Richelieu of 11 May 1753 (see Appendix B); and also Maupeou's view that the King should ask him to bring the remonstrances (AAE, MD, France 1344, ff. 226 and 232: letters to Richelieu of 15 and 22 May).

evening Louis XV gave Richelieu a reply; with it was enclosed a second letter, also addressed to the marshal, containing the King's views on the situation. Richelieu was instructed to show them both to Maupeou, a task which he performed later that night.[157] In the first letter the King again stated that he would not see the remonstrances.[158] The second letter, however, was an extraordinary document calculated to impress the first president. While he appeared to exonerate Maupeou, the King expressed his impatience with the *Parlement* in the strongest terms, saying that it had strayed beyond its bounds and that he would enforce his will upon it, even to the point of bloodshed. But he added:

> S'il [le Parlement] me demande pardon, s'il obéit à ce que je lui ay commandé, avec joie je lui renderés le pouvoir que je lui avois confié. mais après toutes les incartades que j'ay vu, je ne souffrirés jamais qu'il puisse me remettre dans les mêmes embarras. le per. pt. étant le chef que je lui ay donné, avec grande satisfaction je le voirés porteur des soumissions de mon parlement, et des ordres que j'aurés à lui donner pour les faire exécuter.[159]

The King probably wanted to frighten the first president into proposing a way of ending the crisis; in conversation with Maupeou Richelieu was to raise again the question of the *déclaration* transferring the *Parlement* to Pontoise and also to encourage him to offer his suggestions for a new law on denial of sacraments.[160]

Maupeou was not shaken by this piece of crude diplomacy. The letter he wrote to the King on the morning of 12 May is unfortunately lost, but its contents may be gleaned from Maupeou's correspondence with Richelieu; the first president sought to justify the conduct of the *Parlement*[161] and effectively thwarted Richelieu's scheme for an unconditional registration of the *déclaration*. He told the marshal a few days later

---

[157] AAE, MD, France 1344, f. 234: Maupeou to Richelieu, 24 May 1753; and f. 236: Richelieu to Maupeou, Marly, 28 May 1753 (copy). The King's letters (printed in Appendix B) were written at 5 p.m. Richelieu also conveyed verbal instructions to Maupeou on the evening of 11 May (see f. 236).

[158] See Appendix B. There was a rumour that the King had been shown a garbled version of the remonstrances by D'Argenson; see BN, MS franç. 8496, pp. 171ff; and also AAE, MD France 1344, f. 226: Maupeou to Richelieu, 15 May 1753. Richelieu doubted the accuracy of these rumours (see BVC, RP, xlii (catalogue no. 63), f. 253: draft of a reply to Maupeou).

[159] See Appendix B.

[160] Cf. AAE, MD, France 1344, f. 237: Richelieu to Maupeou, 28 May 1753 (copy); and also what is implied in Maupeou's letter to the marshal quoted on p. 187.

[161] The existence of this letter can be established by a close scrutiny of the Richelieu–Maupeou correspondence; see AAE, MD, France 1344, f. 225: Maupeou to Richelieu, 12 May 1753; f. 226: same to same, 15 May 1753, taken with Richelieu's draft of a reply (with its reference to 'votre dernière letre' to the King) in BVC, RP, xlii (catalogue no. 63), f. 253; AAE, MD, France 1344, f. 228: Maupeou to Richelieu, 21 May 1753 (with its reference to the 'lettres' entrusted to the marshal); and Richelieu's letter of the same day (f. 230) refers to more than one letter sent by the first president to the King through his agency (copy).

... je me suis cru obligé de ne pas dissimuler à S. Mté. la position actuelle de la portion du Parlement transféré à Pontojse, qui se trouve liée de telle manière par les différents arrêtés de la Compagnie, qu'elle ne pourroit sans se déshonorer enregistrer purement et simplement cette déclaration; si elle le faisoit, et vous en tomberés d'accord, ne deviendroit-elle pas par une conduite si peu conforme à son devoir inutile à Jamais à son service?[162]

The first president later maintained that the King's letter had inhibited him from proposing any scheme that did not conform to it and had made it improper, on the other hand, for him to advise the King to impose his will on the *Parlement* when he, the first president, knew that it was not prepared to obey. He preferred to await the King's orders and omitted to send in suggestions for a new law.[163] Ysabeau tried in vain to get him to change his mind.[164] In the afternoon Maupeou and the other members of the *grand'-chambre* left for Pontoise.[165]

The first president's attitude was disingenuous, and it undoubtedly failed to convince either Richelieu or the King.[166] But it was also the understandable response of a man who had been ill used by the Government on several occasions. Besides, Maupeou knew that if he and the *grand'chambre* did not stand by the *enquêtes*, the *enquêtes* would not stand by him. They had become his main source of support: they soon became his main source of strength.

Historians agree that the crisis of May 1753 occurred because the *Parlement* refused to obey the wishes of Louis XV. But they have not laid sufficient stress on the fact that the crisis arose out of the King's inability to resolve the conflict over denial of sacraments by means of a new law that was acceptable to the clergy and the *Parlement*. The letters patent did not resolve that conflict and were also unacceptable to the *Parlement*. Moreover, the King's refusal to receive the remonstrances and the part played by the first president are other aspects that have been generally passed over by historians in their explanation of the crisis. Finally, the Government's use of force needs to be seen more as an attempt to impress the *parlementaires* and to induce their leaders to negotiate, than as an indication of the real strength of the French Crown. The King's advisers had also paid scant attention to the mood of the Parisian public. Dr Jeffreys, who was keeping Lord Hardwicke's son, Philip Yorke, informed of political developments, wrote to him on 9 May: 'The common People in general are on the side of the Parl'., and I think the ministry very wrong to have pushd things to such

---

[162] *Ibid.*, f. 226: Maupeou to Richelieu, 15 May 1753.
[163] *Ibid.*, f. 235: Maupeou to Richelieu, Pontoise, 24 May 1753.
[164] *Ibid.*, f. 225: Maupeou to Richelieu, 12 May 1753.   [165] Barbier, *Journal*, v, p. 388.
[166] Cf. AAE, MD, France 1344, f. 219: note in Richelieu's hand.

extremities.'[167] Perhaps the Government itself became belatedly aware of the potentially dangerous force of what was loosely termed 'public opinion'. On the day when the members of the *enquêtes* and *requêtes* left Paris, the police banned a performance of Corneille's *Don Sanche d'Aragon*, at the Comédie Française. About five hundred people had been lucky enough to see the play the previous evening and to hear the lines:

> Lorsque le déshonneur souille l'obéissance
> Les rois peuvent douter de leur toute-puissance:
> Qui la hasarde alors n'en sait pas bien user
> Et qui veut pouvoir tout ne doit pas tout oser.[168]

The allusion was probably not lost upon them.

---

[167] BL, Add. MSS 35,630, f. 85ᵛ: letter of 9 May 1753.
[168] Régnault, *Christophe de Beaumont*, i, p. 245; H. Carrington Lancaster, *The Comédie française, 1701–1774: plays, actors, spectators, finances* (Philadelphia, Transactions of the American Philosophical Society, xli, 1951), p. 774: *Don Sanche d'Aragon* was performed on 5, 7, and 9 May. *Les Femmes savantes* was given on 10 May, and *Tartuffe* on 11 May, both to smaller audiences. The lines from the play come from Act 2, scene i.

7

THE TRANSFER OF THE
PARLEMENT TO PONTOISE
AND THE EXILE OF THE
ENQUÊTES AND *REQUÊTES*,
1753

> Ce qui en soi n'étoit qu'une dispute en matière de religion,
> est devenue bientost un sujet de discorde entre le minis-
> tère ecclésiastique, et la magistrature séculière: et
> aujourd'hui c'est enfin la triste occasion d'une espèce de
> scission dans l'ordre mesme de temporel et du civil, entre
> le Prince et ses principaux officiers.
>
> *Gilbert de Voisins, in a memorandum (1754)*

FROM MAY 1753 until September 1754 a third of France was without its
normal appellate jurisdiction and higher court of law; this event naturally
had serious repercussions. The reasons why the cessation of service lasted so
long are complex and emerge only from a close study of the various moves
that were made to break the deadlock reached in May 1753. The first of
these moves concerned the *déclaration* sent on 12 May transferring the
Parlement to Pontoise.[1] The *grand'chambre* was given an opportunity of
resuming the full duties of the *Parlement*; it had only to register the *déclaration*
as it stood and not subject to the *arrêtés* of 5, 7, and 9 May. It had been
suggested to Maupeou that if the *grand'chambre* seized that opportunity, the
Government might then bring out a new law to end the conflict over denial
of sacraments. But Maupeou had already ruled out this possibility in his
letter to the King, where he stated that the *grand'chambre* could not register
the *déclaration* as it stood without dishonouring itself.[2] However, there
remained other possibilities. If the *grand'chambre* were to refuse to register
the *déclaration* on the pretext that a law transferring the *Parlement* as a body
could not be registered without the participation of the *enquêtes*, the King

---

[1] BN, JF 309, f. 264: D'Argenson to the *procureur général*, 12 May 1753 (letter enclosing
déclaration and *lettres de cachet* dated 12 May (f. 267). These papers were awaiting Joly de
Fleury on his arrival at Pontoise on the night of 12 May.

[2] See Chapter 6, pp. 186–7.

would have a plausible reason for reuniting the *grand'chambre* and the *enquêtes*. It seems that this suggestion was also made to Maupeou and emanated from members of the Government.[3] Another plan was suggested to the *gens du roi* by President Molé on 12 May, when the *déclaration* reached Pontoise. His idea was that the *grand'chambre* should register the *déclaration* subject only to supplications being made to the King about the disadvantages of a translation of the *Parlement*. The *gens du roi* could then go to the King with the suggestion that if he allowed the *grand'chambre* to pass a few sentences that infringed the letters patent of 22 February, the *parlementaires* would be willing to resume their duties, having obtained some satisfaction.[4]

The *déclaration* was read and discussed on 13 May at a meeting held by the first president and attended by the *présidents à mortier*, the *rapporteur* (the Abbé d'Héricourt), and the *gens du roi*. It was identical to the one issued on a similar occasion in 1720, except that the preamble containing an injurious reference to the *Parlement* had been omitted; the Government clearly wished to appear conciliatory.[5] But most of those who attended the meeting were still embittered; they were in no mood for a compromise.[6] The *grand'chambre* debated the *déclaration* four days later. The *gens du roi* had concerted an *arrêté* with President Chauvelin on the lines of President Molé's suggestion. But it was not adopted; perhaps it would have rallied more support had many members of the *grand'chambre* not been under the impression that supplications to the King would not be favourably received.[7] As the first president had predicted, the *déclaration* was registered subject to the *arrêtés* of May. In a letter to his father the *procureur général* had already foreseen the consequences of the decision:

> Si les choses se passent ainsi, qu'elle [*sic*] espérance peut on avoir que les lettres de cachet pour reprendre le service le fasse [*sic*] reprendre, ou que de nouvelles lettres de jussion pour enregistrer les lettres patentes de surséance puisse [*sic*] produire des Remontrances? Le party est donc pris (en enregistrant comme je l'ay marqué) de ne pas reprendre le service et de continuer à rendre des Arrests sur les anciennes et nouveles [*sic*] procédures; par cette conduite Le Gouvernement sera très embarassé [*sic*] car une nouvelle translation ne fera ny reprendre le service ny n'empêchera de suivre les Procédures

---

[3] BVC, RP, xiv (catalogue no. 35), f. 12[r.v]: Ysabeau to Richelieu, 1 Mar. 1754. It is interesting to note that Ogier – a man who was in Rouillé's confidence – observed that the *grand'chambre* could have refused to resume its duties without mentioning the May *arrêtés*; Ogier to G. F. Joly de Fleury, 18 May 1753, in BN, JF 2103, f. 71.

[4] *Ibid.*, f. 51: *procureur général* to his father, 13 May 1753.   [5] *Ibid.*

[6] *Ibid.*, f. 43: same to same, 14 May 1753; f. 45: Jean-Omer Joly de Fleury to his father, 14 May 1753. President Gilbert, a protégé of the Maréchal de Noailles, was unusually bitter and uncompromising.

[7] *Ibid.*, f. 74: note in the hand of the *procureur général*.

et nous sentons qu'on forçera la cour à disperser la grande chambre, et à
établir à Paris une commission pour Juger comme on fit en 1720.[8]

His analysis proved to be correct. The decision of 17 May became a
stumbling block in attempts to resolve the dispute.

The first president had made his position clear in a letter to Richelieu
two days before the debate. Maupeou claimed that the dispute could be
solved only if the King received the remonstrances and issued a new law.
He suggested that the King should order him to bring the remonstrances.
Before he could offer any suggestions concerning a new law, he needed to
know the difficulties that had stood in the way of the various draft
déclarations. He pointed out that the King could naturally discuss this matter
with him, if he adopted his suggestion about the remonstrances.[9] On 16
May Maupeou asked the *gens du roi* on behalf of all the presidents to use
their influence to secure a law. The *gens du roi* obtained permission to go to
Marly three days later to confer with members of the Government. The
day before they left, the *procureur général* received an encouraging message
from Machault: 'il est fort à désirer que les dispositions des esprits soient
telles que le Roy puisse en estre satisfait. Je vous assure que personne ne le
souhaîte plus que moi.'[10] At Marly, they found the ministers, including the
Comte d'Argenson, generally responsive to the idea of a 'law of silence' on
the religious disputes. The chancellor cast a damp over it, as they might
have expected. They all thought the law would have to define *Unigenitus*
with care and that on the question of the competence of the courts it should
simply follow the ruling contained in the *arrêt de conseil* of 21 November
1752. The law should also end the various judicial proceedings that were
pending, by means of an amnesty. However, the Government laid down
two conditions: the *grand'chambre* should resume its full duties before the law
was sent and it should agree to register the new law without the *enquêtes*, if
necessary. The *gens du roi* knew that these conditions could not be fulfilled
(especially the second, for the *grand'chambre* was certain to insist on the
recall of the *enquêtes* as a preliminary to the registration of the law).
Nevertheless, they urged the ministers to start negotiations with the first

---

[8] *Ibid.*, f. 60: *procureur général* to his father, 16 May 1753. See also Ysabeau's observation in a
letter to Richelieu of 5 June 1753: 'une autre raison pour laquelle selon moy, Le Roy ne
doit pas insister sur La Reprise du service par La grande chambre seule, c'est que cette
division de la grande chambre et des enquestes ... auroit L'air d'une Espèce de surprise,
qui n'est pas digne de la Majesté du Roy, qui est le maistre, qui doit toujours agir en
maistre, et qui doit estre toujours obéi, parcequ'il ne doit ordonner que des choses possibles'
(AAE, MD, France 1344 f. 240ᵛ; quoted with slight variations and erroneously ascribed to
an *avocat général*, in Soulavie, *Mémoires du Maréchal de Richelieu pour servir à l'histoire de Louis
XIV, de la Régence, de Louis XV et quatorze premières années du règne de Louis XVI* (London,
Marseille and Paris, 1790–3), 9 vols., viii, p. 291).

[9] AAE, MD, France 1344, ff. 226–7: Maupeou to Richelieu, 15 May 1753.

[10] BN, FJ 309, f. 274: Machault to the *procureur général*, 18 May 1753.

president without delay.[11] For his part, Jean-Omer Joly de Fleury had already picked up governmental hints about the desirability of abolishing some of the troublesome chambers of the *enquêtes* and *requêtes*. His aged father was busily drafting a memorandum on the subject; it was probably intended for the Comte d'Argenson.[12]

The first president heard a report of these discussions from the *gens du roi* on 20 May.[13] The following day he heard privately from Richelieu that the King could not change his mind about the remonstrances. The marshal had found the proposal unrealistic, and he now strongly advised the first president to put forward other suggestions for ending the crisis.[14] Ysabeau was instructed to tell Maupeou that Richelieu hoped he would do everything in his power to vindicate himself in the eyes of the King and to clear himself of the charge of being in league with the Comte d'Argenson.[15] In this way Richelieu tried to frighten Maupeou into being more co-operative. But Maupeou held firm. He expressed regret that his suggestions had not found favour with the King, and in the same letter he strongly denied the charge made concerning his relations with the Comte d'Argenson.[16] As Maupeou's letters were shown to the King and others (including perhaps the Comte d'Argenson himself), the effect – intended or not – of the first president's open denial of the charge of collusion was to cast doubt on the marshal's own motives and to undermine his position as a negotiator; it is possible that Richelieu's oral advice had been designed to embroil Maupeou in some intrigue directed against D'Argenson.[17] At any rate, all that Richelieu was able to obtain from Maupeou was the plan of a new law; the first president sent it off on 24 May.[18] It is possible that Maupeou's confidence stemmed from the fact that overtures were also being made to

---

[11] BN, JF 2103, f. 64: *procureur général* to his father, 17 May 1753. For his part, Maupeou did not think the *gens du roi* should go to Marly (*ibid.*, f. 82: Jean-Omer Joly de Fleury to his father, 20 May 1753). It is interesting to note that a meeting of the *Conseil des dépêches* was held on 19 May (see *Mémoires du Duc de Luynes sur la cour de Louis XV (1735–1758)*, ed. L. Dussieux and E. Soulié (Paris, 1860–5) (hereafter cited as Luynes, *Mém.*), xii, p. 454).

[12] BN, JF 2103, f. 72: Jean-Omer Joly de Fleury to his father, 18 May 1753; JF 568, f. 371: G. F. Joly de Fleury to Jean-Omer Joly de Fleury, 19 May 1753 (draft in JF 2103, f. 77); ff. 375–8: the memoir by the former *procureur général* (draft in JF 2103, ff. 78–80).

[13] BN, JF 2103, f. 86: Jean-Omer Joly de Fleury to his father, 21 May 1753.

[14] BVC, RP, xlii (catalogue no. 63), ff. 252–3: Richelieu to Maupeou, draft of a letter written between 15 and 17 May 1753.

[15] AAE, MD, France 1344, ff. 230–1: Richelieu to Maupeou, 21 May 1753, copy. Ysabeau's instructions led to a misunderstanding between Richelieu and Maupeou. It seems that Ysabeau omitted to show Maupeou a letter from the King to Richelieu (now lost) in which the conduct of the first president and of his son was severely criticised. On this incident see also *ibid.*, ff. 232–3: Maupeou to Richelieu, 22 May 1753; ff. 219–22: Richelieu to Maupeou, draft of a letter that was probably written on 23 May 1753; ff. 234–5: Maupeou to Richelieu, 24 May 1753; and ff. 236–7: Richelieu to Maupeou, 28 May 1753 (copy).

[16] *Ibid.*, f. 232–3: Maupeou to Richelieu, 22 May 1753.

[17] Cf. Richelieu's irritated comments in *ibid.*, f. 220 and f. 236 (letters to Maupeou).

[18] *Ibid.*, ff. 221–2: Richelieu to Maupeou; ff. 234–5: Maupeou to Richelieu, 24 May 1753.

him by the Prince de Conty; he had been to see the prince at his country seat at Vauréal on 23 May and had returned there the next day with President de Novion, one of his close associates. While he waited to learn how his plan was received he continued to help the *gens du roi* in their own attempts to persuade leading *parlementaires* to agree on the terms of a 'law of silence'. He also delayed proceedings in cases of denial of sacraments which now formed the sole occupation of the *grand'chambre*.[19]

Maupeou's plan consisted of four articles. Firstly, the King should order his subjects to respect the authority of *Unigenitus* and forbid them to protest against the bull and the nature of its acceptance by bishops (including the Explanations of 1720). Secondly, he should forbid anyone to break the peace, 'soit par l'exigence d'aucun genre de signature, soit même par des interpellations indiscrètes'. Thirdly, he should order the bishops to watch over the execution of the law and to ensure that their priests exercised their ministry only in accordance with the canons prescribed in the kingdom and that there was no public denial of the sacrament, 'sous le prétexte du Déffaut de représentation de billets de confession ou D'acceptation de la Bulle'. Fourthly, the King should formally annul the judicial proceedings that had been taken and prescribe silence on these questions to his magistrates, who would at the same time be entrusted with the task of punishing those who broke the law.[20] These proposals reveal Maupeou's ignorance of the difficulties surrounding the introduction of a new law on denial of sacraments; but then, as he was prone to remind people in a sullen way, he had not been taken into the King's confidence when the various drafts had been under consideration. It was perhaps unfairly that his suggestions were dismissed by the King in a curt note to Richelieu on 30 May:

Le projet de déclaration du premier président ne vaut rien du tout.

Le premier article révolteroit le clergé. Le second ne vaut rien parce qu'il parle de signature. Et le troisième de même: il n'y a que la fin de bonne.

Si l'on me présente des projets de déclarations, je les ferai voir au premier président avant que de les envoyer au parlement.

Du reste, je m'en rapporte à tout ce que j'ai déjà dit.

Voilà bien du temps perdu sans justice pour mes sujets, et je ne veux pas que cela dure encore.[21]

---

[19] The first president had presented his respects to the prince at Vauréal on 19 and 21 May; his visits on 23 and 24 May had a more serious purpose; see BN, JF 2103, f. 87: Jean-Omer Joly de Fleury to his father, 22 May 1753; f. 102; Joly de Fleury to Rouillé, 26 May 1753; and fr. 104: Rouillé to Joly de Fleury, 27 May 1753. Maupeou lent himself to a postponement of the Loos affair (f. 89: *procureur général* to his father, 22 May 1753) and to the suppression of an illicit edition of the remonstrances (f. 106: note in the hand of the *procureur général*).

[20] AAE, MD, France 1344, ff. 234–5: Maupeou to Richelieu, 24 May 1753.

[21] Soulavie, *Mémoires du Maréchal de Richelieu*, viii, pp. 289–90. The original of this letter is now lost, but a comparison of the text with Maupeou's letter cited in note 20 naturally

The King's letter virtually ended Richelieu's negotiation with Maupeou. But although the Government was already considering the measures that it would have to take to ensure the administration of justice, the King continued to promote negotiations through his cousin, the Prince de Conty. Conty had for many years been engaged in that esoteric exercise in paradiplomacy known as the *Secret du Roi*. As a negotiator he was advantageously placed at court and also in the country, for his estates, L'Isle-Adam and Vauréal, were close to Pontoise. He was a leading advocate of a law of silence, an idea that probably had the best chance of success because it avoided the difficulties faced by those who tried to define *Unigenitus* and to determine the scope of the 1695 edict.

On 19 May, two days after the registration of the *déclaration* transferring the *Parlement* to Pontoise, the prince had taken up residence at Vauréal. He summoned the first president and a couple of leading *parlementaires* to tell them that he wished to be a mediator in the dispute. He laid down certain conditions, declaring that the King would treat only with the *grand'chambre*, which now had full powers to act on behalf of the *Parlement* as a whole. As evidence, the prince pointed to the *arrêté* of 9 May and to the registration of the decision to transfer the *Parlement*. On that basis the prince offered them a law of silence.[22]

There were two major obstacles to the proposed plan. Firstly, the reaction of the members of the *grand'chambre* who were sounded was, at least initially, unenthusiastic. Some were not convinced that they could act on behalf of the *Parlement* in the absence of their exiled colleagues. Moreover, they felt that the precedent of the Law of Silence of 1717 was not an encouraging one. The second obstacle to the success of Conty's negotiation was the attitude of the exiles themselves and its repercussions at Pontoise.

The *enquêtes* and *requêtes* had been exiled in groups of about thirty to the towns of Poitiers, Vendôme, Clermont, Châlons-sur-Marne, Angoulême, Bourges, and Montbrison. At Bourges, the colony was made up of four *presidents* and councillors from the 1st *enquêtes*, six from the 2nd *enquêtes*, two from the 3rd *enquêtes*, five from the 4th *enquêtes*, six from the 5th *enquêtes*, three from the 1st *requêtes*, and three from the 2nd *requêtes*.[23] Although the Government had thus sent *parlementaires* from different chambers to each

leads one to assume that it is authentic. I believe the King's letter to have been written on 30 May; Maupeou returned it to Richelieu the same day (see AAE, MD, France 1344, f. 238: Maupeou to Richelieu, 30 May 1753; and also f. 236).

22 BN, MS franç. 7570 (Durey de Meinières Papers), f. 350, 'no. 67': 'Copie d'une Lettre anonime qui accompagnoit les mémoires dont je reçus le Paquet le 17 juin à dix heures du soir'. The letter is dated 12 June 1753 from Paris. (As the foliation of this volume is defective, the original numbering of some of the documents has also been included in the reference.)

23 See Chapter 6, note 143.

Plate 15 The Prince de Conty, engraving by A. Romanet after a painting by
Le Tellier

place of exile, the result was that, whether by accident or by design, the
chief *zélés* all found themselves in Bourges: Durey de Meinières, Clément de
Feillet, Lambert, Rolland de Challerange, Robert de Saint-Vincent, and
Rolland d'Erceville.[24] A discreet watch was kept on the exiles by the
intendants, but there was no ban on their holding meetings in private or
having contact with friends in Paris or at Pontoise.[25] The content of the
talks at Vauréal was soon leaked to the exiles at Bourges by sympathisers in
Pontoise or in Paris.[26] The indiscretions led three members of the 'colony'
there to prepare separate memoirs. The first, written by Lambert, the chief

[24] AAE, MD, France 1345, f. 158: list of exiled and imprisoned *parlementaires* (with some
names in the hand of the Comte D'Argenson).
[25] *Ibid.*, f. 165: copy of the ministerial letters sent to Intendants Blossac (Poitiers) and
Barentin (Orléans), marked 'secret', Versailles, 9 May 1753; AN, O¹ 397, p. 133, no. 255:
Saint-Florentin to La Michodière (Clermont), 21 May 1753, copy.
[26] BN, MS franç. 7570, f. 351: copy of the letter of 12 June (see note 22 above).

author of the *Grandes remontrances*, was sent on 30 May to Paris, probably to Clément de Barville, a lawyer and the youngest of the Clément brothers. There, at least four copies were made of Lambert's memoir. Armed with the copies, an unnamed go-between reached Pontoise at 6 a.m. on 3 June. He rapidly checked and corrected the copies before going on to the house of a 'Madame B.', where he gave them to four members of the *grand'chambre*: Coustard, Fermé, Lattaignant, and the Abbé Boucher. These sympathisers departed at once to communicate the message 'chacun à leur peloton'. In less than two hours all the members of the *grand'chambre* were informed. The talk was all of breaking off the negotiations with Conty. Four senior councillors were deputed to call on the first president the next morning to give him the memoir and to ask him to show it to the prince. Maupeou cannot have been displeased. He went through the motions of consulting the presidents and afterwards handed a copy of the memoir to the prince, striking a note of finality about the negotiations.[27]

The argument of Lambert's memoir was that the point at issue was not a dispute between the *Parlement* and the clergy of France, but the attempt by the clergy to be independent of royal authority. In the circumstances, the *grand'chambre* had no right to act on behalf of the *Parlement* as a whole. Nothing could be done until the King agreed to receive the remonstrances.[28] Undaunted by this intransigence, the Prince de Conty pressed on with his efforts, treating his negotiating partners in a brisk, cavalier manner.[29] If the refusal to receive the remonstrances was an obstacle, could not the *Parlement* recast the substance of the remonstrances in a memoir which the King would then be prepared to accept? The prince hoped to combine this idea with his original plan to secure acceptance for a law of silence. At the beginning of June, he had an audience with the King and he saw most of the ministers afterwards.[30] He consulted leading *parlementaires* as to the possible terms of the law and quickly prepared a draft. His task was made easier by the Joly de Fleury brothers, who had already canvassed support for a law of silence; Conty further obtained material assistance from their resourceful father, who had already elaborated a draft of his own.[31]

[27] *Ibid.*, ff. 288–9, 'no. 27': unsigned note: 'De Pontoise le 4e juin 1753'.
[28] For the text of his memoir, see *ibid.*, 7570, ff. 253–8, 'no. 17': 'Premier mémoire [...] sur la proposition que l'on fait actuellement à Messieurs de Grand Chambre à Pontoise', Bourges, 30 May 1753.
[29] Anonymous letter of 12 June (see note 22 above).
[30] BN, n.a.fr. 23619, f. 145, no. 280: Villevieille to Loménie de Brienne, 8 June 1753 (copy).
[31] What is probably the text of Conty's draft *déclaration* exists in a copy in BN, JF 2103, f. 196. Machault sent the copy to the former *procureur général* on 7 June 1754, saying that it had been drawn up the previous year (f. 195). The *déclaration* consists of a short preamble and five articles. Conty's secretary (Monnin) came to work at the house of the former *procureur général* (f. 132: *procureur général* to his father, 20 June [1753]). Ysabeau reported that Joly de

The first president took the view that the *grand'chambre* would not be willing to register a law without the exiled colleagues. However, despite the impact of Lambert's memoir, those opposed to Conty's plan feared that there were waverers in the ranks of the *grand'chambre*, especially after the prince had suggested the presentation of a memoir by the *Parlement* as a means of overcoming the problem of the remonstrances. They therefore circulated Lambert's memoir among the exiled *parlementaires* in the other towns, urging them to adopt it and to forward their endorsement to the first president and to known sympathisers in the *grand'chambre*.[32] The colony at Bourges reacted swiftly to Conty's second proposal. Durey de Meinières had another memoir ready by 4 June.[33] He rejected the expedient for circumventing the King's refusal to receive the remonstrances. The president felt the issue of the remonstrances was too important to be set aside. A second memoir, by Robert de Saint-Vincent, took the same view: 'les Remontrances sont le mémoire du Parlement. Il est tout fait. Il ne faut que le lire, pourquoi en demander un nouveau.'[34] He suspected the ministry of seeking to divide the *parlementaires* and to compromise the first president. Robert's memoir reflected the cynical attitude which the exiled *zélés* had towards the King's ministers:

> Ils espèrent que pendant que se dressera le mémoire, le Parlement rendra la justice. Par là, ils se trouvent débarrassés de la situation serrée où ils se trouvent. L'ordre judiciaire est rétabli pour un moment, mais ils s'embarrassent peu de remédier véritablement aux maux. Ils espèrent que le mémoire sera long à dresser, les vacances viendront, on y répondra comme on voudra ou même on n'y répondra point ... Pourvu que les ministres ne se trouvent point dans un embarras qui les pressent de trop près, ils s'embarrassent très peu du reste. Les mémoires dressés par la dernière commission pour la pacification des troubles sont un bel exemple de L'utilité d'un mémoire qui seroit dressé par le Parlement dans ces circonstances.[35]

A third memoir, by Drouyn de Vandeuil, was also opposed to Conty's proposal.[36]

Fleury was said to be the author of the draft; AAE, MD, France 1344, f. 256: letter to Richelieu, 9 July 1753. For the activity of the brothers Joly de Fleury in favour of a law of silence, see BN, JF 2103, ff. 87, 89, 94–5 (G. F. Joly de Fleury's draft of the preamble for such a law), 97, and 98 (for a remark to the effect that G. F. Joly de Fleury had sent the *procureur général* a set of articles for a law of silence).

[32] See the anonymous letter of 12 June (note 22 above).

[33] BN, MS franç. 7570, f. 261ʳ–262ᵛ, 'no. 30': '1ᵉʳ mémoire sur la 2nd négociacion (M. le. P.)', 4 June 1753 (heading in the hand of Durey de Meinières).

[34] *Ibid.*, f. 264: 'Second mémoire sur la seconde Proposition (M. Robert)', 4 June 1753 (note in the hand of Durey de Meinières); BPR, LP 42, p. 249: 'Projet de conciliation' (5 June 1753) and replies from Durey de Meinières, D[rouyn] d[e] V[andeuil] (p. 252), and Robert de Saint-Vincent; BN, JF 2103, f. 128: *Procureur général* to his father, 18 [June 1753].

[35] BN, MS franç. 7570, f. 265ʳ.   [36] *Ibid.*, ff. 290ʳ–295ʳ, 4 June 1753.

The usual channels relayed these views to the other exiles and to Pontoise. Conty's negotiation suffered a setback. Someone, possibly Monnin, the prince's secretary and agent, wrote to Angran, another influential member of the colony at Bourges. Did the exiles wish to compromise all chances of a settlement? What should be the terms of a new law on the current religious disputes? The letter reached Bourges on 9 June, and four days later Angran despatched an unambiguous reply: 'Nous sommes préparés à demeurer dans le lieu de nos exils jusqu'à ce qu'il ait plu au Roy de recevoir nos remontrances.'[37]

Although a rumour circulated that Conty had already told the King on 1 June that the negotiations were over,[38] there is a great deal of evidence to the contrary. The next day the Comte d'Argenson ushered the venerable President de Montesquieu into the King's presence. As director of the French Academy, he had been summoned to be told that Louis XV vetoed the election of Piron to that august body in deference to the wishes of the clergy, whose long collective memory associated the poet with the authorship of an obscene ode to Priapus.[39] The incident is well known, except in two respects. Firstly, Louis XV also told Montesquieu that he did not want the Academy to elect a lawyer to the vacant seat either.[40] This was doubtless his way of expressing displeasure with the legal fraternity for its habitual support of the *Parlement*. Secondly, it is possible, in the light of what was to follow, that the King asked Montesquieu, the most respected thinker of the age, to draft a memorandum on the disputes for him and also to reason with the lesser minds of the colony at Bourges.[41] However, Montesquieu was an outsider, perhaps only an outside hope, and it is clear that the King continued to encourage insiders like Conty to pursue their negotiations. Seemingly concerted moves were now directed at the exiles. From Pontoise the Abbé du Trousset d'Héricourt wrote to Bourges and President Moreau de Nassigny to Châlons. Their letters have not survived, though the abbé's is known to have stated that, in the absence of the exiles, the *grand'chambre* could represent the *Parlement* as a whole and register laws.[42] At Conty's request old Joly de Fleury wrote to Angran on 14 June, the prince discreetly providing the courier. Ever prolix, the former *procureur général* filled eight sides of paper lambasting the Bourges memoirs and the

[37] *Ibid.*, f. 314ᵛ, 'no. 41': 'Réponse fait par M. Angran à la lettre le (sic) 9 partie le 13e juin 1753' (note in the hand of Durey de Meinières).

[38] *Ibid.*, f. 315ʳ, 'no. 39': 'Extrait d'une lettre de Paris du 13 juin'.

[39] *Ibid.*, f. 316ᵛ; Robert Shackleton, *Montesquieu: a critical biography* (Oxford, 1961), pp. 384–5.

[40] BN, MS franç. 7570.

[41] Louis Gazier, 'Une lettre inédite de Montesquieu', *Revue d'histoire littéraire de la France*, xiv (1907), pp. 121–2.

[42] BN, JF 2103, f. 128: *procureur général* to his father, 18 [June 1753]: BN, MS franç. 7570, f. 289ʳ.

Grandes remontrances: 'on ne parle point ainsi à son souverain ny à ses confrères'.[43] In another move the next day, President Gilbert wrote an equally strongly worded letter to an unnamed exile at Bourges attacking the memoirs and extolling the merits of the proposed law of silence in respect of both *Unigenitus* and of the ban on all further controversy:

> il me paroît qu'en ne donnant à la Constitution aucune qualification, en ne parlant ni de respect ou de soumission, elle la fait beaucoup reculer et met à l'écart la déclaration de 1730. C'est aussi un grand coup que le Roi impose silence sur la constitution, non provisoirement, comme en 1717, mais à perpétuité ...[44]

He drew attention to the different ways in which the legal and judicial competence of the *Parlement* was implicitly recognised in the draft law.

In another, parallel, move, the Prince de Conty's agent, the *procureur* Desjobert, arrived in Bourges on 20 June with the probable intention of creating a rift between the exiles. Several of them had not been consulted by the writers of the memoirs sent to Pontoise, and they included Monsieur Boutin, who had, after all, been courteously, albeit wrongly, credited with the authorship of the *Grandes remontrances*. Monsieur Desjobert went to see him with a letter of credence from the prince.[45]

On 17 June Conty had obtained the King's permission to show the draft law to three senior members of the *grand'chambre*: the first and second presidents (Maupeou and Molé), and the *rapporteur* (Du Trousset d'Héricourt). Louis XV had told him that if the negotiation had not succeeded by the end of the week, steps to ensure that justice was administered would be announced.[46] The prince's aim was to get the law of silence in the form of a *déclaration* speedily registered by the *grand'chambre* acting on behalf of the *Parlement*. The three *parlementaires* saw the draft at Vauréal on 20 June. They were satisfied with it, but they asked that two stipulations should be added; one to enjoin ecclesiastics to conform with received and established canons of the Church in the exercise of their ministry, and another to declare those who disobeyed the law punishable as 'perturbateurs du repos public'. Conty returned to Versailles to obtain the King's consent to these additions.[47] Even if he succeeded, he still had to reckon with the opposition

---

43 BN, MSS Autographes Rothschild, vi, 322: G. F. Joly de Fleury to Angran, 14 June 1753. On the background to this démarche, see BN, JF 2103, f. 142: *procureur général* to his father, 23 June 1753.

44 BN, MS franç. 7570, f. 319ʳ, 'no. 41 bis': 'Extrait d'une lettre écrite par M. Gilbert le 15 juin 1753' (note in the hand of Durey de Meinières).

45 According to Rolland d'Erceville's memoirs; see F. Vilaire, 'Le Parlement exilé à Bourges en 1753', *Mémoires de la société historique, littéraire, et scientifique du Cher*, 4th series, xxvi (Bourges, 1912), pp. 231–42: p. 236.

46 BN, JF 2103, f. 128 (see note 42 above); f. 125: *procureur général* to his father, 'Dimanche, dix heures du soir', [17 June 1753].

47 *Ibid.*, f. 129: same to same, 19 [June 1753]; ff. 133–4, 21 [June 1753].

that was growing in Pontoise. On 20 June the *procureur général* thought that at least fourteen members of the *grand'chambre* would vote against a registration of the law without the *enquêtes*; the remaining thirty were still undecided.[48] Two days later he put the number of the opposition at seventeen and argued that, if a further five or six votes had to be excluded from the reckoning because of the rules about kinship, there might not even be a majority to carry the registration. The opposition's argument was naturally that if the *grand'chambre* registered the *déclaration* without the *enquêtes*, the latter would disown them and make a protest when they were eventually reunited.[49]

The argument seemed well founded in the light of the news from Bourges. Drouyn de Vandeuil's reply of 20 June to Du Trousset d'Héricourt was negative: so too was a reply made the same day by Clément to an unnamed correspondent.[50] Moreover, during the night of 19/20 June an amazing document arrived in Bourges.[51] In it the exiles were urged to break the deadlock by accepting the idea of a parliamentary memoir in which the content of the remonstrances would be decanted for willing royal consumption. The proposal was not new, but the purpose of the anonymous document was clearly to sink Conty's scheme for the registration of a law of silence by the *grand'chambre*. The document contained some startling revelations. No hopes could be pinned on the King: he was totally absorbed in his pleasures. There were plans afoot for the wholescale suppression of parliamentary offices, for which the clergy of France was willing to pay the reimbursement to the holders. Did the exiles seriously think that they could count on the long-term loyalty of the *grand'chambre* to the common cause? Were they aware that Conty had sent one of his agents to Bourges to stir up those colleagues whom they had not consulted when drafting their various memoirs and letters? The exiles were told that the *grand'chambre* and the ministers were behind Conty's moves. These moves were, however, unconnected with the proposal for a parliamentary memoir, which had originated with one man:

---

[48] *Ibid.*, f. 131: same to same, 20 [June 1753].

[49] *Ibid.*, ff. 135–6: same to same, 22 June 1753; AAE, MD, France 1344, ff. 247–8: Ysabeau to Richelieu, 20 June 1753.

[50] BN, MS franç. 7570, ff. 431ʳ–322ᵛ, 'no. 44': 'Copie de la Réponse faitte par M. Drouin de Vandeuil à M. L'abbé d'héricourt, à Bourges ce 20e juin 1753' (note in the hand of Durey de Meinières); ff. 323ʳ–324ʳ, 'no. 45': 'M. Clément, 20e juin 1753' (note by Durey de Meinières).

[51] *Ibid.*, ff. 325ʳ–331ᵛ, 'no. 43': '2nd Négociation. Mémoire arrivé à Bourges dans la nuit du 19e au 20e juin, dans lequel on propose de convertir les remontrances en un mémoire qui seroit présenté. *Na.* Ce mémoire est pour appuyer le projet du 5e juin et pour répondre à celuy de M. de Vandeuil du 10e juin et en peu de mots aux premiers mémoires de M. le Pt. de Meinières et de M. Robert de St. Vincent' (note in the hand of Durey de Meinières). Observations made by Clément de Feillet have been copied in the margin of the memoir.

un seul particulier qui est dans l'amitié du Roy traite avec lui immedi-
atement. Il est vrai qu'il en communique avec Mr le Garde des Sceaux. Mais
personne de la cour, pas même le Roi ne le sait. Si les autres ministres en
avoient la moindre connaissance, ils le traverseroient de toutes leurs forces.
L'accomodement [*sic*] qu'ils adoptent, le seul dont la grand'chambre ait
connaissance est celui dont le Prince de Conty s'est chargé.[52]

This passage points to the Richelieu/Machault faction as the originator of
the document. Although this faction probably succeeded in exposing
Conty, hitherto the honest broker, as an agent of the *grand'chambre* and of
the ministry and in revealing the tactics of his agent at Bourges, it failed to
persuade the exiles to adopt the idea of a memoir to the King. The exiles
remained intransigent.

Conty returned on 22 June and saw his three leading *parlementaires* again
at Vauréal the next day. He told them that he had encountered resistance
at Versailles to the proposed changes; this was hardly surprising as the
King had earlier rejected Maupeou's proposals, which were similar. But
Conty was hopeful and intended to see the King again.[53] Two days later
D'Ormesson went to Vauréal to propose a solution that had been devised
by President Gilbert. Under this plan the *déclaration* would be sent to the
grand'chambre, which, upon receiving it, would send a deputation to the
King to ask for the return of the *enquêtes* and *requêtes*, in order to register the
déclaration with them. The King would reply that the cessation of service
was an obstacle to their return and order a resumption of service; the
grand'chambre would obey and send another deputation; the King would
then announce that he recalled the exiles to Pontoise; and the *déclaration*
could then be registered by the whole *Parlement*. Conty thought the scheme
practicable, as long as the *déclaration* was not sent to the *Parlement* before the
return of the exiles,

> ... parce que L'on pourroit craindre qu'en l'envoyant d'avance elle ne
> fut tellement ébruitée que les Evéques ne fissent L'impossible pour la
> traverser.[54]

Some modifications were accordingly made to the plan. However, there
were only a few days left to win support for it among the members of the
grand'chambre, as the King wanted the whole question settled before the
court moved to Compiègne at the end of the week.

There were between forty-four and forty-eight active members of the

---

[52] *Ibid.*, ff. 327ᵛ–328ʳ. Durey de Meinières usually arranged meetings with his close colleagues
to discuss the policy to be followed by the exiles; see A. Grellet-Dumazeau, *Les Exilés de
Bourges* (Paris, 1892), p. 164.

[53] BN, JF 2103, f. 139: *procureur général* to his father, 23 June 1753.

[54] *Ibid.*, f. 140: same to same, 25 June [1753]. It is interesting to note that 'Le Roy' is lightly
crossed out in the text and replaced by 'L'on'.

Table 5. *List of the members of the* grand'chambre *who constituted the* Parlement *at Pontoise*

Premier président:	R. C. de Maupeou
Présidents à mortier:	M. F. Molé (1731), A. Potier de Novion (1736), L. Le Peletier de Rozambo (1743), R. N. de Maupeou (1743), L. Chauvelin (1744), P. P. Gilbert (1746), E. F. d'Aligre (1752), G. de Lamoignon (1747).
Conseillers d'honneur:	L. de La Michodière (1740), J. L. P. Le Peletier de Montmélian (1741), C. A. Ferriol d'Argental (1743), F. G. Briçonnet (1745), President P. J. Moreau de Nassigny (1750), C. F. Huguet de Sémonville (1751).
Conseillers clercs:	L. G. Fieubet de Beauregard (1713), Abbé Pajot de Dampierre (1715), Abbé Boucher (1716), Abbé Langlois (1718), Abbé de Salabéry (1720), Abbé Tudert (1724), E. Bochart (1724), Abbé Macé (1724), Abbé de Vougny (1726), Abbé du Trousset d'Héricourt (1730), Chanoine Chaban de la Fosse (1735).
Conseillers laïcs:	J. J. Coustard (1697), A. L. Pinon (1704), P. B. Rolland (1707), C. A. Benoise (1708), M. J. Fermé (1709), S. J. Tubeuf (1708), N. L. Hénin (1709), L. F. de Blair (1709), P. Rulault (1709), A. F. de Louvencourt (1710), E. V. Le Mée (1711), A. Pajot de Malzac (1711), J. A. de Lattaignant (1713), L. F. de Montholon (1713), J. A. de Pomereu (1713), L. Dupré (1714).

grand'chambre present at Pontoise. The higher figure comes from a printed list of addresses, but if one uses the attendance record for an important debate, like that of 28 May, one arrives at the lower figure: nine presidents, six *conseillers d'honneur*, eleven clerical and eighteen lay councillors (see Table 5).[55] By 28 June the shrewd Ysabeau reckoned there were eighteen members of the *grand'chambre* (including President de Maupeou) in favour of registering the *déclaration* and twenty-five against it.[56] Yet arrangements were being made in the event that the *déclaration* might be laid before the *grand'chambre* two days later. Conty saw the King at Versailles on 29 June and explained the position to him; the *procureur général* heard later from the prince that

> ... le Roy ne luy répondant rien et ayant l'air fasché. Le Prince luy avoit demandé s'il vouloit décidé [*sic*] quelque chose, qu'à celà Le Roy avoit répondu que les circonstances étaient telles qu'il luy falloit quelques jours pour y penser; qu'en conséquence le Prince s'étoit retiré en disant qu'il reviendroit pour prendre congé du Roy et qu'ensuite il iroit à L'isle adam.[57]

In an attempt to save the negotiation, the *gens du roi* went to Vauréal on 2 July to propose another expedient; that the *lettre de cachet* to accompany the

---

[55] BN, JF 309, f. 298 (printed list of addresses of the members of the *grand'chambre* at Pontoise); AN, X¹ᴮ 8931 (*Minutes du Parlement*): attendance list for the debate of 28 May 1753.

[56] AAE, MD, France 1344, f. 252: Ysabeau to Richelieu, 28 June [1753].

[57] BN, JF 2103, f. 147: *procureur général* to his father, 1 July [1753]. See also ff. 144 and 146: same to same, 26 and 30 June [1753].

déclaration should be so phrased as to give the impression that the *déclaration* was being issued in reply to the remonstrances.[58] The idea had originated with Ysabeau, resourceful as ever, who explained its purpose to Richelieu:

> Il me paroistroit que par ce moyen, L'arresté du 5 may tomberoit nécessairement parcque La Cessation du service, ne devant durer que Jusques à ce que Il ait plu au Roy [d']écouter favorablement les Remontrances; le Roy donnant une déclaration en conséquence des Remontrances, Le service doit Estre repris.[59]

The *procureur général* gave the prince Ysabeau's draft of the *lettre de cachet*.[60] Conty agreed to propose the plan at his final audience with the King the next day. He inquired whether Ysabeau could assure him that it would lead the *grand'chambre* to resume its duties.[61] In a letter to the *procureur général* which was hurriedly conveyed to the prince at Versailles Ysabeau replied that he could not assure him that it would: 'le ton de fermeté sur lequel on dit que Mr. le P.Pr. s'est monté a doné [*sic*] des forces à plusieurs, et tient les autres en suspens'.[62] He might have added that there was no guarantee that the *enquêtes* and *requêtes* would not still protest if the *grand'-chambre* resumed the full duties of the *Parlement*.[63] There were signs that the exiles at Bourges were not alone in thinking that the *grand'chambre* could not resume these duties or register a new law without them; the exiles at Angoulême had sent a letter to the first president protesting against the registration of the *déclaration* that transferred the *Parlement* to Pontoise.[64]

Under these circumstances it seems unlikely that Conty pressed the King to adopt Gilbert's plan and Ysabeau's addition to it, at least for the time being. Instead he may have persuaded the King without much difficulty that the first president was the chief obstacle to any settlement and that a negotiation with President Chauvelin might have a better chance of success. Ysabeau noted that both Conty and the *procureur général* had a poor opinion of the first president.[65] One of Joly de Fleury's *substituts*, Mayou d'Aunoy, whom the Comte d'Argenson had recruited as a secret informant the previous year, was at a circle at President de Novion's lodgings and

---

58 *Ibid.*, f. 149: same to same, 2 July 1753. Ysabeau had proposed his idea to the *procureur général* in Paris; see AAE, MD, France 1344, ff. 254–5: Ysabeau to Richelieu, 29 June [1753].

59 *Ibid.*, f. 252 (see note 56).

60 For a copy, see BN, JF 2103, f. 224; the important passage occurs on f. 226; see also f. 220 (note).

61 See the letter from the *procureur général* quoted in note 58.

62 BN, JF 2103, f. 223 (copy in the hand of Joly de Fleury); see also ff. 149, 220, and 221 (letter from Conty).

63 See Ysabeau's letter to Richelieu mentioned in note 58.

64 BN, JF 2103, f. 142: *procureur général* to his father, 23 June 1753; for a copy of the letter from Angoulême, see f. 148.

65 AAE, MD, France 1344, ff. 254–5: Ysabeau to Richelieu, 29 June [1753].

heard the *procureur général* openly declare that the first president had never wanted to register the law of silence.[66]

At any rate, the Government did not announce its plans for the administration of justice, and Conty went to L'Isle-Adam to conduct fresh negotiations. He saw Chauvelin there on 7 July. In his eagerness to become first president should the negotiation succeed, Chauvelin had not forgotten to cover his traces by announcing in Pontoise that he was going to Paris. But it seems that the Maupeous were on the alert; the Chevalier de Maupeou,[67] a hearty soldier and the younger son of the first president, turned up unexpectedly at L'Isle-Adam, allegedly to pay his respects to Conty, his former commander, and quickly spread the news that Chauvelin was there when he got back to Pontoise. Chauvelin was not liked by his colleagues, and the incident aroused their hostility. Conty also consulted D'Héricourt and another *conseiller clerc*, Salabéry, a protégé of Machault and of Madame de Pompadour.[68] Before he left for Compiègne he invited Presidents Molé and Gilbert to have dinner with him on his return, but Gilbert declined the invitation, and Molé promptly retired to the seclusion of his seat at Méry, which was admittedly within easy reach of L'Isle-Adam. Chauvelin lacked support not only because of his unpopularity but also because his patron did not have a following at Pontoise. Mayou reported to the Comte d'Argenson that he had encountered no one there who was fond of Machault, adding that money had not been offered to procure support:

> il n'y a pas eu de bons du Roy non plus, c'est aussi un fait certain. Soyez persuadé que Rien ne se passera à Pontoise que vous ne soyez très bien instruit.[69]

Chauvelin's initial chances of success were therefore not great.

There is little trace of these negotiations. Some evidence suggests that in the course of his discussions with Chauvelin and others, Conty conceded that it was impossible for the *grand'chambre* to register the *déclaration* or even to resume service without the *enquêtes*.[70] At Compiègne he was nevertheless encouraged to pursue the negotiation, for his return to L'Isle-Adam was

---

[66] BUP, CA 42/IV: [Mayou d'Aunoy] to the Comte d'Argenson, 21 June/3 July 1753. On Mayou d'Aunoy, see Appendix A.

[67] Charles Victor René, Chevalier de Maupeou, a knight of the Order of Malta; colonel of the Regiment of Bigorre Infanterie; 1748, *maréchal de camp*; M. de Saint-Allais and M. de La Chabeaussière, *Nobiliaire universel de France, ou Recueil général des généalogies historiques des maisons nobles du Royaume* (Paris, [reprint 1872]), 21 vols., xx, p. 304, and F. A. Aubert de La Chesnaye des Bois, *Dictionnaire de la noblesse* (Paris, 1770–86), 15 vols., xiii, col. 480.

[68] BUP, CA 42/IV: [Mayou d'Aunoy] to the Comte d'Argenson, 9 July 1753.

[69] *Ibid.*, same to same, 12 July 1753.

[70] AAE, MD, France 1344, f. 256: Ysabeau to Richelieu, 9 July 1753. It is possible, judging from this account, that Ysabeau had talked to Salabéry.

followed immediately by Chauvelin's departure for Grosbois, the seat of his formidable uncle, the exiled keeper of the seals; Mayou d'Aunoy understood that the purpose of Chauvelin's visit was to prepare a plan of conduct with the assistance of his capable and resourceful uncle. Chauvelin returned to Pontoise three days later and submitted his plan to the prince.[71] D'Argenson's informant reported with certainty a few days later that Chauvelin had recommended that the *déclaration* should be sent to the *grand'chambre* for registration subject to a second registration when the whole *Parlement* was reunited. As this plan was unlikely to succeed, some believed that Chauvelin had merely acquitted himself of a promise made to the prince and was now working on an entirely new draft for a *déclaration* with the help of his uncle and in concert with Machault, the *procureur général*, Salabéry, and D'Héricourt.[72] On the other hand, D'Ormesson came away from a visit to L'Isle-Adam at this time with the distinct impression that Conty still wanted to act on Ysabeau's plan for sending the *déclaration* with a *lettre de cachet* followed by a deputation.[73] These accounts are a little confusing, though not necessarily contradictory. At any rate, it seems that during Chauvelin's absence from Pontoise the first president and his son went to L'Isle-Adam and warned the prince that, if the *déclaration* were sent to the *grand'chambre*, 'on feroit un arrêté tout sec sans ordonner une députation'.[74]

Conty left for Compiègne on 16 July; his purpose appeared to be to show Chauvelin's plan to the King.[75] It is interesting to note that the usually well-informed Marquis d'Argenson wrote in his journal on 24 July that the prince had shown the King a memoir prepared by Chauvelin's uncle, the former keeper of the seals.[76] While he was away the opposition in Pontoise was encouraged in its attitude by the arrival of over twenty letters sent from Bourges in reply to the one sent there anonymously by the Abbé d'Héricourt.[77] The purpose of D'Héricourt's letter had been to convince the

---

[71] BUP, CA 42/IV: [Mayou d'Aunoy] to the Comte d'Argenson, 16 July 1753.

[72] *Ibid.*, same to same, 18 July 1753. Mayou claims that the *procureur général* was having daily meetings with Chauvelin. There is no trace of the *procureur général* being involved in these negotiations in his papers, though there is some indication that D'Ormesson played some part in them and kept Joly de Fleury informed. Jean-Omer Joly de Fleury does not allude to the negotiation in his letters to the Comte d'Argenson. Although the *procureur général* was said to be a friend of Machault, his family were on the whole *clientèle* of D'Argenson.

[73] BN, JF 2103, f. 168: *procureur général* to his father, 'Lundi' [16 July 1753].

[74] *Ibid.*; see also *The collection of autograph letters and historical documents formed by Alfred Morrison* (2nd series, London, 1882–93), i (1893), p. 79: Comte d'Argental to his wife, 'ce mardi matin', [17 July 1753]. Mayou reports the first president as saying that the subject of the *Parlement* had not even been mentioned in the course of his visit (BUP, CA 42/IV: letter of 16 July 1753).

[75] *Ibid.*: [Mayou] to the Comte d'Argenson, 16 July 1753.

[76] *Journal et mémoires du Marquis d'Argenson*, ed. E. J.B. Rathery (Paris, 1859–67) (hereafter D'Argenson, ed. Rathery), viii, p. 83, and also pp. 85 and 92.

[77] BN, JF 2103, f. 156: Jean-Omer Joly de Fleury to his father, 16 July 1753.

exiles of the merits of the draft *déclaration*, of which they had been shown a copy.[78] Many of the replies were of an offensive nature; in one letter, for instance, the negotiators of Pontoise were taken to task in a passage that somehow betrays the smugness of its author:

> Le caractère des négociateurs, les principes qui les font agir, ne permettent aucune illusion. Ce sont des personnes qui n'ont aucune connoissance des loix, des ordonnances, qui ignorent la méthode d'examiner les affaires en magistrat, c'est à dire avec cet amour et cette recherche de la justice qui place toujours les principes à la tête des décisions, qui part du vrai et ne tend qu'au vrai, qui voit le mal et en cherche sincèrement le remède, qui croiroit, en usant du palliatif, manquer autant au devoir qu'en excitant et entretenant le mal … Il est même difficile de supposer aux négociateurs une volonté sincère d'éteindre à perpétuité les troubles qui désolent le Royaume … Consommés dans la finesse la plus déliée, ils ne cherchent qu'à séduire des magistrats simples et droits par état.[79]

In these letters the argument was often at variance with the position adopted by the *Parlement* since 1730 and, in some cases, since 1720, in that *Unigenitus* was not even regarded as a *jugement de l'église universelle en matière de doctrine* or as a *loi de l'église et de l'état*.[80] The exiles spurned the negotiation and rejected the *déclaration*, which they had not even bothered to read.[81]

Montesquieu's intervention was equally unsuccessful. In his attempts to reason with those whom the King described as 'de furieux écrivains', he had written at length on 9 July to someone at Bourges, probably Durey de Meinières, explaining that the *Parlement* had a duty to the nation, not on such matters as the administration of the sacrament, or points of honour: 'Vous nous devez la conservation de notre constitution.'[82] That was surely more important. For the rest, a new law that followed the remonstrances was in itself a reply to those remonstrances. What more was necessary? Such elevated thoughts elicited little positive response from his correspondent, and some references from *L'Esprit des lois* and the *Lettres persanes* were carefully turned against their author in the reply.

The opposition in Pontoise was further encouraged by a curious belief

---

[78] Mayou saw a letter which the councillor Lattaignant had received from his son in Bourges; the son declared that an unknown man, dressed as a courrier, had brought them a copy of the *déclaration*, which the exiles had not even taken the trouble to read; BUP, CA 42/IV: letter of 16 July 1753 mentioned in note 71.

[79] Quoted in Grellet-Dumazeau, *Les Exilés de Bourges*, pp. 388ff.; see also p. 142 for the date (10 July 1753). Grellet-Dumazeau's work is an insipid paraphrase of a lively account of the exile at Bourges left by Durey de Meinières; this account is in AN, KK 821.

[80] BUP, CA 28/V: Jean-Omer Joly de Fleury to the Comte d'Argenson, 19 July 1753. The *gens du roi* were shown several of these letters at Méry.

[81] *Ibid.*, 42/IV: [Mayou d'Aunoy] to the Comte d'Argenson, 16 July 1753.

[82] Gazier, 'Une lettre inédite de Montesquieu', p. 124; Robert Shackleton, 'A supposed letter of Montesquieu in 1795', in *Studies in Eighteenth-Century French Literature presented to Robert Niklaus*, ed. J. H. Fox *et al.* (Exeter, 1975), pp. 228–9.

that the Government's silence stemmed from weakness. Jean-Omer Joly de Fleury was convinced that if the *déclaration* were to be sent, the *grand' chambre* would act as the first president had predicted; it would simply pass an *arrêté* to the effect that it could not register with the *enquêtes*, and it would make no *démarche* to ask for their recall.[83] The *avocat général* was also convinced that pressure was being brought to bear on individual members of the *grand'chambre*; he did not mince matters:

> Ce sont les Imbéciles du Grand banc et de La grand-chambre qui mènent tout le reste, Entre eux se tiennent les conciliabules, Le Presid*t*. de Maupeou les échauffe Et on voit les Partys que l'on croyoit assurés varier du soir au lendemain.
>
> Que nous ayions, nous autres gens du roy, causé en particulier avec quelqu'un de ceux sur lesquels ils comptent, aussitôt on le chambre et on luy fait faire une confession de ce qu'il a dit, et s'il a foibli, on le remonte.[84]

The attitude of the *grand'chambre* would possibly have been different if the first president had chosen to exert his influence in favour of a settlement. Instead he played a passive rôle and sheltered behind the will of others. It was said that he was involved in a court intrigue with the Comte d'Argenson; this was an allegation he strenuously denied, and the evidence for it is nothing more than the suspicion expressed by some of the *parlementaires*. It is more likely that his conduct stemmed from wounded pride and from a belief that it was his duty simply to await the King's orders. However, the equivocal behaviour of his son, President de Maupeou, casts some doubt on his noble-mindedness and Olympian detachment. President de Novion, their close associate, was known to be stirring up the *zélés* in Pontoise.[85]

On 29 July a decision to settle the whole affair appeared to have been taken at Compiègne. After a meeting with the King, Conty sent the Chevalier de Maupeou to explain the arrangement to the first president. Conty then left for Paris after telling the chancellor that he would return two days later to work out the details of the plan with him.[86] But nothing was done. The main reason was probably that the King was still undecided on many points, having by now received conflicting advice from all quarters. On 1 August he sent a long *questionnaire* to the Maréchal de Noailles at Maintenon. He wanted to know whether a law of silence would remedy the present troubles or whether it would help to alleviate them. He asked for Noailles's opinion on whether the *grand'chambre* would register the law without the *enquêtes* and resume its duties if he gave the order, or

---

83 See letter mentioned in note 71.
84 BUP, CA 28/V: Jean-Omer Joly de Fleury to the Comte d'Argenson, 19 July 1753.
85 *Ibid.*, 42/IV: [Mayou] to the Comte d'Argenson, 31 July 1753; and D'Argenson, ed. Rathery, viii, p. 90.
86 BN, JF 2103, f. 180 *procureur général* to his father, 31 July [1753].

whether such an order might not give rise to a further act of disobedience. Alternatively he wanted to know whether Noailles thought that, if the *grand'chambre* asked for the return of the exiles in order to be able to register the law, he should grant this request, perhaps on condition that the *grand'chambre* should first resume its duties. He also questioned the marshal about another possibility: that he should reunite the *Parlement* without being asked by the *grand'chambre* and before he sent the law with the order for the resumption of service.[87] In effect the King was still searching for a solution that was compatible with his dignity.

Another reason why Louis XV hesitated to take action was probably the political crisis in Rouen. The *Parlement* of Rouen had imposed a fine on the bishop of Evreux for having allowed a *curé* to refuse the sacrament to a dying priest. On 1 August the *Parlement* passed a *décret d'ajournement personnel*[88] on the bishop, but was prevented from notifying it by the military *commandant* of Normandy, the Marquis de Fougères, who arrived at noon with orders from the King. In his presence the *arrêts* in the case were crossed out in the register by the *greffier*, who stayed behind to perform the task only because he had been handed a *lettre de cachet*, unlike the *parlementaires*, who were able to leave the room in protest. The next day the *parlementaires* decreed that they would remain assembled, 'tout service cessant', until they had presented remonstrances to the King.[89] The Government took steps to make sure that the neighbouring province of Brittany remained quiet: La Bourdonnaye, the military *commandant*, was sent to Rennes.[90] In these circumstances the King may well have felt that the time was not right for a settlement with the *Parlement* of Paris. Finally, there was perhaps a third, less important, reason why the King held back; he may have been irritated at Conty's active participation in a dispute between the princes of the blood and the House of Rohan over the use of appellations attached to princely rank: Madame de Pompadour was on the side of the Rohans.[91]

At Pontoise the circumstances were still no more favourable to a settlement than they were at court. In the first place, the Rouen affair also had serious repercussions there, as D'Argental (one of the *conseillers d'honneur*) succinctly described in a letter to his wife:

---

[87] *Correspondance de Louis XV et du maréchal de Noailles* ed. C. Rousset (Paris, 1865), ii, pp. 328–34.

[88] On *décrets d'ajournement personnel*, see p. 116.

[89] On the Rouen affair, see Luynes, *Mém.*, xiii, pp. 35–6.

[90] FL, Tocqueville MSS, 10/65: Bidé de La Grandville to Lamoignon, 8 Aug. 1753.

[91] D'Argenson, ed. Rathery, viii, pp. 86–9; E. J. F. Barbier, *Chronique de la régence et du règne de Louis XV (1718–1763), ou Journal de Barbier* (Paris, 1866), 8 vols. (hereafter Barbier, *Journal*), v, pp. 401–3. The dispute was over by 10 August (Luynes, *Mém.*, xiii, p. 54). See also Conty's letter of 29 June 1753 to an unknown correspondent reproduced in *Musée des*

L'affaire du parlement de Rouen achève de tourner les têtes; elle marque, dit-on, que le gouvernement n'a jamais eu aucun désir sincère de concili-ation. Mr le prince de Conti a été duppe ou trompeur. Il est clair qu'on veut pousser les parlements jusqu'à la dernière extrémité et établir le despotisme sur leur ruine. Il ne faut pas se fier à des paroles. Ce qui auroit paru convenable et suffisant ne l'est plus. 1° le retour des confrères; 2° une satisfaction entière pour le présent; 3° une seureté la plus grande pour l'avenir: voilà le discours que l'on tient. Il y en a même qui vont jusqu'à dire que nous ne devons pas nous contenter qu'on finisse avec nous, et qu'il faut qu'on termine en même temps avec le parlement de Rouen.[92]

The advocates of conciliation were in a weak position. When the Bourges memoirs and some of the letters appeared illicitly in print they thought it prudent not to denounce them before the *grand'chambre*, though they knew that it was essential for them to show that these publications did not represent their own way of thinking.[93] Secondly, there was no one left who was prepared to risk his reputation by engaging in negotiations: Chauvelin and Salabéry were discredited, and the first president had no intention of losing the confidence of the rest of the *Parlement*.[94] And finally, there was no longer a sense of urgency at Pontoise. The *parlementaires* were in comfort-able lodgings in the town, and their friends and relatives came to visit them. The first president kept open house at Saint-Martin (his pension had not been stopped) and the richer presidents followed his example: in this way a *conseiller* could usually go the rounds of the dinner tables. There was plenty of varied hunting on the Prince de Conty's estates; and in high summer there were parties with the ladies on the river at Vauréal followed by fireworks. As the lawyer Moreau noted on his visit to friends in the *Parlement*: 'la bonne chère et l'air de gaîeté de Pontoise ne présentent point l'idée d'un exil bien désagréable'.[95]

---

archives nationales: documents originaux de l'histoire de France, ed. F. A. Maury (Paris, 1892), pp. 596–7; on Conty's movements at this time, see Luynes, *Mém.*, xiii, pp. 19–20.

[92] *Collection of autograph letters ... formed by Alfred Morrison*, i, p. 82: letter dated 'ce mardi matin' [7 Aug. 1753]; see also BUP, CA 42/IV: [Mayou] to the Comte d'Argenson, 7 Aug. 1753; and BUP, CA 28/V: Jean-Omer Joly de Fleury to the Comte d'Argenson, 10 Aug. 1753.

[93] *Collection of autograph letters ... formed by Alfred Morrison*, i, p. 80: D'Argental to his wife, 'ce mercredi matin', [8 Aug. 1753]. Cf. BN, JF 2103, f. 187: Jean-Omer Joly de Fleury to his father, 8 Aug. 1753.

[94] When he visited Pontoise on 7–8 August, the lawyer Moreau observed that Chauvelin and Salabéry and a few others were discredited there; see the extracts from his diary printed in J. N. Moreau, *Mes souvenirs*, ed. C. Hermelin (Paris, 1898, 1902), 2 vols., i, p. 392.

[95] *Ibid.*, pp. 390–2; BUP, CA 42/IV: [Mayou] to the Comte d'Argenson, 2 Aug. 1753; and D'Argental's delightful letters to his wife printed in *Collection of autograph letters ... formed by Alfred Morrison*, i, pp. 79–83. At Pontoise the *Parlement* held its meetings in the refectory of the Cordéliers, and the first president took up residence at the *Vicariat* and later at the château de Saint-Martin on the outskirts of the town; see E. Mallet, *L'Installation du parlement à Pontoise en 1753* (Pontoise, 1926), p. 17.

The life of the exiles was not unbearable either. At Bourges a bored provincial society welcomed them with alacrity; in return they explained *Unigenitus* to their hosts, who, until that moment, had somehow managed to lead their lives without reference to the bull. In the weeks that followed, the *parlementaires* were also entertained in a princely way at Turly, the country seat of the archbishop of Bourges, where Cardinal de la Rochefoucauld took them on a tour of the house and showed them his newly installed *lieux à l'angloise*. It was the occasion of a *faux pas* by Monsieur Boutin of the 1st *requêtes*, another honorary author of the remonstrances, a 'new man', a financier's son with short and ugly legs. According to Durey de Meinières:

> M. Boutin s'écrie à la vue de ces lieux à l'angloise que Son Eminence est d'autant plus admirable qu'étant au dessus des foiblesses humaines, elle veut s'en accommoder.

This comment on the cardinal's sanitary arrangements fell suitably flat.[96] The *parlementaires* admired the way La Rochefoucauld punctiliously carried out his diocesan visitations on horseback. Only occasional reminders of the political crisis now reached Bourges: letters and memoirs from old Joly de Fleury aimed at convincing young Angran of the error of his views and expressing surprise at such folly: 'la pluspart de Messieurs reçus depuis 20 ans pense le contraire de ce que nous pensions lors de leur réception et surquoy nous n'avons jamais varié'.[97]

The court returned to Versailles on 11 August. Two days later the *Parlement* of Rouen resumed its duties, the King having agreed to receive its remonstrances only on that condition. The attention of the Government again turned to Pontoise. If a settlement was not reached before 7 September, the Government would have to provide for the administration of justice during the vacation because the *grand'chambre* would not set up a vacation chamber without the *enquêtes*. The Comte d'Argenson asked Jean-Omer Joly de Fleury for information about the arrangements made in 1720 to deal with a similar situation.[98] At the same time Conty once more made overtures to the first president. Maupeou went shooting with the prince at L'Isle-Adam on 20 August and visited him at Vauréal the next day.[99] Conty was proposing once again that the *déclaration* should be sent to the *grand'chambre*, which would then depute the *gens du roi* to tell the King

[96] Grellet-Dumazeau, *Les Exilés de Bourges*, pp. 152 and 195 (from the account by Durey de Meinières in AN, KK 821, ff. 10–11).

[97] Rogister Collection, Durham: G. F. Joly de Fleury to Angran, 10 July 1753; see also his letter to Angran of 2 July in the Bibliothèque municipale de Rouen, MSS, Collection Duputel, iii, no. 338.

[98] BUP, CA 28/V: Jean-Omer Joly de Fleury to the Comte d'Argenson, 16 Aug. 1753.

[99] *Ibid.*, same to same, 21 Aug. 1753; BN, JF 2103, f. 173: *procureur général* to his father, 'mercredi 22' [Aug. 1753]; *Collection of autograph letters … formed by Alfred Morrison*, i, pp. 80–1: D'Argental to his wife, [21 Aug. 1753].

that it could not register the law without the *enquêtes* and to ask for their return; the request would be granted and the whole *Parlement* would be reassembled at Soissons or Moulins for the registration of the law.[100]

Although the first president made some attempt to enlist support for Conty's proposals from members of the *grand'chambre*, he quickly satisfied himself that the plan had no chance of success on account of the attitude of that convenient entity, the 'gens vifs', and doubtless gave the prince the same answer as before. It is possible that the plan might have been more successful if some of the presidents had taken a firm line with Maupeou. But only President Turgot took part in these negotiations, and he was a junior and rather disingenuous member of the *grand banc*; Molé spoke only belatedly in favour of a *démarche*; Gilbert and Chauvelin informed Conty that they did not wish to be involved in the negotiations.[101]

It was, however, the King's reply of 2 September to the remonstrances of the *Parlement* of Rouen which destroyed the remaining chances of a concili-ation. In the reply the King stated it as his intention that *Unigenitus* should continue to be regarded as a 'rule of Church and State' and that all *arrêts du conseil* that were notified to the *Parlement* should be executed without there being any need for letters patent.[102] The reply naturally created a stir at Pontoise. The *procureur général* thought it had destroyed all faith in the Government;

> Il est effectivement bien triste que l'on se soit expliqué comme on a fait sur Les Arrests du Conseil d'Evocation et de Cassation. Cet article de la Réponse est regardé comme une Dèclaration de guerre à toutes les Compagnies.[103]

If the reply was intended to frighten the *grand'chambre* into submission, it failed in its purpose. Some claimed that it was the work of those who wanted to thwart Conty's negotiation.[104] Nevertheless, the *parlementaires* thought it likely that the Government had taken a decision about them;

---

[100] BUP, CA 28/V: letter quoted in note 98. D'Argental thought Maupeou had probably confirmed Conty in the belief that the *grand'chambre* would not make a *démarche*, or else that he had put forward an earlier suggestion which he had made, that the King should assemble all the *parlementaires* in one place and keep them there until the whole affair was settled, one way or another (*Collection of autograph letters ... formed by Alfred Morrison*, i, p. 81).

[101] BUP, CA 42/IV: [Mayou] to the Comte d'Argenson, 21 Aug., 23 Aug., and 7 Sept. 1753; *ibid.*, 28/V: Jean-Omer Joly de Fleury to the same, 4 Sept. 1753.

[102] For the text of the reply and of the chancellor's speech to the deputies from Rouen, see Barbier, *Journal*, v, pp. 411–13; Luynes, *Mém.*, xiii, pp. 45–6, 55; see also BN, JF 2103, f. 188.

[103] *Ibid.*, f. 174: letter to his father, [5 Sept. 1753]; f. 175; same to same, [6 Sept. 1753]. Jean-Omer Joly de Fleury wrote in the same vein to the Comte d'Argenson (see letter mentioned in note 101 above).

[104] *Collection of autograph letters ... formed by Alfred Morrison*, i, pp. 82–3: D'Argental to his wife, 'ce mardi matin' [4 Sept. 1753].

they were therefore a little surprised to find that they were allowed to break up for the vacation on 7 September.[105]

On 18 September the King set up a commission composed of six councillors of state and twenty-four *maîtres des requêtes* to act as a vacation chamber in Paris until the *rentrée* of the *Parlement* at Pontoise on 11 November. Its meetings were to be held in the hall of the Convent of the Grands Augustins.[106] Jean-Omer Joly de Fleury had assured the Comte d'Argenson some weeks earlier that a commission would encounter little difficulty in trying criminal cases:

> ... vous voyés toujours, Monsieur, que par des arrêtés de la Commission on peut sans ordre du roy et sans contrainte faire venir les Prisonniers et de secondes grosses de leur procès au greffe de La Commission. Pour le Châtelet même cela est inutile: La commission peut juger sur les minutes de châtelet ainsi que la tournelle le fait souvent.[107]

Despite these helpful suggestions, the ministers were apprehensive: on 22 September the council forced the chancellor to invite the *procureur général* to a meeting to advise him on the procedure which should be followed by the new court. Joly de Fleury, who had fled to Epône to avoid being involved, declined the invitation. Lamoignon did not insist.[108]

The important question was whether the *Châtelet* and the other lower jurisdictions of the *ressort* would recognise the Commission. The Government forced the issue here by requiring these jurisdictions to register the letters patent setting up the Commission. This course had not been followed in 1720 or in 1732,[109] and it is not clear why it was adopted on this occasion. The *Châtelet* was the court of the *prévôt* of Paris. As there was no *bailliage* court in the capital, the *Châtelet* was immediately subordinate to the *Parlement*. In some respects its competence extended to the rest of the Kingdom because it tried cases arising from acts that bore the seal of the *vicomté* of Paris. The *Châtelet* was composed of a *lieutenant civil* (D'Argouges de Fleury), a *lieutenant criminel* (Nègre), two *lieutenants particuliers* (Lenoir and Guérey de Voisins) and forty-seven councillors, together with a few honorary councillors. In rotation they worked the four services of the court: criminal, *parc-civil*, *présidial*, and *chambre du conseil* with the aid of a *procureur de roi* and his staff.[110] There was a certain social cachet attached to these

---

[105] *Ibid.* See also BUP, CA 42/IV: [Mayou] to the Comte d'Argenson, 7 Sept. 1753.

[106] Barbier, *Journal*, v, p. 418.

[107] BUP, CA 28/V: letter of 21 Aug. 1753 mentioned in note 99 above.

[108] BN, JF 1497, f. 229: note in the hand of the *procureur général*; f. 230: Lamoignon to the *procureur général*, 22 Sept. 1753; f. 231: *procureur général* to Lamoignon, Epône, 24 Sept. 1753 (draft in the hand of Jean-Omer Joly de Fleury); f. 232: Lamoignon to the *procureur général*, 25 Sept. 1753.

[109] Barbier, *Journal*, v, p. 422.

[110] M. Marion, *Dictionnaire des institutions de la France aux xvii⁰ et xviii⁰ siècles* (Paris, 1923, reprint, 1968), pp. 88–90.

offices. On 28 September the *Châtelet* resolved that it could not register the letters patent establishing the Commission because these had not been registered at the *Parlement* in the first instance.[111] Its refusal marked the beginning of a long and inconclusive struggle between the Government and the court. The King quashed the decision of 28 September by an *arrêt du conseil* and ordered the Commission to proceed to register the letters patent at the *Châtelet*. Three members of the Commission accompanied by their *greffier* – *greffiers* were invaluable on these occasions – went there on 5 October, the offending *arrêté* was struck off the register and the letters patent transcribed. As the councillors of the *Châtelet* were divided, they postponed discussion of what had taken place until after the recess. At their *rentrée* on 22 October, the *lieutenant civil* produced a *lettre de cachet* forbidding them to hold an assembly other than for the purpose of discussing the internal affairs of the *Châtelet*. They made a formal record of the various orders they and the *lieutenant civil* had received, and they again postponed their debate.

Their resistance then took a different form. One of their sentences was confirmed by the Commission, and they received the order to carry it out. They were also instructed by the Commission to arrange for a prisoner to be tortured (the *question préparatoire*). The *Châtelet* deferred the execution of both decisions. The Commission promptly notified the *lieutenant civil* that the sentences had to be carried out and also instructed the *greffier* of the *Châtelet* to bring the register to the Grands Augustins so that the *arrêté* of 22 October could be struck out. The two officers duly complied with these orders. But again the *Châtelet* passed a motion that 'Messieurs de la commission' had no jurisdiction over them and they protested against the notifications made to the *lieutenant civil* and to the *greffier*. They also followed the example of the *Parlement* in asserting the claim that their records could not be removed without their authorisation, and they reaffirmed their previous decisions. Accordingly the Commission once more ordered the *greffier* to bring them the minutes of the *Châtelet*.[112] And so the conflict continued, broadening out into the issue of the recognition of the Commission and of its successor court, the *Chambre Royale*, by the other subordinate courts of the vast jurisdiction of the *Parlement* of Paris: the numerous *bailliages* and *sénéchaussées*. In the meantime, the Commission barely survived on a diet of

---

[111] Barbier, *Journal*, v, p. 420; and D'Argenson, ed. Rathery, viii, p. 133. For the deliberation of the council of the *Châtelet* and the text of its *arrêts* on these matters, see AN, Y 9303 *bis* to 9303; U 1089 no. 96; BN, n.a.fr. 22257, ff. 91–2. To have registered the letters patent would, in the opinion of the magistrates, have been contrary to the terms of the edict of Blois (art. 97 and 98), the edicts of Jan. 1597 (art. 12) and May 1616 (art. 9). Magistrates, they pointed out, could be fined for contravening legislative acts in accordance with an *arrêt de règlement* of the *Parlement* of 5 July 1726.

[112] Barbier, *Journal*, v, pp. 422–30; D'Argenson, ed. Rathery, viii, pp. 143, 149.

criminal cases. As Jean-Omer Joly de Fleury had suggested, prisoners could always be hauled out of the Conciergerie and tried. Two rapists from Châteauroux were sentenced on 11 October, and eight other cases were dealt with before the *rentrée* of the *Parlement*.[113]

As the time approached for the *rentrée* of the *Parlement* at Pontoise, the Government gave careful consideration to the implications of the political situation. Ministers belatedly studied the question whether *arrêts du conseil* evoking cases or quashing judgements needed letters patent and therefore formal registration at the *Parlement*. On this question the *Parlement* of Paris was not alone in thinking that letters patent were necessary; the same view was expressed in the remonstrances of the *Parlement* of Rouen.[114] As the subsequent history of the reign shows, it was a view that was shared by French *parlementaires* generally. In a private exchange of views with the former *procureur général*, the minister Rouillé differed with him on the issue. If letters patent were required and became law only once they had been registered, the *Parlement* could refuse to register them and simply continue its judicial proceedings; the King's will would be without effect ('ce qui n'est pas proposable'). Rouillé conceded that over legislation the position was different, but thought that in judicial matters letters patent would be justified only if the *Parlement* were prepared to register them first and to complain about them afterwards.[115]

Joly de Fleury's view (contained in a memoir which he produced at this time) was that, as it stood, an *arrêt du conseil* was simply an account by a clerk or a minister of a decision reached in the King's council: 'ce n'est point un pareil titre qui puisse parler avec empire aux cours souveraines, qui exige d'elles et l'obéissance et l'obligation de faire obéir les autres'. The King himself had to speak directly – *Louis par la grâce de Dieu* – to those who had to obey his commands – *à nos amés et féaux*. A signature and a seal also required marks of authenticity. Joly de Fleury denied that evocations of cases to the Royal Council would be ineffective if they had to be registered with letters patent. If these were sent, the *Parlement* had either to register them at once or make remonstrances; under the second option it would have to suspend its judicial proceedings until it received a reply to the remonstrances. The *Parlement* would not have all the power. That could happen only if it refused to register or if it made remonstrances without suspending its proceedings. In both these cases of resistance to his will, the King should use his authority. Whether legal proceedings and court sentences could be quashed as part of the ordinary judicial process or as part of an extraordinary procedure was open to debate. Both interpreta-

---

[113] BN, JF 309, ff. 209–10.   [114] BN, JF 1497, f. 159.
[115] BN, JF 1052, f. 94: Rouillé to G. F. Joly de Fleury, 20 Sept. 1753.

tions were buttressed by an array of precedents, but in either case, letters patent were required.[116] Joly de Fleury managed to find thirty-seven instances of letters patent of evocation to the Royal Council being registered at the *Parlement* between 1719 and 1750.[117]

Such views were not willingly accepted by ministers. Jean-Omer Joly de Fleury supplied the Comte d'Argenson with a copy of his father's memoir. He also discussed it with his brother-in-law, the minister Saint-Contest.[118] He found the ministers of one voice: 'de quelque manière que la volonté du roy soit communiquée, on doit y obéir'. When he read this passage in his son's account of the discussions, the former *procureur général* scrawled in the margin: 'ce propos n'est pas raisonable [*sic*]'.[119] The debate grew in importance as the reign progressed, especially in the years 1765–7, though it would be mistaken to see it as part of some concerted onslaught by the *parlements* on royal authority following the Seven Years' War.[120] The issue was already present in 1753 and probably earlier.

The Government's chief source of concern remained the act of disobedience of the *Parlement* of Paris. D'Ormesson's father, the *doyen* of the Royal council, confided to the *gens du roi* that plans had been submitted for the suppression of parts of the existing *Parlement*.[121] No trace of these plans has been found. But some idea of the difficulties involved in a suppression of this kind may be gained from the memorandum on the subject which Joly de Fleury had prepared for one of his sons back in May.[122] The former *procureur général* was by no means unsympathetic to the idea: in his opinion the abolition of two or three chambers of the *enquêtes*, for instance, would usefully rid the *Parlement* of young troublemakers. The remaining chambers could absorb the resultant workload. However, he pointed out that the Government would have to decide whether or not the officeholders would receive financial compensation for the loss of offices that were their property; it was clearly impracticable for the Government to reimburse them,

---

[116] *Ibid.*, ff. 99–112: '3ᵉ mémoire envoyé' (in the hand of G. F. Joly de Fleury). It is possible that a request to President Gilbert for permission to consult the celebrated MSS collection of his brother-in-law, President de Cotte, was made by the former *procureur général*; see ff. 95–6: copy of a letter to Gilbert of 2 Oct. 1753. Joly de Fleury may have sent a copy of his memoir to the Prince de Conty on 15 Oct. (see f. 3: an undated annotated letter from the prince).

[117] *Ibid.*, f. 117.

[118] BUP, CA 28/V: Jean-Omer Joly de Fleury to the Comte d'Argenson, 19 Oct. 1753; BN, JF 1052, f. 97: [same] to [G. .F. Joly de Fleury], Epône, 11 Oct. 1753.

[119] *Ibid.*, f. 131.

[120] Cf. Michel Antoine, *Le Dur Métier de roi. Etudes sur la civilisation politique de la France d'Ancien Régime* (Paris, 1986), p. 198.

[121] BN, JF 1497, f. 235: Jean-Omer Joly de Fleury to his father, 28 Nov. 1753. The *gens du roi* had been to Fontainebleau at the beginning of November, when they saw D'Ormesson.

[122] BN, JF 2103, ff. 77–80: draft memorandum for Jean-Omer Joly de Fleury, 19 May [1753]; JF 568, ff. 375–8 (an identical copy), f. 371: G. F. Joly de Fleury to Jean-Omer Joly de Fleury, 19 May 1753.

and though Joly de Fleury did not say so, the other alternative, that of an outright confiscation, was alien to contemporary notions of kingly justice. Moreover, the Government could not satisfactorily assign to the lower jurisdictions the duty of trying some of the more important cases that normally fell within the attributions of the *Parlement*. Such a step would have to be preceded by a reform of those jurisdictions. Otherwise, a single *bailli*, like the one at Vincennes for instance, could try cases without appeal; over a quarter of the *bailliages* had only one officer. If the reform consisted of allowing only the larger presidial *bailliages* to try cases without appeal, then care had to be taken to exclude such cases as those concerning the status of persons, the position of heirs, and ecclesiastical matters which were all too delicate to be left entirely to the country justices.[123] Changes of this importance could not be undertaken without misgivings: their implications were greater than even questioning contemporaries realised.

In the light of these considerations it is hardly surprising that Louis XV should have preferred to make another attempt to force the *Parlement* into submission. On 7 November the first president received a *lettre de cachet* exiling him to Soissons, and the next day the other members of the *grand'chambre* were also exiled there.[124] The *Parlement* had thus ceased to exercise any functions. Some ministers hoped Maupeou would now make a *démarche* by writing to the King from Soissons (where the intendant, his kinsman Méliand, was conveniently placed to act as an intermediary), but their hopes were disappointed.[125] On 11 November the King set up a special court, the *Chambre Royale du Louvre*, to dispense justice in place of the *Parlement*; it was composed of eighteen councillors of state and thirty-six *maîtres des requêtes*. The letters patent creating the *Chambre Royale* were registered by the court itself two days later. On 18 November a further set of letters patent were issued separating the court into civil and criminal divisions. Finally, on 22 December letters patent in the form of a *déclaration* (registered on 4 January 1754) entrusted the *Chambre Royale* with all cases pending before the *Parlement*.[126] La Rochefoucauld confided to Durey de

[123] *Ibid.*, f. 376.

[124] BN, JF 309, f. 7: note in the hand of Jean-Omer Joly de Fleury, 7 Nov. 1753; f. 13: Maupeou to the *procureur général*, 9 Nov. 1753; f. 16: printed list of the members of the *grand'chambre* who were sent to Soissons.

[125] See the remarks made in February 1754 by *Avocat général* d'Ormesson to Ysabeau which the latter reported to Richelieu: BVC, RP, xiv (catalogue number 35), no. 8: letter of 1 March 1754; and a letter of 21 November 1753 from the well informed and influential financier Pâris-Duverney to the Abbé de Bernis in *Correspondance du Cardinal de Bernis, Ministre d'Etat avec M. du Vernay, conseiller d'état, depuis 1752 jusqu'en 1769* ('Londres et se trouve à Paris chez Buisson', 1790), i, p. 78.

[126] For the text of the letters patent of 11 November 1753 establishing the *Chambre Royale du Louvre*, see Luynes, *Mém.*, xiii, pp. 108–10; for the other royal acts, see BN, JF 308, ff. 282, 283, and 289; for the official records of the *Chambre Royale*, see AN, X^{1B} 9688–9689.

Meinières at Bourges that the plans for the new court had been ready for three months.[127] No evidence has yet come to light to substantiate the suggestion made by the Marquis d'Argenson that the Government intended to persuade the *Grand Conseil* to take the place of the *Parlement*.[128]

Louis XV outlined his purpose in a letter to the chancellor on 13 December:

> J'ay établi la chambre royale au lieu et place du parlement jusqu'à ce qu'il m'ait donné des marques de soumission, et que je les aie acceptées, et je veux que tout ce qui ressortit du parlement la reconnoisse; et c'est ce que je soutiendrés de tout mon pouvoir.[129]

The letters patent setting up the *Chambre Royale* accused the *Parlement* of dereliction of duty, and it seems that some ministers hoped that this would at last provoke Maupeou into writing to the King in defence of the *Parlement*; they were again disappointed.[130] Hence the King could succeed in his stated aim only by making the *Chambre Royale* an effective threat to the position of the *Parlement*.

---

[127] AN, KK 821, f. 10ᵛ.   [128] D'Argenson, ed. Rathery, viii, p. 29.
[129] FL, Rosanbo MSS, 1/3/50.
[130] See Ysabeau's letter to Richelieu of 1 March 1754 (note 125 above).

8

⤴

THE EXILE OF THE
GRAND'CHAMBRE
AND THE RETURN OF THE
PARLEMENT, 1753–1754

C'est le Roi seul qui s'est servi de conseil à lui-même à
l'occasion du rappel du parlement: c'est son véritable
amour pour ses sujets qui l'a déterminé à leur rendre des
juges ...
>   *First President de Maupeou to a* parlementaire,
>   *1 August 1754*

THE MEMBERS of the *grand'chambre* made their way to their place of exile.
The *gens du roi* were included in the proscription.[1] As they had received
advance warning of the King's order, they decided to steal a march on the
présidents à mortier to get the best lodgings for themselves. At 10 p.m. on the
evening of 6 November, upon returning to the family seat at Fleury after
their final audience with the King at nearby Fontainebleau, the *avocat
général* and his brother sent an express message to their secretary in Paris.
Woken in the middle of the night, the poor man was instructed to find four
lodgings ('chauds et commodes') for them at Soissons before the town was
flooded with the servants of the presidents bent on the same purpose. They
wanted a kitchen, dining-room, with accommodation for a cook and a
maître d'hôtel. It was better for the *procureur général* and D'Ormesson to be
together, while Jean-Omer Joly de Fleury and their new, young, colleague,
Bochart de Saron, the third *avocat général*, preferred separate apartments:
each needed a room, closet, *garde-robe* (all within easy reach if possible),
stables, lofts, rooms for coachmen. 'M. d'Ormesson, mon frère et moi',
wrote Jean-Omer Joly de Fleury, 'nous aurons chacun notre lit. M. de
Saron pourra bien ne pas en avoir d'abord.' Perhaps Bochart de Saron was
expected to spend his first night gazing at the firmament, an interest which

---

[1] BN, JF 309, f. 7: note in the hand of Jean-Omer Joly de Fleury, 7 Nov. 1753; f. 13: First
President de Maupeou to the *procureur général*, Bruyères, 9 Nov. 1753; f. 16: printed list of the
members of the *grand'chambre*.

led him some thirty years later to determine that Herschel had discovered not a comet but a new planet beyond Saturn, Uranus; and this before the Revolution sent him to the scaffold, like Lavoisier, that other scientist of whom the Republic had no need. The secretary was told to put suitable pressure on the local representative of the *parquet*: 'la considération du procureur du roi à Soissons se réduira en politesses extrêmes à son égard, si les logements n'étaient pas convenables'.[2] Presumably they obtained what they wanted, and some idea of their style of living may be gleaned from a note of a consignment of wines and liqueurs which their secretary received for their use from Châlons-sur-Marne: fifty bottles of red Champagne, twenty-four bottles of liqueur wines (Lunel, Malaga, and muscat), and twenty-one bottles of liqueurs bearing exotic names such as *huile de Vénus*, *crème des Barbades*, and *parfait amour*.[3] These were some of the compensations or stimulants of the hectic life of the *gens du roi*.

Several obstacles had to be overcome if the new *Chambre Royale* was to fulfil its purpose adequately. In the first place, the senior councillors of state were markedly unenthusiastic about their new judicial duties. They complained to the chancellor about the arrangements for the inaugural session of the new court; according to Jean-Omer Joly de Fleury:

> ils [les conseillers d'état] prétendent que si c'est *conseil* mr le chancelier doit toujours y présider, que si c'est *tribunal* c'est une dérogation à leur état et que c'est faire d'eux un second grd. Conseil.[4]

They did not obtain satisfaction; for the chancellor attended only the inaugural session. They had also criticised the procedure laid down in the original draft of the letters patent, which had to be hastily revised. If the young and ambitious *maîtres de requêtes* saw the *Chambre Royale* as an opportunity to display their zeal, the councillors of state were afraid that the King's authority and their own dignity would be compromised in an unsuccessful venture; Jean-Omer Joly de Fleury observed, 'que les conseillers d'état pensent que cette besogne ne vaudra pas grand-chose'.[5] Besides, and this may have been a more important consideration, the D'Ormessons, the Gilbert de Voisins, the Le Peletiers, all had sons, brothers, and other relatives to place or consider in the *Parlement*; although they would have

---

[2] Jean-Omer Joly de Fleury to De la Roue (secretary), Fleury, 6 Nov. 1753, published in Albert Grün, 'En revenant de Pontoise', *Feuilles d'histoire du xviie au xxe siècle*, vi (1911), pp. 388–91. For the scientific activity of J. B. G. Bochart de Saron (1730–94), the last first president of the *Parlement*, see Adolphe Wattinne, *Magistrats célèbres du xviiie siècle* (Paris, 1941), p. 301, and the *Encyclopédie de la Pléiade*, v (i) *Histoire de la Science des origines au xxe siècle*, ed. Maurice Daumas (Paris, 1957), p. 729.

[3] Grün, 'En revenant de Pontoise', p. 391.

[4] BN, JF 1497, f. 225: letter to his father, 9 Nov. 1753.

[5] *Ibid.* same to same, Epône, 14 Nov. 1753.

denied it, there was perhaps a trace of passive resistance stemming from family interest in their attitude to the *Chambre Royale*.[6]

Secondly, there was again the question of the recognition of the court. What would be the attitude of the *Châtelet* and the other lower jurisdictions, the *bailliages* and the *sénéchaussées*, to the *Chambre Royale*?[7] On 10 November a councillor of the *Châtelet*, Roger de Monthuchet, a sick man recovering from a leg operation, was arrested and taken to the Bastille.[8] The ostensible reason was that he had been responsible for the suppression of certain pamphlets that were sympathetic to *Unigenitus*. But the chancellor told a deputation from the *Châtelet* on 14 November that his release depended on the future conduct of his colleagues, and it seems therefore that the Government was trying to intimidate them.[9] Six days later the *Châtelet* registered the letters patent establishing the *Chambre Royale*, though only with the clause, *du très exprès commandement du roi*.[10] The *Chambre Royale* ordered the *lieutenant criminel* of the *Châtelet* to receive an *information* from a party in a criminal case. The *lieutenant criminel*, Nègre, was a sick man whose duties were taken in rotation on a monthly basis by the two *lieutenants particuliers*, Lenoir and Guérey de Voisins.[11] Guérey de Voisins was on duty in November, and he refused to receive the *information*, saying that he did not recognise the decisions of the *Chambre Royale*. The senior members of the *Chambre Royale* told the chancellor they would have to take proceedings against Guérey de Voisins and that their decisions could be effective only if accompanied by *ordres particuliers*. The chancellor pleaded for them with the King:

> Le refus fait par le Sr Guérey de Voisins d'exécuter un arrest de la Chambre Royalle s'il n'est pas punis entraisnera celuy de touts les officiers du chastelet mesme de ceux qui sont les mieux intentionnés pour le service de V.M. qui

---

[6] Dr Jeffreys wrote to Philip Yorke that, of the members of the *Chambre Royale*, 'some few are men of Reputation and Ability, but the majority is compos'd of young men quite ignorant of Business – the Procureur General is not above 20 years of age': BL, Add. MSS 35,630: letter of 12 Dec. 1753. In fact, the *procureur général* (Bourgeois de Boynes) was thirty-four and was generally considered fairly capable.

[7] BN, JF 309, ff. 209–10.

[8] BL, Egerton MSS 1667: 'Livre d'entrée des prisonniers de la Bastille' (1734–54), f. 184. The order was dated 9 Nov. 1753. Luynes mistakenly states that another councillor, Quillet, was also sent to the Bastille at this time (*Mémoires du Duc de Luynes sur la cour de Louis XV (1753–1758)*, ed. L. Dussieux and E. Soulié (Paris, 1860–5) (hereafter cited as Luynes, *Mém.*), xiii, p. 107). Quillet was not sent to the Bastille until April 1754 (Egerton MSS 1667, f. 195); BN, MS franç. 22105, f. 63.

[9] *Journal et mémoires du Marquis d'Argenson*, ed. E. J. B. Rathery (Paris, 1859–67) (hereafter cited as D'Argenson, ed. Rathery), viii, p. 163; BL, Add. MSS. 35,630, f. 109^v: Jeffreys to Yorke, 14 Nov. 1753.

[10] E. J. F. Barbier, *Chronique de la régence et du règne de Louis XV (1718–1763), ou Journal de Barbier* (Paris, 1866), 8 vols. (hereafter Barbier, *Journal*), v, p. 440; D'Argenson, ed. Rathery, viii, pp. 165–6.

[11] BN, n.a.fr. 22257; f. 96: note of 7 Dec. 1753.

n'ozeront pas avoir une autre conduitte que luy dans la crainte de se déshonorer, Il y a actuellement de gros procès pendants en la chambre Royalle dont il sera nécessaire de renvoyer au chastelet l'exécution suivant l'ordre judiciaire; ce qui ne pourra se faire vû la désobéissance du chastelet.[12]

The King agreed that proceedings should be started against Guérey de Voisins,[13] but they were not allowed to go beyond the stage of a *décret d'ajournement personnel*, and the *lieutenant particulier* was probably encouraged to go into hiding.[14] The King possibly felt that the threat of further action would be sufficient to restrain the *Châtelet* from committing more acts of disobedience. Moreover, on 1 December the duties of *lieutenant criminel* fell to Lenoir, who had shown himself willing to co-operate with the Government.[15] But the *Châtelet* reacted strongly to the decree passed on Guérey de Voisins, to the continued imprisonment of Roger de Monthuchet, and also to a ban imposed on their debates; on 7 December they ceased their service.[16] D'Argouges de Fleury, the *lieutenant civil*, was eager to assist the Government (after all, one of his sons was a member of the *Chambre Royale*); he was also fairly adroit. He went to Versailles on 9 December, and when he learned that the Government intended to issue *lettres de cachet* to all the members of the *Châtelet* ordering them to resume their duties, he persuaded the King that the measure would have a better chance of success if no mention of the *Chambre Royale* was made in the *lettres de cachet*.[17] The plan worked, except that the *Châtelet* indicated its continued unwillingness to recognise the *Chambre Royale* by a decision to make representations to the King.[18] On the advice of D'Argouges de Fleury and Lenoir, and under pressure from the chancellor and the committee of the *Chambre Royale*, the King willingly ordered the sending of further *lettres de cachet* which formally insisted upon a recognition of the *Chambre Royale* by members of the *Châtelet* and the execution of its decisions without discussion.[19] But the *Châtelet* merely treated these *lettres de cachet* as another item to be included in their representations. The terms of the representations adopted on 18 December were explicit: the *Châtelet* recognised only the *Parlement* as its superior and asked the King for its recall. And although the *Châtelet* continued to

---

[12] FL, Rosanbo MSS, 1/3/46: letter of 27 Nov. 1753; original spellings.
[13] *Ibid.*, 1/3/47: Louis XV to Lamoignon, 27 Nov. 1753.
[14] J. M. J. Rogister, 'Missing pages from the Marquis d'Argenson's journal', *Studies on Voltaire and the Eighteenth Century*, cxxvii (1974), pp. 218–19 (entry for 21 Dec. 1753).
[15] Barbier, *Journal*, v, p. 444.   [16] *Ibid.*, pp. 444–5; Luynes, *Mém.*, xii, p. 119.
[17] FL, Rosanbo MSS, 1/3/50: Louis XV to Lamoignon, 13 Dec. 1753; Luynes, *Mém.*, xiii, pp. 119–20.
[18] Barbier, *Journal*, v, p. 446.
[19] FL, Rosanbo MSS, 1/3/48: Lamoignon to Louis XV, 13 Dec. 1753 (copy); 1/3/50: Louis XV to Lamoignon, 13 Dec. 1753 (cited above, note 17); Barbier, *Journal*, v, pp. 447–8; and D'Argenson, ed. Rathery, viii, p. 184.

perform its duties, it took care to decide cases without pronouncing definite sentences susceptible of appeal.[20]

The *Chambre Royale* obtained the King's permission to arrest Guérey de Voisins (who was in flight anyway) and to cancel an embarrassing visit to the *Châtelet* for the annual *séance des prisonniers*.[21] The King told the chancellor to see all the members of the *Châtelet* in groups in order to ascertain their sentiments, to reassure some of them and to put others in fear of family disgrace; but the chancellor's remarks had little effect on them.[22] On 22 December an *arrêt du conseil* was notified to the *Châtelet* ordering it again to recognise the *Chambre Royale* and forbidding all representations on the subject; *lettres de cachet* were also sent to the five *commissaires* who were preparing the representations. As there was not a quorum that day, the *Châtelet* postponed its debate until 29 December, when it was again postponed until 15 January despite another *lettre de cachet* which ordered the immediate registration of the *arrêt du conseil*. The *Châtelet* now planned to make representations in support of its right to make such representations.[23] After a plethora of *lettres de cachet*, there was little the Government could do which would not bring the King's authority further into disrepute. The King therefore allowed the matter to rest. Besides, he had no choice if he wished to retain the services of the *Châtelet*, meagre as they had become. Much of the responsibility for dealing with the courts fell on the Comte d'Argenson and he was ill at this time. The chancellor did not have the same influence over the King. In what was perhaps a reference to Louis XV, Lamoignon confided to D'Argenson on 24 January: 'j'ay parlé très vivement sur le chastelet et la chambre royalle; j'ai esté écouté tranquillement et sans contradiction. Du surplus, je ne sçais que penser.'[24]

Much research still remains to be done on the response of the *bailliages*, *sénéchaussées*, and other lower courts to the creation of the Commission and the *Chambre Royale*. In 1755, one of the *zélés*, Le Febvre de Saint-Hilaire (5th *enquêtes*), conducted a private inquiry into their conduct during the exile of the *Parlement*.[25] He faced a problem that has continued to baffle

[20] *Ibid.*, p. 188.

[21] FL, Rosanbo MSS, 1/3/52: Lamoignon to Louis XV, 17 Dec. 1753 (with the King's reply); 1/3/53: same to same, 18 Dec. 1753 (also with the King's reply).

[22] *Ibid.*, 1/3/55: Louis XV to Lamoignon, 18 Dec. 1753; Rogister, 'Missing pages from the Marquis d'Argenson's journal', pp. 218–19 (entry for 21 Dec. 1753); Barbier, *Journal*, v, p. 450.

[23] *Ibid.*, pp. 451–63; D'Argenson, ed. Rathery, viii, pp. 190, 196–7, 207–8, and 213.

[24] BUP, CA 30: letter from Versailles of 23 Jan. 1754; on D'Argenson's absence from the councils of government, see AS, Turin, Lettere ministri, Francia 190, f. 191ᵛ: Sartirane to Charles-Emmanuel III, Paris, 17 Dec. 1753 (in cipher); and BL, Add. MSS 35,445 (Hardwicke Papers), ff. 477, 487, and 493: 'nouvelles à la main'.

[25] BPR, LP 531, 'Supplément à la Chambre Royale: Bailliages 1753-1754', *passim*; Le Febvre de Saint-Hilaire to De Chévigné, 28 June 1755 and the latter's reply of 1 July 1755 and letter of 5 Aug. 1755.

historians: that of compiling a complete and accurate list of the courts. Using personal knowledge and contemporary sources, such as an *arrêt* of the *Parlement* of 14 December 1740 listing the courts and Chasot de Nantigny's recently published *Tablettes de Thémis*,[26] he arrived at total figures that fluctuated between 152 and 190 courts for the jurisdiction of the *Parlement* of Paris. Writing in 1972, the historian Philip Dawson observed that 'enumerating the lawcourts and the judges of the ancien régime is a task complicated by problems of definition, by changes from time to time in the number of jurisdictions and the numbers of offices legally in existence, and by the fluctuating number of vacant offices'.[27] He put the total number of *bailliages* (in which he includes *sénéchaussées*) at 143 in 1789; again, different sources are used, some courts are added and others subtracted to arrive at that figure.[28] Fortunately, in the Joly de Fleury papers there is a printed list of lower jurisdictions to which ordnances, edicts, *déclarations*, letters patent, and *arrêts* were sent: the list was probably an updated version of the 1740 one, and it was used by the *procureur général* in 1769 for a particular inquiry that had to be conducted on a systematic basis. This list gives a total figure of 158 jurisdictions.[29]

Le Febvre de Saint-Hilaire managed to obtain information about the conduct of 124 courts, and of these he found that 104 had recognised the Commission and the *Chambre Royale*. They included the important *bailliages* of Montargis, Orléans, Sens and Troyes. The remaining twenty courts had not been sent the letters patent creating the two royal jurisdictions. Le Febvre de Saint-Hilaire listed thirty-one courts about which he had obtained no information; if one removes five doubtful ones from his list, that number comes down to twenty-six.[30] But in any case, on the basis of the total figure of 158 from the 1769 printed list, it is clear that over 65 per cent of the courts had recognised the jurisdictions set up to carry out the duties of the *Parlement* during its exile.

It would be unwise to conclude simply from these figures that the Government had scored a triumph in securing a high level of recognition for its courts. Firstly, some courts had delayed their decision until the *rentrée* in November in the belief that the *Parlement* would by then have been

[26] Louis Chasot de Nantigny, *Tablettes de Thémis* (Paris, 1755), 2 vols.
[27] Philip Dawson, *Provincial magistrates and revolutionary politics in France, 1789–1795* (Cambridge, Mass., 1972), p. 347; M. Marion, 'A propos de la géographie judiciaire de la France sons l'ancien régime: la question du ressort des présidiaux', *Revue historique*, lxxxix (1905), pp. 80–8, publishes a document which lists only the more important *bailliages* and *sénéchaussées*.
[28] Dawson, *Provincial magistrates*, pp. 30 (note 4), 37 (Table 1), 350–6 (Table A1 and notes).
[29] BN, n.a.fr. 22150, ff. 327–328ᵛ: 'Liste alphabétique des Bailliages, Sénéchaussées & autres jurisdictions Royales auxquels on envoye les Ordonnances, Edits, Déclarations, Lettres patentes & Arrêts' (4to).
[30] BPR, LP 531 (no foliation).

recalled.[31] Secondly, some small *bailliages* had waited to see how the more important ones in their province or *pays* would react. The *procureur du roi* at Yenville waited for the officers at Orléans to register, which they did after having been enjoined to do so; Yenville then followed their example, along with Boiscommun, Neuville-aux-Bois, and Yèvre-le-Châtel. Montargis registered, and Châteaurenard, Lorris, and Gien followed suit.[32] Thirdly, several courts registered under duress. Bourgeois de Boynes, the *procureur du roi* for both the Commission and the *Chambre Royale*, was known to take a firm line with recalcitrant magistrates, so that at Laval, for instance, when the local *procureur du roi* threatened to write to him, the president and *juge royal* of the *bailliage* agreed to register the letters patent.[33] Fismes, Châlons-sur-Marne, Reims, Cognac, Saint-Pierre-le-Moutier, had argued that they did not have to register the letters patent, but they sent their criminals to the Commission for trial.[34] They persisted in their stand but later agreed to register. Senlis used the phrase 'du très exprès commandement' (indicating duress) in the registration, and in consequence the officers of the *bailliage* were summoned to appear before the *Chambre Royale*.[35] Fourthly, at some courts, registration caused division, or was the result of existing division, amongst the magistrates. At Bellême the *lieutenant civil* was dying, and it was the *procureur du roi* who called for the registration in face of the opposition of the *lieutenant particulier*: he secured a registration, but the lawyers boycotted the court.[36] At Sens, the *lieutenant général* recognised the Commission on his own authority, thereby antagonising his colleagues. When the *déclaration* establishing the *Chambre Royale* was sent, he absented himself and, to his surprise, his colleagues registered it.[37] Finally, the Government had to deal with the resistance of those jurisdictions which refused to recognise the royal courts. The large *sénéchaussées* of Abbeville and Angers refused to recognise the Commission. The *lieutenant particulier* at Angers wrote to the *procureur général* of the *Parlement* asking for instructions, but he received no reply. His colleague at Abbeville refused to have the letters patent registered, but obeyed a *lettre de cachet* to attend upon the Commission.[38] The letters patent were not registered at Amiens, Chinon, Lyon, Mortagne, and

---

[31] BN, JF 309, f. 158: Paulze de Chassagnol (*procureur du roi* at Montbrison) to Bourgeois de Boynes, 6 Oct. 1753.

[32] BPR, LP 531 (Le Febvre de Saint-Hilaire inquiry).

[33] BN, JF 309, f. 160: Bourgeois de Boynes to Paulze de Chassagnol, 18 Oct. 1753; on Laval, see BPR, LP 531: note in De Chévigné's hand.

[34] AN, X¹ᴮ 9689: 'Chambre Royale du Louvre 1753–1754': *Conseil secret, Registre des assemblées*, 11 Dec. 1753 to 22 Aug. 1754.

[35] BN, JF 309, f. 227: 'Mémoire pour le Sr. Bonhomme, pourvu des offices de Président Lieutenant général de Senlis demandant s'il peut poursuivre sa réception' [12 Nov. 1753].

[36] BPR, LP 531 (Le Febvre de Saint-Hilaire inquiry).   [37] *Ibid.*

[38] BN, JF 309, ff. 108, 111.

Montbrison.[39] The immediate vicinity of the exiled *parlementaires* also discouraged some courts from recognising the Commission and the *Chambre Royale*. Pontoise was an example followed in turn by Soissons.[40] In January 1754 the Abbé du Trousset d'Héricourt wrote to his friend Président Hénault from Soissons:

> Je crois que le sisthème de la chambre royalle [*sic*] est absolument manqué. Il y a dans ce voisinage trois ou 4 gros bailliages, vous couperiés plustost 4 testes que de faire exécuter un de leurs arrêts et tous les autres suivront l'exemple du chastelet.[41]

At Bourges the *procureur du roi* pretended that he had not received the letters patent and hurriedly left for his country seat; when he learned that the local director of post was coming to deliver them to him personally, he vanished.[42] The officers of these courts were probably afraid that if they recognised the Commission or the *Chambre Royale*, the *Parlement* would take disciplinary action against them on its return.

The Government's relative success in securing recognition for its two courts can be attributed to three factors. Firstly, the rôle of the *procureur général* of the *Parlement*: Joly de Fleury systematically refused to give advice to his many subordinates who looked to him for guidance.[43] Secondly, while the *procureur général* remained passive, his equivalent at the *Chambre Royale*, Bourgeois de Boynes, an ambitious young administrator, was extremely active.[44] The intendants and their subdelegates were also exerting considerable pressure on the lower courts.[45] Sometimes this pressure was resisted with dignity, especially when it created personal dilemmas, as in the case of Le Mareschal, the *lieutenant particulier* of the *bailliage* and presidial court of Beauvais. He was not only *avocat du roi* and a councillor at the presidial court, but also the local subdelegate. He

---

[39] BN, JF 308, f. 174 (note in the hand of the *procureur général*) about Mortagne and Chinon, where the *lieutenants généraux* were prosecuted by the commission; f. 180: Lenée (*lieutenant général* at Chinon) to the *procureur général*, 31 Aug. 1754; JF 309, f. 105 (Amiens), f. 134 (Lyon), f. 167 (text of a decision taken at Montbrison, 23 Oct. 1753). On Lyon, see also D'Argenson, ed. Rathery, viii, pp. 196–7.

[40] BN, JF 309, f. 206 (Pontoise).

[41] BN, n.a.fr. 10235 (Hénault Papers), f. 15: letter of 12 [Jan 1754]. Though it is unsigned this letter is in the abbé's handwriting; cf. BN, MS franç. 7573 (Durey de Meinières Papers): letters of an unnamed lady to an exile at Bourges; f. 129: letter of 12 Nov. 1753: 'il [Du Trousset d'Héricourt] va loger à Soissons chès l'Evêque avec l'abbé de Salabéri'.

[42] A. Grellet-Dumazeau, *Les Exilés de Bourges* (Paris, 1892), pp. 180–1.

[43] BN, JF 308, f. 309ff: letters from *procureurs du roi* at Châtillon-sur-Marne, Morêt, Ribeaumont, Meaux, Troyes, and Gannat to the *procureur général*, with a copy of the latter, reply thanking them for keeping him informed about 'l'exercice de votre ministère' (f. 308).

[44] He suspended and imprisoned Lenée, the *lieutenant général* of Chinon, who was thereby prevented from continuing proceedings in a case of rape.

[45] BPR, LP 531: copies of letters from Blossac (intendant of Poitiers) of 15 Dec. 1753 and Bertier de Sauvigny (intendant of Paris) of 5 Dec. 1753 to their subdelegates were obtained clandestinely and published.

explained his position to the intendant, Bertier de Sauvigny, to whom he owed a debt of gratitude. If orders were sent for the registration of the letters patent for the Commission, he could not execute them:

> Je vous prie de vous souvenir alors que je suis membre de ma compagnie, que par état je me dois à elle et à ma charge, que je pense comme elle, et que je ne pourrois pas me déterminer à agir contre elle et contre ses membres, et que je n'y suis point obligé par état.[46]

It was in his absence that the officers of the *bailliage* agreed under duress to register the letters patent.[47] Finally, there was a great deal of ignorance on the part of local justices about what was taking place, as their letters to the *procureur général* reveal; Château-du-Loir and Niort registered the letters patent, but sent the certificate of registration to Joly de Fleury instead of to Bourgeois de Boynes. One court simply addressed it to 'M. le procureur général en son hôtel à Paris'.[48] The letters received by Joly de Fleury also revealed the deep and instinctive attachment of the *bailliages* and *sénéchaussées* to the *Parlement*. In the remaining decades of the ancien régime, it proved possible to foster a desire for greater independence from the *Parlement* among the more important courts of its jurisdiction, but that desire was not much in evidence in 1753–4.

The chief obstacle to the success of the *Chambre Royale* was the unwillingness of *procureurs*, lawyers, and litigants generally to bring civil actions before it. Criminal actions might give the court some scope for activity, but the royal council's own lawyers were too inexperienced in the work to handle civil actions, as the wise Pâris-Duverney predicted to the Abbé de Bernis. 'Si les Avocats et les procureurs au Parlement se dévouoient à cette nouvelle cour', he commented, 'il me semble que l'ancienne auroit beaucoup à perdre'.[49] But the *procureurs* and lawyers wished to retain the goodwill of the *parlementaires*. The richer *procureurs* were apparently supporting the poorer ones during the crisis. They and prospective litigants probably also had doubts concerning the ultimate validity of judgements given by the *Chambre Royale*.[50] On 3 December the King issued letters

---

[46] Bibliothèque municipale, Beauvais (Oise), MSS, Collection Bucquet, vol. lxxxv, ff. 501–2: Le Mareschal to Bertier de Sauvigny, 28 Oct. 1753 (copy).

[47] *Ibid.*, ff. 385–6, 496–510.

[48] BN, JF 309, f. 134 (Château-du-Loir) and f. 186 (Niort); f. 136 (for the address on the envelope).

[49] Pâris-Duverney to Bernis, 21 Nov. 1753 in *Correspondance du Cardinal de Bernis, Ministre d'Etat avec M. du Vernay, conseiller d'état, depuis 1752 jusqu'en 1769* ('Londres et se trouve à Paris chez Buisson', 1790), i, p. 78.

[50] BL, Add. MSS 35,630 (Hardwicke Papers), f. 118: Jeffreys to Yorke, 26 Dec. 1753. Amongst those who refrained from resorting to legal action at this time was the Prince de Croÿ. He felt he had a case against the House of d'Harcourt, but agreed with his *procureur* to go to court only 'dès qu'il y aurait un Parlement': *Journal inédit du Duc de Croÿ, 1718–1784*, ed. Vicomte de Grouchy and P. Cottin (Paris, 1906), i, p. 238.

patent authorising and compelling the *procureurs* to perform their duties before the *Chambre Royale*.[51] The measure was unwise. Lamoignon had to inform the King ten days later that only one *procureur* had come forward with a case to be heard; there were still only four by the end of the month. The chancellor and the committee of the *Chambre Royale* were painfully aware that success in attracting them turned on the outcome of the *Châtelet* affair.[52] It was probably in order to provide the *Chambre Royale* with some work that the Government entrusted it on 4 January with all the cases that were pending before the *Parlement*.[53] But by February it was clear to observers that the new court was simply maintaining a semblance of activity by postponing business from one day to the next.[54]

By mid-January 1754 the return of the *Parlement* was again being considered. Before his departure for Languedoc Richelieu arranged a meeting between Machault and Ysabeau on 16 January.[55] Ysabeau prepared an ingenious plan and sent it to Machault a fortnight later.[56] The main feature of Ysabeau's plan was that the return of the *Parlement* should be formally requested by the princes and the peers. Machault, and probably also the King, did not want the participation of the princes and the peers in the matter. As Machault did not like the plan, Ysabeau produced another in the light of his suggestions. The main feature of the new plan was that the whole *Parlement* was to be transferred to Soissons, a decision that would be presented simply as an act of clemency on the King's part. The *déclaration* of transfer would contain an injunction to the *parlementaires* to resume their duties. The *lettre de cachet* that came with the *déclaration* would, however, be conciliatory in tone. The *Parlement* would register the *déclaration*; the first president would report to the King, who could then make a full and encouraging reply which would be favourable to the *Parlement*. Unfortunately, the evidence does no more than allude to the proposed content of the King's reply: it seems that the intention was that the King should ask the *Parlement* for a memoir on the subject of denial of sacraments.[57] Machault certainly insisted that the *Parlement* had to resume its

---

[51] For a copy, see BN, JF 308, f. 286 *et seq.*

[52] FL, Rosanbo MSS, 1/3/48: Lamoignon to Louis XV, 13 Dec. 1753 (copy); see also Barbier, *Journal*, v, p. 454; D'Argenson, ed. Rathery, viii, p. 200.

[53] For a copy of these letters patent, see BN, JF 308, f. 289 (and also f. 287, for letters patent on the procedure to be followed). The letters dated back to 22 December.

[54] See e.g. a pamphlet entitled *Lettre à un gentilhomme de province* ... *3 février 1754*, in BN, JF 1497, f. 205 *et seq.*

[55] Richelieu left for Languedoc (where he was to preside over the Estates) on 20 January and was not back at court until the following June. During that time Ysabeau kept him informed of developments concerning the *Parlement*.

[56] AAE, MD, France 1344, ff. 257–61: Ysabeau to Richelieu, 15 Feb. 1754.

[57] *Ibid.*; BVC, RP, xiv (catalogue no. 35), ff. 9–13: Ysabeau to Richelieu, 1 March 1754; BN, JF 2103, f. 195: Machault to Joly de Fleury, 7 June 1754; f. 194: Joly de Fleury to

duties before the matter of its remonstrances could be considered. At the same time he surprised Ysabeau by his appreciation of the need to support the *Parlement* in its legitimate rights:

> Il regarde ce corps comme nécessaire à l'Etat et au Roy et pouvant mesme estre très utile à tout ministre qui aura de bonnes intentions, et qui ne doit point craindre d'estre Eclairé dans sa conduite; si ces sentiments sont sincères, Il y a plus à Espérer de luy que je ne l'aurois cru, Une plus longue connoissance pourra me mettre en Etat de démesler le vray.[58]

It is possible that his concern for the *Parlement* came from a growing awareness that its services might shortly be required for the registration of new financial measures.

The new plan took into account the realities of the situation. As it was clear that no move, such as a request for the recall of the *enquêtes*, could be expected from the *grand'chambre*, the King had to take the less dignified alternative of re-uniting the *Parlement* under the guise of an act of clemency. The plan had a number of advantages. As the *Parlement* was not being transferred directly to Paris, the place it was being transferred from did not have to be mentioned in the *déclaration*; there could therefore be no objection from the *enquêtes*. Moreover, in case the *parlementaires* chose to abide by the May *arrêtés*, the Government would find it less embarrassing to have them in Soissons than in Paris.[59] For the plan to succeed it was necessary to summon the first president in order to persuade him to co-operate; it was also necessary to enlist support for the plan among the exiles.[60] But Machault chose instead to make another attempt to topple the first president. Maupeou was pressed by Gilbert, Salabéry, and D'Héricourt to write a letter asking for the recall of the *Parlement*, and they tried to induce Molé, as second president, to write the letter if Maupeou persisted in his refusal. Ysabeau told Richelieu:

> Il ne faut pas estre sorcier pour deviner l'auteur de la division, qui se cache sous les noms de MM. Gilbert, Salabéry et D'Héricourt; Le Pᵗ. amy [Chauvelin] de M. Le G. des Sc. fera de son mieux pour embarquer dans quelque fausse démarche, M Le PP et M le Pᵗ. Molé, et ce ne seroit pas estre trop maladroit de les faire périr dans la mesme nasselle [*sic*].[61]

Machault, 7 June 1754 (copy); and AAE, MD, France 1344, ff. 241–2: Ysabeau to Richelieu, 8 June [1754].

[58] *Ibid.*, f. 259: Ysabeau to Richelieu, 15 Feb. 1754.

[59] Ysabeau thought the argument that the *Parlement* was obliged to abide by the May *arrêtés* could be fought on the grounds that the proposed *déclaration* did not simply contain an order to resume service, but also a new item, viz. the translation of the *Parlement* (see BVC, RP, xiv (catalogue no. 35), f. 9ᵛ).

[60] AAE, MD, France f. 258: Ysabeau to Richelieu, 15 Feb. 1754. Ysabeau began to sound out the exiles.

[61] BVC, RP, xiv (catalogue no. 35), f. 11ᵛ: Ysabeau to Richelieu, 1 Mar. 1754.

On 17 February three ministers (probably Machault, Rouillé, and Saint-Florentin) told the *gens du roi* that from the start Maupeou could have settled the whole affair to the satisfaction of all concerned. The *gens du roi* were clearly intended to communicate this impression to the exiles at Soissons; a list of the opportunities that had been missed by Maupeou was even circulated there. Copies were also circulated at Soissons and at Bourges of a letter that purported to show that Maupeou was a tool of the Comte d'Argenson, reputed by Machault's adherents to be the enemy of the *Parlement*.[62] Ysabeau thought Machault was misguided and correctly predicted that he would not succeed in his aim:

> Par ce qui me revient de L'impression de ses opérations, sur les esprits, on tentera Inutilement de détacher MM des enquêtes de M. Le PP., Ils disent nettement que M Le PP ne peut se séparer d'eux, et conséquemment, qu'ils doivent compter sur luy ...[63]

These manoeuvres failed; they also brought delays.[64] An encouraging sign, however, was that the response of the exiles to the proposals had been favourable. Ysabeau found that the exiles did not object to the idea of resuming their duties as an act of obedience; they were more interested in *Unigenitus*, and they wished to introduce an *appel comme d'abus* over the execution of the bull because ecclesiastics persisted in describing it as a rule of faith.[65]

Circumstances made it increasingly unwise for the Government to delay a settlement much longer. There was the need for money. But there were also other considerations. Cases of denial of sacraments were no longer chiefly limited to the vast jurisdiction of the *Parlement* of Paris. The *Parlements* of Rouen, Rennes, Toulouse, Aix, and Bordeaux had also begun to prosecute priests and even bishops; the agents general of the clergy were naturally demanding redress.[66]

At a meeting of the *Conseil des dépêches* on 1 March, Noailles and Rouillé apparently opposed, though without success, the annulment of sentences given by these *parlements*: the request for annulment had been made by the agents general.[67] At Toulouse, the quashing of two sentences by the council at the end of April angered the *enquêtes*, who demanded the right to take

---

[62] *Ibid.*, ff. 12ʳ–13ʳ. [63] *Ibid.*, f. 13ᵛ.

[64] On 23 March D'Ormesson reported that the division at Soissons was no longer so great, and that President Chauvelin was on speaking terms with the first president. There was still an atmosphere of suspicion: 'Les Maupeoux débitent qu'il [President Gilbert] a des entretiens avec Mr Ch[auvelin], et il ny a pas un mot de vray': BN, JF 309, f. 35: letter to the *procureur général*.

[65] BVC, RP, xiv (catalogue no. 35), ff. 8–11: Ysabeau to Richelieu, 1 Mar. 1754.

[66] Michel Antoine, 'Le Conseil des dépêches sous le règne de Louis XV', *Bibliothèque de l'Ecole des chartes*, cxii (1954), p. 138.

[67] Luynes, *Mém.*, xiii, pp. 178, 425.

part in drawing up remonstrances. Moreover, they claimed that the permission of the *grand'chambre* was not necessary for holding an assembly of the chambers (in spite of a *déclaration* of 11 June 1687 registered by the *grand'chambre* on behalf of the whole *Parlement*). First President de Maniban wrote to the chancellor, his brother-in-law:

> L'exemple des Parlements de Bordeaux, de Rouen, d'Aix et de Bretagne, qui traitent toutes les affaires de sacrements à l'assemblée des chambres, donne bien de la force et de la vivacité aux chambres des Enquêtes; et leur donne bien des partisans à la Grand chambre, et à la Tournelle, indépendamment du Jansénisme et du grand nombre de gens qui veulent brouiller les cartes, et faire parler d'eux à quel prix que ce soit.[68]

Lamoignon and Maniban persuaded the archbishop of Toulouse not to notify the *arrêts en cassation* to the *Parlement*.[69]

From late February until the beginning of April the Government was also involved in a bitter conflict with the *Châtelet* over a case of denial of sacraments; in the course of that conflict Messieurs Bourdin, a *procureur*, and Quillet, a councillor of the *Châtelet*, were sent to the Bastille on 10 March and 8 April to join Monsieur Roger de Monthuchet.[70] The Government had tried to arrest another councillor, Monsieur Pelletier, but he could not be found. Instead, the police ransacked his home, seizing family papers, including title deeds and notarial acts, as well as documents relating to Pelletier's judicial cases. With that illogicality that seems to be a characteristic of the police state throughout the ages, the three officers took the councillor's musical scores but were not interested in his Latin texts.[71] The papers were not returned until a month later.[72] For the prisoners, life in the Bastille must have been near unbearable. On 15 July the prison doctor found Roger de Monthuchet in a state of deep melancholia which, he felt, could lead to the scurvy: 'd'autant plus', he reported to Berryer, the lieutenant general of police, 'qu'il est d'un tempérament fort sec et qu'il a le sang âcre; il pleure comme un enfant'.[73] He thought the prisoner should be allowed to take the air for an hour each day. D'Argenson (who had himself twice been lieutenant general of police in his youth) wrote to tell Berryer that the King allowed the three men to walk in the prison garden on

---

[68] FL, Tocqueville MSS, 33/149: letter of 14 May 1754.
[69] *Ibid.*, 33/150: Maniban to Lamoignon, 18 May 1754.
[70] On the affair of Saint-Nicholas-des-Champs, see BL, Egerton MSS 1667, ff. 185, 192; Luynes, *Mém.*, xiii, p. 426; D'Argenson, ed. Rathery, viii, pp. 239, 244, 246, 267–72; BN, MS franç. 22105 (Anisson-Duperron Collection, xlv), f. 107 (Bourdin), f. 178 (Quillet).
[71] *Ibid.*, ff. 226–30. The raid was carried out by the lieutenants Christophe and Le Clerc de Brillet, accompanied by Monsieur Jannel, whose other duties included opening the mail and keeping Louis XV regularly informed of its contents (see Eugène Vaillé, *Le Cabinet noir* (Paris, 1950), p. 155).
[72] BN, MS franç. 22105, f. 242: Berryer to the Comte d'Argenson, 3 May 1754.
[73] *Ibid.*, f. 89: Boyer, *médecin ordinaire du roy*, to Berryer, 15 July 1754.

condition that they did not encounter each other, 'et qu'ils ne puissent abuser de la permission qui leur est accordée'.[74] Although the *Châtelet* effected its *rentrée* quietly on 22 April despite these arrests, the Government could not expect that it would remain docile for long. Moreover, the sudden death of Lenoir deprived the King of a loyal servant and D'Argouges de Fleury of a valuable associate.[75]

There was another consideration which the Government could not overlook. In the same way that the religious disputes had led to public discussion of ecclesiastical questions, so now the division within the civil order gave rise to discussion of questions concerning the constitution and the nature of royal authority. Gilbert de Voisins wrote at Easter, in a private memorandum on the situation:

> Aujourdhui ce sont les fondements mesmes de la constitution et de l'ordre de l'état qu'on met en question, les différends degréz d'autorité et de pouvoir, les règles et la mesure de l'obéissance. Ces mistères d'état se traittent indiscrèttement sous les ieux du vulgaire.[76]

The situation owed much to the efforts of the pamphleteers and their elusive network of patrons, printers, and booksellers. The Government naturally viewed this development as a threat to the established order. If a closer examination of pamphlets that supported the *parlementaires*' cause does not lend substance to that view, political pamphleteering of a kind not witnessed since the Fronde a century earlier was nevertheless a potentially subversive element, even if the Government may have increased its impact by encouraging its use by opponents of the *Parlement*.[77] Fundamentally the debate resolved itself into two untenable positions: the *parlementaire* side argued that the *Parlement* 'obeyed in disobeying' or was, to borrow Diderot's phrase, 'pour le roi contre le roi'; the Government's side held that, although the King's power was absolute, he could not be a despot. Accordingly, in the public debate, 'ministers and *parlementaires* on one level, and

---

[74] *Ibid.*, f. 95: Comte d'Argenson to Berryer, Compiègne, 27 July 1754. For a recent study of arbitrary imprisonment under the *ancien régime*, see Claude Quétel, *De par le Roy: essai sur les lettres de cachet* (Toulouse, 1981).

[75] FL, Rosanbo MSS, 1/3/58: Lamoignon to Louis XV, 22 Apr. 1754. Just before his death, President Chauvelin expressed his concern to the *procureur général*, lest the post be filled by the wrong person: BN, JF 309, f. 38: letter of 23 [Apr. 1754].

[76] AN, K 698 (Gilbert de Voisins Papers), unnumbered memoir of thirteen pages, following no. 144 in the file.

[77] For an account of the pamphlet war, see J. M. J. Rogister, 'The crisis of 1753–1754 in France and the debate on the nature of the Monarchy and of the Fundamental Laws', in *Herrschaftsverträge, Wahlkapitulationen, und Fundamentalgesetze*, ed. R. Vierhaus (Studies presented to the International Commission for the History of Representative and Parliamentary Institutions, lix, Göttingen, 1977), pp. 105–120; and the same author's 'Parlementaires, sovereignty, and legal opposition in France under Louis XV: an introduction', *Parliaments, Estates and Representation*, vi (1986), pp. 25–32.

pamphleteers and possibly their readers on another, were unwilling to take up extreme positions or to probe too deeply into the basis of government. It seems that on all sides in 1753–4 there was an important measure of general agreement on two points: the first was that the king's sovereignty and power were absolute, and the second was that he exercised his power in such a way that it could be distinguished from despotism and was in accordance with the traditions and customs of the French Monarchy.'[78] There was a consensus.

The position could change, however, and public debate, if prolonged, could eventually become subversive. In September 1752 Rouillé, outraged at the number of pamphlets that were appearing at that time, wondered whether the police was doing its job properly: 'est-ce la fautte de la police, ou n'est-elle plus autorisées [sic] comme elle l'étoit autrefois?'[79] The police seemed unable or unwilling to prevent the publication of works such as Le Paige's *Lettres historiques sur les fonctions essentielles du Parlement*, a significant treatise which gave currency to the concepts which some *parlementaires* held about the nature of the French Monarchy.[80] Yet the police was well organised and increasing its overall efficiency during this period.[81] As its surviving records amply demonstrate, it could catch individual authors, printers, or distributors, but it was less effective in dealing with a tentacular network, like that of the *Nouvelles ecclésiastiques*, for instance.[82] This pro-Gallican and pro-Jansenist paper was firmly established in 1731 and resembled, as one historian has written, 'an efficient military machine employing multiple printers and a squad of agents and distributors each ignorant of the identity of his colleagues'.[83] Probably some of the

[78] Rogister, 'The crisis of 1753–1754 in France', pp. 119–120; and 'Parlementaires, sovereignty, and legal opposition', p. 31. Diderot's phrase comes from the article 'Parlementaire' in the *Encyclopédie*, xii, p. 69a (quoted in John Lough, *The Encyclopédie* (London, 1971), p. 325).

[79] BN, JF 1493, f. 153: Rouillé to G. F. Joly de Fleury, 7 Sept. [1752].

[80] Louis-Adrien Le Paige (1712–1802), a lawyer at the *Parlement* who worked for the Prince de Conty as *bailli* of the Temple. He wrote many pamphlets and two extended works, of which this was the most important.

[81] On the police, see the introduction by A. de Boislisle to his edition of the *Lettres de M. de Marville, lieutenant général de police, au ministre Maurepas (1742–1747)* (Paris, 1896), i, pp. i–ci; and the more recent work by Suzanne Pillorget, *Claude-Henri Feydeau de Marville, lieutenant général de police de Paris 1740–1747, suivi d'un choix de lettres inédites* (Paris, 1978), pp. 72–191.

[82] See Robert Shackleton, 'Deux policiers du xviiie siècle: Berryer et D'Hémery', in *Thèmes et figures du siècle des Lumières: mélanges offerts à Roland Mortier*, ed. Raymond Trousson (Geneva, 1980), pp. 251–8. For an account of a successful police raid, see J. S. Spink, 'The clandestine book trade in 1752: the publication of the *Apologie de l'abbé de Prades*', in *Studies in eighteenth-century French literature presented to Robert Niklaus*, ed. J. H. Fox, M. H. Waddicor and D. A. Watts (Exeter, 1975), pp. 243–56.

[83] D. A. Coward, 'The Fortunes of a Newspaper: the *Nouvelles ecclésiastiques* 1728–1803', *British Journal for Eighteenth-Century Studies*, iv (1981), p. 7; see especially Françoise Bontoux, 'Paris janséniste au xviiie siècle: les *Nouvelles ecclésiastiques*', *Mémoires publiés par la Fédération des sociétés historiques et archéologiques de l'Ile de France*, vii (1955 [1956]), pp. 205–20.

pamphlets that appeared on the *parlementaire* side were products of this network.[84]

The role of periodicals and of the press generally in pre-revolutionary France has received attention in recent years from a school of historians working in the United States. Unfortunately, the work of this school is not sufficiently based on the study of original source material, other than the press itself. According to one of these historians, printed editions of remonstrances – and, therefore, presumably by extension the press and the pamphlets as well – were 'directed, not so much at the Crown as to an educated reading public', but he does not identify or quantify this educated public.[85] Moreover, this line of argument overlooks the reality of the situation: that the authorities, whether the Government or the *parlementaires*, believed that 'the public', however one defined it, had no part to play in the disputes beyond the peculiarly French notion that it was best to have common sense and one's fellow men and women on one's side. Even the implication that press coverage in the *Gazette de Leyde*, for example, played a part in discrediting the Crown's attempts at resolving the crisis in 1753–4 is exaggerated.[86] The indiscretions committed and relayed by *parlementaires* themselves in letters to each other or in circulating their manuscript memoirs had a more important influence in that process. While it can be argued that foreign periodicals that were tolerated in France, such as the *Gazette de Leyde*, which had no more than about 400 French subscribers, provided increasing coverage of political events, it is doubtful whether this highlighting had much impact on those who took decisions. Finally, it is difficult to agree with the view that 'the existence of the *Gazette de Leyde*, relatively controlled though it was, meant that the principle of public participation in politics had won some tangible acceptance in France long before the Revolution'.[87] There was no 'public' participation in politics in

[84] Le Paige, for example, wrote occasionally for the *Nouvelles ecclésiastiques*; see J. M. J. Rogister, 'Louis-Adrien Le Paige and the attack on *De l'esprit* and the *Encyclopédie* in 1759', *The English Historical Review*, xcii (1977), pp. 522–39. On the anti-*parlementaire* side the literature has been studied in a somewhat assertive manner by L. de Santi, in 'L'Abbé Capmartin de Chaupy', *Revue historique de Toulouse*, xv (1928), pp. 115–45, 181–200.

[85] Carrol Joynes, 'The *Gazette de Leyde*: the opposition press and French Politics, 1750–1757', in *Press and politics in pre-revolutionary France*, ed. Jack R. Censer and Jeremy D. Popkin (Berkeley, 1987), p. 142.

[86] Joynes, 'The *Gazette de Leyde*', p. 152. The same author mistakenly writes that all 250 members of the *Parlement* were exiled in May 1753 (pp. 151 and 156) and that, somehow, the 'rump parliament that remained in Paris [sic] after the exile' was transformed into the *Chambre Royale* (p. 153), and that the *bailliages* and *sénéchaussées* had refused to recognise the new court (p. 154).

[87] Jeremy D. Popkin, 'The *Gazette de Leyde* and French Politics under Louis XVI', in Censer and Popkin (eds.), *Press and politics*, p. 130; p. 86 (for the French subscription figures). See also Keith Michael Baker, 'Politics and the public opinion under the Old Régime: some reflections', *Press and politics*, p. 210: 'French politics burst out of the absolutist mold' [in the 1750s]; and Jeremy D. Popkin, 'The Revolutionary origins of political journalism', in *The*

1753–4. Anyone seeking to participate actively from outside the magic circle would have gone straight to the Bastille. The majority of the people were like spectators at the play, free to cheer or to boo; and even then, they would probably be watched and reported by one of Berryer's informers.

After Easter 1754 a denouement of the crisis was in sight. No settlement could be reached without the concurrence of the first president. His position was stronger than ever, especially after an epidemic swiftly carried off his chief rival President Chauvelin on 29 April (and Chauvelin's death was followed by that of President Gilbert on 12 May). New men were eager to step into dead men's shoes. D'Ormesson had been promised the first presidency that became vacant; he was loath, however, to disburse 17,500 *livres* for it and to leave the congenial society of the *gens du roi*. Jean-Omer Joly de Fleury was in line to succeed him as first *avocat général*, and he quickly hinted to the Comte d'Argenson that he would himself need financial assistance from the Government. D'Ormesson obtained the promise of Chauvelin's *présidence à mortier* on 2 May.[88] At the same time the boredom of life in Soissons coming after the hard winter of 1753–4 had begun to have its effect on the *parlementaires* and even on the first president himself. Mayou wrote to the Comte d'Argenson from there on 23 April:

> Si toutes les façons de penser pouvoient devenir uniformes, vous verriez le filz et le père se plier comme deux Serpents – je vois cela de loin par quelques discours que le président de Maupeou m'a tenus en disant qu'il étoit tems que tout cela finisse.[89]

Nevertheless, Maupeou still showed no sign of wishing to make the first move. It was perhaps in order to induce the Government to take the initiative that Jean-Omer Joly de Fleury was unusually charitable and understanding about Maupeou's reticence in a letter of 10 May to the Comte d'Argenson:

> On se sert de tout lorsqu'il s'agit de bien faire: mais comme je ne voudrois pas luy imputer ne d'être pas animé de ce désir, il faut croire qu'il en a été détourné par une timidité, mal entendue peut-être, de ce que penseroit le reste de sa compagnie d'une démarche marquée de sa part. Il faut convenir que l'on est à plaindre d'être à la teste d'un corps auquel on n'a pas résisté quand il estoit tems de le faire, Ensuite on est subjugué, et on ne peut plus

---

French Revolution and the creation of modern political culture, vol. i: *The political culture of the Old Regime*, ed. Keith Michael Baker (Oxford, 1987), pp. 203–21, where the argument overlooks the importance of *nouvelles à la main* during the period.

[88] BN, JF 309, f. 44: D'Ormesson to the *procureur général*, 30 Apr. 1754; BUP, CA 28/VI: Jean-Omer Joly de Fleury to the Comte d'Argenson, 12 May 1754; BN, MS franç. 7573 (Durey de Meinières Papers), f. 122ʳ: note about D'Ormesson's appointment.

[89] BUP, CA 42/V: see also BN, JF 309, f. 41: D'Ormesson to the *procureur général*, 28 Apr. 1754, and f. 42: same to same, 29 Apr. 1754.

reprendre le ton d'autorité si nécessaire à celuy auquel le roy confie le soin de présider son parlement.[90]

The Government grudgingly made a gesture. On 21 April the Abbé Chauvelin, who had been imprisoned first in the Benedictine penitentiary of the Mont-Saint-Michel and later at the castle in Caen, was transferred to the château de Vincennes on compassionate grounds, as he was seriously ill with scurvy. The bishop of Bayeux had not wished him to die in his diocese because he did not want any trouble over the last rites. The Comte d'Argenson planned to send him to Argentan, but yielded to pressure from the abbé's brother, who was an intendant of finance. As the Sainte-Chapelle at Vincennes was a royal peculiar, the archbishop of Paris had no say there if the last rites had to be administered to the sick man. Once released from the fortress by the sea, the abbé began to recover his strength and was soon able to see his friends.[91]

Everything also turned upon the King. He had been subjected to constant but unhelpful pressure from the chancellor, whom one well-informed lady compared to the mechanical automaton which had recently been the rage at Versailles. She told a friend:

> cette beste au dessou de l'ottomat, parle au Roi quant il lui plait à toute heure, le plus hardiment et avec autant de confience que la raison même en pourroit avoir. Il lui fait voir sans cesse que son autorité est compromise dans la conduite de ses parlemens, que les inconvéniens qu'ils luy répettent dans leurs remontrances, sont sans principes et deviendront dangereux s'il se relachoit sur la rigueur qu'il doit garder avec eux.[92]

It was about this time that a dialogue is alleged to have taken place between the King and his witty captain of the guards, the Duc d'Ayen:

> Duc d'Ayen, venez-vous de voir l'automate?
> Sire, répondit-il, je sors de chez M. le Chancelier.[93]

At last Louis XV made up his mind. On 3 June he wrote to Maupeou ordering him to come to Versailles the next day (without going through

---

[90] BUP, CA 28/VI.

[91] BN, MS franç. 7573, f. 134: a lady to a president (probably Durey de Meinières), 22 Apr. 1754. Durey de Meinières notes (f. 127) that these letters were 'd'une Dame à un de Mrs. du Parlement exilés à Bourges'. The identity of this well-connected lady has not yet been established; she entertained both Machault and D'Argenson at her table; she was possibly Madame d'Arty (1710–65), a natural daughter of the banker Samuel Bernard, and Conty's Egeria at L'Isle-Adam for over twenty years. On the appalling conditions at the Mont-Saint-Michel, see Claude Quétel, *De par le Roy*, pp. 56–61.

[92] BN, MS franç. 7573, f. 135: the same lady's letter of 30 May 1754.

[93] Charles Collé, *Journal et mémoires sur les hommes de lettres, les ouvrages dramatiques et les événements les plus mémorables du règne de Louis XV, 1748–1772*, ed. H. Bonhomme (Paris, 1868), i, p. 417. The automat was on view in April.

Paris); the King said he wished to talk to him at 8 p.m.[94] That evening the first president gave the news to senior *parlementaires*, and he left Soissons at 3 o'clock in the morning.[95] Before Maupeou arrived the chancellor was having his customary audience with the King. Lamoignon took his leave, and as Rouillé was entering the room, also to work with the King, Louis XV said to the usher, in a splendid understatement, '*un* premier président doit venir à huit heures'.[96] When Rouillé left, Maupeou in his robes was ushered in; he was with the King for over an hour. For the first president this long private audience was a great honour and a considerable triumph. What exactly was said between them remains a mystery. On his return to Soissons the next day the first president called together the members of the *grand'chambre* and told them, according to Ysabeau, that the King had informed him of his wish to end the unfortunate state of affairs which had arisen. The King had indicated his intention of settling the matter himself and had asked for his suggestions. Maupeou had replied by stressing the need to recall the whole *Parlement* to Paris. The King had listened favourably to the suggestion but had not committed himself to it.[97] The King's aim had clearly been to sound the first president and to secure his co-operation; he had succeeded in doing both.

It is not clear whether anyone in particular had influenced the King in his decision to summon the first president. The former *procureur général* gathered as much information as he could on the subject without arriving at any firm conclusions. He was told by someone at court that Conty was behind the move. He also learned that on the evening when Maupeou saw the King, D'Argenson was in the vicinity of the palace, in a house belonging to his mistress, Madame d'Estrades, off the avenue de Versailles: it was possible that Maupeou had stopped there on his way back to Soissons. On the other hand, there was a rumour that while Maupeou was with the King, Machault was with Madame de Pompadour in her apartment on the ground floor; Joly de Fleury wondered whether Machault had joined the King and Maupeou by using the private staircase (see Figure 4, p. 73).[98] Four days after the meeting Ysabeau went to Arnouville at Machault's request to discuss the changes that might have to be made to their plan in the light of the latest developments; Ysabeau came away with the impression that Machault did not know exactly what had

[94] BN, JF 309, f. 70: D'Ormesson to the *procureur général*, 3 June [1754]. There is a plausible version of the King's letter in AN, K 698, no. 62.

[95] BN, MS franç. 7573, f. 155: 'nouvelles à la main'.

[96] BN, JF 309, f. 71: G. F. Joly de Fleury to the *procureur général*, 'mercredi' [9 June 1754].

[97] AAE, MD, France 1344, f. 242: Ysabeau to Richelieu, 8 June [1754], 1 p.m.; BN, n.a.fr. 10235 (Hénault Papers), f. 21: [Du Trousset d'Héricourt] to Hénault, Soissons [10 June 1754].

[98] See letter mentioned in note 96 above.

been said between Maupeou and the King.[99] Although Conty and D'Argenson may have had more influence in the decision than Machault, it is on the whole more likely that Louis XV had simply acted on his own initiative and left everyone else more or less in the dark about his plans.

The King still had the same choice between two solutions: either he could ask the *Parlement* for a memoir, as Ysabeau and the *procureur général* suggested, or he could bring out a law of silence, as Conty had always advocated. The first course was a means of gaining time. But Louis XV preferred the second alternative, perhaps because he was afraid that any memoir would appear in print.[100] Machault also reverted to the idea of a law of silence; at the same time, however, he wanted the *Parlement* recalled on terms that were honourable for the King. There is some evidence to suggest that he was now pressing for a law against cessation of service. The *procureur général* appears to have betrayed details of this plan to the Prince de Conty, who thwarted it by disclosing them to *parlementaires*; the result was that the King could not adopt a plan that had been made public.[101] The blow was felt keenly by Machault. The King continued to employ Conty.

Machault was dining in Paris with an unidentified lady (who was in contact with Durey de Meinières at Bourges) on 15 June when the news was brought to them that the letters of recall for the *parlementaires* had been given to the staff of Saint-Florentin's ministry three days previously but had been countermanded in a matter of hours. Machault was taken aback and intended to go the next day to Versailles to find out what had happened.[102] When he returned on 20 June he again dined with the lady. While he appeared satisfied, he was clearly pessimistic about the state of affairs, and he told her: 'il faut que le Parlement revienne'. After emphasising to his hostess that he wanted to concert things with Durey de Meinières in future, he asked her to find out whether Maupeou still had the confidence of the *Parlement* in spite of the public knowledge that he was secretly in league with the Comte d'Argenson. Machault had received confirmation of this secret entente during his stay at Versailles. The keeper of the seals swore that he had not himself been consulted by the King.[103]

[99] See f. 241 of the first letter referred to in note 97 above.
[100] *Ibid.* See also BN, JF 2103, f. 195: Machault to G. F. Joly de Fleury, 7 June 1754; and f. 194: copy of Joly de Fleury's reply, 7 June [1754].
[101] AAE, MD, France 1344, f. 243: Ysabeau to Richelieu, 8 June [1754]; 11 p.m.; f. 249: same to same, 21 June [1754]; BVC, RP, xiv (catalogue no. 35), f. 55: same to same, 10 July 1754. It is interesting to note that it was the *procureur général* who told Ysabeau in February that Conty was capable of thwarting negotiations that were not conducted through him: AAE, MD, France 1344, f. 260.
[102] BN, MS franç. 7573 (Durey de Meinières Papers), f. 136: letter from an unidentified lady probably addressed to Durey de Meinières, 18 June 1754.
[103] *Ibid.*, f. 137: letter from the same lady, 22 June 1754.

Details concerning the negotiations of July which finally led to the recall of the *Parlement* to Paris are scanty. The King seems to have excluded his ministers from these negotiations, which he conducted with Conty's assistance. It is interesting to note that at about the same time as he had written to Maupeou, the King sent a letter to La Rochefoucauld at Bourges asking him to come to Versailles; it was probably at the King's request that the cardinal kept the news secret until the eve of his departure from Bourges a fortnight later, on 14 June.[104] La Rochefoucauld saw the King briefly on 21 June,[105] and had discussions with several bishops and the agents general two days later. He had another royal audience on 29 June, this time in the company of the archbishop of Paris and the former bishop of Mirepoix, probably to discuss new church appointments for priests who were under sentence from the *Parlement*.[106] Dr Jeffreys heard a rumour that the Maréchal de Belle-Isle and President Hénault went to see the archbishop in the week of 7–13 July, and that after they had reported to the King they were sent to Soissons to negotiate with the first president and to order him to attend the King at Compiègne on 14 July. Belle-Isle was certainly in Soissons on 13 July, though on a visit that had been announced a long time beforehand; still, as he had previously conveyed a message to Maupeou, who was his kinsman, he may have done so again on this occasion. The King, who had worked with Conty the previous evening, saw the first president in private for an hour and a half on 14 July.[107] Maupeou told D'Ormesson that he had provided the King with the remaining information he required to make his arrangements. Maupeou was authorised to inform all the *parlementaires* that the King had forgiven the *Parlement* and would at any moment give the order for its recall.[108] Maupeou did not say

---

104 AN, KK 821 (Durey de Meinières's account of his exile), ff. 218 and 222; BUP, CA 28/VI: Jean-Omer Joly de Fleury to the Comte d'Argenson, 13 June 1754.

105 AN, KK 821, f. 222ᵛ: BN, MS franç. 7573 (Durey de Meinières Papers), f. 137.

106 BN, JF 309, f. 86: J.-F. Joly de Fleury (councillor of state) to his brother the *procureur général*, 'Dimanche matin' [30 June 1754]; AN, KK 821, f. 222; Luynes, *Mém.*, xiii, p. 434 (states that the King saw the prelates separately). The King received them after he had seen Conty. Bouettin was given the abbacy of Orgny in Burgundy at this time; see D'Argenson, ed. Rathery, viii, p. 318; and A. Gazier, *Histoire générale du mouvement janséniste depuis ses origines jusqu'à nos jours* (Paris, 1924), 2 vols., ii, p. 63 (note 1).

107 For these details, see BVC, RP, lxvii, f. 126: Mademoiselle de Charolais to Richelieu, 'à Compiègne ce 15' [July 1754] (nineteenth-century copy); BN, JF 309, f. 89: D'Ormesson to the *procureur général*, 13 July 1754; BL, Add. MSS 35,630, f. 159ʳ: Jeffreys to Hardwicke, 16 July 1754. There is a note in the papers of Durey de Meinières to the effect that Noailles had been sent on 18 May to tell Beaumont on behalf of the King that he could no longer rely on *arrêts du conseil* being issued as in the past (BN, MS franç. 7573, f. 176). There was a lengthy meeting of the *Conseil des dépêches* the day before the first president came to Compiègne (see Antoine, 'Le Conseil des dépêches', pp. 138–9).

108 BN, JF 309, f. 94: D'Ormesson to the *procureur général*, 15 July 1754; for copies of Maupeou's letter to the *parlementaires* of 15 July, see AN, U 1089, no. 1 *bis* (5) and BN, JF 1482, f. 172. At Bourges the letter had been sent to Durey de Meinières, who replied on behalf of the 'colony' there: BN, MS franç. 7573, f. 110.

what other measures the King planned to take; however, D'Ormesson did glean a little information from him which he communicated to the *procureur général*:

> on ne sçaura ce que le roy doit envoyer au parlement que lorsque nous y entrerons à la première assemblée pour l'apporter. M[r] le P[r]. P[dt]. nous a tous prévenus par ordre du roy, ajoutant seulement que ce sera l'ouvrage d'un prince qui connoit toute l'étendue de son authorité. On fait remarquer que ce mot a trait au clergé et au parlement également.[109]

Maupeou's letters of recall were sent on 15 July, and it looked as if the other letters were about to be despatched; indeed on 19 July President Hénault, the close friend of the Comte d'Argenson, wrote from Compiègne to the former Swedish ambassador, Baron Scheffer: 'le Roi rappelle enfin son parlement et lui fait grâce'.[110] But still the King did not give the order. The reason for the delay is not known. Conty was in an agitated state when he saw the King on 21 July, and one observer wrote:

> M Le Prince de Conti a parlé à une personne de L'affaire en question, comme n'étant point prête à finir, et ayant reçu de nouvelles entraves.[111]

These difficulties appear to have been overcome; on 27 July D'Argenson was ordered to write to Saint-Florentin with instructions to send off the letters of recall.[112] It seems unlikely that the important ministerial changes of 28–29 July (which followed the death of Saint-Contest on 24 July) were connected with this decision.[113] However, those changes were certain to have an effect on the political settlement. Machault left the *Contrôle général* for the Marine at his own request,[114] but his departure must have been

---

[109] BN, JF 309, f. 95: D'Ormesson to the *procureur général*, Soissons, 16 July 1754.

[110] *Ibid.*, f. 84: same to same, 17 July 1754; and *Lettres inédites de madame du Deffand, du président Hénault et du comte de Bulkeley au baron Carl Fredrik Scheffer, 1751–1756*, ed. Gunnar von Proschwitz, (Studies on Voltaire and the Eighteenth Century, x) (1959), p. 372; Pâris-Duverney announced the news to Bernis on 24 July: *Correspondance du Cardinal de Bernis*, i, pp. 110–11.

[111] BN, MS franç. 7573, f. 112: anonymous letter to Durey de Meinières, Compiègne, 21 July 1754; AS, Turin; Lettere ministri; carteggio diplomatica: Francia, 190, f. 193a: Sartirane to Charles-Emmanuel III, Compiègne, 22 July 1754 (in cipher).

[112] BN, MS franç. 7573, f. 93: D'Argenson to Saint-Florentin, 27 July 1754 (copy in the hand of the *parlementaire* L'Averdy, who clearly had contacts in one of the ministerial departments). The letters for Bourges had to be despatched by Saint-Florentin. The letters of recall for the *grand'chambre* reached Soissons on 30 July. On 23 July the first president had prudently informed the rector of the university that he was 'dans l'impossibilité de prévoir le jour où je pourrois assister à la distribution des prix qui se fait ordinairement dans les premiers jours du mois prochain': AN, M 71, no. 213.

[113] The King appointed Rouillé to succeed Saint-Contest at the Ministry of Foreign Affairs on 28 July, and the following day he appointed Machault to the Marine in his place and Moreau de Séchelles to the *Contrôle général*. For an interesting account of these changes, see *Journal inédit du duc de Croÿ*, i, pp. 273–9.

[114] See *Correspondance du maréchal de Noailles*, eds. C. Rousset (Paris, 1865), ii, pp. 334–5: Louis XV to Noailles, 30 July 1754.

welcomed by Maupeou as well as by the leaders of the clergy. In the letters of recall the King ordered the *parlementaires* to go to Paris on 1 September; they were not allowed to leave their place of exile before 20 August except with the chancellor's permission (and they could not in any case go through Paris).[115]

Two new pieces of evidence indicate that the King used the time that remained before the return of the *Parlement* to draft a new law. The evidence consists of two letters that were certainly written to Conty. In the first, dated 2 August, the King gave his opinion on a draft submitted by the prince:

> ... je lis et relis tous les jours le projet des lettres-patentes. Je passe tous les adoucissements pour le parlement, mais vous ne rabattez rien pour le clergé et cela m'effraie à juste titre, je pars toujours d'icy mardi: si vous veniez icy comme le Ch. de M. vous le propose cela fairait plus de mal que de bien. Je seray, vendredi à Versailles et samedi à vous s'il est nécessaire ...[116]

The second letter was written on 9 August from Bellevue; not only does it help to explain the genesis of the law of 2 September 1754, but it also provides an insight into the King's methods:

> Je vous ay mandé ce qui me faisoit de la peine dans le projet de lettres patentes: je vous le renvoie avec quelques notes que j'y ay faites. Je vous en envoie aussy un autre fort imparfait, mais qui vous prouvera que ma teste travaille: j'avay ramassé des fragments de droitte [*sic*], et de gauche, et ils sont très mal cousus. faites vos réflexions et donnés-les moy par écrit car de longues audiences de vous fonts trop de bruit, et je vous avoue que celà ne s'inculpe jamais dans ma teste comme ce que je lis, et que je réflechis soit le jour soit la nuit quand je ne dors pas ...[117]

This evidence lends support to the view that Louis XV drafted the law of silence himself with some assistance from Conty. The chancellor and the ministers appear to have had little or no part in the preparation of the law,

---

[115] BN, MS franç. 7573, f. 93; AN, O¹* 397, f. 137ᵛ (no. 1006): Saint-Florentin to Méliand (intendant at Soissons), 27 July 1754 (copy).

[116] BN, Cabinet des MSS, Fichier Charavay, 117 (LOUIS): côte 8mm/261: unsigned a.l., 1 p. in 4to, Compiègne, 2 Aug. 1754; and the catalogue, *Autographes et documents historiques: Collection du Professeur Chevassu*, for the sale held at the Nouveau Drouot, Paris, on 23/24 October 1980, lot no. 198. The reference to the 'Ch. de M.' is probably to the Chevalier de Maupeou. The King's movements were as he described them in this letter, cf. Luynes, *Mém.*, xiii, pp. 308-9 and *Journal inédit du duc de Croÿ*, i, pp. 286-7. The present whereabouts of the letter are unknown.

[117] Bibliothèque municipale, Nantes, MSS Collection d'autographes (Fonds Labouchère), vol. 650, no. 19. A reference to a letter from Warsaw in the King's letter strongly reinforces the view that it was addressed to Conty, a perennial candidate for the Polish throne who was involved in the *Secret du roi*. The prince's audiences were indeed attracting comment; see Luynes, *Mém.*, xiii, pp. 434-5; BN, MS franç. 7573, ff. 105, 110.

though the King probably did not send it to the *Parlement* without having first asked them for their opinion at a meeting of the council.

The agents of the Government were conscious of the need to avoid all provocation that might conflict with the King's peaceful intentions. Lamoignon de Malesherbes, the director of the *Librairie*, required Diderot to remove a controversial article on *Unigenitus* from the forthcoming volume of the *Encyclopédie*. The article, which was by the Abbé Mallet, was deemed too favourable to the bull. The chancellor supported his son's action of 22 July in removing the article, despite pressure from Bishop Boyer.[118] The article had already been set up in print. Cardinal de Tencin heard about it and asked his friend the chancellor whether he might be allowed to read the banned article.[119] Lamoignon complied with his request. Tencin heartily approved of Mallet's text: 'c'est dommage qu'il ne soit pas publié'.[120] Caution had prevailed, however, and Mallet, who had been expecting a good fee for his labours, was given a royal pension of 1,500 *livres* instead.[121]

The first president returned to Paris on 27 August: his residence, the *hôtel du bailliage*, was illuminated, and a large crowd assembled outside, lit a bonfire, and made merry until the morning.[122] The *Chambre Royale* was abolished, and the various prisoners were released.[123] There were more scenes of enthusiasm when the *Parlement* reassembled for the first time on 4 September:

> La grand sale [*sic*] du palais, toutes les galéries [*sic*] et les cours du palais étoient pleines de monde, on s'y étouffoit. A mesure que les présidents et conseillers arrivoient c'étoient des acclamations de vive le Roy et le parlem^t.

---

118 R. N. Schwab, W. E. Rex, and John Lough, 'Inventory of Diderot's *Encyclopédie*', *Studies on Voltaire and the Eighteenth Century*, lxxx (1971), pp. 149–83 (for an account of these events by Mrs Robert Senghas and the text of the banned article); see also Douglas H. Gordon and Norman L. Torrey, *The censoring of Diderot's Encyclopédie and the re-established text* (New Yoprk, 1947), *passim*; on the Abbé Edmé Mallet (1715–55) see Robert Shackleton, *The 'Encyclopédie' and the Clerks* (The Zaharoff Lecture, Oxford, 1970), p. 10–11 (which contains the curious statement that Mallet had the reputation of being a Jansenist) and the more non-committal entry in John Lough, *The contributors to the Encyclopédie* (London, 1973), pp. 90–1. See also Mirella Brini Savorelli, 'La bolla *Unigenitus* nell *Encyclopédie*', *Rivista critica di storia della filosofia*, xxx (1975), pp. 167–72.

119 BN, n.a.fr. 31 (autographes), f. 165: Tencin to Lamoignon, 3 Aug. 1754 (with annotation that a reply was made on 11 August).

120 Bibliothèque municipale, Lyon, MS 1884: Tencin to Lamoignon, 5 Sept. 1754, quoted in J. Sareil, *Les Tencin: histoire d'une famille au dix-huitième siècle d'après de nombreux documents inédits* (Geneva, 1969), p. 407. Sareil's argument that Lamoignon cannot have been responsible for banning the article because he sent a copy of it to Tencin is unfounded in the light of the evidence.

121 See the letter from the *parlementaire* Rolland de Challerange of 30 July 1754 reproduced in Gazier, *Histoire générale du mouvement janséniste*, ii, p. 52 (note 2); *contra* Sareil, this account is correct.

122 D'Argenson, ed. Rathery, viii, p. 342; BL, Add. MSS 35,630, f. 167^v: Jeffreys to Yorke, 4 Sept. 1754; AN, U 1089, no. 1 *bis*, no. 7.

123 BN, MS franç. 22105 (Anisson-Duperron Collection, xlv), f. 219: D'Argenson to Berryer, 1 Sept. 1754.

suivis de battemens de mains et des pieds si considérables qu'à la force d'entendre on n'entendoit plus rien. Les acclamations ont redoublé, lorsque les prisoniers d'état ont paru, et surtout lorsqu'on a aperçu M. le premier Président.[124]

As the *parlementaires* were still in the dark about the King's intention, their uneasiness must have impinged upon their enjoyment of the scene.

The previous day, the Bastille yielded up the last prisoner, Monsieur Bourdin, the *procureur* at the *Châtelet*. By the end of his stay he had one consolation: the prison authorities had given him all the books that he had asked for. Well, not quite: they had given him everything except Quesnel's *Nouveau testament en françois, avec des Réflexions morales sur chaque verset.*[125] No Jansenism in gaol!

---

[124] AN, 4 AP 189 (Loménie de Brienne Papers): anonymous note between nos. 30 and 31.
[125] BN, MS franç. 22105, ff. 175–7.

CONCLUSION

THE 'LAW OF SILENCE',
2 SEPTEMBER 1754

> Il faut partir de la position où l'on est et empêcher qu'elle
> n'empire, ce que je regarde comme infaillible, si la
> déclaration du 2 septembre est le dernier mot.
> *Bishop of Grenoble to the Comte d'Argenson, November 1754*

THE KING's *déclaration* had been sent to the *procureur général* on 2 September, and the first president and the *gens du roi* had only one day in which to examine it before it was presented to the assembly of the chambers (though it had probably been shown privately to Maupeou, as well as to Cardinal de La Rochefoucauld, a fortnight earlier).[1] If it resumed its duties, the *Parlement* would only have three days to run: on 8 September the vacation began. In the preamble of the law the *parlementaires* were severely censured for having ceased the administration of justice and refused to resume their duties. Although the King confirmed his willingness to listen to what the *Parlement* might have to say, he remained uncompromising on the subject of the remonstrances of April 1753.[2] He declared that, after having made the

---

[1] BN, JF 308, ff. 228, 236, and 238. On 14 August Louis XV had instructed Lamoignon or one of the ministers to summon Maupeou to Versailles on the 20th; see his letter in BN, Cabinet des MSS, Fichier Charavay, 117 (LOUIS), côte JC 405/84 and 525/100; *Journal et mémoires du Marquis d'Argenson*, ed. E. J. B. Rathery (Paris, 1859–67) (hereafter cited as D'Argenson, ed. Rathery,), viii, p. 339. Perhaps the first president was shown the draft on this occasion. The *déclaration* and accompanying letters patent were sent by the Comte d'Argenson to the *procureur général*: BN, JF 308, f. 238: covering letter of 2 September. Joly de Fleury informed Maupeou of its arrival, and the first president replied that as the *procureur général* had seen fit to show it to him, they could meet the next day with the *gens du roi* (f. 236). D'Ormesson had observed: 'J'imagine que le paquet annoncé vaudra la peine que l'on quitte tout pour le voir' (f. 228: letter of 2 Sept. to the *procureur général*).

[2] AN, K 698, no. 64[2]: *Déclaration du Roi, donnée à Versailles le 2 septembre 1754* (Paris, Imp. Royale, 4to), pp. 1–2. The text of the law is also conveniently reproduced in *Les Remontrances du Parlement de Paris au xviii͏ᵉ siècle*, ed. Jules Flammermont (Paris, 1888–98), 3 vols. (hereafter referred to as Flammermont, *Rems.*), i, pp. 610–11, and in *Mémoires du Duc de Luynes sur la cour de Louis XV (1753–1758)*, ed. L. Dussieux and E. Soulié (Paris, 1860–5) (hereafter cited as Luynes, *Mém.*), xiii, pp. 340–2. For the text transcribed officially by the *Parlement* see AN, X¹ᴬ 8760, ff. 1–3.

parlementaires feel the effects of his displeasure, he now willingly made them feel the effects of his clemency by recalling them from exile. He added that he had decided to reassemble the *Parlement* in Paris to hear his orders. The *déclaration* contained three stipulations: an order to the *parlementaires* to resume their accustomed duties in Paris; an injunction on the *Parlement* to enforce the rule of silence which had long been imposed on the religious disputes; and an order to suspend the judicial proceedings that had been taken (with certain exceptions, the judgements that had been delivered were also to remain without effect). The delicate question of the transfer of the *Parlement* was thus eluded by means of a verbal subtlety. The precise terms of the second stipulation were naturally of particular importance:

> ... ayant reconnu que le silence imposé depuis tant d'années sur des matières qui ne peuvent être agitées sans nuire également au bien de la Religion et à celui de l'Etat, est le moyen le plus convenable pour assurer la paix et la tranquillité publique; [Nous] enjoignons à notre Parlement de tenir la main à ce que d'aucune part il ne soit rien fait, tenté, entrepris, ou innové qui puisse être contraire à ce silence, et à la paix que nous voulons faire régner dans nos Etats; luy ordonnant de procéder contre les Contrevenans, conformément aux Loix et Ordonnances.[3]

This stipulation enabled the *parlementaires* to regard the use of confession certificates as contrary to the Law of Silence; it consequently allowed them to punish offenders. In this way the King had tipped the scales in favour of the *Parlement*.

When the *déclaration* was laid before the assembly of the chambers on 4 September, D'Ormesson in his *réquisitoire* as *avocat général* urged the magistrates to register it. He described the new law as the fruit of the King's pains and labours. A tense debate ensued in which the first president had an altercation with Durey de Meinières. Four courses of action were proposed: to appoint *commissaires*, to postpone the assembly to the next day, to register the law 'purely and simply' as it was the work of the Monarch himself, not to register the law on account of the offensive nature of the preamble. These views were then reduced to two: to appoint *commissaires* and to postpone the assembly to the next day. The stalwarts of the *grand'chambre* threw their weight behind the second opinion and carried the day. Despite this tactical victory, the first president had difficulty in concealing his despair at the turn of events.[4] As the assembly broke up, the

---

[3] *Déclaration du Roi*, p. 3.
[4] AN, U 1089 no. 1 *bis*: item no. 8. According to an unsigned note in Italian in the papers of the papal nuncio, only forty-two magistrates wanted to register the law as it stood, fifty-eight were for appointing *commissaires*, and seventy-one for not registering the law at all; the first two groups had then joined forces and ensured the subsequent passage of the law: BL, Add. MSS 20,659 (Gualterio Papers), f. 93. The figures quoted seem too high for a single round of voting.

parlementaires had once again to face the applause of the crowds thronging the *grande salle* and the galleries. Maupeou was besieged by a group of ladies who tried to present him with a bouquet, a crown of laurels, and a written compliment. He accepted the bouquet but declined the rest. However, as the crown of laurels was being thrust in the air while he was being pressed to accept it, he finally took it and got his servants to hide it away.[5]

The following day twenty-five different views were expressed in the course of a debate lasting nearly eight hours. They were again reduced to two: that the *Parlement* should resume its duties while petitioning the King to withdraw his *déclaration*, and that the *déclaration* be registered with a clause stating that there should be no innovation in the 'external and public administration of the sacraments'. With the second alternative the *arrêté* would also state that the *Parlement* did not accept the charges levelled against it in the preamble of the *déclaration*, and that a deputation would be sent to the King to justify its conduct. The second view prevailed by nineteen votes. Again, there was a furious row between Maupeou and President Durey de Meinières, who wanted to reject the law. Durey de Meinières finally changed his mind, declaring that it was not the first president's anger that was causing him to do so.[6]

The result had been achieved through the subtle use of a procedural device. There were two linked *arrêtés*: the first, which was secret, ordered the registration of the law according to the terms of the second. This second *arrêté* (known confusingly as the *arrêté particulier*) substantially reproduced the terms of the majority view at the end of the debate and was eventually printed with the text of the law. The first *arrêté* also stated that representations would be made to the King as follows:

(1) que son Parlement ne peut se dispenser de lui faire connoistre que la dispersion des membres qui le composent, et ce qui s'en est ensuivy, est d'un exemple dangereux et porte même atteinte aux Loix fondamentales du Royaume et est une source de maux pour les sujets dudit Seigneur Roy;

(2) qu'il est important que ledit Seigneur Roy ne refuse pas de recevoir les remontrances que son Parlement croit Luy devoir représenter pour le bien de son service sur la seule imputation de la nature des objets qui doivent entrer dans lesdites remontrances.[7]

---

[5] AN, 4 AP 189 (Loménie de Brienne Papers): item between nos. 30 and 31 and headed '4 7bre 1754).

[6] AN, U 1089 no .1 *bis*: unnumbered item on the debate of 5 Sept. before item no. 10; BN, n.a.fr. 8448, ff. 27–8.

[7] The secret *arrêté* was not reproduced by Flammermont in his account of the proceedings at the *Parlement*; cf. *Rems.*, i, pp. 612–14; for the original *minute* signed by the first president, see, AN, X^{1B} 8931 under the date, and for the text transcribed in the registers, see AN, X^{1A} 8489, f. 301^{r,v}; see also AN, U 1089, no. 1 *bis*, item 10.

Thus had the matter of the *Grandes remontrances* been raised after all. The procedural device was probably the work of Maupeou, perhaps acting in concert with the King. It meant that the *parlementaires* could make their long-standing protest to the King, but that its formal link to the registration of the new law remained secret.

The same evening the *procureur général* wrote to the chancellor reporting the outcome of the debate and requesting an audience with the King to ask him when he would receive the deputation of the *Parlement*. His letter did not arrive at Versailles before 10 o'clock at night.[8] Earlier that evening, at just about the time when the debate of the *Parlement* had been drawing to a close, the King had returned from the hunt. The Duchesse de Luynes, one of the Queen's ladies-in-waiting, noted that he looked very worried ('très soucieux'):

> son débotté fut court et silencieux. Il renvoya ses enfants et appela d'un ton dur M. le Prince de Conti avec lequel il passa dans son cabinet.[9]

The next day the chancellor told the *procureur général* to come to Versailles that very evening for his audience. The King told him he would receive the deputation on 7 September at noon.[10]

The *zélés* had one day left in which to try and wreck the settlement. After the debate on 5 September the first president had refused a demand from the deputies of the *requêtes* for an assembly of the chambers on the grounds that he had not been told its purpose. The next day, while the *procureur général* was on his way to Versailles, the *enquêtes* and *requêtes* provoked an assembly of the chambers by simply moving into the *grand'chambre* during the *audiance*. Maupeou had to suspend the *audiance*, and when he expressed surprise at the conduct of the intruders, Drouyn de Vandeuil told him he had no right to insist upon knowing the reasons why members of the *Parlement* might wish to call for an assembly of the chambers. A dangerous precedent was being set. There was a heated discussion between Maupeou and the two deputies from the chambers of *requêtes* (Moron and Hocquart). Finally, the first president succeeded in breaking the deadlock by eliciting from them what they wished to discuss. Durey de Meinières wanted a debate on whether the officers of the *Châtelet* should not be called to give an account of what had taken place in the absence of the *Parlement* and on whether regulations should not be made for the guidance of the vacation

---

[8] BN, JF 308, f. 217: *procureur général* to the chancellor, 5 Sept. 1754 (copy); f. 216: Lamoignon to the *procureur général*, 5 Sept. 1754, 10 p.m. As the *Parlement* had formally resumed its duties, the chancellor despatched the commission for the vacation chamber.

[9] *Lettres inédites de la Reine Marie Lecksinska* [sic] *et de la Duchesse de Luynes au Président Hénault*, ed. Victor des Diguères (Paris, 1886), p. 231: Duchesse de Luynes to President Hénault, 5 Sept. 1754; BL, Add. MSS 20,659 (Gualterio Papers), f. 93.

[10] BN, JF 308, f. 211: Lamoignon to the *procureur général*, 6 Sept. 1754, noon.

chamber, which would be taking over the duties of the *Parlement* two days later. Maupeou agreed to the request to hold the assembly. On the first proposal President Molé weighed in at once with the argument that it was dangerous and contrary to the King's stated desire for silence to prevail on the current disputes. He narrowly carried the day, by seventy-six votes to seventy-three. Durey's proposal about the vacation chamber was postponed until the deputation had returned from Versailles the next day. To make matters worse, there was a rumour that the archbishop of Paris had just sanctioned a refusal of the sacrament.[11]

The first president and the deputation of the *Parlement* went to Versailles on 7 September. Maupeou's speech was an expanded and oratorical version of the unpublished *arrêté*, including its reference to the remonstrances.[12] When he came to the passage when he told Louis XV that truth had reached him 'sans autres secours que vos propres lumières', he glanced meaningfully at all the ministers present. The *Parlement*, he continued, exercised that portion of his authority which the King had entrusted to it, but it would preserve that authority which the Monarch held from God and which had to be transmitted entire to his most distant posterity. At this point Maupeou, with a touching expression on his face, looked at the Dauphin. Luynes was told by an observer that the most skilful actor could not have played his part with more pathos.[13] As the *parlementaires* had now resumed their duties, the King's reply, doubtless agreed beforehand, was conciliatory and, more significantly, did not question the terms of the *arrêt d'enregistrement*.[14] At 7 p.m. the deputies were back in Paris for the assembly of the chambers. Molé's motion that the first president's speech and the King's reply should be registered was carried unanimously. Then the debate was opened on Durey de Meinières's proposal that guidelines should be issued for the vacation chamber on the precedent of 1752. Molé argued that the circumstances were not the same; in 1752 the juridical competence of the *Parlement* was in question; now the situation had changed because of the new law and the King's reply to the deputation. His view prevailed. Another motion, this time from President Bernard de Boulainvilliers (2nd *enquêtes*), that the first president should concert measures with the King to secure the release and reinstatement of magistrates who had been the victims of the *Chambre Royale*, was not even put to the vote. The pro-clerical Pajot de Malzac proposed that Maupeou should use his influence on behalf of ecclesiastics who had been the victims of *lettres*

---

[11] BS, MS 801 (Durey de Meinières Papers), ff. 53–4 (debate of 6 Sept. 1754).
[12] For the speeches see Flammermont, *Rems.*, i, pp. 612–14.
[13] Luynes, *Mém.*, xiii, p. 348.
[14] BN, JF 308, f. 210: note in the hand of the *procureur général*.

de cachet, but he had no following either.[15] The crisis was over and the *Parlement* then adjourned until 27 November, leaving the vacation chamber with the unenviable task of coping with any cases that might arise.

Despite the unanimous decision to register the text of the proceedings at Versailles, many *parlementaires* had found the first president's speech distasteful: 'bas et rampant, et peu convenable à la dignité de la Compagnie' was how one of them described it.[16] Before they left the *Palais*, they went back to their chambers. The message came that Maupeou wanted them to send deputies to his residence so that they could draft a ban on derogatory references being made about the Commission and the *Chambre Royale*. Although Maupeou was only following a precedent of 1720, his proposal caused offence and was rejected by all the chambers. To mark their disapproval, the magistrates decided not to pay him the courtesy call that was customary at the end of the parliamentary year.[17] Maupeou's ephemeral crown of laurels was decidedly turning into a more permanent crown of thorns.

Doubtless exhausted by the dramatic events of the three days that had passed since the *Parlement* had reconvened in Paris after its exile, the first president and his colleagues of the *grand banc* attended the King's *lever* at Versailles on 8 September. They were rewarded for their pains, for Louis XV engaged Maupeou and Molé in a lengthy exchange of conversation. There was cause for mutual satisfaction.[18]

The same could not be said of the King's relations with his leading clerics. On 3 September Louis XV had summoned Cardinals de La Rochefoucauld and Soubise together with the archbishops of Paris and Narbonne to Choisy to read them the text of the new law. From what little can be pieced together about this meeting, their reaction was one of protest. As they offered no alternative solutions of their own, the atmosphere was distinctly cool. The King curtly told them that he wanted silence on the religious disputes and that he had given orders to the *Parlement* to ensure that it was observed. Rounding on Beaumont, Louis XV added: 'et vous, Monsieur l'archevêque de Paris, soyez à l'avenir plus modéré'. Beaumont had the presence of mind to retort words to the effect: 'ma conscience ne me permet aucun accommodement'.[19]

---

[15] BS, MS 801, ff. 55–6 (debate of 7 Sept. 1754).   [16] *Ibid.*, f. 56.   [17] *Ibid.*
[18] Luynes, *Mém.*, xiii, p. 347.
[19] According to the version given by the Marquis de Stainville in his despatches to the Emperor: AS, Florence: Segretaria Ministero Esteri, no. 2296, Francia: Carteggio col il Marchese Stainville no. 4; nos. 163 (6 Sept. 1754) and 164 (15 Sept. 1754). Stainville gives Beaumont's rejoinder but was not sure of its accuracy. For another version (with slight variants in the words spoken), see AN, K 698 no. 68 (quoted in Père E. Régnault, *Christophe de Beaumont* (Paris, 1882), 2 vols., i, p. 271). For other comments on these meetings, see BUP, Archives d'Argenson, CA 23: Jean de Caulet (Bishop of Grenoble) to the Comte d'Argenson, 8 Dec. 1754; and D'Argenson, ed. Rathery, viii, p. 354.

The prelates were in a quandary. After the registration of the Law of Silence, they apparently contemplated holding a juridical assembly, but Beaumont was opposed to it.[20] La Rochefoucauld and several bishops saw Beaumont again on 8 September, and that clerical spy, the Abbé de Villevieille, informed the new papal nuncio that they were now expecting the Pope to come to their assistance.[21] The nuncio had already been approached by Beaumont and was subsequently praised by Cardinal Valenti, the papal secretary of state, for the prudent way in which he had handled this overture.[22]

Monsignor Luigi Gualterio, whose uncle, a friend and correspondent of Saint-Simon, had also been nuncio to France, had succeeded the irascible Durini. He had arrived in July and had already encountered La Rochefoucauld on his journey to Versailles. Valenti's instructions required him to keep on good terms with Bishop Boyer, who knew Rome well by virtue of his duties and whose zeal was felt to be great. Gualterio was also to show consideration towards the archbishop of Paris and the two cardinals, La Rochefoucauld and Soubise.[23] He could not have taken up his duties at a more difficult time, but he fortunately possessed the requisite qualities of patience, tact, discretion and judgement. Some, though not all, of these qualities were shared by his counterpart, the new French ambassador in Rome, the Comte de Stainville, the future Choiseul, whose political and diplomatic career had just begun.[24]

For his part Pope Benedict XIV was already preparing himself for a more direct involvement in the affairs of the French Church. Cardinal de Tencin was sending him advice and explaining the complex French legal terminology. On 9 October Valenti outlined the Pope's position in a letter to the nuncio. The main point, as Benedict XIV saw it, was the need for the bishops to be united so that their conduct could be uniform in voice and in deed. The unity among the *parlementaires* had been their source of strength; the bishops needed to achieve as much if they wished to make some impact on the King. The Pope was willing to help, but he wanted first to see what steps the French episcopate, and especially Cardinal de La Rochefoucauld, intended to take.[25] These men – Benedict XIV, Gualterio, Stainville, La Rochefoucauld – were all to play an important part in the events of the years that followed.

---

[20] BL, Add. MSS 20,669A (Gualterio Papers), f. 14: Abbé de Villevielle to the nuncio, 8 Sept. 1754.

[21] *Ibid.*, f. 16: same to same, 9 Sept. 1754.

[22] *Ibid.*, Add. MSS 20,651, f. 62: Valenti to Gualterio, 11 Sept. 1754 (in cipher).

[23] *Ibid.*, f. 10: same to same, 17 July 1754.

[24] Rohan Butler, *Choiseul*, vol. i: *Father and son, 1719–1754* (Oxford, 1980), pp. 1074–8.

[25] For Tencin's rôle see abbé P. Richard, 'Le Secret du pape – un légat apostolique en France (1742–1756)', in *Revue des questions historiques* xcii (1912), pp. 395–6; for La Rochefoucauld's possible rôle, see BL, Add. MSS 20,651, f. 97: Valenti to Gualterio, 9 Oct. 1754 (in cipher).

The vacation chamber avoided trouble, largely through the efforts of its president, Le Peletier de Rosambo. One of the nuncio's informants described him as a man who was attached to the Church like his father, the former first president, and who had often been the target of those whom the informant described as the 'fougueux du parti républicain'.[26] The *zélés* later complained about his conduct of business. Durey de Meinières wrote in his parliamentary diary:

> On ne l'amenoit que difficilement à délibérer sur les objets les plus intéressans et les plus pressans. Il remettoit toujours après les séances du service ordinaire que souvent il allongeait afin qu'on eût moins de temps. Il retardoit l'expédition des arrests qu'on rendoit afin de diminuer la fréquence des occasions d'en rendre, et par là augmentoit le mal par la lenteur de l'application du remède.[27]

Le Peletier de Rosanbo clearly possessed the usual attributes of a *président à mortier*, but he was no match for the Joly de Fleurys. The *procureur général* briskly launched an appeal *comme d'abus* against two decisions of the chapter of Orléans. The chapter had decreed that one of its members, Canon Cogniou, could receive the last rites only if he withdrew an appeal he had made to a future council of the church and accepted *Unigenitus* 'purely and simply'. The chapter had appointed three canons to administer the sacrament to him only if these conditions were fulfilled. On 11 October the vacation chamber upheld the appeal *comme d'abus* and ordered the three canons to comply with the Law of Silence and to end the scandal created by their refusal to administer the sacrament to Cogniou. Those who had taken part in the second deliberation of the chapter received a collective fine of 12,000 *livres*; failure to pay it would lead to seizure of temporalities.[28] With the Law of Silence behind them, the *gens du roi* had felt less inhibited about resorting to the powerful weapon of the appeal *comme d'abus*, and the magistrates had flexed their collective muscle in ordering the administration of the sacrament, albeit in a circuitous way. A pattern was being set.

By 23 October the Pope was willing to accede to the wish of several French bishops that he should write to the King, but he did not want his letter to do more harm than good. He did not wish it to appear that he was writing under pressure from the bishops, but he was eager to have the views of Beaumont, of the two cardinals, and of those who were in charge of the affairs of the Church.[29] A week later Valenti sent Gualterio the draft of the Pope's letter: 'una sua patetica Lettera, e tutta confidenziale'. The letter

[26] BL, Add. MSS 20,660, f. 15: unsigned report to Gualterio, 21 Sept. 1754.
[27] BS, MS 801, f. 57 (debate of 12 Nov. 1754).
[28] Luynes, *Mém.*, xiii, pp. 375–6.
[29] BL, Add. MSS 20,651, f. 105: Valenti to Gaulterio, 23 Oct. 1754) (in cipher).

was not a remonstrance, but an expression of faith in the King. Gualterio was to present it quietly ('senza strepito') to Louis XV, but only after having communicated it under the seal of secrecy to Beaumont and a few others.[30] Gualterio received the letter on 10 November and decided to show it only to Beaumont.[31] The archbishop's reaction was favourable, though he did not like the Pope's reference to the Law of Silence; he wrote to the nuncio the next day:

> mais tout bien examiné, il y a d'allieurs [sic] tant de bon dans la pièce que vous m'avés communiquée que je crois que vous pouvés suivre le projet que vous avés formé de la faire passer sans aucun délai à son addresse.[32]

Gualterio immediately transmitted the Pope's letter to the King. Benedict XIV expressed himself in terms of great warmth towards Louis XV but reminded him that the Law of Silence had not changed the rights of the Church. The King had wisely imposed silence on the disputes but his intention had not been to take away from the Church what God had given or place the control of the sacraments in the hands of secular magistrates. However, the absence of all reference to the preservation of episcopal authority in this matter saddened and tormented the French clergy.[33]

The Pope had stated the position in the way in which the French bishops themselves were beginning to view it. Evidence for this may be found in the voluminous correspondence between the Comte d'Argenson and the bishop of Grenoble, Jean de Caulet. The latter's reputation for writing letters of extraordinary length became legendary (as late as 1800 Stendhal referred to it when writing to his sister), but seems not to have deadened his impact on the minister or even on the King, also the recipient of his bulky missives.[34] Like D'Argenson, Caulet had belonged to the clientèle of the late Duc d'Orléans. D'Argenson had been a member of the duke's household; Caulet had enjoyed the protection of the duke in the latter's capacity as provincial governor of Dauphiné.[35] The minister and the bishop now contemplated the prospect of the assembly of the clergy which was due to hold its next quinquennial meeting the following year. On 11 November the bishop wrote to Louis XV on the subject. In his covering letter to D'Argenson he made the point that, while the assembly would be useful in

---

30 *Ibid.*, f. 114: same to same, 30 Oct. 1754 (in cipher).
31 For evidence that Gualterio showed the Pope's letter only to Beaumont, see BL Add. MSS 20,651, f. 149: Valenti to Gualterio, 4 Dec. 1754.
32 *Ibid.*, f. 115: Beaumont to Gualterio, 'ce Lundi au soir', [11 Nov. 1754].
33 *Ibid.*, ff. 116–17 (text of the Pope's letter to the King of 30 Oct. 1754 in Italian), ff. 118–19 (in French); for a better French translation, see AAE, CP (Correspondance politique), Rome 815, ff. 136–9.
34 Louis Bassette, *Jean de Caulet, Evêque et Prince de Grenoble (1693–1771)* (Grenoble, 1946), p. 135; the letters from the bishop to the Comte d'Argenson are in BUP, CA 23.
35 Bassette, *Jean de Caulet*, p. 127.

a number of ways (perhaps a delicate reference to its being asked to vote the usual subsidy to the Crown), if the state of affairs created by the Law of Silence remained unchanged, there would be trouble as the assembled bishops would seek redress of their grievances: it was not an encouraging prospect.[36] Caulet was fighting against D'Argenson's inclination to allow the King time to come round to his way of thinking. A week later Caulet sent another letter to Louis XV urging him to adopt the policy of keeping the balance between the parties:

> Votre Majesté me permettra, Sire, de le lui dire: ce point de vue n'a pas été rempli par celui qu'elle a honoré de sa confiance dans la rédaction de la Déclaration du 2 septembre.[37]

The bishop seemed not to know that the King had devised the law himself, and D'Argenson the courtier was naturally reluctant to take up the cudgels.

Yet, by all accounts, the Comte d'Argenson was now the most influential member of the Government. Back in August the Sardinian minister at Versailles, the Comte de Sartirane, had sought to interpret the ministerial changes of July for the benefit of his royal master in Turin. In his view D'Argenson had had a greater part in these changes than his rival Machault, who had been forced to leave the field of battle. It was Machault's tenure of the controller generalship of the finances that had put him at loggerheads with the clergy over the *vingtième* (and his subsequent attempts to extract from it a statement of its wealth) and with D'Argenson over the funds for the Department of War. The result had been that D'Argenson had supported the clergy while Machault had supported the *Parlement*. Now that Machault was in charge of the Navy, he no longer had anything to do with the clergy or with supplying funds to the minister of War; indeed, he would have to treat the new *contrôleur général* with care if he wanted to obtain the funds he needed for the Navy. It was here that he was at a disadvantage; his successor, Moreau de Séchelles, was an intimate friend of both the Maréchal de Belle-Isle and of the Comte d'Argenson. Although Moreau de Séchelles probably owed his appointment to the Prince de Soubise and to Madame de Pompadour, the links between the

---

[36] BUP, CA 23: letter to the Comte d'Argenson of 11 Nov. 1754. One of the nuncio's informants was relatively sanguine about the clergy's position after the law of silence. 'Toutes les Déclarations et particulièrement celle de 1730 conservent leur force et leur autorité. On n'ordonne que le silence sur ce qui y est porté. Voilà en quoi la nouvelle Déclaration paroît étrange. Mais on ne pouvoit rétablir la paix dans l'Eglise et dans l'état que par ce moyen'; BL, Add. MSS 20,660, f. 17: undated and unsigned letter. On the 1695 edict the King's position remained that of the *arrêt du conseil* of 21 November 1752 which had been a source of such disappointment to the clergy as it implicitly confirmed the competence of the royal courts in certain cases of denial of sacraments (*ibid*).

[37] BUP, CA 23: bishop of Grenoble to the King, Verdun, 11 Nov. 1754.

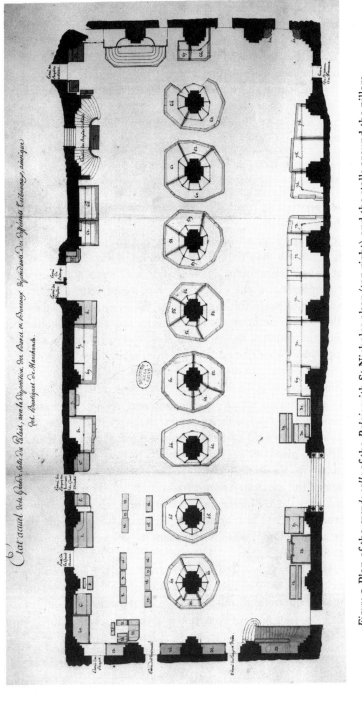

Figure 5 Plan of the *grande salle* of the *Palais* with St Nicholas altar (top right) and the stalls around the pillars (from the Archives de Paris)

latter and D'Argenson had not yet been completely severed. Sartirane thought D'Argenson had been able to weave a delicate web between himself and Madame de Pompadour, the Prince de Conty, and the Prince de Soubise. Even the transfer of the harmless Rouillé from the Navy to Foreign Affairs was the work of the same party: according to Sartirane, Rouillé was just an 'entrepôt' until someone better could be found for the post. Sartirane's analysis seems on the whole confirmed by other sources, although he was careful to allow for the possibility of error when he wrote warily to Charles-Emmanuel III:

> ... V.M. sent fort bien qu'on ne peut rien assurer sur des sistèmes de cour, et surtout de celle-ci, qui sont sujets à mille différentes variations.[38]

If Sartirane's analysis was probably correct at the highest level, it did not encompass the refinements and twists lower down the scale. D'Argenson may have been a supporter of the clergy, but he also had his following in the *Parlement*; Machault may have been the friend of the *Parlement*, but its first president was no friend of his. Hence, Sartirane's view of the situation between the *Parlement* and the clergy was less sound. He thought that without the support of Machault the *Parlement*, 'humiliated after its longest period of exile', would be more restrained in its proceedings against the clergy; whereas the bishops, to whom La Rochefoucauld had communicated the King's instructions, would refrain from taking any measures that caused trouble.[39] He was mistaken in both these assumptions.

Although the *Parlement* did not formally reconvene until 27 November, there was one occasion on which its members met before that date. The 'Red Mass' traditionally marked the *rentrée*, the start of the new parliamentary year, and it was held on 12 November, the day after the feast of St Martin. That year about ninety *parlementaires*, having donned their red robes, assembled in the *grand'chambre* before the service. President de Maupeou alone of the *présidents à mortier* had turned up. The absence of the others, noted Durey de Meinières, 'fut trouvé tout à fait déplacé dans les circonstances actuelles'.[40] The magistrates quickly dealt with another stage in the Orléans affair before it was time for them to process to the *grande salle* (see Figure 5) for the mass.

The Mass of the Holy Ghost, commonly known as the 'Red Mass', was a ceremony that traditionally attracted crowds of onlookers perched in the precarious wooden booths and stalls that encased the massive pillars of the *grande salle*. This occasion was no exception and these uncomfortable places

---

[38] AS, Turin, Lettere ministri, Francia 191, f. 201b: Sartirane to Charles-Emmanuel III, 5 Aug. 1754; cf. *Mémoires du Président Hénault*, ed. F. Rousseau (Paris, 1911), pp. 207–9; Butler, *Choiseul*, i, pp. 1061–2 (based on Choiseul's account).

[39] *Ibid.*   [40] BS, MS 801, f. 57ʳ (entry for 12 Nov. 1754).

cost as much as 6 or 12 *livres* enabling the stallkeepers to make a handsome profit.[41] Preceded by his chaplain, his secretaries, his equerry, and followed by the presidents and councillors, each chamber in turn filing past, the first president, resplendent in his *mortier* and with his fur *épitoge* over his red robes, advanced amidst the applause of the crowd towards the St Nicholas altar in one corner of the vast hall. He and the presidents sat on the gospel side of the altar, while the *doyen* and the councillors were on the epistle side. The celebrant, always a bishop, made his entry and the choir sang the *Kyrie*. The most intriguing part of the ceremony took place after the offertory, when the first president left his place and went up level to the bishop's throne where he would do two curtseys to the altar, one to the left and one to the right. Upon returning to his place he curtseyed in the same manner to the presidents, to the councillors, and to the *gens du roi*. The presidents then followed his example, performing the same curtseys to the altar and to the rest of the *Parlement*. As these curtseys involved bending the knees, 'le plus bas que faire se peux [*sic*] à la manière des femmes',[42] this singular practice invariably attracted the curiosity of the crowds, which on this occasion repeatedly clapped as the first president acquitted himself manfully of this seemingly feminine ritual.[43] Perhaps, in the seclusion of their stately *hôtels* in the Marais, the absent *présidents à mortier* had relished the thought of the Maupeous, *père et fils*, on their own, bobbing up and down as they curtseyed to one another.

With less than a fortnight to go before the start of a new parliamentary year under the hopeful signs engendered by the Law of Silence, the magistrates may not have had much time or inclination to reflect on the momentous events of the passing year, or to speculate upon what the new would bring. However, as we take leave of them at the close of their *messe rouge* and on their way to the splendid banquet given for them by Maupeou in the *salle Saint-Martin* of his official residence, it is necessary to draw a number of conclusions about those events of 1753–4.

In the first place, few of those who were concerned with these events seem to have realised at the outset that a religious dispute, which had admittedly become a source of discord between the clergy and the royal courts, would lead to the disruption of the civil order over a large part of France. If that development had been foreseen, the crisis of May 1753 might well have taken a different turn. Instead the ordinary administration of justice was interrupted for over a year with serious results: important and urgent cases were left without trial; numerous subordinate jurisdictions which needed to be supervised – however inadequately – by the *Parlement*

---

[41] *Ibid.*; on the *messe rouge* see BS, MS 435: 'Le Premier Président du Parlement de Paris dans l'exercice de ses fonctions' by Boizot (1747), p. 229.

[42] BS, MS 435, p. 225.   [43] BS, MS 801, f. 58r.

were left to themselves; and the general policing of the *ressort* became less effective. The special courts which were set up were no substitute for the *Parlement* because lawyers, *procureurs*, and litigants did not resort to them, despite the fact that they were recognised by most of the subordinate jurisdictions. Although the *Chambre Royale* represented only a superficial attempt to replace the *Parlement*, the experience had revealed the difficulties involved in such an enterprise. The *Parlement* was a venerable institution that even in exile inspired loyalty and fear in those who depended upon it. As it had long occupied an important place in the political and judicial order, its necessity was apparent to many and its return seemed inevitable to all.

Secondly, the division within the political order and its effects could be ended only by the recall of the *Parlement*. But this course presented two major difficulties; first, the recall had to be effected in a manner that was honourable for the King, and secondly, it had to be accompanied by a decision on the current disputes. The King's authority had already been weakened by the resistance of the *Parlement*; there was a danger that it could be further weakened by the recall. For a long time the Government and the *gens du roi* hoped that the first president would make a *démarche* that could be seen as an act of submission. Maupeou made no such move. His attitude was held to be very suspect in some quarters, perhaps not without reason. But it also has to be seen in the light of the effects of the exile of the *Parlement*. The *parlementaires* could no longer act as a body, only as individuals or as a group of individuals; hence they hesitated to take steps that might compromise them with their colleagues. The members of the *grand'-chambre* were deterred from taking the initiative in negotiating with the Government by the thought that the *enquêtes* would disavow any steps they might take. The first president did little to dispel that belief. For these reasons the negotiations did not succeed. Indeed, the negotiations probably had the effect of prolonging the resistance of the *parlementaires* because they were seen as an indication of the Government's weakness. The solution of the crisis needed to take a different form and to come at a time when exile had begun to weigh heavily upon the *parlementaires*. Louis XV seems to have realised that the dispute had to be settled with the *Parlement* and not with the *parlementaires*. For that reason it was necessary to recall the *parlementaires* to Paris as a preliminary step. Naturally the King would have liked the *grand'chambre* to ask for their recall. This had proved impossible, and he was obliged to make arrangements that he may have considered less dignified. Nevertheless, by his repeated delays he managed to end the exile without appearing to yield to any pressure. The settlement that he then imposed on the *Parlement* skilfully combined an order to resume duties with an important concession on the subject of confession certificates. From the

King's point of view the settlement had two main advantages. He had made the *parlementaires* resume their duties without having openly yielded to them on the subject of the remonstrances. And he could point out to the clergy that the legal position of *Unigenitus* and the respective rights of the royal and ecclesiastical courts were not brought into question by the terms of the new *déclaration*. The King had taken a risk with the *déclaration*. If the *Parlement* had declined to register it, he would probably have had to resort to a *lit de justice*, which in turn might have led to another cessation of service. But the majority of the *parlementaires* were in no mood to reject the settlement. And the King was careful not to jeopardise its chances of success; in particular, he resisted the desire to introduce a law against cessation of service at the same time, as Machault had advocated.

For the period 1737 to 1754 much evidence has been adduced here to suggest that the intrigues at court and at the *Parlement* fuelled the political crises that developed over the application of *Unigenitus* or the passage of financial legislation. Certain *parlementaires*, or groups of *parlementaires*, could be and were manipulated by powerful ministers at court by means that are not always directly apparent to the historian. Some of those intrigues were inherent in the nature of the office-holding system of the *ancien régime*. Others stemmed from the workings of the governmental system, which had been shown to be unsatisfactory in the sense that ministers all too often gave the impression of a house divided, thus triggering off hopes and intrigues amongst *parlementaires*. Outside that system Louis XV came increasingly to play an indirect, secretive, personal rôle in the exacerbation or resolution of the disputes. It is possible that the King's secret policy had simply been one of keeping the balance between the Clergy and the *Parlement*. Such a policy was perhaps practical in political terms, but it created great legal and constitutional problems. The forces in the balance were not evenly matched in law: the Clergy of France was a body which looked to the King as its natural protector, while the *Parlement* was his chief court of justice, an emanation of his own sovereign authority. Many of the problems which Louis XV encountered, if such was his policy, stemmed from this legal imbalance. In practice, the policy of holding the balance had certain advantages as it kept both the Clergy and the *Parlement* largely dependent on the King. However, it contained risks.

Within the *Parlement*, the crisis of 1753 had demonstrated how, in certain circumstances, the otherwise monolithic control of the *présidents à mortier* and of the *grand'chambre* could collapse, albeit temporarily. At the same time, intrigues gathered momentum, and the shortcomings of ministers or *parlementaires* bore consequence, only because of the way this closed world regarded certain issues as explosive. The status of *Unigenitus* was a theological, legal, and political minefield. The minefield would in time have to be cleared once and for all. A 'law of silence' which merely ordered people to keep away from the minefield could work only in the short term.

As the chief protagonists in the dispute, the King and the *Parlement* eventually resolved their differences and agreed on the compromise solution of 1754 without any pressure from outside the existing narrow political structure. 'Public opinion' had played no part in that resolution, despite the flutter of the *gazettes*, the pamphlets, and the ubiquitous *nouvelles à la main*.

The events of 1753–4 revealed that the real strength of the King's authority lay in the chain of authority which derived from it by a process of delegation. In that chain the *Parlement* was the most important link. Only when the chain was broken did contemporaries become aware of its existence and importance; for the Government could not replace it by mere acts of authority. Although there were undoubtedly measures that the Government could take (and indeed intended to take) to tighten its hold on the *Parlement*, yet the fact remains that the exercise of royal authority depended of necessity on the willing co-operation of those to whom an important part of that authority was delegated. Few people dared to admit this fact, but everyone accepted its corollary, which was that the King's authority ought not to be risked if there was a serious likelihood of its being respectfully disobeyed.

APPENDIX A

NOTE ON THE COMTE
D'ARGENSON'S INFORMANTS

(See p. 113 n. 75 and p. 204 n. 55.)

The Comte d'Argenson received secret information about debates inside the *Parlement* from at least two sources: Jean-Baptiste-Maximilien Titon, an influential councillor at the 5th chamber of the *enquêtes* and, from 1753 onwards, at the *grand'chambre*, and from Louis Mayou, a *substitut* of the *procureur général*. Titon was not only present at assemblies of the chambers, but was also an active participant in the debates. By virtue of his position Mayou could not be present at such assemblies, but he sought to glean as much information about them as he could.

In an entry in his diary for 30 March 1752 the Marquis d'Argenson wrote:

> M. Titon, doyen de la cinquième chambre, qui a joué longtemps le rôle de saint et de janséniste, a reviré totalement du côté de la débauche et est l'espion visible de mon frère. Il va à ses audiences publiquement lui rendre compte de tout et prendre ses ordres.[1]

The Fonds d'Argenson on deposit at the University of Poitiers contains forty-four letters, mostly unsigned, addressed by Titon to the Comte d'Argenson or to his first secretary Dupin at the latter's address in the rue Saint-Honoré, 'près les Jacobins'. A study of these letters confirms the statement made by the Marquis d'Argenson that Titon was his brother's spy in the *Parlement*. The letters span the period 1752–6 with some significant gaps (1753 and much of 1755).[2]

Jean-Baptiste-Maximilien Titon was the son of Jean-Jacques Titon

---

[1] *Journal et mémoires du Marquis d'Argenson*, ed. E. J. B. Rathery (Paris, 1859–67) (hereafter cited as D'Argenson, ed. Rathery), vii, p. 177.

[2] BUP, Archives d'Argenson, CA 54: *dossier* Titon: five dated letters (1752–6) and thirty-eight undated letters.

(1665–1740), who became a *maître des comptes* in 1692. His date of birth figures on a print: 13 June 1696, two years after his father's marriage to Jeanne-Hélène de Saint-Mesmin. The Titons were a family of the Parisian bourgeoisie ennobled in 1672 through the office of *secrétaire du roi*; there is the suggestion that the family was Scottish in origin. The founder of the family fortune was Titon's grandfather, Maximilien (1631–1711), Seigneur d'Ognon, Lançon, Istres, and master armourer of Paris. He was a protégé of Louvois and became *directeur général des manufactures et magasins d'armes du roi*. His wife, Marguerite-Angélique Bécaille (died 1721), whom he married in 1656, became the *nourrice* of Louvois's children.[3] The couple had three sons: Louis-Alexandre, Jean-Jacques, and Evrard, better known as Titon du Tillet (1677–1762), the originator of the celebrated bronze Monument to Genius which bears the name of the *Parnasse françois*.[4] Some indication of the wealth of Maximilien Titon is provided by the size of the donations he made to his sons: 250,000 *livres* to the eldest and 150,000 each to Jean-Jacques and Evrard.[5] He built a colossal house, 'La Folie Titon', in 1673 at 31 rue de Montreuil; at his death the major part of it passed to Evrard (another part became the Reveillon factory).[6]

Jean-Jacques was seigneur of Plessis-Choiseul, Chambant and Aumont and had served as a musketeer and captain in the Regiment of Navarre. He became a captain of the Regiment of Bombardiers, being present at the siege of Philipsburg in 1688. He was wounded in the shoulder at the siege of Mainz and switched to a career in finance. Jean-Baptiste-Maximilien was the elder of his two sons (the younger, Daniel-Jacques, followed in his father's footsteps as a *maître des comptes*).[7]

Although the evidence is lacking, there is a strong likelihood that

---

[3] Christine Favre-Lejeune, *Les Secrétaires du Roi de la grande chancellerie de France: dictionnaire biographique et généalogique (1672–1789)* (Paris, 1986), 2 vols., ii, pp. 1262–3 (entry under Titon); François Bluche, *L'Origine des magistrats du Parlement de Paris au xviiiᵉ siècle* (Paris, 1953–4[1956]), p. 400.

[4] On Evrard Titon du Tillet, see Judith Colton, *'The Parnasse François': Titon du Tillet and the origins of the Monument to Genius* (New Haven, Conn., and London, 1979).

[5] Favre-Lejeune, *Les Secrétaires du Roi*, p. 1262. On Maximilien Titon's activity as an armourer in Charleville, see Christiane Lacombe, 'Manufactures d'armes, xviiᵉ et xviiᵉ siècles' in *Monuments historiques*, cxxxviii (Aug.–Sept. 1983), pp. 30–5.

[6] On 'La Folie Titon', see the catalogue of the exhibition held at Bagatelle and at the Musée Carnavalet (13 July 1978–28 January 1979): *De Bagatelle à Monceau 1778–1978: les folies du xviiiᵉ siècle à Paris* (Paris, 1978), p. 66, nos. 140 and 141 (with illustration). There was another house, built in 1665, at 57 rue du Temple (then rue Sainte-Avroye). Largillière, a near neighbour and friend of the Titons, painted several portraits of them; see *Portraits and figures in paintings and sculptures 1570–1870: Summer exhibition 15 June–26 August 1983*, Heim Gallery, London, Exhibition catalogue 36 (London, 1983), no. 9: portrait (1713) of Madame Titon de Cogny, second wife of J. B. M. Titon's first cousin (plate 9). Largillière also did a portrait of Marguerite Bécaille.

[7] F. A. Aubert de La Chesnaye des Bois, *Dictionnaire de la noblesse* (Paris, 1770–86), 15 vols., xii, col. 23: entry under Titon.

Jean-Baptiste-Maximilien was sent to the famous Jesuit college of Louis-le-Grand in the rue Saint-Jacques, where his uncle Evrard had gone before him.[8] As he was born in the same year as the Comte d'Argenson their stay at Louis-le-Grand probably overlapped from 1709 onwards.[9] In a letter, which can be dated to 1756, Titon described himself to D'Argenson as 'un ami de plus d'un demi-siècle'.[10]

Titon was received into the *Parlement* as a councillor of the 5th chamber of *enquêtes* on 22 January 1717 and had become its *doyen* by the time he moved to the *grand'chambre* in 1753. A zealous opponent of *Unigenitus*, he was arrested along with Abbé Pucelle in 1732. He was an active participant in the convulsionary *séances*, and the following year he was put under surveillance by the police; the surveillance was ended after protests had been made to the keeper of the seals, Chauvelin.[11] In 1721 Titon had married Marie-Louise Oudaille (died 1748), daughter of Jean-Baptiste Oudaille, seigneur of Villotran, receiver of the *grenier à sel* of Pontoise.[12] There was one son of the marriage, Jean-Baptiste-Maximilien-Pierre Titon de Villotran (1727–94), who also went into the *Parlement*.[13]

Titon's motivation in becoming a spy is difficult to discern. The Marquis d'Argenson established a curious link between his spying activity and his supposed lapse from Jansenism into debauchery. Even if such a link existed, the evidence for his debauchery is slender: the unexplained presence in the file of letters at Poitiers of a copy in his hand of what was then an unpublished licentious poem by Collé,[14] and an intriguing bequest in his will, made in 1766. The bequest of 300 *livres* of *rentes viagères* is made to one Marguerite David

---

[8] On Titon du Tillet at Louis-le-Grand, see Colton, '*The Parnasse François*', p. 13.

[9] On the organisation of the college, see E. M. J. P. Dupont-Ferrier, *Du Collège de Clermont au Lycée Louis-le-Grand 1563–1920*, 3 vols. (Paris, 1921–5). The records of the college have largely disappeared. On the passage of the D'Argenson brothers at Louis-de-Grand, see René Pomeau, *D'Arouet à Voltaire 1694–1734* (Oxford, 1988), p. 53; and the earlier work by Henri Beaune, *Voltaire au collège: sa famille, ses études, ses premiers amis: lettres et documents inédits* (Paris, 1867), pp. cxxv–cxlv. On the curriculum of studies, see René Pomeau, 'Voltaire au collège', *Revue d'histoire littéraire de la France*, lii (1952), pp. 1–10.

[10] BUP, CA 54: no. 16: 'Copie d'une lettre au c. d'a' dated 'ce 13' [1756].

[11] B. Robert Kreiser, *Miracles, convulsions, and ecclesiastical politics in early eighteenth-century Paris* (Princeton, N.J., 1978), pp. 237, 299n, and 302. According to Augustin Gazier, Titon appears with the Abbé Pucelle and another, unidentified, *parlementaire* in Jean Restout's print of Carré de Montgeron kneeling at the tomb of the Deacon Pâris in the cemetery of Saint-Médard (7 September 1731): *Histoire générale du mouvement janséniste depuis ses origines jusqu'à nos jours* (Paris, 1922), 2 vols., i, p. 297n. Gazier described Titon as 'vertueux' (p. 302).

[12] Favre-Lejeune, *Les Secrétaires du Roi*, ii, p. 1263.

[13] Joël Félix, *Les Magistrats du Parlement de Paris 1771–1790: Dictionnaire biographique et généalogique* (Paris, 1990), p. 231.

[14] BUP, CA 54: no. 34: 'Marmotes': the poem was finally published in 1807 with variants as 'L'Irrésolue comme ça'; see *Recueil complet des chansons de Collé* (Hamburg and Paris [Brussels, 1864]), pp. 8–10.

née le dix-sept juillet mil sept cent cinquante deux, baptisée à St Nicolas des Champs, mise en nourrice à Jouy, depuis pensionnaire à St Mandé, actuellement chez le Sr. et De. Gar, m[aîtr]e ciseleur, graveur sur métaux.[15]

Further provision for an eventual dowry was made in the will.[16] Was Titon perhaps the girl's father? The year of her birth is the same as that of the entry in the Marquis d'Argenson's journal.

However, other reasons can be adduced to explain Titon's rôle as a secret informant. He seems to have been short of money and eager to obtain face-saving honorary posts outside the *Parlement*. On 20 October 1752 he wrote to the Comte d'Argenson from his estate at La Neuville, near Beauvais:

> Voilà, dit-on, le moment où vous devez renouveller les baux. Mr. Duverney ne demande pas mieux que d'obliger son ancien ami Pierron et moy. Je vous conjure de me donner cette preuve de bonté. Je lis dans votre cœur que vous le désirés. S'il n'étoit pas possible de faire entrer actuellement M. Mazières, qui certainement vous convient par sa probité, et capacité, et qui s'arrangera aisément avec la compagnie, accordés moy en attendant d'être en croupe avec quelqun [*sic*] de confiance. J'attend [*sic*] tout de vous, et de vous seul. Que deviendrois-je si vous me refusiés?[17]

Even when allowance is made for stylistic hyperbole, this sounds like a desperate plea. Presumably Titon had a private arrangement with Charles de Mazières that if this financier became a farmer general, he would be remunerated by him. If Mazières was not included in the renewal of the *bail*, or contract, between the Crown and the new consortium of farmers general, then Titon hoped he would get a *croupe*. In this context, a *croupe* was a fixed share in the profits of a farmer general payable to an individual designated by the King. As such individuals did not contribute to the advances of funds made by the farmer general to the Crown upon the signature of a *bail*, the practice was not popular with the tax farmers unless they owed the renewal of their *bail* to the goodwill of the individuals concerned.[18]

It seems that Titon obtained a *croupe* in partnership with Mazières and

---

[15] AN, Minutier central, *Etude* LII, no. 467: Holograph will of J. B. M. Titon of 26 March 1766, p. 5.

[16] *Ibid.*, p. 6.   [17] BUP, CA 54: unnumbered but dated letter.

[18] On the system of *croupes*, see Marcel Marion, *Dictionnaire des institutions de la France aux xviie et xviiie siècles* (Paris, 1923, reprint), p. 160; and especially Yves Durand, *Les Fermiers généraux au xviiie siècle* (Paris, 1971), pp. 108–14. Louis XV himself had a *croupe* in various financial affairs. Charles de Mazières became an honorary farmer general and died in 1783 leaving debts of over a million and a half *livres* (Durand, p. 173); in 1752–3 he was part of a syndicate formed to exploit the sale of Sèvres porcelain (Durand, pp. 139–40); the contract of marriage of his daughter in January 1755 was signed in the presence of the Comte d'Argenson, of the latter's mistress, the Comtesse d'Estrades, and of Machault (Durand, p. 366).

another person (possibly his old friend Pierron, a *substitut* of the *procureur général*) though only through the influence of 'mr. le m. de r. [?Richelieu] qui m'a fait connaître Mr. Duvernai'.[19] At the end of September 1754, he was pleading again with the Comte d'Argenson that he should not be denied 'des preuves d'amitié que l'on accorde à tant d'autres'.[20] A month later he expressed his gratitude to the minister. D'Argenson and Machault seemed prepared to work together on his behalf, and the keeper of the seals had written to his successor at the *contrôle général* about the promises made to Titon: a rate of a *sol* (presumably per *livre*) on the *Caisse de Poissy* due to be renewed in 1755 and another *sol* in an unnamed *sous-ferme*.[21] However, the question is whether these promises were honoured. Titon wrote to Dupin on 3 July 1755, having heard that the arrangements for the *Caisse de Poissy* were going to be made during the court's sojourn at Compiègne. He begged Dupin:

> J'ose vous supplier d'y songer à moy, sans préjudice, car outre que le mal est pressant, il est grand, n'ayant de ma vie trouvé une main secourable. Je dépose mes peines dans votre sein et dans celui de M. le C.D. sous la protection desquels je veux vivre et mourrir.[22]

Titon remained dissatisfied. On 4 February 1756 he told Dupin that he had seen D'Argenson the previous Thursday at the Invalides.

> Je luy ay dit que je vous avois arraché un secret que par bonté vous n'aviés pu me cacher. J'ay reconnu auprès de luy ce que je sçai parfaitement, que je suis bien peu de chose, et qu'on pense me faire beaucoup d'honneur de me laisser parler un moment sans m'écouter.[23]

After this sarcastic expression of his feelings, Titon was again received by the minister, this time at the Louvre and with what he described to Dupin as 'les grâces qui me flattent'. However, he obtained nothing on his new requests for a share in the supply either of horses to the artillery or of gun-carriages. On the first, he was told that it had gone to 'les Gueldres'; and on the second that, as an economy measure, the task would be given to the *magazins*. Titon knew that the second statement was untrue. Moreover, he knew that others were being more active than the Comte d'Argenson in obtaining shares for their *protégés* in the renewal of the judicial contracts. He urged Dupin:

> Revenés promptement et chargés-vous d'obtenir de quoy faire vivre un vieillard qui en vérité ne devroit n'être [*sic*] plus dans le cas de demander.[24]

---

[19] See letter cited in note 10 above.
[20] BUP, CA 54, no. 26: letter dated 'ce samedy 28' [Sept. 1754].
[21] *Ibid.*, no. 23: letter dated '22 8bre au soir' [1754].
[22] *Ibid.*, unnumbered but dated letter to Dupin, 3 July 1755.
[23] *Ibid.*, unnumbered but dated letter to Dupin, 4 Feb. 1756.   [24] *Ibid.*

On 18 June the Marquis d'Argenson noted in his diary:

> Mon frère a mécontenté M. Titon conseiller au parlement, qu'il avait gagné à la cour, de façon que ce conseiller ne garde plus aucune mesure. Cet homme est outré en toutes choses, et va partout déclamant contre la personne de ce ministre.[25]

Yet later that year Titon sent Dupin a copy of a long letter which he had addressed to the Comte d'Argenson, adding the intriguing comment: 'quand on est amoureux, et qu'on n'a jamais manqué à rien à quelqun [sic] qui nous manque en tout, on est piqué avec raison'.[26] In his letter to the minister Titon gave several instances in which D'Argenson had overlooked him over the previous two months. The first concerned the death of 'Mr Châteauvillars', who had held a commission of which Titon's grandfather had been the first holder and originator. This was presumably a reference to François-Bruno Le Blanc de Châteauvillard (born *c*. 1711), who was *commissaire des guerres* in 1745, living at the Invalides.[27] Titon felt he would have made a worthy successor to him in the post despite his lack of expertise:

> J'en remplirois les fonctions avec zéle [*sic*], et l'on sçait que souvent ceux qui s'acquitent [*sic*] le mieux des devoirs de leur état y sont entrés sans en sçavoir un mot.

The second instance related to Mazières's withdrawal from the *croupe* ('dans le m .. [?]'). It would have been simple and fair to merge his share with that of Titon and his other partner. However, D'Argenson had insisted on adding one Lisladot to their number at a higher share, thus reducing the value of the share held by Titon and his partner. On this occasion they also lost the attendance and secretarial dues which Mazières had shared with them. A third complaint was that the commission of *intendant des postes*, which was in D'Argenson's gift, had also eluded Titon (it had gone to Jannel on 30 December 1755).[28] Finally, the death of another *parlementaire*, Davy de La Fautrière, led to his post as intendant of the Invalides being given to the Comte de Maillebois, D'Argenson's nephew.[29] As the minister had given the post to Davy in the first place only because he thought Titon had not wanted it, his friend resented being passed over, especially in favour of a military man who had already reached the exalted

---

[25] D'Argenson, ed. Rathery, ix, p. 285.   [26] Letter cited in note 10 above.

[27] See Favre-Lejeune, *Les Secrétaires du Roi*, ii, p. 807 (Le Blanc de Châteauvillard) and 1081 (Piquefeu).

[28] On Jannel's appointment, see D'Argenson, ed. Rathery, ix, p. 167; Eugène Vaillé, *Le Cabinet noir* (Paris, 1950), p. 163 and the same author's *Histoire générale des postes françaises*, vol. vi: *La Ferme générale et le groupe Grimod–Thiroux (1738–1789)* (Paris, 1956), p. 7.

[29] On Davy de la Fautrière, see p. 50 note 68.

rank of *lieutenant général*. What would a man like Maillebois do in such a menial post?

> On le décorera comme on voudra, ce sera toujours un garde à chiens, un quelqu'un fait pour feuilleter, déchiffrer et arranger des papiers, et étoit-ce le moment d'en changer la nature, pouvant le donner à un ami de plus d'un demi-siècle? Les parents méritent beaucoup, mais vous connoissés son prix.[30]

On 19 September Titon again expressed his despair at not having obtained this post:

> Eh bien! Monsieur, s'il est quelqu'un dans le monde qui vous sois aussi imperturbablement attaché, dont le cœur soit tout à vous, et qui voudrois n'agir que pour le prouver, présentés ce quelqu'un! Mais si cela n'est pas vous ne pouvez le faire sans injustice et sans m'exposer au mépris. Toute la France sçait mon attachement pour vous. Vos enemis m'en ont puni. Il y a donc quelque raison de refus. Cette pensée m'accable. Mettés-vous un moment à ma place et rappellés tout ce que vous m'avés refusé![31]

These last letters were written at a time when Titon was still providing the minister with much useful information about what was taking place inside the *Parlement*. Perhaps further research will one day shed some light on why a man of Titon's background was short of funds and why the Comte d'Argenson was unable or unwilling to do more for him. Perhaps the very public nature of Titon's attachment to the minister had damaged his chances.

With the fall of the Comte d'Argenson in February 1757, Titon's hopes of grafting himself on the military establishment so closely linked to his family's tradition were finally dashed. This was a poor return for a man who in July 1753 had taken advantage of the passage at Sainte-Ménehould of D'Argenson's friend, the Maréchal de Belle-Isle, to slip him a list for the minister of 'the most seditious and more insolent' of his colleagues of the *Parlement* exiled with him in neighbouring Châlons.[32]

Subsequent information about Titon is sparse but not without interest. On 29 November 1759, while out hunting with his son and others on land at Beaumont belonging to the abbot of Marcheroux and adjoining his own properties at La Neuville and Villotran, he encountered a poacher. Régnier, a miller, shot a hare from his mill and recuperated his prey in front of the huntsmen, declaring loudly: 'qu'il se f... des conseillers, qu'ils les traiteroient de même s'il les rencontroit'. The two Titons went up to the mill, but Régnier had already fled with the hare, leaving his aged father to

---

[30] Letter cited in note 10 above.
[31] BUP, CA 54 no. 17: letter to the Comte d'Argenson, 'ce 19 7bre' [1956].
[32] *Correspondance du Comte d'Argenson, ministre de la guerre: lettres des Maréchaux de France*, ed. Marquis d'Argenson (Paris, 1924), pp. 237–8: Maréchal de Belle-Isle to the Comte d'Argenson, Commercy, 23 July 1753.

face the angry huntsmen. Régnier *père* threatened to strike Titon *père* over the head with a hammer, but was restrained by a timely warning from Titon de Villotran. Régnier exclaimed: 'qu'il se f ... de MM. Titon, du Parlement, de la Justice, de M. Le Curé, comme des Enfans de cœur'. The huntsmen then allegedly searched and set fire to the mill, and they so frightened the elder Régnier that he died four months later.[33]

This unfortunate incident was part of a broader conflict between Titon and a farmer called Philippart, whom he accused of threatening behaviour towards a gamekeeper. The conflict gave rise to lengthy and inconclusive proceedings before several courts while Philippart and others were thrown in gaol. When he came to draw up his will in June 1766 Titon was still marked by the affair, and while he left it on record that there had been a plot against him he expressed Christian remorse at the fate of Philippart and the others who were still languishing in prison without trial.[34]

His uncle, Titon du Tillet, having died in 1762, the councillor tried to unload the cumbersome *Parnasse françois* upon the King.[35] Already, in 1757, he had indicated to the Marquis de Marigny, the *directeur général des bâtiments*, that he would gladly relinquish the *Parnasse*, which he was due to inherit, in favour of a royal pension. On 18 June 1766 he wrote to Marigny expressing his gratitude to the King for accepting the *Parnasse*, while again stressing his own political and financial problems.[36] Almost a year later he received a royal pension of 6,000 *livres*.[37] He did not have long to enjoy it, for he died in Paris on 28 July 1768. He was presumably buried at Saint-Mandé, as he had requested in his will. He was survived by his second wife, Antoinette Brochette Ponçin, who was the executor of his will, by Titon de Villotran, who later suffered a revolutionary death, and perhaps by the mysterious Marguerite David.[38]

Another of the Comte d'Argenson's informants in the *Parlement* was one of Joly de Fleury's *substituts*. Little is known about him. Louis Mayou d'Aunoy was christened at Taponnat (Charente) on 5 October 1715. He became a *substitut* in 1745. He joined the Maupeou *Parlement* in 1771 and was a councillor at the *Grand conseil* between 1774 and its suppression in 1791. He died in 1794.[39] The *Almanach royal* of 1762 (p. 108) gives his

---

[33] BN, JF 369, *dossier* 4188, ff. 284ᵛ (p. 4 of a printed *mémoire*) and 289 (p. 3 of another *mémoire*).

[34] AN, Minutier central, *Etude* LII, 467: Titon's will, pp. 1–3.

[35] Colton, 'The Parnasse François', p. 181: letter of 6 Dec. 1757.

[36] *Ibid.*, pp. 183–4.   [37] *Ibid.*, p. 181.

[38] The will was 'insinué' (a form of probate) at the *Prévôté de Paris* on 22 Dec. 1768: Archives de Paris, DC6 250, f. 93ʳ. At Titon's death seals had immediately been placed on his effects in Paris.

[39] Information kindly supplied by Professor Michel Antoine.

address as rue de la Mortellerie 'à coté des Audriettes'. Mayou sent over four hundred and fifty confidential reports to D'Argenson over the period 1752–6. They were unsigned and for further security the ones from Pontoise were addressed to 'Mademoiselle Fournier, rue de la Harpe à Paris'. This lady may have been related to Fournier, who was a doctor to the Duc d'Orléans and to President Hénault and, therefore, possibly to the Comte d'Argenson, who had been a member of the ducal household.[40] Mayou's links with D'Argenson and his family were very close. He corresponded with the minister's son, the Marquis de Voyer, in 1765 over the comte's succession, and on a letter of 12 October 1770 Voyer scrawled the words 'Mon cher Mayou'. Mayou continued sending rather less interesting reports – indeed at times they were simply well-informed newsletters – to the Comte D'Argenson's nephew, assistant, and successor at the Ministry of War, the Marquis de Paulmy, between 1754 and 1766;[41] and these were used in part by Charles Aubertin in his *L'Eloquence politique et parlementaire en France avant 1789, d'après des documents manuscrits* (Paris, 1882),[42] though he was unaware of the identity of their author. In a letter of 30 December 1757 Mayou described himself as linked to Paulmy by friendship 'et par les liens du sang'.[43] The nature of this family link still eludes the researcher. Mayou's château was at Aulnoy, near Coulommiers.

It is interesting to compare the fate of men like Titon and Mayou with that of the *nouvelliste* who was Philip Yorke's informant.[44] There are now strong reasons for thinking that this unnamed spy was one Bousquet (or Bosquet) de Colomiers, a native of Toulouse. Firstly, an *à la main* of 17 September 1752 from the informant concerning Cardinal de Tencin is almost identical to an item of the same date in Bousquet's *gazette*, which was found by the police when they eventually arrested him.[45] Secondly, the date of the *à la mains* forwarded to Philip Yorke coincide with those of Bousquet's activity as a gazetteer. When he forwarded the last two *à la mains*, which were dated 1 and 9 November 1752,[46] Dr Jeffreys wrote to Philip Yorke: 'I am sorry to tell you they will probably be the last you will receive, at least from the same Author; the poor Fellow was last week sent to the Bastille and all his

---

[40] See *Lettres inédites de la Reine Marie Lecksinska [sic] et de la Duchesse de Luynes au Président Hénault*, ed. Victor des Diguères (Paris, 1886), p. 400.

[41] EN, MS franç. 14039.   [42] See pp. 269–72.   [43] BN, MS franç. 14039, f. 232.

[44] See p. 108 note 43.

[45] Cf. BL, Add. MSS 35,445 (Hardwicke Papers), f. 313 with Paul d'Estrée, 'Nouvelles à la main de Bosquet de Colomiers (avril–novembre 1752)', in *Souvenirs et mémoires*, vi (Jan.–June 1901), p. 413. The identification of Bousquet de Colomiers with Philip Yorke's informant is also made, but not demonstrated, by Larry Bongie in 'Les Nouvelles à la main: la perspective du client', in *De bonne main. La communication manuscrite au xviii⁰ siècle*, ed. François Moureau (Paris and Oxford, 1993), pp. 134–42, especially pp. 137–42.

[46] BL, Add. MSS 35,445, ff. 339 and 343.

papers seized ...'[47] Jeffreys was writing on 14 November, and indeed Bosquet had been taken to the Bastille on 8 November (on an order of 23 October signed by the Comte d'Argenson).[48] On 14 February 1753 Dr Jeffreys wrote: 'our a la main author remains in the Bastille ...'[49] In fact, Bosquet had been released three days previously and had left the capital for Toulouse, his place of exile, on 2 March.[50] 'Our gazeteer is at last released out of the Bastille', wrote Jeffreys on 23 March, 'but upon condition of his writing no more a la mains'.[51] Bosquet had built up an important clientèle including the Dutch ambassador, the archbishop of Narbonne, and the intendant of Languedoc.[52] Dr Jeffreys had difficulty in finding an adequate replacement for him, and on 25 July 1753 he wrote to Philip Yorke: 'Our new a la main writer is so very dull that there is no danger of his being sent to the Bastile [sic].'[53] Indeed, the new man simply gave them details of the King's movements.[54]

Titon and Mayou had been highly placed insiders who provided secret information to a minister of state, whereas Bosquet was an outsider seeking to penetrate the secrets of state for the benefit of other outsiders. For that reason his à la mains, which contained what the police described as 'des articles très hardis et très repréhensibles',[55] had predictably landed him in the Bastille.

[47] BL, Add. MSS 35,630 (Hardwicke Papers), f. 58.
[48] BL, Egerton MSS 1667: 'Livre d'entrée des prisonniers de la bastille' (1734–54), f. 137.
[49] BL, Add. MSS 35,630, f. 69^v.
[50] Bibliothèque de l'Arsenal, Paris, Archives de la Bastille, 12,495, f. 110; Archives de la Préfecture de Police, Paris: Aa 7, no. 786.
[51] BL, Add. MSS 35,630, f. 76^r.   [52] Paul d'Estrée, 'Nouvelles à la main', p. 385.
[53] BL, Add. MSS 35,630, f. 98^r.
[54] BL, Add. MSS 35,445, ff. 364 et seq.
[55] Bibliothèque de l'Arsenal, Arch. Bastille, 12,495, f. 110.

APPENDIX B

TWO LETTERS OF LOUIS XV
ON THE CRISIS OF 1753

(See p. 179 n. 127.)

Historians have usually attached doubtful value to the two lives of the Maréchal de Richelieu which were published at the end of the eighteenth century; J. L. G. Soulavie's *Mémoires du Maréchal de Richelieu pour servir à l'histoire de Louis XIV, de la Régence, de Louis XV et des quatorze premières années du règne de Louis XVI* (London, Marseille and Paris, 1790–3), 9 vols.; and the *Vie privée du Maréchal de Richelieu contenant ses amours et intrigues, et tout ce qui a rapport au divers rôles qu'a joués cet homme célèbre pendant plus de quatre-vingts ans* (Paris and Maestricht, 1791), 3 vols., ed. J. B. de Laborde and L. F. Faur. These authors claimed to have based their works on Richelieu's papers, and Soulavie claimed in addition to have used those of President Durey de Meinières and of President Rolland d'Erceville. Historians have long been sceptical about these claims, particularly in the case of Soulavie.[1] But the latter's biographer, A. Mazon, had shown as early as 1893 that some of the papers used by Soulavie had found their way into the archives of the Quai d'Orsay.[2] These papers included part of the correspondence between Richelieu and Maupeou in May 1753 with also a number of letters from Ysabeau on the exile of the *Parlement*.[3] These documents were used to a

---

[1] J. Flammermont, 'Les Papiers de Soulavie', *Revue historique*, xxv (1884), p. 113; and A. de Boislisle's introduction to the *Mémoires du Maréchal de Richelieu, 1725–1757* (Paris, 1918), pp. xviii, lxx.

[2] A. Mazon, *Histoire de Soulavie (naturaliste, diplomate, historien* (Paris, 1893), p. 162; and the same author's *Appendice à l'Histoire de Soulavie* (Privas, 1901). On Soulavie see also the introduction in Pierrette Jean-Richard and Gilbert Mondin, *Un collectionneur pendant la Révolution: Jean Louis Soulavie (1752–1813)* (Catalogue of the XVᵉ exposition de la Collection Edmond de Rothschild, Musée du Louvre, 20 April–24 July 1989, Paris, Réunion des Musées nationaux, 1989), pp. 1–18.

[3] AAE, MD, France 1344, ff. 218–61. There is also a copy that seems to have belonged to Richelieu of Rolland d'Erceville's memoirs (f. 280ff). These papers were confiscated from Soulavie by the Imperial Government in 1811 (Mazon, *Histoire de Soulavie*, ii, p. 152).

limited extent in 1891 by M. Marion for his *Machault d'Arnouville: étude sur l'histoire du contrôle général des finances de 1749 à 1754.*[4] Other portions of that correspondence have now been found scattered among the Richelieu Papers kept in the Bibliothèque Victor Cousin at the Sorbonne.[5] They include more letters from Ysabeau and two letters from Louis XV. From a study of these new documents it becomes apparent that the King's letter of 11 May 1753 published by Laborde was genuine and differed only slightly from the original text. As this letter aptly illustrates the King's superficial view of the situation in 1753 and of the place of the *Parlement*, it seems useful to republish it here from the original, with in addition the unpublished text of the King's covering letter to Richelieu (which clearly establishes that the other letter was intended to be shown to the first president).

I.

à versailles ce 11 May 1753 jour anniversaire de fontenoy

ma façon de penser est cy jointe en réponse à la lettre que vous m'avés remise, ainsi que du papier qui y étoit joint. J'ay sçu avant que vous en eussiés parler [*sic*] à m^e. de pompadour que vous étiés chargé de me faire voir les remontrances avec ce qu'elles contenoient. Je ne pourois n'y [*sic*] les voir, n'y [*sic*] les recevoir.[6]

2.

puisqu'on m'a dit que vous prenés intérest au parlement je ne suis point fasché de trouver une occasion de vous dire ma façon de penser laquelle j'ay puisée dans ce que j'ay vu, ce que j'ay sçu, et ce que j'ay lu.

le parlement a été de tous temps opposés [*sic*] aux rois, ou régents, et moy qu'on sçait qui aime la paix, il m'a choisy pour me dire des choses qu'ils n'avoient encore jamais osé dire aux souverains mes prédécesseurs. J'ay bien voulu patienter l'année dernière, et vous en avés été témoing occulaire, et auriculaire, sans je croy qu'il y ait paru au dehors, et de là je suis indifférent, mais si vous m'aviés vu en dedans, vous m'auriés trouvé bien diférent [*sic*]. Je n'attribue point au p^er. p^t. ce qu'il ma dit parcequ'il ne pouvoit guère faire autrement, mais à qui le mérite? poussé à bout comme je le suis je ne puis plus diférer [*sic*] à faire sentir à mon parlement que je suis le maître absolu, et que puissance vient de dieu, et que je ne dois quà lui d'en rendre compte au jour qu'il me retirera de ce monde, mais pour lors ils auront un autre maître non moins le maître, mais peutêtre plus vif que moy. Je suis roy, et le maître, ou c'est le parlement, personne ne pense ce d[erni]er je croy, mais beaucoup imagine tout comme, hors [*sic*] je ne veux point détruire le parlement mais je

---

[4] Published in Paris, 1891; see pp. 350ff. thereof.
[5] BVC, RP, xiv (catalogue no. 35), ff. 8–13 and 55–6; xlii (no. 63), ff. 164–6, 252–3.
[6] *Ibid.*, f. 164.

le veux réduire dans les justes bornes pour lesquels il a été institué, ainsy il faut qu'il plie, ou moy. Moy j'y metterés toute la force que dieu a mis dans mes mains, et y repandrés mon sang avec grand plaisir. s'il me demande pardon, s'il obéit à ce que je lui ay commandé, avec joie je lui renderés le pouvoir que je lui avois confié. mais après toutes les incartades que j'ay vu, je ne souffrirés jamais qu'il puisse me remettre dans les mêmes embarras.

le p^er. p^t. étant le chef que je lui ay doné, avec grande satisfaction je le voirés porteur des soumissions de mon parlement, et des ordres que j'aurés à lui donner pour les faire exécuter.

l'on m'a fait plusieurs fois condescendre à bien des choses que je regrette autant présentement, qu'elles étoient peu de mon goust pourlors. mais dans ce moment-cy, je n'écouterés rien qu'on ne se soit soumis, et que je n'en aie les plus sûres preuves. je n'aime pas plus l'authorité des prestres en temps qu'ils veulent sortir de leurs bornes mistiques, mais je veut qu'on rende à dieu ce qui est [à] dieu, et à ceesar ce qui est à ceasar. hors ceasar ne tient que de dieu ce qui est à ceesar, mais il ne le laschera à personne sur la terre françoise.

vous pouvés communiquer cecy à qui vous voudrés, n'étant pas fait pour vous seul, ainsi vous en fairés l'usage que vous jugerés à propos. Je ne le signe pas non plus: vous cognoissés assés mon écriture pour être bien sur qu'il est bien de moy, mais je le fairois avec grand plaisir s'il le faloit, même d'une autre couleur.

à versailles le 11e. may *1753*. à cinq heures du soir.[7]

The existence of these letters also helps to confirm the authenticity of a third letter from Louis XV to the marshal on the subject of Maupeou's suggestions for a *déclaration* (see Chapter 7, p. 193). The letter is lost, but internal evidence suggests that it has been accurately reproduced by Soulavie in the *Mémoires du Maréchal de Richelieu*.[8]

---

[7] *Ibid.*, ff. 165–6; cf. *Vie privée du Maréchal de Richelieu*, ed. Laborde and Faur, iii, pp. 231–3(or pp. 362–3 in some copies).

[8] The Richelieu Papers at the Bibliothèque Victor Cousin also help to authenticate a letter from Christophe de Beaumont to the King of which only a copy survives in the library of the Museum Calvet in Avignon: see Chapter 3, p. 80 n. 38.

Index

Long entries in this index comprise two types: the analytical (see e.g. entry for '*arrêts du conseil*'), and the narrative (see e.g. entry for 'Argenson, Marc Pierre de Voyer de Paulmy'). In the latter type the 'subheadings' are pointers to the narrative rather than analytical classifications, and it cannot be assumed that all page refs. following a pointer in a narrative entry relate exclusively to that pointer.

DATE DUE

HIGHSMITH #45115